D1338073
…3759 8
a30213 003037598b
WITHDRAWN
FROM STOCK
…IL LIBRARY

The U.S. Multiregional Input-Output Accounts and Model

Volume VI of Multiregional Input-Output Analysis Edited by Karen R. Polenske

This is the sixth and final volume in a series entitled *Multiregional Input-Output Analysis,* edited by Karen R. Polenske. The present volume was written by the editor. It contains a review of the history of national, regional, and multiregional accounts; a detailed description of the multiregional input-output (MRIO) accounting conventions; a summary of major multiregional modeling; a presentation of the theoretical MRIO model; and a summary description of the data sources and estimation procedures used to assemble the data for the MRIO accounts. Base 1963 and projected 1980 data are provided in the appendix. Other volumes in the series contain detailed explanations of the data sources and estimation procedures used to assemble state estimates of 1947, 1958, and 1963 final demands and outputs, employment, and payrolls; state estimates of 1963 technology and interregional trade flows; and 1970 and 1980 state projections of final demands.

Volumes in this series include:

State Estimates of the Gross National Product, 1947, 1958, 1963
Karen R. Polenske, Carolyn W. Anderson, Richard Berner, William R. Buechner, Bo Carlsson, Orani Dixon, Peter Dixon, W. Norton Grubb, Frans J. Kok, Mary M. Shirley, James F. Smith, and Isabelle B. Whiston

State Estimates of Outputs, Employment, and Payrolls, 1947, 1958, 1963
John M. Rodgers

State Projections of the Gross National Product, 1970, 1980
Raymond C. Scheppach

State Estimates of Technology, 1963
Karen R. Polenske, Carolyn W. Anderson, Orani Dixon, Roger M. Kubarych, Mary M. Shirley, and John V. Wells

State Estimates of Interregional Commodity Trade, 1963
John M. Rodgers

The U.S. Multiregional Input-Output Accounts and Model
Karen R. Polenske

The U.S. Multiregional Input-Output Accounts and Model

Karen R. Polenske
Massachusetts Institute
of Technology

Lexington Books
D.C. Heath and Company
Lexington, Massachusetts
Toronto

206294
HC 110.I57

Library of Congress Cataloging in Publication Data

Polenske, Karen R
The U.S. multiregional input-output accounts and model.

(Multiregional input-output analysis; v. 6)
Bibliography: p.
1. United States–Economic conditions–1945– –Mathematical models.
2. United States–Industries–Mathematical models. 3. Interindustry economics.
I. Title. II. Series.
HC101.M85 vol. 6 [HC106.7] 330.973'092s
ISBN 0-669-02173-3 [339.2'3'0973] 78-332

Copyright © 1980 by D.C. Heath and Company

All rights reserved. No part of this publication may be reproduced or transmitted in any form or by any means, electronic or mechanical, including photocopy, recording, or any information storage or retrieval system, without permission in writing from the publisher. This book was prepared with the support of DOT Grant No. DOT-OS-30104 and EDA Grants No. OER-544-G-76-28, No. OER-544-G-77-14, and No. OER-544-G-78-8. However, any opinions, findings, conclusions, or recommendations herein are those of the author and do not necessarily reflect the views of the funding agency.

Published simultaneously in Canada

Printed in the United States of America

International Standard Book Number: 0-669-02173-3

Library of Congress Catalog Card Number: 78-332

QUEEN MARY
COLLEGE
LIBRARY

Contents

List of Figures

List of Tables

Preface

The multiregional input-output (MRIO) accounts and model described in this book are the result of research conducted between 1967 and 1972 at the Harvard Economic Research Project for the Economic Development Administration, U.S. Department of Commerce. The project was closed June 30, 1972, and the multiregional research was transferred to the Department of Urban Studies and Planning, Massachusetts Institute of Technology, where it is being continued. The present focus of the research is on the use of the accounts and model for multiregional policy analyses related to transportation, employment, energy, and the environment.

A substantial amount of the MRIO accounts data was assembled by the staff of Jack Faucett Associates, Inc., under subcontracts with the Harvard Economic Research Project or under separate contracts with the Office of Business Economics–for the interregional trade flows–and with the Office of Civil Defense and the Institute of Defense Analyses–for an initial set of 1963 output estimates. All of the remaining data were originally assembled at the Harvard Economic Research Project under a contract with the Office of Economic Research of the Economic Development Administration, U.S. Department of Commerce. Additional agencies that had become interested in the overall multiregional project supplied part of the funds to complete the contract in 1970. These agencies are the Office of Systems Analysis and Information, Department of Transportation; the Bureau of Labor Statistics, Department of Labor; the Office of Civil Defense, Department of Defense; and the Bureau of Mines, Department of the Interior. During the period 1971-1972, extensive revisions were made to all the data under a contract between the Office of Systems Analysis and Information, Department of Transportation, and the Harvard Economic Research Project. Additional revisions were made during 1972-1973 under a contract between the Office of Systems Analysis and Information, Department of Transportation, and the Department of Urban Studies and Planning, Massachusetts Institute of Technology. Some of the policy analyses cited in the text were conducted at the Massachusetts Institute of Technology with grants from the University Research Program, Department of Transportation (1973-1976), and from the Economic Development Administration, Department of Commerce (1976 to the present).

Chapter 1 contains a review of the history of national, regional, and multiregional accounts, thus providing the context for the assembly of the MRIO accounts. To document the multiregional accounts, it was necessary to provide an extensive description of the national accounting conventions as well, because of the lack of updated written documentation of the national accounts. This description is provided in chapter 2. In chapter 3, a history of multiregional modeling is provided, and the primal, dual, and truncated dual versions of the MRIO models are described.

In chapters 4 through 7, the data sources and estimation procedures used to assemble the MRIO accounts are summarized from the extensive descriptions provided in the previous five volumes of this series [181; 182; 191; 192; 198]. Additional theoretical and empirical studies related to the data assembly are covered in these chapters as well, thus providing a complete and up-to-date description of all data sources and estimation procedures used.

Acknowledgments

I sincerely thank all the people who assisted directly or indirectly with the completion of this the final volume. Members of the MRIO research staff assisted with many of the theoretical and empirical studies conducted after completion of the initial set of accounts upon which the discussion in chapters 1 through 3 is based. Special thanks are extended to Patrick Del Duca, Denise DiPasquale, Margaret C. Feiger, F. Ron Jones, Gary M. Kaitz, Nathaniel K. Ng, Gregory G.Y. Pai, Ruth E. Rowan, Ananna S. Tse, and William H. Crown.

I received invaluable assistance during the past few months from William H. Crown, who commented on some of the chapters and who did all the computer runs presented in appendix B. In addition, Kit-Fong Teoh helped with checking the references and with proofreading the manuscript. Julie C. Sarason made a significant contribution to all phases of the final editing, typing, and proofreading. She was assisted by Priscilla Kelly, Blake Smith, and Marie Southwick. Susan R. Brown showed exceptional skill as she assisted with the proofing and checking of the master proof.

Selected chapters of the manuscript were reviewed by Philip M. Ritz and Daniel H. Garnick, Bureau of Economic Analysis, U.S. Department of Commerce, both of whom helped to clarify the descriptions (chapters 1 and 2) of the accounting conventions used at the Bureau of Economic Analysis. Their quick responses were appreciated.

I am especially grateful for the contributions made by Jack G. Faucett, of Jack Faucett Associates, Inc., and Irene S. Raught. Both read the entire manuscript, helping to find inconsistencies, omissions, and errors. In addition, both provided the moral support required for this ten-year writing project. Without them, the manuscript would never have been completed. To Irene, I owe a special thanks for the substantial improvements she made in the writing and presentation of the material as she edited and typed the many different versions of the manuscript.

None of the research reported here could have been completed without the use of unpublished data, computer programs, and other materials that were available at the Harvard Economic Research Project during the years (1966-1972) the basic research was being done. Wassily Leontief was responsible for providing his colleagues with this rich historical set of information.

I would also like to express my deep gratitude to M.N. Lewis, copyeditor, and to Joe Crowley at Jay's Publishers Services, both of whom made valuable contributions as each book in the series of six volumes entered into the final publication stages.

I appreciate the facilities made available to me at the Netherlands Institute for Advanced Study as I did the final proofing of this sixth volume.

Finally, I thank my parents and also Kenneth Moody and Caroline Moody for providing me with hospitable environments during my working "holidays" here and abroad.

Needless to say, I accept responsibility for any errors that are present in the manuscript.

List of Abbreviations

AEC	Atomic Energy Commission
BEA	Bureau of Economic Analysis
BFDC	Bureau of Foreign and Domestic Commerce
BLS	Bureau of Labor Statistics
CBP	*County Business Patterns*
CCC	Commodity Credit Corporation
Census	Bureau of the Census
CES	Consumer Expenditures Survey
CMI	*Census of Mineral Industries*
CP	Census of Population
DOD	Department of Defense
DOT	Department of Transportation
DRI	Data Resources, Inc.
DUD	Distribute the Undistributed
DUSP	Department of Urban Studies and Planning
EDA	Economic Development Administration
EM	Emergency Model
ERS	Economic Research Service
FEA	Functional Economic Area
f.o.b.	free on board
FPA	Federal Preparedness Agency
FTC	Federal Trade Commission
GNI	Gross National Income
GNP	Gross National Product
GPFCF	Gross Private Fixed Capital Formation
GRI	Gross Regional Income
GRP	Gross Regional Product
HERP	Harvard Economic Research Project
ICC	Interstate Commerce Commission
IDIOM	Income Determination Input-Output Model
INFORUM	Interindustry Forecasting Model
IO	Input-Output
IRIO	Interregional Input-Output
JFA	Jack Faucett Associates, Inc.
MPS	Material Products System
MRIO	Multiregional Input-Output
NASA	National Aeronautics and Space Administration
NBER	National Bureau of Economic Research
NINV	Net Inventory

NIPA	National Income and Product Accounts
NIPCE	National Income Personal Consumption Expenditures
NPA	National Planning Associates
NTB	Net Trade Balance
NTIS	National Technical Information Service
OBE	Office of Business Economics
OCD	Office of Civil Defense
OEEC	Organization for European Economic Cooperation
PCE	Personal Consumption Expenditures
POSTDUD	Postdistribute the Undistributed
PREDUD	Predistribute the Undistributed
Prime Contracts	*Military Prime Contract Awards by Region and State*
R&D	Research and Development
RFF	Resources for the Future
RIMS	Regional Impact Multiplier System
Shipments	*Shipments of Defense-Oriented Industries*
SIC	Standard Industrial Classification
SLG	State and Local Government
SIR	Service Industry Residual
SMSA	Standard Metropolitan Statistical Area
SNA	System of National Accounts
STRI	State Transfers-In
STRO	State Transfers-Out
Survey	*Survey of Current Business*
UN	United Nations
USDA	United States Department of Agriculture

The U.S. Multiregional Input-Output Accounts and Model

1 National, Regional, and Multiregional Economic Accounts

One purpose of the study presented here was to construct a consistent and comprehensive set of multiregional accounts for the United States. Another was to formulate and implement a general multiregional input-output model that could be used for a variety of regional economic policy analyses. Consideration was first given to the types of regional analyses for which the accounts would be used. Important decisions then had to be made as to what the specifications of the accounting framework should be; what types of data should be assembled; what methodologies, criteria, and data sources should be used for assembly of the data; and, finally, how the multiregional model should be formulated and implemented. To an extent, all of the decisions were interrelated. Prime importance, however, was attached to the development of a multiregional accounting framework that could provide an accurate and consistent industrial and regional data base.

Major economic policy issues usually relate to structural and institutional problems within the economy. Although some investigations have been made of structural relationships at the national level, no systematic investigations of them at the regional level have been possible because of the lack of a comprehensive multiregional data base. An in-depth understanding of the various structural issues affecting different people and regions in the United States requires comparative analyses of two or more regions. At a minimum, therefore, multiregional data must be available for production, consumption, employment, and prices, as well as for the shipments of commodities between any two regions. The multiregional input-output accounting structure and model developed for the present study help assure that the multiregional data assembled and the empirical results of the different regional and multiregional studies using both the data and model are comprehensive, consistent, and accurate. Inherent within such an accounting structure and model is the institutional framework within which prices are formulated and production, consumption, employment, and transportation take place. In keeping with the purposes expressed above, the major contributions of the present study include formulation of a detailed multiregional input-output (MRIO) accounting framework; construction of a 1963 set of MRIO accounts; and extensive documentation of the methodologies, criteria, and data sources used to construct those accounts. The historical development of the national, regional, and multiregional accounts that led to the MRIO accounts is reviewed in this chapter; the reasons for choosing the MRIO accounting framework are explained in detail in chapter 2 as the accounts are described.

For the present study, a complete set of 1963 MRIO accounts was assembled to correspond to the 80-order Office of Business Economics (OBE) industrial classification for 51 regions (50 states plus the District of Columbia). Supplemental historical data were assembled for 1947 and 1958 for outputs, employment, payrolls, and six components of the gross regional product (final demand), but only for 49 regions because of limited availability of data for Alaska and Hawaii. The six final demand components were projected to 1970 and 1980 for 51 regions independently from the MRIO model, the projections being made in the late 1960s. The industrial and regional classifications are given in the appendix, tables A-1 and A-2, respectively. Although a uniform set of criteria was applied to the assembly of the data, the methodologies and data sources necessarily varied with each major component of the accounting system. A series of consistency checks, described in chapters 2 through 7, was made during each stage of the data assembly and of the model implementation. (Also, refer to a report by Polenske, Anderson, and Shirley [180, pp. 44–56].)

The work was officially begun in March 1967; the basic data assembly was completed and the column-coefficient version of the MRIO model was formulated and implemented by December 1970. Extensive testing of the data and model was done and major revisions to the accounts were made in 1971 and 1972. Throughout the study, high priority was given to providing comprehensive descriptions of methodologies and data sources, noting especially ambiguities and obvious errors in the data. A thorough documentation of the methodologies and statistical sources used for the data assembly has been furnished in the five previous volumes of this series [181; 182; 191; 192; 198]; the complete MRIO accounting framework, the structure of the theoretical model, a summary of the data assembly, and a review of some of the regional policy analyses for which the data and model have been used since 1972 are provided in the present volume.

The discussion in this volume will be restricted to the income and product and input-output accounts. Thus, other U.S. economic accounts, such as the foreign transactions, gross saving and investment, personal income and outlay, and government receipts and expenditures will be discussed only as they implicitly relate to the income and product and input-output accounts. Although the term *social accounts* is commonly used in accounting literature, *economic accounts* will be used instead in the present text because of the numerous connotations now given to the word *social* in the economic literature. *Social accounts* was originally used by Hicks to distinguish social accounts from private accounts, the former referring to the accounts for an entire community or nation and the latter to those for individual firms [78, p. vi]. Also to avoid confusion, *income and product accounts* will refer to the value added and final demand portions of the input-output system, while *input-output accounts* will refer to the more comprehensive set of economic accounts with intermediate transactions included.

In the remainder of this chapter, the historical development of national, regional, and multiregional accounts is summarized. The brief review of the history of national accounts in the first part of the following section is important, because almost all the issues concerning regional and multiregional economic accounting relate to similar issues that have been discussed for many years at the national level.

History of National, Regional, and Multiregional Economic Accounts

There is no one correct form for national, regional, or multiregional accounts, but collectors and users of accounting statistics constantly interact, and as a result, the structure of the accounts and the data used change radically over time. Different conceptual accounting frameworks have been developed for countries with different economic systems. But even in countries with similar economic systems, vastly different methodologies have been established for collecting and tabulating the data; consequently, while economic accounts may be assembled using a uniform accounting concept, they will usually vary significantly from country to country and over time in their content and coverage. The development of the System of National Accounts (SNA), adopted by the United Nations in 1952 and revised in 1968, has contributed to substantial standardization of the basic structure of economic accounts in the various countries [223]. A detailed discussion of the old and the new SNA is contained in the book by Ruggles and Ruggles entitled, *The Design of Economic Accounts* [195, pp. 16–37].

Even with the SNA, however, accounts vary from country to country for several reasons. The types of data available to users depend partly upon what data have been collected originally; which of them have been processed, transformed, and published and in what ways the processing and transforming have been done; and what computation facilities are used for processing and publishing them on a timely basis. All of these, in turn, depend largely upon the strengths and weaknesses of various political, economic, and social factions in a country. This may be belaboring an obvious point, but the historical process that led to the present set of multiregional accounts should be borne in mind for evaluation of their usefulness and for determination of which changes can and should be made to them.

In the remainder of this section, special attention is directed, first, to the conceptual basis of the economic accounts, and, second, to the distinction between income and product accounts and input-output accounts.

Three basic concepts of economic accounts have been developed during the past 300 years: the comprehensive production concept, the restricted material production concept, and the restricted market production concept. Only the highlights of these developments will be discussed here, since an excellent and comprehensive survey of the historical development of national accounts in relationship to economic theory in the United States and other countries is available in the two-volume work by Studenski [210; 211].

For the United States and most other western countries, the comprehensive production concept is used. This concept provides a measure of the total value of all goods and services produced in an economy in a given time period. It was developed in the seventeenth century as a result of production and national income measurement attempts by the English and French analysts, William Petty, Gregory King, Pierre le Pesant Sieur de Boisguillebert, and Seigneur Sébastien le Prestre de Vauban. A major factor contributing to the present widespread use of the comprehensive production concept was the successive refinements in the accounting concepts made by Alfred Marshall in publications such as *Economics of Industry* [131] and *Principles of Economics* [132]. The development of the comprehensive production concept was, of course, vital for the elaboration of the macroeconomic theory of Keynes.

The two other economic accounting concepts are used in some countries. The one most widely used is the restricted material production concept set forth by Adam Smith and reformulated and extended by Karl Marx. It is now employed by most countries adhering to the Marxian economic ideology. Smith was influenced by the Physiocrats' concept that only agricultural activity was *productive*, because only agriculture returned a net income, that is, returned more to the producer than the value of the labor employed and the capital expended. By modifying the basic distinction between *productive* and *nonproductive* labor, Smith extended the concept of productive labor to include all labor employed in producing material goods. Thus, the value of the labor engaged in agriculture and manufacturing activities as well as in the commerce and the transportation of goods was included as part of the national income. For the measurement of national income, Marx adopted Smith's general definitions of productive and nonproductive labor, modifying the interpretations and expanding upon them as he developed various theories and concepts, such as the theory of surplus value, the labor theory of value, and the exchange value and use value of commodities. Productive labor, as defined by the Marxian theory of value, is therefore "labor used in the direct acquisition of goods of nature (agriculture, forestry, extractive industries), in their processing (processing industries, construction) and in their distribution (transport and trade)" [quoted in 224, p. 372].

The different conceptual bases for measuring national income and product using the western system of national accounts (SNA) or the eastern material products system (MPS) present difficulties for comparison of national aggregates between countries. Some of these difficulties are covered by Stone in his essay "A Comparison of the SNA and the MPS" [206, pp. 201-223]. It is important to stress that in the case of the restricted material production concept, only the total value of all goods produced in an economy is measured, the value of services being ignored.

The third concept, that of the restricted market production, has been used by a few analysts in East European countries, such as Poland and Hungary. It is less restricted than the material production concept in that it includes the value of both goods and services, but is more restricted to the extent that it includes only those goods and services produced for the market. Thus, the value of the services of government and other collectives not controlled by market forces is excluded. The rationale for making these exclusions, according to Studenski, "is contradicted by innumerable examples" [211, p. 27].

The MRIO set of accounts is based upon the comprehensive production concept. While no strong demand seems to exist in the United States to change to one of the other basic economic accounting concepts, many differing opinions are expressed concerning the method of valuing individual elements in the accounts. From time to time a question of greater concern has been raised: Should the economic accounting framework be restricted to the income and product accounts, or should it also encompass intermediate transactions as in the input-output accounts?

The income and product accounts are subsets of the more comprehensive economic accounts represented by the input-output accounting system, in which the intermediate sales of goods and services are double-counted. On the one hand, the income and product subsets of data have certain advantages for some economic measurements because the value of the income received and the goods and services produced is counted only once, either as the value of payments to the primary factors of production (labor, land, and capital) in the income accounts or as the value of goods and services sold to final users in the product accounts.

On the other hand, the income and product accounts have a decided disadvantage for many other economic analyses in that an important series of transactions is omitted, namely, the sales of one establishment to another. The sales and purchases involved, for example, in transforming iron ore into steel and then into a small nail that is used to hold apparatus required for the production of wine from grapes are not recorded in the national income and product accounts. Only the purchases of the wine by final consumers and the payments to the primary factors of production used to produce the iron ore, steel nail, grapes, wine, and so forth are ever shown.

The intermediate transactions, however, can be specified and traced in considerable detail in the input-output accounts. For an increasing number of economic studies and for planning purposes, the details of all sales and purchases, not just the final ones, are important and essential to determine. It is therefore this complete set of accounting transactions that will be described in detail at the multiregional level in chapter 2. But first, a brief review of the history of the

U.S. national, regional, and multiregional economic accounts is presented. The discussion in the national accounts section relies heavily upon the work of Carson [13], Duncan and Shelton [280], Ruggles and Ruggles [195], Stone [204], and Studenski [210; 211], as well as upon the 50th anniversary volume of the *Survey of Current Business,* which contains special contributions relating to economic accounts by Carter and Leontief, Jaszi, Kuznets, Ruggles and Ruggles, Samuelson, and many others [276]. The focus of the national section will be on the major events and issues that affected the assembly of the MRIO set of accounts.

National Economic Accounts

The history of national economic accounts is a relatively long one. Petty formulated the concept of national income about 1665. The first estimates, dated 1696, were made by King [210, p. 13]. One of the earliest economic accounting frameworks was Quesnay's *Tableau Economique,* published probably in 1758 [108, p. x]. His tableau, which showed the flow of national income from the agricultural sector to the rest of the economic system, was also, of course, an important precursor of the present input-output system of accounts. Since the 1930s, considerable impetus has been given to the development and use of national economic accounts by the macroeconomic theories and policies based upon Keynes' book *The General Theory of Employment, Interest, and Money,* published in 1936 [100].

During the 1920s and on through the 1950s, pioneering work, which eventually led to the widespread acceptance and use of national economic accounts, was done by scholars in many countries. The importance attached to national economic accounting by the world community of scholars is perhaps indicated by the fact that by 1973, five years after the establishment of the first Nobel Memorial Prize in Economic Science, two of the first six economists who had won the prize did so primarily for work related to national economic accounting. Simon Kuznets won the prize in 1971 for his seminal work on national income and product accounts, and Wassily Leontief won it in 1973 for being the "sole and unchallenged creator of the input-output technique." The significant contributions made by Kuznets and Leontief will be reviewed in terms of four major events that occurred in the official publication of the U.S. national economic accounts, namely, the publication of (1) national income statistics; (2) national product statistics; (3) national income and product accounts; and (4) a coordinated set of national income and product and national input-output accounts.

National Income Estimates

The official publication by governments of national accounting statistics and the methodologies used for assembling them was important for their present extensive use. National income statistics were published in Australia, the first country in which they were published by a government, in 1886. In 1904, however, Australia stopped publishing the statistics, and no estimates were published officially in other countries until the 1920s and 1930s. Then, between 1925 and 1939, nine other countries published national income statistics on an official basis [210, p. 151]. In the United States, national income estimates were first published officially by the Bureau of Foreign and Domestic Commerce (BFDC) of the Department of Commerce in cooperation with the National Bureau of Economic Research (NBER). This was done in 1934, making the United States the seventh country to publish official estimates.[1] Because the U.S. estimates were compiled at the BFDC in response to the June 1932 Senate Resolution Number 220 (sometimes referred to as the La Follette resolution), they were first submitted to the Senate (in 1934) as a report entitled *National Income, 1929-32* [264]. Kuznets directed their compilation at the BFDC. The estimates were published in the same year and with the same title by the NBER, with Kuznets as the author [112].

The correlation of a world depression during the 1930s and the official acceptance of national income measures may not have been accidental, according to the director of the OBE (now the Bureau of Economic Analysis) since 1963, George Jaszi:

> A forward leap in the development of national income statistics at a time when the economy is under unusual strain is not unique to the U.S. of the thirties. The takeoff of NIP [national income and product] accounting in seventeenth-century England was closely linked to a fiscal emergency which led to the conversion of an essentially feudal system of taxation to one appropriate to a commerical economy. English national income statistics took another quantum jump in the wake of the Industrial Revolution, when another fiscal crisis was resolved by the introduction of the income tax. The association between the flowering of NIP accounting and profound changes in the structure of the economy attests to the pertinence of this branch of economic statistics. [94, p. 184]

In the United States, the official publication of the national income estimates at the BFDC was preceded by earlier publications by individuals—such as those by George Tucker, in 1843 and 1855; Ezra C. Seaman, in 1852; Charles B. Spahr, in 1885; Willford I. King, in 1915; B.M. Anderson, Jr., in 1917; David Friday, in 1918; and Adolph C. Miller, also in 1918—and by organizations—such as those by the FTC, in 1926; the National Industrial Conference Board, in 1927; and the NBER in the 1930s [13, pp. 153-155]. The contributions by the NBER were especially important. In 1921 and 1922, the NBER published two volumes by Mitchell, King, Macaulay, and Knauth containing estimates of national income and its distribution from 1909-1919 [142; 143]. These volumes were followed by estimates of the 1919 distribution of income in 1922 by Knauth [105], estimates of 1920-1922 income and employment by industrial origin in 1923 by King [102], and estimates of 1919-1921 state incomes in 1925 by Leven [120]. Another national income study by King was published by the NBER in 1930 [103]. In 1929, Kuznets joined the staff of the NBER and prepared an article, entitled "National Income," for the *Encyclopedia of the Social Sciences,* published in 1933 [111]. In January 1933, he was assigned to work on the previously mentioned study at the Department of Commerce, and the final report of that study was submitted to the Senate less than a year later—on January 4, 1934. Some of the NBER staff members participated in making the estimates by checking and revising completed entry books sent to them after the preliminary data had been assembled at the BFDC [13, p. 157]. Subsequently, when the Department of Commerce began official publication of national income estimates, the NBER continued to maintain an active interest in national income measurement and in 1936 established the Conference on Research in Income and Wealth, the papers from the annual conferences appearing in a series of volumes still being published.

The official estimates of national income statistics appeared in the *Survey of Current Business* (known as the *Survey*), a publication of the Department of Commerce, starting in 1934. Updates of the original 1929-1932 estimates were published in the January 1935, August 1935, November 1935, and July 1936 issues of the *Survey.* By 1940, income estimates were being published on an annual basis both for the nation and for states. Monthly estimates were published for the first time in the February 1938 issue of the *Survey.* After Kuznets left the BFDC, the national income measurement work, which included responsibility for the publication of the estimates, was directed first by Robert F. Martin and then by Robert R. Nathan. [280, pp. 78-82]

The next major turning point was the expansion of the estimates to include national product estimates as well.

National Product Estimates

After completing the national income study at the BFDC in 1934, Kuznets returned to the NBER. His next important contribution was *National Income and Capital Formation, 1919-1935,* which was published by the NBER in 1937 [113]. In it, he provided, among other things, detailed definitions of the measurement of gross national product (GNP) and net national product and described the way to apportion GNP between gross capital formation and consumers' outlay. Two other scholars, Clark Warburton and Lauchlin Currie, were developing national product estimates during the 1930s. The first national product estimates were probably those for 1919-1929 made by Warburton. They were published in an article in the *Journal of the American Statistical Association* in 1934. His article also "appears to be the first use in print of the term gross national product" [13, p. 162]. While Warburton's GNP estimates were the first and Kuznets' were the most detailed, a third set of estimates, contained in a 1935 memorandum by Currie, Assistant Director of Research and Statistics, Board of Governors, Federal Reserve System, "is distinguished from the two other sets of estimates because it was specifically designed to aid in policy analysis" [13, p. 165].

The expansion of the official national economic estimates to include measurements of the gross national product in addition to the gross national income did not occur until May 1942, at which time an article containing GNP estimates for 1929-1941 made by Milton Gilbert and R.B. Bangs was published in the *Survey* [57]. Regular publication of quarterly GNP estimates began soon thereafter, in the August 1942 *Survey.* All the GNP estimates were made in the Final Products Analysis Section, which had been established in the BFDC in 1940 [280, p. 83]. Jaszi feels that an earlier establishment of the product side of the accounts would have been beneficial. He states:

> Calculation of a national product measure would have added greatly to the usefulness of the accounts for economic analysis and would have been feasible, given the state of the art. I am inclined to ascribe its omission to lack of statistical creativity, but this is only a hypothesis. [94, p. 184]

It should be stressed, however, that the initial national product estimates were not made within a complete national accounting framework. That development was the next major turning point for the national economic accounts.

National Income and Product Accounts

The next important development was the coordination of the national income estimates and the national product estimates into a single accounting framework. In 1947, a set of six accounts was published for the year 1939, with the first table being called National Income and Product Account [280, p. 94]. The report containing the six accounts was published as a Supplement to the *Survey,* a practice that has since become customary with major revisions.

Although work of the individual scholars in other countries will not be reviewed here, special mention should be made of the significant contributions made to national economic accounting by Richard Stone. His work has been influential not only in the United Kingdom, but also in the League of Nations, the Organization for European Economic Cooperation (OEEC), and the United Nations (UN). His work on the SNA accounts for the UN influenced the restructuring in the 1960s of the U.S. economic accounts. According to Carson, Stone's article in the League of Nations document *Measurement of National Income and the Construction of Social Accounts* "stands as a landmark in the development of the economic accounting approach" [13, p. 178]. As director of the National Accounts Research Unit of the OEEC, Stone was responsible for the preparation of the OEEC standard system of national accounts, which was later (1952) modified and adopted by the UN. In addition, he chaired an Expert Group that met for four years to advise the UN Secretary General concerning the revisions to the SNA, published in 1968 [223, p. iv]. Most important in terms of this discussion is the fact that in *Input-Output and National Accounts* [204], published in 1961, Stone illustrated the way in which the estimates in the income and product accounts could be coordinated with those in the input-output accounts. That coordination was the next major turning point in the development of the U.S. economic accounts.

Coordinated National Economic Accounts

Beginning in 1947, the income and product accounts were published annually, with considerable detail stressing the various industrial, occupational, and other organizational structures of the national economy. Many of these national data were even provided on a monthly or quarterly basis. It was not until 1959 that a decision was made to construct and publish the national income and product accounts in coordination with the input-output accounts. Estimates from the two coordinated accounts were not actually published until 1965.

To avoid confusion later, the most important changes in the names of the government agency responsible for the national economic accounts are given here. The first income estimates were made by the Economic Research Division of the BFDC. This division was abolished in 1939, and the National Income Section was made a division [280, p. 82]. During the 1930s and 1940s, the Office of Business Economics (OBE) was part of the BFDC. The OBE was established as a primary organization of the Department of Commerce on December 1, 1953, and the BFDC ceased to exist [276, p. 178]. Functions previously performed by the OBE were transferred in January 1972 to the Bureau of Economic Analysis (BEA) to be part of the Social and Economic Statistics Administration of the Department of Commerce. The 1963 input-output table, with which the MRIO accounts described in this volume were linked, was published while the agency was still referred to as the Office of Business Economics. For consistency with the five previous volumes in this series, the earlier name will be used throughout this volume, except in a few special cases, and will be referred to as the OBE. It should be noted, however, that the first official national input-output table was constructed at the Bureau of Labor Statistics (BLS) in the Department of Labor rather than at the OBE.

The construction of the first official U.S. input-output table by the BLS in the early 1940s was supervised by Leontief. In 1928, he had joined the staff at the NBER, where he worked for a year or more on the basic conceptions of the input-output framework. In 1932, he became a member of the faculty at Harvard University and was given a small amount of money to continue his input-output research. His first input-output table, a 41-industry table for 1919, was published in *The Review of Economic Statistics* in August 1936 [121] (the same year that Keynes' *General Theory* was published). Government officials were quick to recognize its usefulness for national economic analyses, and Leontief was requested to construct a 1939 table for the BLS. That table, which contained 38 endogenous industries, was prepared by BLS staff members working at Harvard under Leontief's direction [7, p. 8–7]. Marvin Hoffenberg, who was then associated with the BLS, supervised the preparation of the table [122]. The 1919 and 1939 tables, as well as a table for 1929, are included in Leontief's book *The Structure of American Economy, 1919–1939* [122], a book that provides much of the underlying theory for the discussion presented in chapter 3 of the present text.

The first national input-output table published by the government was a 20-industry version of the 1939 table. It was published by the BLS in 1945 [7]. A 45-industry table for 1947 was prepared from data for about 450 industries and published in a May 1952 article by Evans and Hoffenberg (two members of the BLS staff) [32]. In October 1952, a 192-industry version of the same 1947 data was published by the Division of Interindustry Economics at the BLS [295]. Since then, four additional input-output tables providing industrial detail for between 80 and 500 industries have been published—the 1958 table in September 1965 [278], the 1963 table in November 1969 [269], the 1967 table in February 1974 [260], and the 1972 table in February 1979 [190], the first two by the OBE and the last two by the BEA. Official work on input-output had been discontinued at the time a 1954 table should have been published. Thus, with the exception of 1954, official tables have been published for every major industrial census year since 1939. The interindustry accounts are now published in full detail (370-order to 500-order) for each census year, and "annual" tables that are updates of the previous benchmark table are available for the six years: 1961, 1966, 1968, 1969, 1970, and 1971.[2] Starting with the publication in 1975 of the 1968, 1969, and 1970 U.S. input-output tables, the BEA expected to publish tables in lesser detail (80-order) on an annual basis. According to Young and Ritz of the BEA, the objective is to publish updated annual tables within three years after the year of reference [262, p. 1]. As discussed later, the objective has not been realized.

Two important issues influenced the timing and the manner in which the input-output accounts were coordinated with the income and product accounts. The first concerned an assumption by some policymakers and members of the business and academic communities that the use of the input-output technique implied acceptance of a planned economy and of all the controls on production and distribution that were used by the Soviets in the 1940s and 1950s. The second was a diversity of opinion among economists as to how the national economic accounts should be structured. Although the most relevant history relating to both issues will be reviewed here, their exact impact on U.S. input-output work specifically and national accounts work generally is difficult to determine.

During the 1950s, the cold war intensified an already existing fear of government planning. The 450-order 1947 input-output table was one of the planning tools included in a large U.S. Air Force planning project, Scientific Computation of Optimum Programs, known as Project SCOOP.[3] The 190-industry version of this table, prepared and published by the BLS, became known as the Emergency Model (EM), because the data were used for economic analyses and planning related to the Korean War. Since the work on the 1947 table cost approximately $4 million, with a large part of the funds coming from Project SCOOP, input-output work became part of a careful assessment that began when the Korean War ended, in 1953. Roger Keyes, Deputy Secretary to Charles E. Wilson, Secretary of Defense, was asked to review the project and evaluate the usefulness of the EM model as a planning tool. Stephen DuBrul of General Motors was critical of the work. Probably as a result, in part, of DuBrul's criticism, Keyes recommended withdrawing the Department of Defense support of the BLS input-output work. As a result, funds were cut back in 1953 and discontinued entirely in 1954. The decision to cut back the funds and later to discontinue them directly affected the employment of more than 100 government statisticians and economists. Some of these employees who dispersed to other government agencies or to academic institutions and private businesses continued with input-output work in their new positions and were instrumental in helping to revive it in the government later.

During the Eisenhower administration, the important role the input-output framework could play in the organization of consistent and systematic accounting statistics was overlooked by many people, partly, at least, because of the prevailing concern that its use could lead to a Soviet type of planned economy. Of course, this response must be seen in light of the fact that the greatest impact of the cold war was occurring during the 1950s. In their review of input-output research at the NBER 1952 national accounts conference, Evans and Hoffenberg allude to a deep-seated resistance to the input-output accounts:

> An illusory fear is that the [input-output] approach constitutes a potentially undesirable planning device. The word "planning" has acquired a rather unsavory semantic content, especially when linked with the word "government." It has come to imply some kind of belief that productive operations should be directed by a central authority; in other words, a belief in some form of socialism. This has been extended to imply that any device that might make planning more practical is somehow undesirable. When clearly stated, this is an obvious *non sequitur.*
>
> A good deal of misunderstanding about what the interindustry-relations approach can do, or is intended to do, undoubtedly comes about

> through the vague meaning of the word planning. . . . The suggestion that interindustry relations, as a technical device, might help to make socialism more "practical" is arguable but irrelevant. . . . Another fear of misuse related to planning is that input-output methods may somehow be used in connection with the imposition of production controls and materials allocations. . . . [33, pp. 120–121]

This is perhaps why Jaszi appears to be surprised at the later acceptance of input-output accounting methods by the business community, with the most successful businesses doing large-scale planning every day. In 1971, he stated:

> In the light of the experience of the Bureau of Labor Statistics with input-output work, we were somewhat apprehensive about the reception that our work would receive from business, but we were pleasantly surprised. We found that input-output had a large, receptive, and growing audience, particularly among business economists. [94, p. 186]

According to Carter, Leontief's theory has never been as well received in the United States as abroad, where it has had far-reaching acceptance among economists [17, p. 58].[4]

In the 1950s, advocates of input-output work were confronted not only by the cold-war antiplanning factor, but also by disagreement among the economic analysts themselves concerning whether or not the national income and product accounts (NIPA) should be coordinated with the input-output accounts, and, if so, in which way it should be done. Leontief was one who argued for such a coordination, maintaining that the national accounts data published at that time contained inconsistencies, and that these would best be determined and corrected through use of a more complete accounting framework. At the 1952 NBER national accounts meetings, Liebling presented a general outline of the similarities and differences in the two accounts, the relationships between them, and the types of analyses for which each was best suited [128]. Some analysts were reluctant to try to coordinate the two sets of accounts, partly because the inconsistencies Leontief mentioned were present in all the published NIPA data from 1929 on, and revising such a long time series of data would be an enormous and expensive undertaking. The extent and nature of the revisions to be done were the subject of lengthy debates.

It was not until 1959 that input-output research was officially resumed, this time as an accounting program coordinated with the overall national accounting program of the OBE. Goldman, Marimont, and Vaccara have stated that the request to resume the input-output research came from the Bureau of the Budget:

> The [input-output] program was instituted in the latter half of 1959 in response to a recommendation of the National Accounts Review Com-

> mittee which was set up at the request of the Bureau of the Budget to evaluate the national accounts work of the United States. One of the principal recommendations made by the Review Committee was that input-output accounts be prepared regularly as an important and integral component of the national accounts. [60, p. 10]

A preliminary version of the 1958 direct input coefficients was made available to the Harvard Economic Research Project by the OBE in 1963, and preliminary estimates of the row distributions of the output (rather than the actual interindustry flows), direct input coefficients, and direct and indirect coefficients were published in the November 1964 *Survey* [60].[5] However, official publication of the actual 1958 interindustry flows, including revised tables of coefficients, was delayed until the September 1965 *Survey* [278]. As Leontief and others had predicted, the simultaneous construction of the two sets of accounts, with the input-output accounts used as cross-checks of the NIPA statistics, showed many inconsistencies in the latter. The NIPA staff did not want the 1958 input-output flows to be published until the NIPA data from 1929 on could be revised; otherwise, revised NIPA statistics could have been published in 1964 only for the year 1958. While all the NIPA data from 1929 through 1964 were revised, the most detailed revisions were made only for the data from 1946 through 1964. The revised 1929–1964 NIPA statistics, which were at this point almost fully coordinated with the national input-output accounts, were published in the August 1965 *Survey* [273], one month before the publication of the full details of the 1958 input-output table.[6]

Although not directly a part of the history of national economic accounts, three important developments that affected the way in which input-output accounts were used during the 1950s through the 1970s should be mentioned. One major development was the start of the input-output projection work in 1962 at the BLS. When input-output work was resumed in 1959, only the portion of the work concerning the construction of the input-output accounts became the responsibility of the OBE. Then, in 1962, Congress appropriated funds for an Interagency Growth Project. The Division of Economic Growth, headed by Jack Alterman, was established at the BLS as part of the Growth Project, with responsibility for the projection of the input-output coefficients and the final demands. For the initial projections to 1970, a large portion of the work was done for the BLS at the Harvard Economic Research Project. The coefficient projection work was supervised by Anne P. Carter [16] and the personal consumption expenditures projections by Hendrick Houthakker [84]. Projected tables are now a part of the routine work of the Division of Economic Growth, presently headed by Ronald E. Kutscher. These projected national input-output tables are used in a wide variety of economic studies, and the coefficients form the core of most of the large national econometric forecasting models.

Another significant development was the extension of linear economics to the linear programming technique, which is a generalization of the input-output technique. In static input-output models, the technologies are given, while in linear programming models, alternative combinations of feasible technologies are examined to determine the optimal combination, given a set of constraints and an objective function. Input-output theory and linear programming theory are two of three important areas of linear economics that were developed between 1928 and 1947, the third being game theory. There was considerable interaction among the developers. As an example, George B. Dantzig (who developed the linear programming theory in the United States and the simplex method of solution), Marshall K. Wood, and others doing economic planning work for the U.S. Air Force used the 1947 input-output data for many of their linear programming analyses [280, pp. 196–197].

A third significant development was the revolution in computer technology, without which linear programming models and input-output models would have remained only academic exercises. Perhaps the way in which the impact of this advancing technology can best be seen is in terms of the amount of time required to invert an input-output matrix. In the 1950s, the inversion of a 10-industry input-output table, using the hand calculators available at that time, took about a week to complete and check. In 1951, it took 56 hours to obtain the general solution of the input-output inverse on the Mark II computer for the 41-industry 1939 input-output table. By 1969, it took only 36 seconds to invert a 100-industry matrix on the IBM 7094 and, using an optimized program, about 26 seconds on the IBM 360/65, and about 10 seconds on the CDC 6600 [171, p. 14]. This tremendous reduction in computation time means that many input-output analyses that formerly either would have been impossible to do or would have required weeks, months, or years to complete, can now be done. Although other countries use computers extensively for the assembly of input-output accounts, it should be noted that computers are used only to a very limited extent for this purpose by the members of the BEA staff. This fact will be discussed in the next section in conjunction with some other issues that arise concerning the national accounts.

Until 1965, the emphasis in the input-output research was mainly on the use of the input-output system as an economic analytical tool rather than as an accounting structure. Now, however, national input-output tables are routinely assembled and published as an integral part of the U.S. national accounts and form the benchmarks for the national income and product accounts. As is evident from the preceding discussion, economic factors are only one of the determining elements in the evolutionary process of the development of the national economic accounts; political factors, such as the cold war, also played a vital role. The impact of certain social factors will be discussed in the following section as the national accounting issues that have had the greatest influence on the development of the MRIO accounts are presented.

Major National Accounting Issues

Three major issues involving the U.S. accounts will be discussed to provide additional background of the present study. They concern the refinement of concepts of income and product to make the accounts as comprehensive as possible; data collection, assembly, and documentation for the accounts; and the time lags in publication of statistics. This is not intended as a comprehensive overview of all issues, but will indicate some of the major factors that have affected the types of multiregional accounts that can be constructed, especially in the United States.

Refinement of Concepts of Income and Product. For a period of time in the 1950s and 1960s, people from universities, business, and the government held joint meetings to discuss national accounts concepts and to propose changes in them. Some of the arguments presented at those meetings as to what to include in or exclude from the accounts are documented in NBER publications, such as the Conference volume *A Critique of the United States Income and Product Accounts* [162] and *Input-Output Analysis: An Appraisal* [156]. In 1956, a National Accounts Review Committee was formed at the request of the Bureau of the Budget with, as noted earlier, one of the major recommendations resulting from the review being the resumption of input-output work by the federal government as part of a coordinated national economic accounts program [152]. In addition, articles concerning the valuation issues appeared in many of the mainstream economic journals. Major consideration, for example, was given both to the examination of specific items to include in or exclude from the NIPA and input-output statistics and to the determination of methods of calculating the various components of the accounts. According to Carson, discussion centered on the treatment of interest on government debt, corporate profits tax, inventory valuation adjustment, and imputations [13, p. 180]. Of these, the one of most relevance to the MRIO accounts was the imputations made for personal consumption expenditures.

To obtain a measure of the value of purchases made by private consumers that can be compared over time and between countries, several items of imputed consumption must be estimated and added to actual consumer purchases. At present, imputations are made for food and fuel produced and consumed on farms; food, clothing, and housing furnished in kind to employees; space rental value of owner-occupied dwellings; and services rendered without explicit charge by financial intermediaries. In 1963, of the total GNP, $49,179 million, or over 8 percent, represented imputations.

There are many arguments among economists as to whether or not to include as part of the GNP the value of any imputations, and, if so, which ones. A main argument for their inclusion is that it would allow better data comparisons to be made over time and between countries. Jaszi claims that there has been an "impressive record of failure to rationalize the existing imputation procedure or to develop a reformed one" [94, p. 219]. Rationalizations for imputations seem to depend on both the existing economic structures and the existing social structures of a country. Thus, the existence of private property (and the resulting income accruing, say, to owners of apartments) presents some of the economic rationale for trying to make an imputation for the rental value of owner-occupied housing. This imputation is said to be needed to improve intertemporal and intercountry comparisons because the proportion of dwelling units rented versus those owned will alter significantly over time and from country to country; thus, making the imputation reduces some of the unrealistic variations that would affect accurate comparisons. In the United States, the rental value of owner-occupied housing is one of the largest imputed expenditures, comprising about 81 percent of the total value of imputed 1963 personal consumption expenditures [272, p. 153].

Various arguments are advanced to justify exclusion of the services rendered by housewives. Jaszi, for example, favors their exclusion because he in general favors making imputations for the least possible number of items, and he states that there are too many difficulties associated with making this particular exclusion [94, p. 220]. Nevertheless, the current social revolution concerning the role of women will certainly compel some rethinking on whether or not to make this imputation, which is estimated by Heilbroner and Thurow to be at least 18 percent of the GNP [75, p. 339]. According to them, the main reason for the exclusion of housewives' services from the accounts is probably that calculation of the market value of the services of women who keep house is "far from simple" due to the large variations in the amount of housework performed in different stages of the life cycle, the difficulties in determining the dollar value of the services, and the problem of determining what to do with the unpaid labor of men working at home as "carpenters, plumbers, bartenders, etc." [75, p. 339]. The difficulties are real. The rationale, however, appears dubious, in view of the extensive calculations and the vast amount of information required for making other imputations, such as the rental value of owner-occupied dwellings—a large and difficult figure to obtain. Rather, here is a case where social factors have obviously played a role in the decision as to what will and will not be valued. The possible regional and income-group differences in the number of women working outside the home argue strongly for inclusion of the value of housewives' services in the multiregional economic accounts.

Because Rosen in his book *National Income* [193, pp. 117-171] presents a thorough discussion of many of the other issues raised in the 1950s in relation to the definition and estimation of national income and product, additional comments will not be provided here.

Questions related to the logistics of assembling the accounts, which, as suggested earlier, are of particular significance in terms of restrictions placed upon the assembly of the MRIO accounts, will now be discussed.

Data Collection, Assembly, and Documentation. Three areas of particular concern about national accounts data are their collection, assembly, and documentation. A few surveys are made by the BEA to collect primary data for items such as professional incomes, international investment, and plant and equipment expenditures. But most data are assembled by the BEA staff from published and unpublished primary statistics provided by the Bureau of the Census (Census), Internal Revenue Service, Bureau of Labor Statistics, Office of Management and Budget, Treasury, and other federal agencies, as well as from many sundry sources. The Census is responsible for general-purpose statistical programs, while data from most of the other organizations are obtained as by-products of their principal activities [94, p. 194]. Thus, in the case of the national economic accounts, almost all the statistics used, with the exception of those collected by the BEA, are collected by agencies for purposes mainly unrelated to the accounts.

The principal task of the BEA staff, then, is to construct the diverse primary data as a coherent set of accounts. Census data are crucial as they are used not only in constructing the accounts, but their availability also determines the year in which a benchmark can be established. Since the publication in 1936 of Leontief's first input-output article, the major industrial censuses were taken for the years 1939, 1947, 1954, 1958, 1963, 1972, and 1977. As mentioned earlier, it is therefore not a coincidence that, with the exception of 1954, input-output tables were assembled for the same years. The input-output data for these years form the benchmark for the national income and product accounts. Interpolation, extrapolation, and various other estimation techniques are required to estimate many of the data for both accounts. Users always seem somewhat taken aback when they realize that many of the accounts data are estimates rather than actual figures. The prevalence of estimates and the many sources from which even actual data must be assembled are two of the reasons why a thorough documentation of the estimation procedures and data sources is so important.

Although both national income and product data were published as early as 1942, an annual publication was not begun until 1947, when "the National Income Division [of the OBE] cast its published data into an accounting form for the first time" [195, p. 9]. These data were published in a Supplement to the *Survey,* entitled *National Income and Product Statistics of the United States, 1929–46*, with a presentation of six accounts but with no documentation of the methodology [280]. This was followed by another major national income and product Supplement in 1951 [280]; however, it was not until the publication of *National Income, 1954 Edition* [271] that extensive documentation of the national income and product accounts was provided. In fact, that is still (as of 1980) the only comprehensive description available that provides details on constructing the accounts.

Updated descriptions of some methodologies are available, but these are sketchy and are not available in a single document. To obtain a current description of the composition of the data, users must refer to several sources other than the 1954 publication, including three publications of the U.S. Department of Commerce: *U.S. Income and Output* [279]; "The National Income and Product Accounts of the United States, Revised Estimates, 1929-64" [273]; and *The National Income and Product Accounts of the United States, 1929-1965* [272]. To save users some time, portions of the three publications have now been grouped with certain other information into a single document entitled "Readings in Concepts and Methods of National Income Statistics" [266]. However, there are ambiguities in the descriptions presented in the combined publication, some methodologies differ now from the ones described, and even with the combination, the definitions and methodologies are incomplete. Furthermore, the documentation does not cover the input-output accounts. One of the best sources for a comprehensive description of the general structure of the national income and product accounts, including details on the revisions made in the 1960s and on the input-output accounts, is Rosen's book *National Income* [193]. However, Rosen does not provide many of the tedious, yet essential, analytical details that are available in the outdated *National Income, 1954 Edition.*

The details provided on the data and the basic input-output conventions used by the BLS staff to assemble the 450-order 1947 input-output table are probably the best input-output documentation that exists anywhere, even though woefully out of date for present use. Some general information appeared in the *Technical Supplement,* published by the NBER [155], while very specific information on each industry was published in mimeographed BLS worksheets [288]. The worksheets proved invaluable in assembling the MRIO accounts and provided some of the basic guidelines for the documentation presented in later chapters of this volume, even though the information they contained related to national, not multiregional, input-output tables.[7]

It was evidently the intention of the analysts conducting the 1947 study to publish a complete documentation of it after the industry reports had been edited "for consistency, clearness, and data disclosures" [32, p. 99], but when the official work on input-output was discontinued in 1954, these plans could not be carried out. The interruption of the analytical work also halted work on documentation, and the funds to do the latter work have not been restored, even though the analytical work was resumed in 1959. Thus, the worksheets remain only in mimeographed form, unavailable to most analysts. Some of the procedures developed for the 1947 input-output table have been changed for the 1958 table and again for the 1963, 1967, and 1972 tables; but, as of 1980, no complete documentation of any of these last four input-output studies has been published, nor, as mentioned earlier, is an updated description of the income and product accounts available.

Jaszi recognizes the problem as one of being unable to obtain sufficient funds, but states,

> It is evident . . . that our users are dissatisfied because we have not furnished enough information on the statistical sources and methods we use in making our estimates. Our users are right. We have in this respect fallen short of desirable goals. The only comfort I have is that the intensity of their dissatisfaction may be due to the fact that we have fallen from very high standards. The only apology I have is that it takes a great deal of skill and effort to write good methodologies and that we have not been able to marshal the resources necessary to parallel our earlier efforts. [94, p. 204]

As noted earlier, the necessary resources in 1947 were $4 million (in current dollars). Costs of assembling the NIPA data are not readily available, but the 1963 national input-output table cost $1,300,000 [62], the 1967 table $2,500,000, and the 1972 table $2,700,000 [110]. In comparison with the 1947 study, however, the documentation provided in these studies is extremely limited.[8] Even if preparation of thorough documentation of both sets of accounts required as much as several million dollars, the benefits to research analysts and policymakers would be worth the expenditures. In terms of benefit-cost calculations or justification of the spending of taxpayers' money, it is impossible to put a dollar value on good documentation. What is the cost of a wrong calculation made by an economic analyst who assumes that a particular component of the accounts is an actual figure when in fact it is based on a much earlier benchmark year and should therefore be adjusted before being used in policy recommendations to business or the government? Unless users put strong pressure on the BEA staff so that they, in turn, can show the need for documentation of the accounts to the officials at the Department of Commerce and the Office of Management and Budget, funds for the work will not be allocated. During the present study, inadequate documentation complicated the effort to assemble multiregional data on a basis consistent with the national aggregates, as it must also hinder important work in many fields.

Publication Time Lags. Publication time lags no longer seem to be a major problem for the national income and product accounts. When input-output data are discussed, however, the question always arises as to why they are so out of date. The time lag in data publication creates a difficult problem not only in input-output work but in all work involving vast sets of diverse economic statistics that must be regrouped within a coordinated framework, especially when there is no central statistical agency. This problem is not unique to the United States. The time lag exists in most countries; notable exceptions are Canada, Norway, and a few other countries, where input-output tables are published within one to three years of the year for which the data were collected. So-called updated annual U.S. national input-output tables are now being published as interim tables between census years, but even these tables usually are not available on a timely basis. For example, a table for 1971 was published in March of 1977 [261], and the table for 1973 will not be available until late in 1979. So far, the stated objective of publishing annual tables within three years after the year of reference has not been met. Part of the difficulty is that the annual tables that should have been published in 1977, 1978, and 1979 are for the years 1973–1975, all of which are subsequent to the main industrial census year of 1972. When the 1972 table was published in 1979, annual tables for 1973 and 1974 were expected to be available by the end of the calendar year 1979, and annual tables for 1975, 1976, and 1977 were expected to be available before the end of the calendar year 1980. On the other hand, the publication of the 1978 table will have to await publication of the 1977 benchmark year input-output table, which, unless previous schedules are improved, will place its publication in the year 1984. Even for the tables relating to the main census year, the time delays seem unreasonable, but no quick solution appears feasible.

In the United States, the delays result partly from the vast number of data to be handled and partly from the need to obtain them from numerous and decentralized statistical sources. Two of the advantages of input-output accounts over other sets of data, namely, the extensive coverage in terms of all industries in the economy and the internal consistency requirements of the accounting structures, actually exacerbate the difficulty of providing timely publications. A major delay in the publication of one census, say the Census of Transportation, will usually delay the assembly of the entire table since final consistency checks are dependent upon the availability of all relevant information. Also, little can be done to reduce the number of transformations required in tabulating data from the numerous sources when the collection of statistics needed for the input-output accounts is largely uncoordinated from agency to agency. Different industrial classifications, for example, have been used in the past for import and export, manufacturing, and transportation statistics, and some data, such as those from certain federal government agencies, are not even classified according to the standard industrial classification or any other industrial classification.

Table 1-1 provides examples to show the extent of the delays that have occurred and are expected to occur in the assembly of U.S. national input-output tables. Because the table is intended just for illustration of the types of problems that arise, only data from the Census are included. The census forms, of course, cannot be filled out by the establishments until the end of the year (or even the year following the year) for which data are required. At least one year has already elapsed before all the forms are received and checked for completeness by the Census. Although the time required for processing the forms has been shortened and their accuracy improved through the use of computers, it still takes another year and a half to two years to process them, to check for missing data, and finally to suppress information that would disclose data for individual companies. The nondisclosure regulation is being

Table 1–1
Schedule of Collection and Publication of Census and Input-Output Data

Year of Input-Output Table (Census Year)	*Year of Census Questionnaire*	*Year Census Data Are Published*	*Year OBE (BEA) Completes National Input-Output Table*	*Time Span (year) (Col. 4 – Col. 1)*
(1)	(2)	(3)	(4)	(5)
1958	1959	1960–1961	1965	7
1963	1964	1965–1966	1969	6
1967	1968	1969–1971	1974	7
1972	1973	1974–1975	1979	7
1977	1978	1979–1980	n.a.	n.a.

n.a. = not applicable

enforced more rigorously now than in earlier censuses. In the 1947 census publications, for example, "nondisclosed" data could often be determined by subtracting from census region control totals the elements for which information was given or by approximating the output figure, say, by referring to the employment figure for the establishment. In the more recent Census publications, two or more elements are suppressed in such cases, with some elements being suppressed only to maintain the nondisclosure rule for one establishment in another state. Careful checking by the Census staff to assure that the nondisclosure rule is strictly enforced of course takes time.

The national input-output staff received preliminary tabulations for the 1977 census in 1979, two years after the census year, and final tabulations are expected to be available by mid-1980, about three years after the census year. As soon as the preliminary estimates are received, work is begun on the regrouping of the statistics into the input-output format, one of the first tasks being to establish preliminary output control totals for each industry. Delays occur in obtaining data from other statistical sources as well as from the Census. For the last four national input-output tables (1958, 1963, 1967, and 1972), the work by the national input-output staff has taken three to four years to complete once final data were received from the Census. The reasons vary. The long delay in publication of the 1958 national input-output table was explained earlier. As noted, it was ready for publication two years prior to the publication date of the final revised estimates.[9]

For the more recent tables, the long delays are attributable to several factors and cannot be greatly reduced without a reorganization of the statistical agencies and a complete restructuring of the types of data collected and of the procedures used for processing them. Although a certain amount of hand reconciliation will probably always be required in constructing input-output accounts, improved computer techniques could be developed and new computer facilities installed that would certainly reduce some of the present delays. Methods can and should be developed to incorporate data directly from census and other statistical forms into the input-output format, thus eliminating the vast number of transformations and reconciliations that are now needed to establish the accounts. Even so, significant reductions of publication time lags probably cannot be effected without a restructuring of the entire statistical collection, management, and processing system to assure that the appropriate data are collected and stored in a form that can be immediately used in the input-output table. As noted earlier, data are obtained from numerous agencies, none of which have collected the data for the primary purpose of constructing input-output accounts. It might well be desirable, in terms of more accurate data and reduced delays in publication of input-output and other economic accounts, to expend more effort in coordinating the various activities of the data collection agencies.

As will be shown in the following section and the next two chapters, almost all of the national accounting events and issues just discussed affected the assembly of regional and multiregional sets of accounts or the implementation of the MRIO model.

Regional and Multiregional Economic Accounts

There is no thorough documentation—such as that provided by Carson, Duncan and Shelton, and Studenski at the national level—of the history of economic accounts at the regional and multiregional levels.[10] The information supplied in this section has therefore had to be pieced together from many different sources and strongly reflects the author's experiences in formulating and constructing the first comprehensive multiregional accounting system for the United States.

Regional economic theory has a shorter history than general economic theory. The same holds true for accounts. Regional and multiregional accounting has a much shorter history than does national accounting in terms of a general discussion of issues, but, as will be shown later, not in terms of actual estimation of the U.S. data. In the preceding section, a more extensive discussion was provided of the national accounts than would usually be included in a book basically devoted to multiregional accounts. This was done partly because many of the fundamental conceptual questions are the same regardless of the level of geographic detail. But another reason for giving so much detail was that the development of the U.S. regional and multiregional economic accounts was strongly influenced by work being done at almost the same time on the national accounts.

Some of the strong parallel trends in the history of national economic accounts and that of regional and multiregional economic accounts is evidenced by the following similarities: Many of the early estimates for both were made at the NBER; the first regional accounts estimates were published at almost the same time as those of the national accounts; income estimates for the regional economic accounts were made first without estimates being made for the product side of the accounts; and the first regional and multiregional input-output estimates were made by analysts or research groups in the private sector, thus outside of the official auspices of the Department of Commerce. On the other hand, some major divergences occur in the historical evolution. The one of most concern is the current lack of official estimates of regional product accounts and of regional and multiregional input-output accounts. A brief review of the major events, literature, and issues concerning U.S. regional and multiregional accounts is given here to indicate the historical context for the MRIO accounts.

Regional Income Estimates

As with the U.S. national economic accounts, the initial focus in collecting regional data was on the estimation of regional income, and major work on these estimates was done at the NBER. In 1922, one year after the first volume on national income estimates for 1909–1919 was published in the NBER series [142], a volume was published, also by the NBER, on state income estimates, which were made by Oswald W. Knauth [105]. The latter volume was followed in 1925 by another volume on state income estimates, this one by Maurice Leven [120]. (He updated earlier estimates by Frederick R. Macaulay.) Both Knauth and Leven had worked on the national income estimates. In 1939, a book by W.M. Adamson providing 1929 and 1935 estimates of income for counties in Alabama was published by the University of Alabama [1].

A substantial amount of discussion of regional income has appeared in various NBER publications. The books by Knauth and Leven have already been mentioned. Beginning in 1939, research on regional income has been reviewed at the NBER Conference on Research in Income and Wealth. Articles that appeared in the NBER publications from those conferences included the following: "Some Problems Involved in Allocating Incomes by States" by R.R. Nathan in 1939 [157] and "Income and the Measurement of the Relative Capacities of the States" by P.H. Wueller also in 1939 [157]; "A Statistical Study of Income Differences Among Communities" by Herbert E. Klarman in 1943 [158]; "Some Effects of Region, Community Size, Color, and Occupation on Family and Individual Income" by D. Gale Johnson in 1952 [159]; and "Regional and National Product Projections and Their Interrelations" by Walter Isard and Guy Freutel in 1954 [160]. In June 1955, regional income was the principal subject of the Conference on Research in Income and Wealth, and the volume entitled *Regional Income,* all of which was devoted to that conference, was published by the NBER in 1957 [161]. It should be noted, however, that all of these NBER publications except the 1954 article, dealt with measures of regional income rather than regional product.

In 1934, the first official national income estimates were published by the Department of Commerce [264]. Five years later, in May 1939, the Department published *State Income Payments, 1929-1937,* by Robert R. Nathan and John L. Martin [151]. This volume initiated the official U.S. state income series. As of the summer of 1980, however, no official estimates have been published for the expenditures side of the regional accounts, nor have there been any official federal publications of state or multiregional input-output tables, although demand for both types of data is strong. Because only regional income estimates have been published officially, the discussion of comprehensive sets of regional and multiregional accounts will be presented first in terms of the literature concerning the accounts and then in terms of accounting issues relevant to the MRIO accounts.

Comprehensive Regional and Multiregional Accounts

As noted at the beginning of this chapter, economic policy issues must be analyzed within a structural framework. This is especially true for analyses of regional and multiregional policies because of the interindustrial and interregional linkages. The reasons for the lack of attention to the official development of accounts at a subnational level are best understood in light of the failure by most analysts and policymakers to ask the appropriate questions. In the 1960s, for example, attention was focused on "pockets of poverty," rather than on the broader structural problems that created those pockets. The situation has worsened, rather than improved. Since the 1960s, emphasis throughout the federal government has been placed increasingly on short-term studies. Yet, in order to understand the nature of problems confronting each region, the structure of the production, consumption, employment, transportation, and other major relations must be analyzed, and to analyze these, accurate and comprehensive sets of regional and multiregional data are required. What is accepted by analysts as being crucial for conducting good national studies is still a largely unproclaimed need (at least in the literature) by most regional analysts, who often make do with fewer than adequate data. The discussion that follows, therefore, is presented with these basic considerations in mind.

The neglect of the regional product side of the regional income and product accounts and also of the multiregional input-output accounts is still evident in official publications of the Department of Commerce, although efforts are being made to construct both types of accounts. Work at the OBE on estimating the state personal consumption expenditures component of gross regional product, for example, was begun in the 1960s, but so far no data have been published. Regional and multiregional input-output accounts have also been largely neglected by the Department until recently. In 1968, Morris R. Goldman, then Deputy Director of the Office of Business Economics, lent cautious support to the development of multiregional input-output tables in his oral presentation at the Regional Science Association meeting in Cambridge, Massachusetts [61]. Since then, a concerted effort has been made by the BEA staff to obtain the funds required to construct multiregional input-output accounts. But funds requested for this new program have been consistently removed from the BEA's budget either at higher levels within the Department of Commerce, such as the Social and Economic Statistics Administration, or even by the Office of Management and Budget. Until such time as the accounts can be assembled by the BEA staff, Daniel H. Garnick, Associate Director for Regional Economics, and Philip M. Ritz, head of the Interindustry Economics Division, at the BEA have been providing moral support for the private effort of the staff at Jack Faucett Associates, Inc., to assemble the 1972 multiregional input-output data.

Thus, only unofficial conceptual frameworks and estimates of regional product accounts and regional and multiregional input-output accounts are available for the United States. Some of the literature relating to those will be reviewed after the general effort by Hirsch and others to establish a systematic set of regional accounts has been discussed.

In the late 1950s, a major examination of problems concerning regional accounts was initiated by Harvey S. Perloff, Director of Regional Studies for Resources for the Future, Inc. (RFF). Hirsch spent a year at the RFF investigating the possibility of developing a system of regional accounts. The RFF then gave him a grant, which enabled him to continue the work at Washington University. The Committee on Regional Accounts was formed in May 1958. The purpose of the Committee was summarized by Hirsch as follows:

> At its 1960 Conference, the Committee investigated major decision-making problems on a subnational level, and attempted to design regional accounts that would aid in the examination of alternative solutions to these problems. The second Conference, held in 1962, attempted to foster a deeper understanding of key elements of regional accounts. The 1964 Conference made a special effort to investigate regional accounts and information systems which would elucidate and provide help for specific regional policy decisions. [82, p. x]

The conferences, which were attended by numerous regional scholars, resulted in three volumes [81; 82; 83]. After 1964, there was a hiatus until 1969, when Hirsch, then at the Institute of Government and Public Affairs at the University of California in Los Angeles, received funding from the Committee for Urban Economics to hold a number of regional accounts conferences. One on Regional Input-Output: Second Generation was held in May 1969 in Washington, D.C., and was attended by twenty-five people from academic institutions, private organizations, and the federal government.

The wide divergences in opinions concerning the role regional and multiregional accounts should play in analytical studies can best be seen by reviewing some of the literature.

Regional and Multiregional Accounting Literature. Numerous articles have been written about the feasibility of extending the national accounts concepts to regional and multiregional levels and about some of the conceptual problems encountered in constructing any set of regional and multiregional accounts. But the only available survey article that is restricted to accounting at the regional and multiregional levels is Stone's "Social Accounts at the Regional Level: A Survey," presented at a 1960 conference on problems of economic development [205]. Even Stone's article, however, is devoted more to an explanation of the various methods of constructing proposed accounts at the regional and multiregional levels and to a description of a specific accounting framework than to a survey of actual accounts, partly because so few accounts were available in 1960. Because of this emphasis, his article will be discussed later.

Before the regional and multiregional accounting proposals made by Stone and others are discussed, three major surveys of regional economic analyses will be reviewed.

General Economic Analyses. Useful, but now very outdated, surveys of general regional and multiregional economic analyses for the United States were made by Meyer in 1963 [133] and by Kerr and Williamson in 1970 [99]; a more up-to-date survey by Richardson was published in 1978 [185]. Each of these articles contains only a brief mention of regional and multiregional economic accounting; thus, a major survey to update Stone's 1960 one is long overdue. The review here will cover only the highlights.

Meyer devotes only two of forty pages to a discussion of regional data and regional income accounting. He apparently did not consider it necessary to review the regional and multiregional accounting literature thoroughly, partly, no doubt, because of the publication of Stone's "excellent recent survey" [133, fn., p. 24]. However, Meyer's lack of attention to regional and multiregional accounting may also have been attributable to the priorities he established for the ongoing research. He wanted relatively fewer regional research funds to be allocated to account development at that time for three reasons. First, he suggested (with debatable justification) that adequate and exceptionally accurate data already existed. He states:

> Indeed, it is hardly any exaggeration to say that regional economics is in many ways one of the most fortunately blessed fields in economics in terms of data availability. [133, p. 52]

Second, he indicated that additional efforts at the regional and multiregional levels should await improvement of the national accounts concepts and data because of the problems being encountered then in assembling those data. Third, he wanted to reduce the level of support for assembling regional accounts and allocate the funds to developing and testing hypotheses [133, p. 53].

Whereas Meyer stresses the need to await improvements in the national accounts and the reallocation of funding priorities, Kerr and Williamson emphasize the inappropriateness of using the same type of accounts for analyzing national and regional issues. At the beginning of their review, they say that theories, principles, and analytical tools have been borrowed by regional economists from the general economic discipline and mention national income accounting as one case in point. In their concluding section, they stress that

> . . . the need still exists for an adequate flow of appropriate data to feed into the economic models. For instance, the form of economic accounting developed at the national level is often inappropriate and sometimes irrelevant and misleading when applied to regional problems. [99, p. 15]

They go on to mention the publications by the Committee on Regional Accounts from the 1960 [83], 1962 [81], and 1964 [82] conferences and an article by Leven [116] as examples of work being done on regional accounting. Even so, neither of these two early reviews of the literature adequately stressed the need for the development of comprehensive regional or multiregional accounts as a basis for analyses.

Richardson poses two almost contradictory views on regional accounting. First, he cannot find justification for funding regional income and product accounts. He states:

> In this context, he [Meyer] questions the need for elaborate systems of regional income and product accounts. . . . With the possible exception of Czamanski (1973), no one makes strong pleas for the construction of such accounts nowadays. [185, p. 3]

Actually, Meyer was asking for the expenditure of less relative effort on regional income and product accounting, not a complete abandonment of effort, as suggested by the above quotation from Richardson's article.

Second, Richardson indicates that resource stock accounts and input-output accounts may "salvage" the regional accounting approach and that the former need more attention.

Richardson is correct in his assessment that few requests for more data have appeared recently in the literature (and also that long-run issues are especially critical in regional analyses). The fact is, however, that requests for data are just not being made in publications. Numerous requests for accounting information and data have been received, for example, by the MRIO research staff at the Massachusetts Institute of Technology from analysts at academic institutions; private industries; and federal, state, and local governments. In addition, many of these research analysts and other interested user groups throughout the country wrote letters to the Office of Federal Statistical Policy and Standards in June 1979 requesting that funds be provided the BEA to assemble state economic accounts. Requests such as these indicate that a great need for up-to-date regional and multiregional accounts does exist.

Since the accounting literature has not been dealt with adequately in any of the general economic surveys of regional analyses, some of the major accounting proposals will be reviewed here.

Regional and Multiregional Accounting Studies. Several alternative proposals for regional and multiregional accounts and their uses for economic analyses have been made. The ones by Stone; Hirsch; Isard; Czamanski; Leven; and Leven, Legler, and Shapiro will be reviewed here. Although Stone's article does not relate to the United States, it is included because of his important influence here and abroad. (The MRIO accounts are not discussed here, because they are dealt with extensively in chapter 2.)

Stone begins his 1960 article by presenting a detailed theoretical discussion of the various ways that economic data can be portrayed at a regional and multiregional level, first for a single indicator, such as income payments, then for more disaggregated data, such as income and product accounts. The article includes a set of 1948 accounts for 12 civil defense regions in the United Kingdom. These data were assembled at the Department of Applied Economics of the University of Cambridge during 1950–1954. Fourteen transactions are recorded for each region. These are separated into production accounts, income and outlay accounts, and capital transactions accounts, with details being provided in the article on the accounting balances that must be maintained. Stone concludes his article with a brief survey of local and regional input-output studies in Belgium, France, Holland, Italy, Japan, Sweden, and the United States. At the time he wrote the article, far more regional and multiregional input-output studies had been conducted in the United States than elsewhere. The article is available in at least two publications, one an original collection of papers, edited by Isard and Cumberland, from the first OEEC study conference on problems of economic development [93] and the other a collection by Stone of his own articles [205].

In a presentation at the American Economic Association meeting in December 1961, Hirsch proposed the establishment by the federal government of a set of regional accounts and also a Department of Urban Affairs [80, pp. 365, 373]. The department has been established, but the set of accounts has not been. The accounting framework that he proposed was to be a three-tier system of integrated national, regional, and intraregional accounts. The national accounts were to be used to obtain regional final demand and also to check against aggregates of the regional totals. The regional accounts, said Hirsch, were a key element in the overall system in that they included an input-output model for the determination of regional interactions. The intraregional accounts, he said, were people-oriented and place-oriented and were dependent upon the collection of adequate data for standard metropolitan statistical areas and other data and upon the availability and use of improved high-speed electronic data-processing equipment by federal, state, and local governments.

Isard devotes a full chapter of his book *Methods of Regional Analysis,* published in 1960, to regional income and product accounts and their estimation [92, ch. 4]. As was customary in much of the early accounting literature, Isard calls all regional accounting *regional income accounting,* but then proceeds to discuss gross regional product as well as gross regional income. He reviews the conceptual problems and methods of measuring regional income and product and the various frameworks for establishing regional economic accounts, referencing seventy-nine regional accounting publications. In the same book, Isard presents a regional accounting framework and his now classic interregional input-output flow table. The latter will be discussed in detail in chapter 2. Mention should be made here, however, of the term *ideal* as it is often used to refer to his proposed interregional table. Its use by regional analysts is based upon a statement made by Isard:

> Although we recognize that such an ideal set of data has not thus far been assembled, we present the outlines of this ideal set because these outlines enable us better to appreciate and evaluate the potentials, problems, and limitations of the interregional input-output approach. [92, p. 319]

Some of the theoretical issues surrounding his interregional accounting framework when used for actual policy analyses, which make it less than ideal for studies such as those related to technological change, are covered in chapter 3.

Czamanski's accounting proposal is a standard comprehensive one, detailing particular ways of constructing accounts for regional income and product, input-output, balance of payments, flow of funds, and wealth (stock). He stresses the need to develop formats of regional economic accounts that vary substantially from their national counterparts. He also discusses both regional and multiregional input-output accounts, but cautions against building and using these accounts in regions in which almost no interindustry flows occur. Finally, he emphasizes the need for stock accounts, which could help link the research of regional economists with that of physical planners. [24, pp. 6–11]

In the book by Leven, Legler, and Shapiro, the discussion of a multiregional accounting system is presented on a much more general level than Czamanski's, with the principal focus on the particular components of accounts that must be taken into consideration rather than on the more technical details concerning how all data can be incorporated into a comprehensive system. They state:

> In sum, the purpose of this study is to consider the important issues involved in, and to make recommendations for the establishment of a regional accounts system for the United States for the purpose of analyzing differential regional changes in income, employment, output, consumption, and population with special reference to the analysis of public sector (mainly federal) programs and policy decisions in those areas affecting, by design or otherwise, the levels of regional development as indicated by the aforementioned variables. [119, p. 7]

They list eleven characteristics that such a system should have, ranging all the way from the rather specific first one, "that it would account for changes in the stock of capital and its utilization as well as changes in utilization of labor services," to the very general eleventh one, that the system should account for "macro measures of the internal spatial form of the region" [119, p. 10]. By this eleventh characteristic, they mean that recognition should be given in the accounts to "potential interaction between the internal arrangements of major cities and their economic performance" [119, p. 148]. It should be noted that Leven's earlier accounting proposal had been of a more standard and less comprehensive kind, setting up regional income and product accounts, regional input-output accounts (focusing on stable technology coefficients), and regional *from-to* accounts (focusing on stable trade coefficients) [118].

The present study is probably the first regional or multiregional one in which an extensive discussion of the general multiregional accounting framework is combined with a discussion of its use in modeling and with details of the data sources and estimation procedures. Because most of the publications do not contain sufficient information for comparisons of proposed and actual regional and multiregional accounting structures, it is not possible to review here the many important ways in which they differ. The publications do, however, contain a fair amount of discussion of various issues related to them, of which the major ones relevant to the MRIO accounts will now be reviewed.

Accounting Issues. Many of the issues present today in constructing income accounts were addressed in the previously referenced 1957 NBER volume *Regional Income* [161] and in the collected papers of the regional accounts meetings in 1960 [83], 1962 [81], and 1964 [82]. Some of the basic issues of regional accounts have centered on what regional classification scheme should be used, whether the accounts should be assembled by separate regional units or by a central agency, how the conceptual framework for regional economic accounts should be specified, publication time lags, and how computational difficulties in compiling such vast arrays of data should be handled.

Regional Classification. The possibilities for area designations are almost unlimited. They include states, counties, cities, standard metropolitan statistical areas, urban areas, state economic areas, census tracts, unincorporated places, city blocks, watershed districts, school districts, utility districts, and so on. Until recently, many of the statistics were collected according to major political units, such as states or counties. Now, effort is being directed more and more toward assembling data for specifically defined areas for which no political authority exists.

A few of the many geographic areas in the United States associated with political authority are states, counties, and cities. The Census and other federal statistical organizations have collected data for these political areas for many years. The first economic census was for "the year 1809, when inquiries on manufacturing were included within the 1810 Census of Population" [235, p. 1]. Mining inquiries appeared in 1840, fisheries in 1880, business and construction in 1929, selected services in 1935, and transporation in 1963 [235, p. 2]. The nine geographic divisions have been used by the Census since the 1909 Census of Manufactures, and the nine divisions are also reclassified into four geographic regions–Northeast, South, North Central, and West. According to Ullman and Klove,

> The set of geographic regions and divisions still used [as of 1957] by the Census Bureau were developed before the turn of the century by Henry Gannett, Geographer of the Census, but the considerations which led to these areas are largely lost to history. . . . The nonmetropolitan state economic areas were defined almost exclusively on the principle of grouping together those counties with similar economic and social statistical indexes. [218, pp. 92, 94]

In addition, many census statistics are provided for geographic areas that are not legally constituted, such as the approximately 230 standard metropolitan areas. The state economic areas are another regional grouping for which no legal authority exists. For the 1950 census, a set of 501 state economic areas was designated by the Census in cooperation with the U.S. Department of Agriculture. These 501 areas were combined into 119 economic subregions for Census use, and Donald J. Bogue in a 1954 article further combined them into 13 economic regions and 5 economic provinces [218, p. 90]. Thus, until recently, the Census has played a critical role in designating geographic areas for the collection of statistics.

For the present study, the state was chosen as the regional unit, because it is a political unit, and policy action relating to it can be taken based upon the outcomes of regional analyses. Also, as Ullman and Klove note,

> States have definite boundaries, completely cover the United States, are readily recognized, and have all types of data available which can

readily be made comparable with the past by simple compilation. [218, p. 99]

Collection Agency. The question of who should collect data is partly answered by determining the regional division for which the data are being collected. If accounts are needed only for the Cambridge school district, say, the Cambridge school district will probably have to expend the time, effort, and money to collect them. However, frequently the same types of data are useful to many different regional groups throughout the country. Then, a central statistical agency should bear the responsibility for the data collection. Such is the case with state accounts data. There are several reasons for giving a central agency the basic task of constructing a general set of state economic accounts or, at least, of coordinating the assembly of the data.

First, economic accounts data assembled by a central agency can be obtained for all regions, with a minimum of effort required to assure that all estimates are internally consistent. Consideration can also be given to the longer-term issues of providing data for multipurposes (rather than just the immediate purpose) and of maintaining consistency with other accounting systems. At present, individual groups assemble their own regional accounts data, using varying methodologies, and provide little or no documentation of the methodologies and data sources used, so that integrating statistics from one region with those from another is difficult or impossible to do. During the past 25 years, for example, U.S. research groups have assembled input-output tables covering different years, regions, and industries and based upon different accounting frameworks. Construction of regional and multiregional economic accounts by a central statistical agency would provide consistent estimates within a common accounting framework that could then be used for comparative regional and multiregional economic analyses.

Second, the uniform accounting framework imposed by a central agency should improve the overall quality and accuracy of regional data. Even if estimates made by individual regional groups were documented so that they could be combined with those made in other regions and if estimates were compiled in each region, the summation of the individual regional data would probably provide an estimate of total GNP and other statistics that would vary widely from the corresponding national aggregates. The variations would be difficult to correct since compilation of the initial data involved many different agencies, some of which may have disbanded by the time checks could be made. In addition, it takes considerable time for a research group to learn the basic methodology of compiling sets of regional accounts. At the same time, even if supposedly the same methodologies are used, the estimates will often vary from, say, one state to another just because analysts in one state will interpret the methodologies differently from the ways in which they are interpreted by analysts in another state. Also, wide variations in the quality of the estimates are bound to occur, because more resources can be allocated to data collection efforts in some states than in others. A compilation of statistics by one central agency would therefore improve the overall quality of the estimates. Moreover, accuracy of estimates made for a comprehensive set of regions covering the entire United States could be checked against U.S. aggregates. These checks could be built in as part of the data assembly effort by a central statistical agency.

Third, given the sizeable economies of scale realized by having one agency responsible for collecting data and constructing estimates for all regions, less overall time, effort, and money would be required to assemble data by a central statistical agency than by having data assembled in each individual region. As a case in point, it now costs the individual states from $50,000 to more than $100,000 to compile data for their input-output tables. A complete set of 51 tables constructed by individual states would therefore cost a minimum of $2,550,000 to as much as $5,000,000, or even more. On the other hand, the 1963 multiregional input-output tables for 51 regions, which were assembled by a single research group, cost only about $750,000 to construct, and the BEA staff has estimated that a 1967 set of tables would have cost about $1,500,000. Economies of scale can definitely be realized when 51 tables are constructed by the same group, using the same methodologies and data sources.[11]

Centralization of the regional data assembly efforts would therefore allow state decision makers and analysts to improve and expand the official data with supplemental statistics peculiar to their states and to investigate specific state policy issues. Because most regional economic research units probably encounter opposition to the allocation of adequate funds for data assembly, the statistics are often hastily compiled, almost no consideration is given to maintaining consistency with other classification systems (industrial, regional, foreign trade, etc.), and the methodology is seldom documented. Other research groups have no way of ascertaining how the estimates were calculated and so cannot change or improve them. Also, they have no basis for determining how accurately the statistics have been estimated and compiled and therefore how reliable the accounts are. If the basic sets of regional accounts were to be routinely assembled by one central agency, only a small fraction of the total cost of compiling a reliable set of accounts for each region would be incurred, and it should be easier to insure that the accounts are accurate and consistent and that the methodology is documented.

Conceptual Framework. Many of the conceptual issues are the same for national and for regional and multiregional economic accounts. The problems encountered in making imputations, defining final and intermediate production, using constant or current dollars, separating capital and current accounts, and so on, arise for either set of estimates. Some conceptual issues, however, are specific to regional and multiregional economic accounts. These will be dealt with in more detail here.

One of the major conceptual difficulties in establishing a regional accounting framework has stemmed from the need to differentiate between where income is earned and where it is received and between where a product is bought and where the buyer lives. Personal income and product accounts can be specified at the regional level by where the income recipients work, or where they live, or where they spend their money. Variations therefore occur in the way in which the data are collected and published.

There is also a problem in determining the regional location of consumption for an individual firm or a government body, since the region where the good or service is used may not be the same as the one where it is recorded as a purchase. The central office of a firm, for example, may record a capital purchase that then appears under the gross private fixed capital formation sector of final demand for the particular region where the office is located, but this capital good may be used by a plant situated in any one of a number of regions in which the firm operates. Similarly, with the public sector, the purchase of a good or service may be recorded in the accounts of a federal government agency in Washington, D.C., whereas the actual consumption may occur in one of the regions, or even overseas. Because the desired income or product accounts concept will undoubtedly change from one economic analysis to another, regional data should preferably be provided for each type of basic location concept or be capable of being easily transformed from one definition to another.

Publication Time Lags. Only the delays in publishing the MRIO accounts will be discussed here; information concerning the delays that have occurred for other studies is not available. One of the basic requirements in constructing the MRIO accounts was that the data in the state input-output tables when summed should exactly equal the corresponding data in the national table for the given year. As long as this requirement is enforced, the MRIO accounts can never be published prior to the national accounts. The 1963 MRIO accounts were published one year after the 1963 national ones. At this point, it is difficult to predict what the time lags will be if future sets of multiregional accounts are constructed at the BEA.

Computational Difficulties. A few of the past reservations about the feasibility of compiling regional and multiregional economic accounts have undoubtedly been due to the fact that the statistical system requires the handling of millions of figures. Early computer techniques were cumbersome and slow, computer capacities were extremely limited, and massive sets of data, such as those required for a comprehensive set of regional or multiregional economic accounts, could not be effectively and efficiently collected and maintained on a routine basis. Because rapid advances are being made in the capabilities and use of computers, the problems of data collection, storage, and retrieval no longer seem insurmountable. In fact, a completely new approach to national, regional, and multiregional economic accounts may now be feasible, given the recent developments in computer technology.

Conclusion

Major political, economic, and social events have influenced both the timing of the evolution of economic accounting and the conceptual framework adopted in the United States. The world depression in the 1930s, the second world war in the 1940s, the cold war in the 1950s, and the war against poverty in the 1960s were a few of the major influences molding the basic U.S. accounting framework. If the emphasis in the 1970s on short-term analyses that can only lead to stop-gap policies continues into the 1980s, major improvements in the accounting system probably will not occur. On the other hand, if the major structural problems of the economic system and means of overcoming them begin to receive consideration, an entirely new accounting approach, and one that makes use of the tremendous advances in computer technology, may be possible. The MRIO accounts would be only one small, but important, component of such a comprehensive accounting system.

The general structure of interregional and multiregional input-ouput accounts and the specifications of all the major components of the MRIO accounts are presented in the next chapter.

Notes

1. The United States perhaps should be counted as the fourth country to have published official estimates. In 1926, the Federal Trade Commission (FTC) submitted a report to the Senate, prepared by Francis Walker, chief economist of the FTC, entitled *National Wealth and Income,* with estimates of value of product by industry for 1918–1923. The FTC work on the national income estimates, however, was discontinued because of curtailed funding [13, pp. 154–155]. The estimates from the BFDC are generally considered to be the first official ones.

2. The term *order* has been used in some of the national input-output publications in the United States. It refers to the approximate number of endogenous industries in the tables. The 500-order table, for example, actually has 496 detailed endogenous industries, the 370-order table 367, and the 80-order table 79. Because the number of endogenous industries can change, depending upon how *open* or *closed* the system is, a rounded approximation,

rather than a precise number, is sometimes used to specify the table size. In at least some of the current publications of the Department of Commerce, however, a precise industry number is again given.

3. Most of the information in this paragraph was obtained from a Department of Commerce report by Joseph W. Duncan and William C. Shelton [280, pp. 111-112].

4. Some of the worldwide use of input-output techniques was reviewed in April 1979 at the Seventh International Conference on Input-Output Techniques, which was attended by more than 350 input-output analysts from both socialist and capitalist countries. Among that number was the first delegation to attend such a conference from the People's Republic of China. (As mentioned earlier, the use of input-output models in some socialist countries is troubling to certain people in the United States, who assume that their use in capitalist countries implies government planning and control.)

5. It is interesting to note that on the original worksheets for the 1958 table received at the Harvard Economic Research Project, the rows and columns of the table were referred to as sales and purchases, probably reflecting initial hesitation to use the term *input-output,* given the earlier criticism.

6. Duncan and Shelton in their report provide details on decisions that had to be made concerning the integration of the two sets of accounts and discuss some of the problems that remain unresolved [280, pp. 112–114].

7. Much of the credit for completion of the extensive documentation relating to the national tables belongs to Philip M. Ritz, now head of the Interindustry Economics Division of the BEA. He remains to this day a strong advocate of expanded and improved documentation of the input-output accounts.

8. Some documentation of the final demand portion of the 1972 table is being prepared by the BEA staff.

9. The table was made available to the general public only at the 80-order level, though interested users could obtain greater industry detail from unpublished worksheets.

10. In this text, the term *regional* will be used to refer to accounts or models of a single region, while *multiregional* will be used to refer to all accounts or models of two or more regions and also to designate the particular theoretical technology and trade structures discussed in chapter 3.

11. Considering that the 1967 national input-output table cost $2,500,000, expenditures on multiregional accounts are obviously not exorbitant. The lower cost for multiregional than for national tables is partially explained by the fact that the 1967 national table has 480 industries, while the 1963 multiregional table has only 80.

2 Multiregional Input-Output Accounts

In this chapter, the general background and specific details of the multiregional input-output (MRIO) accounting framework will be presented, following a brief discussion of the current set of MRIO accounts and the relationship between the MRIO and the interregional input-output (IRIO) accounting frameworks.

Background of the Multiregional Accounts Study

As was noted in chapter 1, one of the purposes of the present study was to establish and construct a consistent multiregional accounting framework for the United States, providing detailed documentation of data sources and estimation procedures. The state data for those accounts were obtained from numerous sources when actual data were available. When they were not available, several different estimation procedures had to be used.[1] It was therefore imperative that the data be assembled within a consistent accounting framework. An accounting framework is like a crossword puzzle in that one wrong entry can affect many other entries. The framework does provide a consistency check on the entries; and it is a useful way to assure that gross errors in estimation are caught; but it does not assure that the accounts will be 100 percent accurate.

Although national economic accounts are now routinely published for the United States, the lack of consistent sets of regional data and disagreements among analysts over the conceptual definitions required for the assembly of regional statistics delayed the compilation of regional and multiregional economic accounts. The set of multiregional data that has been assembled in the present study is the most comprehensive that has ever been available for the U.S. economy using a common industrial and regional classification scheme and covering all industries in the economy. For all the data assembly, of course, a considerable amount of research effort was required to assure consistency among all the data components. A basic consistency requirement, for example, was that the state data in the set of interindustry tables assembled for the MRIO accounts had to sum to the corresponding national input-output data. The decisions as to selection of years, industrial classification, and regional classification were crucial in determining the data to be used in the accounts and their accuracy and consistency. Those decisions will be reviewed here, before the specific IRIO and MRIO accounting frameworks are described.

Selection of Years

Since one requirement was that the national and multiregional sets of accounts had to be consistent, the selection of years for the MRIO accounts was governed by the years for which national input-output tables can be constructed. In turn, as noted in chapter 1, the national tables can only be reliably constructed in the United States for years in which major statistical censuses are taken. Thus, in 1967, when the MRIO study was begun, the years from which a selection could reasonably be made were 1947, 1958, and 1963. (No national input-output table had been officially published for 1954, another census year, so that year was excluded from consideration for the MRIO tables.) The intent was to have as current a set of accounts as possible; therefore, when the choice had to be narrowed to only one year, 1963 was chosen, in spite of the fact that the exact publication date of the 1963 national input-output table was still to be determined and that all the MRIO data were to sum to those national data.

The construction of output, employment, payroll, and final demand data for 1947, 1958, and 1963 was begun on the assumption that a complete set of MRIO accounting data could be obtained for all three years. As the work progressed, however, it became evident that the interregional trade-flow data, especially, but also the state technology data, for 1947 and 1958 would be far too difficult and too expensive to assemble. Because 1963 was the first year for which a census of transportation existed, interregional trade estimates for earlier years would have had to be determined by relying primarily on the annual publications of *Carload Waybill Statistics* by the Interstate Commerce Commission, a data source that was not considered to be as accurate as the census of transportation source and which covered only rail shipments. For state technology estimates, the main source of detailed industry technologies (the 1963 data having yet to be published) was the 1947 national input-output table. But adjustments made to the 80-order 1947 national table in the 1960s had not been made to the 450-order 1947 data that were required for the technology estimates. Thus, both trade and technology estimates for 1947 and 1958 posed serious data assembly problems.

There were four major reasons that the data assembly on all data components other than trade flows and technology was continued for 1947 and 1958 even though 1963 had been chosen as the base year. First, the work on the 1958 estimates was continued in case 1963 national data might not be available prior to the fall of 1970, when the MRIO data assembly was to be completed. Although it was hoped that 1963 could be used as the base year, many 1963 statistics had still not been published by late 1967, when a decision had to be made as to the continuation of data assembly for 1958. Also, no definite date could be obtained from the OBE for the publication of the 1963 national input-output table. After several delays, it was finally published in November

1969. If the 1963 data had not become available in 1969, the base year for the MRIO accounts would have had to be 1958.

Second, the work on the 1947 state estimates was continued because it was felt that the work already done on them would be extremely valuable for all the MRIO data assembly since extensive documentation of the 1947 national input-output table existed. The documentation of the 1947 table, provided both in the *Technical Supplement* [155] and in the mimeographed worksheets [288], is still (as of 1980–33 years later) far more complete than that available for the 1958, 1963, 1967, or 1972 national input-output tables. However, many of the subtleties of the data and meanings of the methodologies and descriptions in the 1947 documentation could be understood only as the various 1947 state estimates were actually made.

Third, when it was determined that complete input-output accounts could not be assembled for all three years, the availability of state output, payroll, and final demand data for more than one year was still considered desirable. These are the types of data that are in great general demand by research groups and can be used for many regional economic studies in addition to those using the MRIO model.

Fourth, as work proceeded on the 1947 and 1958 estimates, it became evident that determination of the appropriate data source or examination of the reasonableness of the 1963 estimates through cross-checks with other data could best be done with complete sets of 1947 and 1958 data for as many components as possible. Omissions and inconsistencies in the 1963 data sources often became apparent only as estimates were assembled from slightly different sources for 1947 and 1958. Furthermore, the 1947 and 1958 final demand and output data could be used for testing the accuracy of the MRIO model, as explained in chapter 3.

The actual assembly of data for more than one year did not appreciably increase the overall amount of time and money spent. Especially for this first round of constructing MRIO accounts, the major amount of time was spent in determining the definition and composition of each particular data component, establishing procedures for constructing the estimates, locating data sources, and writing the documentation of the procedures, rather than in recording data from the sources and adjusting them to be consistent with the national estimates. The inclusion of data for two additional years, therefore, did not significantly add to the total work of this initial phase of the study.

A complete set of MRIO accounts is presently (as of the summer of 1980) available only for 1963. Because of the impossibility of assembling complete 1947 and 1958 MRIO accounts, comparisons of changes in technology and interregional trade relations cannot be made. However, comparisons can be made of changes in the composition and level of final demand, using both historical (1947, 1958, and 1963) and projected (1970 and 1980) data. For outputs, employment, and payrolls, data were assembled for 1967 as well as for 1947, 1958, and 1963.

Industrial Classification

With certain exceptions, all the statistics for the MRIO accounts were assembled using the 80-order input-output (IO) classification initially employed by the OBE for the 1958 national input-output table. The exceptions were: (1) IO-74, Research & development; IO-81, Business travel, entertainment, & gifts; and IO-82, Office supplies, were eliminated as separate industries. (2) The components of the final demand and value added sectors of the table were adjusted and expanded to reflect specific conventions required for the MRIO accounts. These adjustments are detailed in the section of this chapter describing the MRIO accounting framework. The input-output industrial classification table, with specific standard industrial classification (SIC) components for each industry, is given in table A–1 in the appendix.

Although the same 80-order classification used for the 1958 national input-output table was later employed by the OBE for the revised 1947 table and for the 1963, 1967, and 1972 tables, it should be noted that there were minor modifications in the SIC composition of the industries in the 1963 and 1967 tables and a major modification in the 1972 table. Comparisons from year to year must take these modifications into account. The six specific minor changes that occurred in the definitions of input-output industries between 1958 and 1963 were given in table 1–1 in the first volume of this series [181, p. 16]. Even though the changes were minor, it would have been preferable to use the 1963 rather than the 1958 industrial classification; however, in most cases, it was impossible to adjust the output, employment, payroll, and final demand state estimates for 1947, 1958, and 1963 to reflect these changes since they did not become known until near the completion of the study in the fall of 1970. The only adjustment made to reflect the changes in definition was for IO-74. Research & development. In the 1963 national input-output table, this industry was eliminated, and the data were included in the industries in which the research and development actually took place. This change was made to the 1947 and 1958 data, but for the remaining five industries whose composition changed, the changes were so slight (ranging from less than 1 percent for IO-79, State & local government enterprises, to 4.5 percent for IO-4, Agricultural, forestry, & fishery services) that no modification was made. The comparability of the state data for the three years should not be greatly affected by this lack of adjustment.

The choice of level of industrial aggregation to use was fairly well predetermined by time and budget constraints, combined with the timing of the data assembly (that is, the fact that most of the data had to be assembled prior to the publication of the 1963 national table). When the project was begun, in 1967, the three levels of industrial aggregation that were considered as options were the 450-order 1947 classification, the 370-order 1963 classification, and the 80-order 1958 classification. Because the revisions to the 1947 input-output table had been made only to the 80-order and not to the 450-order data, and because the 1947 national income and product accounts had been revised, the use of the 450-order classification would not only have entailed an unduly cumbersome quantity of data for a pilot study of this type, but the number of data adjustments made to the national table would have created an unwieldy set of transformations for the multiregional accounts and increased the unreliability of the data estimates. Some of the same problems concerning the number of estimates to be calculated would have had to be confronted if the 370-order 1963 classification had been chosen. Given the uncertainty of the availability of the 1963 data before the completion of the study and therefore the lack of any national data except the 80-order 1947 and 1958 national data against which to check the estimates, and given the fact that tables with comparable sets of data for all three years were to be available at the 80-order level of classification, the 1958 industrial classification was used for the MRIO accounts.

Regional Classification

An extensive discussion of the choice of regions was included in chapter 1. As noted there, the choice of a spatial unit for a particular economic analysis will depend upon the analysis that is to be made. Data must sometimes be assembled, for example, by watershed districts for the study of water requirements within a community, by standard metropolitan statistical areas (which may cut across county, state, and other regional boundaries) for urban studies, by railroad territories for commodity movements by rail, etc. For a sizeable number of regional policy decisions, however, the state political body is responsible for implementing the policies, and data compiled by states may be the most appropriate for studies of the economic impact of these policies.

The state was chosen as the regional unit for the MRIO accounts because it was the most detailed spatial unit for which a consistent set of reliable regional data could be assembled. To be exact, all data for 1963 and later years were assembled for the 51 regions mentioned earlier (the 50 states plus the District of Columbia) and are referred to as data for 51 regions, or sometimes as state data. Data for 1947 and 1958 could be assembled only for 49 regions because data for Alaska and Hawaii were not included in most statistical sources for those years. The numbers assigned to the states and used on the worksheets and given in the published tables are shown in table A-2 in the appendix.[2]

Choosing the most appropriate spatial unit for an economic analysis is a pervasive problem and one that has been discussed in most of the literature concerning the establishment and construction of regional and multiregional accounts. During the late 1960s, when the first MRIO accounts were being constructed, two major regional groupings were receiving special attention in the literature. They were the detailed 173 functional economic areas (FEA), which represent combinations of the 3,133 counties and county-type units in the United States, and the very aggregate nine census regions, which represent combinations of the 50 states and the District of Columbia. Some analysts, such as Karl A. Fox [52], have taken considerable pains to show that FEAs would be the most appropriate spatial units for regional economic analyses. The fact remains, however, that there are no consistent and reliable sets of data covering all counties in the United States and all industries in the economy at a detailed level. Furthermore, the problem of nondisclosure, which is discussed later, would have been even more troublesome if the FEA spatial designation had been employed, and the number of rough estimates necessitated by the additional regional detail would have been much greater than the number required for the state estimates.

The only spatial unit other than states, therefore, that was seriously considered for the MRIO accounts was the U.S. census region, of which there are nine. The advantage of this unit is that most census data are published in considerable industrial detail for the census regions. But numerous additional data sources also had to be used for the study, many of which contained data published only by other regional groupings. The data used for the personal consumption expenditures estimates are an example of this. Those data were published in the *Survey of Consumer Expenditures, 1960–61* [294] only for four regions. The state estimates would therefore still have been needed in order to recombine the data into those required for the census regions. Because any regional grouping other than states would have created far more work than time and money allowed and, in the case of the more aggregate regional groupings, would have created a vast amount of detail that would have been unavailable to most analysts, the use of census regions was not considered feasible. This left the state as the logical choice. In any case, state data can always be easily aggregated into some of the more common regional groupings, such as census regions or federal regions, or split into smaller spatial units required for any particular regional study.

The MRIO accounts constructed for the present study are closely related to the IRIO accounts. Because of this relationship, the IRIO framework will be discussed first.

Interregional Input-Output Accounting Framework

The IRIO accounts illustrated in figure 2–1 were formulated by Isard and briefly described in his book *Methods of Regional Analysis* [92, pp. 309–373].[3] The figure represents a large IRIO table, with the rows indicating the industry and

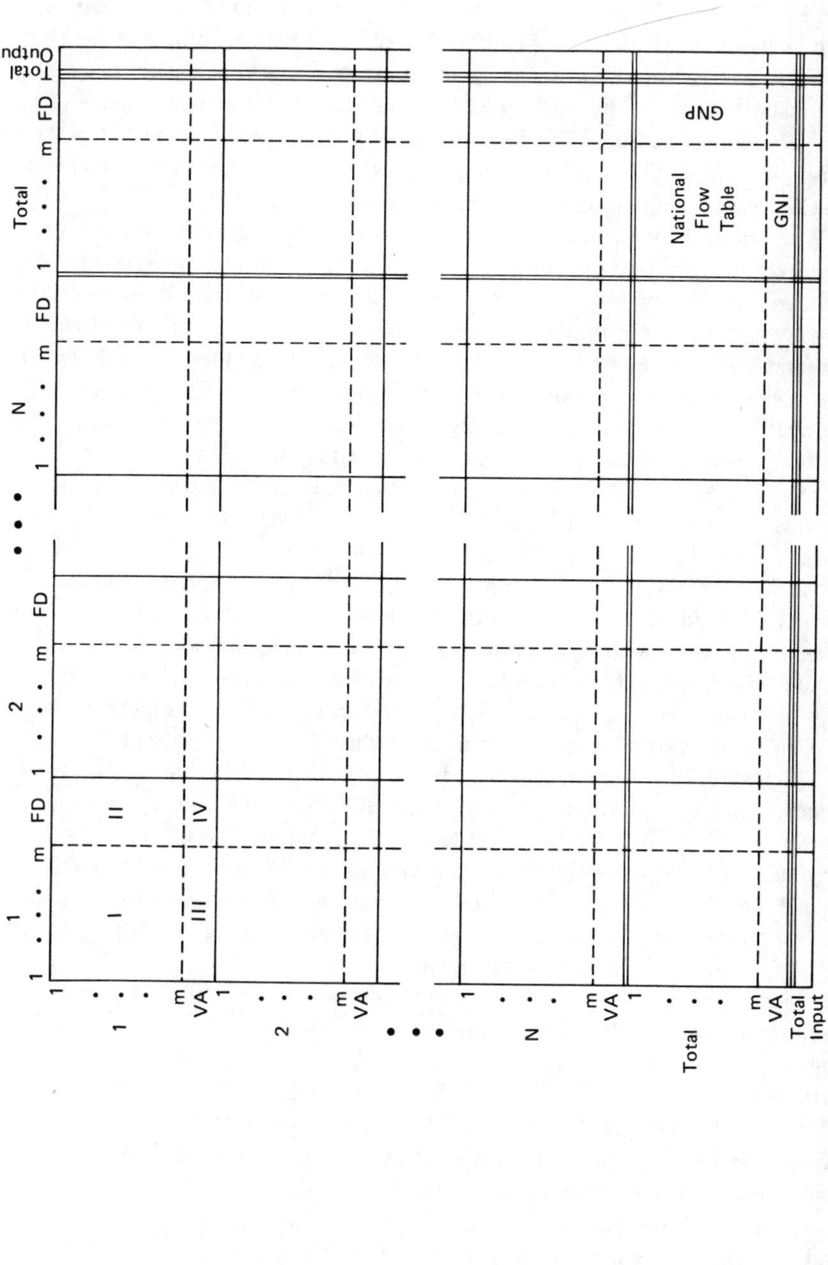

Figure 2-1. Interregional Input-Output Table

region in which a good or service is produced and the columns the industry and region in which a good or service is consumed. The rows and columns in the table are grouped into regional blocks, each block specifying all transactions, namely, the sales and purchases by industries, final users, and factors of production, between any two of the *n* regions. The diagonal regional blocks in the table show the transactions that originate and terminate in the same region, and each regional block off the diagonal shows the transactions that originate in one region and terminate in another. The first horizontal row of regional blocks shows the distribution of all the sales by region 1, and the first vertical column of regional blocks shows the distribution of all the purchases by region 1.

Interindustry sales and purchases are shown in the upper left-hand quadrant, Quadrant I, of each regional block; purchases by final users from intermediate industries are shown in the upper right-hand quadrant, Quadrant II; interindustry payments to factors of production are shown in the lower left-hand quadrant, Quadrant III; and payments by final users to factors of production are shown in the lower right-hand quadrant, Quadrant IV. The sum of the final demand elements in Quadrants II and IV in the first vertical set of regional blocks is given in the corresponding quadrants at the bottom of the table. The total of the elements in Quadrants II and IV, at the bottom of the table, equals the gross regional product (GRP) for region 1, that is, the total value of output purchased in region 1 by final users (private and public consumers and investors). Likewise, the sum of the payments to the primary factors of production (labor, land, and capital) in Quadrants III and IV in the first horizontal set of regional blocks is given in the corresponding quadrants at the right-hand side of the table. The total of the elements in Quadrants III and IV at the right-hand side of the table equals the gross regional income (GRI) for region 1, that is, the total value of income received by all primary factors of production located in region 1. This is the total value of wages and salaries, rent, profits, depreciation, interest, dividends, indirect business taxes, and subsidies received by the primary factors of production. It is often referred to as regional value added.[4] In this text, the terms *regional final demand* and *gross regional product* will be used interchangeably, as will the terms *regional value added, gross regional income,* and *gross regional product originating.* The total gross regional product for a region must equal the total gross regional income for the region.

An example will be used to illustrate the types of transactions that would be recorded in the IRIO table for the United States, where *n* is the number of regions, *m* the number of industries, *p* the number of final demand sectors, and *q* the number of value added sectors. For the example, *n* will equal 51, representing the 50 states plus the District of Columbia, the first of the *m* industries will be livestock, and the *n* regional blocks at the right-hand side of the table and those at the bottom will be disregarded.

In the first row of the table and in the first regional block, there are *m* interindustry elements and *p* final demand elements. The first set of *m* elements in the first row of the table will indicate for Alabama (region 1) the amount of

Alabama livestock output sold to each of the m industries in Alabama, including that sold to the livestock industry itself. The next set of elements, p in number, in the first row in the same regional block will indicate the amount of Alabama livestock output sold to final users in Alabama. In the second regional block, the set of m and p elements will indicate the amount of Alabama livestock output sold to each of the m industries and p final users in Arizona (region 2), and so on for each of the m industries and p final users in each of the remaining 49 regions. Thus, the first m rows in the first horizontal set of regional blocks will designate the output produced by industries in Alabama and distributed to all intermediate and final users throughout the United States, including that designated for foreign export. In the case that no output for a particular industry is produced in the state, all elements in the relevant row will be zero.

The q rows below the m rows in the first horizontal set of regional blocks will show the sales of the services of the q factors of production located in Alabama, first to the m industries and p final users located in the state, then to the m industries and p final users located in each of the remaining 50 regions. The same types of sales data for intermediate industries and factors of production are shown by each of the elements in the rows for the other 50 regions. In the general case, there are $mn + pn$ elements in each row of the table, many of which, of course, may be zero.

While each row in the IRIO table contains specifications as to the output of a particular industry in a given region distributed to industries and final users in each region, each column in the table contains the industrial (or factor of production) and regional detail for the inputs purchased by a particular industry or final user in a given region. The example of the Alabama livestock industry will be used again, this time to describe the elements in the first column of the table. The first set of m elements in the first column of the table will indicate the amount of inputs the Alabama livestock industry purchased from each of the m industries (including itself) in Alabama; the following set of q elements in the first column in the first regional block will indicate the payments made by the Alabama livestock industry to the factors of production located in Alabama. In the second regional block in the same column the set of m and q elements will indicate the amount of inputs purchased from each of the m industries and q factors of production in Arizona (region 2) by the Alabama livestock industry, and so on for each of the m intermediate industries and q factors of production in each of the remaining 49 regions. This purchase information will also be provided for each of the other $m - 1$ industries in Alabama. The next set of p columns in the first group of vertical regional blocks will show the purchases made by the p final users located in Alabama, first the purchases from the m intermediate industries and q factors of production located in Alabama, then those from intermediate industries and factors of production in each of the other 50 regions. The same types of purchase data are then repeated for each of the m intermediate industries and p final users in the remaining 50 regions.

In each column of the table, there are $mn + qn$ elements, many of which may be zero. In the entire table there are $(mn)^2$ intermediate purchases, pn^2 final demand elements, and qn^2 factor of production elements. It should also be noted that as with the national accounts, the sum of each column in the table, representing total outlays by a particular industry in a given region, is equal to the sum of the corresponding row in the table, representing sales of total output by the same industry in the same region. This is assured because if the total revenues received by an industry differ from the total payments made, the difference will show up in the accounts either as a profit or as a loss in the value added portion of the table.

The n blocks at the right-hand side and those at the bottom of the table can now be explained. Each of the former represents the summation, cell by cell, of all the elements in the n blocks in a row for the specific region. In the Alabama livestock industry example, the elements in the first row of the first total regional block specify the total sales of Alabama livestock to each of the m industries and p final users in the United States, now disregarding the regional destination of the output. (Although these blocks are included for the sake of completeness, the data, as far as is known, have not been used for any regional analyses.)

In terms of notations, the elements in each row of each total regional block at the right-hand side of the table are obtained as follows:

Interindustry elements $$x_{ij}^{go} = \sum_{h=1}^{n} x_{ij}^{gh} \qquad g = 1,\ldots,n \quad i,j = 1,\ldots,m$$

Final demand elements $$y_{ik}^{go} = \sum_{h=1}^{n} y_{ik}^{gh} \qquad g = 1,\ldots,n \quad i = 1,\ldots,m \quad k = 1,\ldots,p$$

Value added elements $$v_{sj}^{go} = \sum_{h=1}^{n} v_{sj}^{gh} \qquad g = 1,\ldots,n \quad j = 1,\ldots,m \quad = 1,\ldots,q$$

Value added, final demand elements $$v_{sk}^{go} = \sum_{h=1}^{n} v_{sk}^{gh} \qquad g = 1,\ldots,n \quad s = 1,\ldots,q \quad k = 1,\ldots,p$$

where

x_{ij}^{gh} = output purchased by industry j in region h from industry i in region g

y_{ik}^{gh} = output purchased by final user k in region h from industry i in region g

v_{sj}^{gh} = payment made by industry j in region h to factor of production s in region g

v_{sk}^{gh} = payment made by final user k in region h to factor of production s in region g

o = summation notation for the superscripts.

The n blocks at the bottom of the table, however, are the ones of prime interest for this study, as they form the input-output tables for the multiregional accounts. Again, they represent the summation, cell by cell, of all the elements in the n blocks, but now in a column, for the specific region. (A detailed discussion of the MRIO accounting framework is presented in the next section.) The elements in each column of each total block at the bottom of the figure are obtained as follows:

Interindustry elements $$x_{ij}^{oh} = \sum_{g=1}^{n} x_{ij}^{gh} \qquad h = 1, \ldots, n; \quad i, j = 1, \ldots, m$$

Final demand elements $$y_{ik}^{oh} = \sum_{g=1}^{n} y_{ik}^{gh} \qquad h = 1, \ldots, n; \quad i = 1, \ldots, m; \quad k = 1, \ldots, p$$

Value added elements $$v_{sj}^{oh} = \sum_{g=1}^{n} v_{sj}^{gh} \qquad h = 1, \ldots, n; \quad j = 1, \ldots, m; \quad s = 1, \ldots, q$$

Value added, final demand elements $$v_{sk}^{oh} = \sum_{g=1}^{n} v_{sk}^{gh} \qquad h = 1, \ldots, n; \quad s = 1, \ldots, q; \quad k = 1, \ldots, p$$

where the notations are as defined earlier.

Finally, the elements in the national input-output block in the lower right-hand corner of the table are obtained either by summing, cell by cell, all elements in the n blocks at the right-hand side or those at the bottom of the table as follows:

Interindustry elements $$x_{ij}^{oo} = \sum_{g=1}^{n} x_{ij}^{go} = \sum_{h=1}^{n} x_{ij}^{oh} \qquad i, j = 1, \ldots, m$$

Final demand elements $$y_{ik}^{oo} = \sum_{g=1}^{n} y_{ik}^{go} = \sum_{h=1}^{n} y_{ik}^{oh} \qquad i = 1, \ldots, m; \quad k = 1, \ldots, p$$

Value added elements $$v_{sj}^{oo} = \sum_{g=1}^{n} v_{sj}^{go} = \sum_{h=1}^{n} v_{sj}^{oh} \qquad j = 1, \ldots, m; \quad s = 1, \ldots, q$$

Value added, final demand elements $$v_{sk}^{oo} = \sum_{g=1}^{n} v_{sk}^{go} = \sum_{h=1}^{n} v_{sk}^{oh} \qquad s = 1, \ldots, q; \quad k = 1, \ldots, p$$

where the notations are as defined earlier.

In order to describe the MRIO accounting system, one more set of data, namely, interregional trade flows, must be tabulated from the data illustrated by the large IRIO table in figure 2-1. These flows are obtained by summing all elements in each row of each regional block. Each interregional trade flow represents the amount of commodity i shipped from region g to region h, therefore indicating the total shipment from region g to all intermediate and final users in region h. In terms of notations, these elements are obtained as follows:

Interregional commodity shipments $$x_{io}^{gh} = \sum_{j=1}^{m} x_{ij}^{gh} + \sum_{k=1}^{p} y_{ik}^{gh} \qquad \begin{aligned} g, h &= 1, \ldots, n \\ i &= 1, \ldots, m \end{aligned}$$

where o = summation notation for subscripts and all other notations are as defined earlier.

Interregional flows of factors of production can also be tabulated from the large IRIO table. They are obtained as follows:

Interregional value added shipments $$v_{so}^{gh} = \sum_{j=1}^{m} v_{sj}^{gh} + \sum_{k=1}^{p} v_{sk}^{gh} \qquad \begin{aligned} g, h &= 1, \ldots, n \\ s &= 1, \ldots, q \end{aligned}$$

where all notations are as defined earlier.

The transformation from the IRIO to an MRIO accounting framework is conceptually very easy, as has just been shown. For the present study, the MRIO framework was strongly preferred to the IRIO framework because of the reduced data requirements. It will now be discussed in detail.

Multiregional Input-Output Accounting Framework

One of the major contributions of the present study is the extension of the input-output system of economic accounts from the national to the multiregional level. It is important to have national statistics on industrial production, consumption, price, and so on, but to have those statistics on a multiregional dimension greatly increases the number and enriches the value of the analyses for which they can be used. The complete MRIO accounting system is comprised of two basic sets of data: a set of regional input-output tables and a set of interregional trade-flow tables. To construct the accounts, data were assembled for 79 industries and 51 regions. (These classification schemes are specified in tables A-1 and A-2 in the appendix.) As far as possible, the national input-output accounting definitions and methodologies were used. The limited documentation of the national economic accounts, discussed earlier, created some problems in trying to maintain consistencies between national and multiregional accounts. In addition, some of the definitions and methodologies used for the national accounts were intentionally changed to provide for the regional dimension of the data.

In practice, data were not aggregated from the more detailed IRIO accounts; rather, they were tabulated from sources that contained measures representing as closely as possible the exact MRIO component desired. Data on the industry and region of both producer and consumer, that is, the details necessary to construct IRIO accounts, are not available. From the 1963, 1967, and 1972 Census of Transportation, for example, the amount of a commodity shipped from state to state can be obtained, but more detail on the industrial origin and destination of the commodity cannot.[5] On the other hand, only the region of destination and the industry producing and consuming the commodity are provided in the Census of Manufactures. The specific sources and methodologies used to make the MRIO estimates are given in chapter 4–7.

Basic Accounting Structure

All of the transactions in the input-output portion of the MRIO accounts are provided in terms of current accounts and in producer prices for the 79 industries and 51 regions. Although capital accounts transactions, representing the purchases—both private and public—of plant and equipment, are included only in the final demand portion of the regional input-output tables, the interregional trade tables show shipments of output produced on both current and capital account.

By constructing the input-output tables in terms of producer prices, each input is valued in terms of the cost of producing the good or service before it is transferred from the producer to the purchaser, and, therefore, before the costs of transporting, wholesaling, retailing, and insuring the output are incurred. To transform the input-output tables from a producer-price to a purchaser-price base, transportation, wholesale trade, retail trade, and insurance margin tables are required. These tables contain data with the same industrial and regional classifications as those used for the producer-price table and show the cost markup on the producer price of each input. The sum of each column of these margin tables is entered as part of the relevant row of the producer-price table, that is, the sums of the columns of, say, the transportation margin table are added as part of the respective elements in the transportation row in the producer-price input-output table. Additional details on the use of these margin tables are provided as the state input-output tables are described.

The complete MRIO accounting system is portrayed in figure 2-2, with the regional input-output tables given at the top of the figure and the interregional trade-flow tables at the bottom. The input-output tables contain data

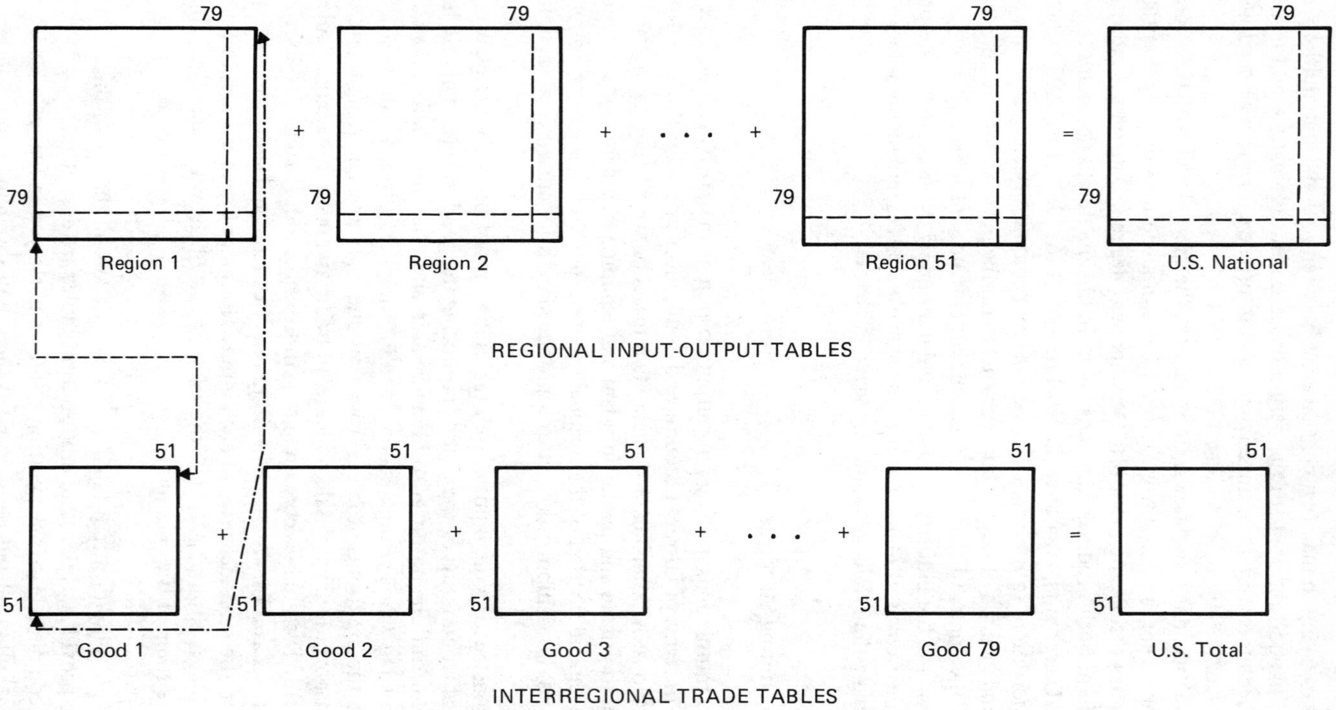

Figure 2-2. MRIO Accounting System–Input-Output and Interregional Trade Consistency

identical in concept to data in the total regional blocks shown at the bottom of the IRIO table in figure 2-1, the components of which have already been briefly described. Since all of the following discussion, unless otherwise specified, relates to accounts constructed using dollar rather than physical units, it should be noted that some of the accounting balances would not be valid for a set of accounts constructed in physical units.

Two of the consistency requirements of the MRIO accounts are illustrated in figure 2-2. As mentioned earlier, one basic requirement in assembling the data is that the elements in the regional input-output tables, when summed for all regions, must equal the corresponding figures in the national input-output table for the same year. This equality is indicated at the top of the figure by the summation sign preceding the national table. The second consistency requirement pertains to the relationship between the data in the regional input-output and interregional trade tables. Both of these balances are crucial for the implementation of the MRIO model, described in chapter 3.

Another consistency requirement is associated only with the IRIO and national input-output tables and therefore does not apply to the regional tables in the MRIO accounts. The user of national input-output tables is accustomed to working with a balanced input-output table, in which the sums of corresponding rows and columns of the table must be equal, since the total value an industry receives for its output in a given year must equal its total outlays in that year. For each input-output table in the MRIO accounts, however, the sums will generally not be equal. The sum of all elements in each row of the regional input-output table gives the total consumption by all intermediate and final users within the region, referred to as *gross regional consumption,* while the sum of all elements in each column gives the total input requirements of each industry within the region, referred to as *gross regional outlays.* But the column sum must also be equal in the accounts to the total value of output, because in any given year the total amount paid out for inputs by an industry must equal the total amount the industry received for its output, as was illustrated earlier through use of the IRIO table. The row sums will therefore be called *gross regional consumption* and the column sums will be called either *gross regional outlays* or, more usually, *gross regional output.* For most industries, the sums of corresponding rows and columns in each input-output table in the MRIO accounts will not be equal, with the differences being attributable to interregional trade. Only if none of the good or service produced by the industry in a given region is traded will the sums be identical. This occurs, for example, for some of the industries in the MRIO accounts, for which the assumption is made that all of a particular output produced in a region is consumed in the same region.

So far, only the input-output tables have been discussed. The trade-flow tables for the 79 industries are shown at the bottom of figure 2-2. Although the 79 industries include the production of both commodities and services, the following description will be simplified by using the term *commodity* to cover both.

Each trade-flow table is square and represents all shipments of one commodity to all 51 regions. Thus, for the MRIO accounts, these tables are 51 by 51. The same regions are listed along the rows and columns of each table. For example, the first row of the first trade-flow table in figure 2-2 shows the total shipments to all regions of commodity 1 produced in region 1. The first element in row 1 represents shipments of commodity 1 from region 1 to region 1; the second element represents shipments of commodity 1 from region 1 to region 2; the third element represents shipments of the same commodity from region 1 to region 3; and so on for each of the 51 regions. The first row sum shows total shipments of commodity 1 produced in region 1. In the MRIO accounting system, this shipments total, which includes shipments to ports for foreign export, must be exactly equal to the total of the first column in the input-output table for region 1, as indicated by the line of short dashes in figure 2-2. In other words, all of a given output that is produced in a region must be either used in that region or shipped to other regions.

The first column of the first trade-flow table in figure 2-2 shows the shipments of the products of industry 1 into the first region from all the regions in the country, including the consuming region itself. The sum of the column equals total consumption of the products of industry 1 in region 1; and in the MRIO accounting system, this equals the first row sum of the input-output table for region 1, as indicated by the line of dashes and dots in figure 2-2. In other words, all of a given output that is consumed in a region must have been either produced in that region or shipped in from other regions. Consistency is thus maintained between the data in the input-output and the interregional trade tables. To obtain exact consistency between the two sets of regional production and consumption figures, secondary products must be double-counted in both sets of tables. This double-counting and the adjustments made to the data in the two sets of tables to achieve consistency are explained later in the chapter.

First, the overall organization of data in the input-output part of the accounts and the very detailed accounting conventions must be explained.

Input-Output Tables

Each state input-output table in the MRIO accounts is 87 by 87, as shown in figure 2-3. The goods or services in a given row are homogeneous for the first 79 rows of the table, with the exception of all entries appearing in column 83, secondary transfers-out. These entries represent goods or services produced by a firm as its secondary products that are not classified in the same SIC category as its major product. Elements composed of heterogeneous commodities do occur in some of the exogenous rows of the table, rows 80 through 86.

The elements in each of the first 79 columns of the table are the purchases made by a particular establishment that may be producing a heterogeneous

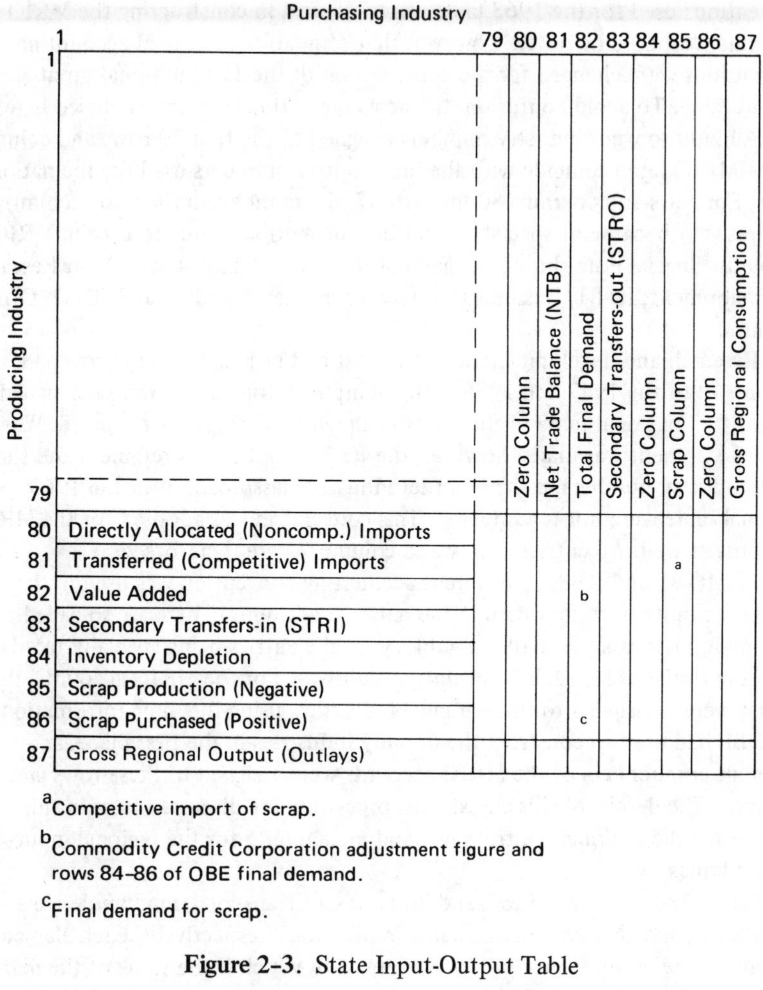

[a]Competitive import of scrap.

[b]Commodity Credit Corporation adjustment figure and rows 84–86 of OBE final demand.

[c]Final demand for scrap.

Figure 2-3. State Input-Output Table

mix of goods or services classified in various SIC categories, and the transactions in columns 80 through 86, excluding column 83, are primarily purchases by final users. The transactions in all columns except 83 and 87 therefore represent what are called the *primary transactions* in the U.S. national accounts, with the secondary output of each establishment being accounted for in column 83. The total consumption in the region is given in column 87. The secondary output of a firm is double-counted in this column. This double-counting of secondary products is discussed further in chapter 5. With the exception of secondary products and a few other accounting items, national input-output accounting conventions used for the 1963 table were followed in constructing the MRIO accounts. It should be noted, however, that some of the national accounting conventions were changed for the construction of the 1972 national input-output table. To avoid confusion, the new conventions are not discussed here.

All input-output industry numbers assigned to the first 79 rows and columns of the MRIO table coincide with the input-output numbers used for the national table. For rows and columns 80 through 87, the numbers in the two accounting systems vary because of special accounting conventions required for the MRIO accounts. Special note should be made of the national industries IO-74, Research & development; IO-81, Business travel, entertainment, & gifts; and IO-82, Office supplies.

Research and development activities that had been specified in row and column 74 of the 1947 and 1958 national input-output tables were reassigned in the 1963 national table to the industry in which the activity occurred. When this reassignment was made, however, the IO-74 number was retained, and the other industry numbers in the 80-order industry classification for the 1963 national table were not renumbered. This convention was adopted for the MRIO accounts as well. All entries in row and column 74 are therefore zero.

For IO-81 and IO-82, a different accounting convention was used in the MRIO accounts from that used in the national accounts. These are so-called dummy industries in the national table, with the entries being specially tabulated from the statistics for each input-output industry. For the MRIO accounts, these entries were reassigned to their original industries, using the same information the OBE had used to construct the dummy industries in the first place, and different components of the MRIO accounts were assigned to these rows and columns. The details of this adjustment procedure are discussed later in this chapter for the national control table and in chapter 5 for the regional input-output tables.

The entries in rows 65, 69, and 70 represent transportation, wholesale and retail trade, and finance and insurance transactions, respectively. Each element contains three components, by far the largest of which is the value of the margins charged on all inputs purchased by the industry represented by the column. It should be noted that in these rows each entry for this margin component represents the costs of *transferring inputs to the purchasing industry,* represented by the column, because this is a producer-price table. In a purchaser-price table, each of these margin entries would represent the costs of *transferring the output of the producing industry,* represented by the column. These margin values were calculated for the MRIO accounts by using the national margins to obtain a percentage markup that was applied uniformly for all regions, because regional margins were unavailable. The second component of each element is the directly allocated value, if any, representing any costs that are not accounted for in the margin tables. The third component of each element is the value of the margins on imports.

To avoid confusion, the quadrant numbers have not been inserted into figure 2-3. However, the input-output table depicted in the figure can be divided into the same four quadrants used for the regional blocks in the IRIO table in figure 2-1. The basic MRIO accounting structure of the four quadrants of each table will be described here, and additional details on the accounting components will be provided in chapters 4-7. Quadrant IV will be discussed as part of both Quadrants II and III, because the data overlap.

As mentioned earlier, the national accounting conventions are not readily available in written form. Whenever applicable, therefore, the specific convention used for the MRIO accounts must be prefaced with a brief description of the basic methods used for the national accounts. The conventions used for the input-output tables will be described first, then those used for the commodity-trade tables. It should be noted that no national conventions existed for constructing the interregional commodity-trade tables.

Quadrant I, Interindustry Sales and Purchases. In each input-output table, the largest block, Quadrant I, represents the interindustry sales and purchases. It is square for the MRIO accounting system, with the number of purchasing industries being exactly equal to the number of producing industries. Rows 1 through 79 represent the producing industries, regardless of their regional location, and columns 1 through 79 represent the purchasing industries in the respective state or region. As mentioned earlier, all entries in row and column 74 are zero.

All entries in columns 1 through 79 of row 11 are also zero, because all private and public purchases from IO-11, New construction, are capital accounts transactions. These purchases of new plant are recorded only in the final demand portion of the table. The column for this industry, column 11, however, does contain some entries, because the construction industry purchases its noncapital inputs on current account, the same as any other industry.

Quadrants II and IV, Final Demand. The entries in columns 80 through 86 in the rectangle at the right of each input-output table, Quadrants II and IV, represent the purchases of goods and services by final consumers (private and public) in the region from intermediate users and factors of production as well as some columns to make the accounts balance. One convention is to identify final demand as all exogenous columns in the table; another is to identify final demand as only those entries making up the gross regional product. Both conventions will be used in the remainder of this text, with clear indications given in each case as to the context in which it is being used. Each column in the final demand portion of the table will now be described.

Column 80. Column 80 is left as a zero column to maintain a square table, thus keeping the same number for corresponding rows and columns, such as secondary transfers-in (STRI) and secondary transfers-out (STRO), which are row 83 and column 83, respectively.

Column 81, Net Trade Balance. Interregional trade flows were assembled for all agricultural, mining, and manufacturing commodities and were estimated for the output of most service industries. No trade data, however, could be estimated for four industries: IO-3, Forestry & fishery products; IO-4, Agricultural, forestry, & fishery services; IO-11, New construction; and IO-12, Maintenance & repair construction. For these industries, it was therefore assumed that the total amount produced in a particular region was consumed in the same region—that the output was not traded between regions.[6]

To balance the figures for the output and consumption of these four industries, an extra column of numbers, shown as column 81 in figure 2-3, was added to each input-output table. Each entry in this column is referred to as the net trade balance, or NTB, in the remainder of the text. Each NTB entry was obtained by subtracting total regional consumption of an industry (the sum of that row) from the total regional output of that industry (the sum of the corresponding column) to obtain the net outflow of production from the state, which could be either a positive or a negative figure. The entries in column 81 should be calculated only after all other entries have been recorded in each state input-output table. In the present system of 80-order accounts, NTB entries appear in column 81 only for rows 3, 4, 11, and 12.

Although trade flows supposedly had been calculated for IO-3, Forestry & fishery products, the trade matrix had no off-diagonal elements (no shipments other than intraregional); yet gross regional output did not equal gross regional consumption for the industry. An entry therefore appears in column 81 for this industry to equate the regional output and consumption figures. Further discussion of this is given in chapter 6.

Column 82, Gross Regional Product. The entries in column 82 represent the total of all purchases by final users in the region in a given year, which is the gross regional product (GRP) of the region. The six major components of the GRP are: personal consumption expenditures, gross private fixed capital formation, net inventory change, net foreign exports, state and local government purchases, and federal government purchases. There is one important change from the national convention for the MRIO accounts. Rather than including net inventory change as part of column 82, only inventory additions are included, with inventory depletions being treated as a separate row (row 84) in the table. It should be noted that the above six components are given as separate columns in the1963 national table and were estimated separately for the MRIO accounts (see chapter 4), but were combined as a single column in the regional input-output tables.

The GRP figures represent the total final purchases in a given year regardless of where the good or service was produced, where the income was earned, or where the purchaser lived. Thus, for example, if a personal consumer lived in Connecticut, earned money in New York, but bought some consumer goods in Massachusetts, the purchases would be recorded in the final demand column of the state input-output table for Massachusetts.

The details of the national and multiregional accounting conventions for the six major components of column 82 are now provided.

Personal consumption expenditures. By far the largest component of the Gross National Product (GNP) is personal consumption expenditures (PCE), which was \$375,540 million in 1963, or 63.6 percent of the GNP. Since 1929, this component as a percentage of total GNP (in constant 1958 dollars) has for the most part remained relatively stable at approximately 60 percent of the GNP. The percentage, however, has varied from an all-time high of 76.9 percent in 1933 (the midst of the depression) to an all-time low of 45.1 percent in 1944 (near the end of World War II).

All purchases of services and durable and nondurable goods by private consumers are included in this component of the GNP, regardless of the length of life of the goods. Thus, durable goods, such as cars, refrigerators, freezers, stoves, dishwashers, washing machines, and television sets, are recorded as part of the current-account transactions of consumers even though they last longer than one year. They are accordingly combined with those goods that are definitely bought and used by private consumers in the given year. The full value of these durable goods therefore is recorded in the year in which they are bought, and no depreciation is calculated for them. The only major exception to this treatment of private consumer durable goods is for the purchase of private residential housing. These purchases are included as part of the structures component of gross private fixed capital formation.

Within each PCE element, the purchases by foreigners and the services rendered to individuals by nonprofit institutions are combined with those of U.S. private residents. The expenditures made by foreign visitors are combined by the Office of Business Economics (OBE) with those made by private U.S. residents because of the statistical difficulties of separating them item by item.[7] The total PCE figure, however, is adjusted in the national table through a single negative entry in the IO-85, Rest of the world industry, in the PCE column to exclude the expenditures by foreigners. Therefore, although each element includes the value of these expenditures, the PCE total represents only the purchases made by U.S. residents. It should be noted that sales to PCE by the nonprofit sector are referred to by the OBE as sales by nonprofit institutions, while sales to gross private fixed capital formation by the nonprofit sector are referred to as sales by nonprofit organizations.

Gross private fixed capital formation. In 1963, gross private fixed capital formation (GPFCF) totaled \$80,510 million, or 13.6 percent of the GNP. The GPFCF component includes only purchases by private business and nonprofit institutions of new durable capital goods (capitalized equipment with a life span greater than one year), of new construction, the net value of used equipment and structures, and miscellaneous overhead and installation charges. Thus, all sales of capital to the government sectors are excluded. Capital formation by the public sector is included as part of government purchases. Because the GPFCF figures are gross measures of fixed capital formation, there is no deduction for depreciation.

All figures in the GPFCF portion of the GNP column represent purchases made on capital account by private firms, while all other private purchases shown in the GNP column of the input-output tables are current account transactions. As explained later, the public purchases shown in the government sector are combinations of current and capital account purchases. Most private firms keep both current and capital accounts for income tax and general accounting purposes. The distinction between the two accounts is related to the length of life of the good, with any good lasting longer than one year being recorded in the capital account records of the firm. Thus, each GPFCF element represents the capital produced and sold by a particular industry in the given year. Because all of the private sector capital sales by each industry are grouped together as a single entry in this GNP component, the private purchaser of the capital good is not explicitly identifiable.

For complete information on the private-sector purchaser as well as producer of capital goods, a capital-flow table is required. It should be emphasized that the U.S. capital-flow tables show a breakdown only of private fixed capital purchases and are available only at the national level. A national capital-flow table deals exclusively with plant and equipment sold on capital account. A given industry produces a certain amount of capital, keeping some for its own use and selling the rest to other industries. At the same time, this industry also buys capital goods from other industries. A prototype of the national capital-flow table is shown in figure 2-4. It is an industry-by-industry table. Because the same industries are listed for the rows and columns, it is a square table, but it need not be so. Each element, b_{ij}, of the table shows the dollar value of capital produced by industry i and bought on capital account by industry j in a given year.[8] The sales on capital account by a particular industry are shown along a given row of the national capital-flow table, while the corresponding column of the table represents purchases of different types of capital goods required by that industry. In a national capital-flow table, the sums of all the rows form a column, indicating how much of the total amount of capital produced in the nation is bought *from* each industry in a given year. This column is the total national GPFCF component of GNP in the input-output table. In contrast, the column sums of the national capital-flow table show how much of the total amount of capital produced in the economy is bought *by* each industry on capital account.

It should be noted that the capital-flow tables indicate only the amount of capital each private industry produces and sells in a given year, not the total

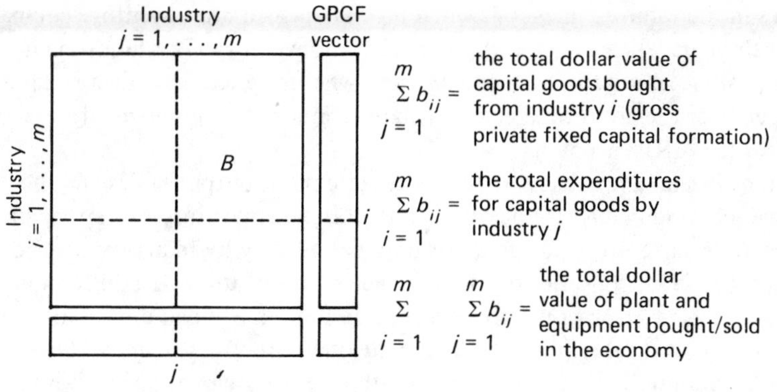

Figure 2-4. National Capital-Flow Matrix

stock of capital of the purchasing or producing industry. To obtain the total amount of capital stock available for private production, a capital-stock table must be constructed. If time series of capital-flow tables are available, data for the capital-stock tables can be calculated by depreciating the capital in the capital-flow tables for each year and summing the results, element by element.

Another important factor that must be noted is that gross private domestic investment and gross private fixed capital formation are two different items in the accounts, with the latter being a subset of the former. Gross private domestic investment represents the sum of gross private fixed capital formation and net inventory change; thus, total private investment will always be larger than total private fixed capital formation unless large inventory depletions occur in a given year.

Net inventory change. In 1963, net inventory change totaled $5,329 million, or 0.9 percent of the GNP. The net inventory change (NINV) component of the GNP represents the overall, or net, change in the physical volume of private inventories for a given year. Entries appear only for the industries that produce commodities, because services cannot, in general, be stockpiled from year to year. Government stockpiles of goods are not included, as they are part of the government sector of GNP. Each NINV element represents a netting in the given year of the value of inventory additions minus inventory depletions for the products of a particular private industry (regardless of which industry actually owns or stores the inventories [60, p. 17]). Thus, each element in the NINV column can be either positive or negative, depending upon the magnitude of the additions relative to the depletions. As just mentioned, however, although the data are reported in terms of dollars, an attempt is made to measure the physical volume of the inventory changes. To do this, an element called *inventory valuation adjustment* is included in the NINV column to adjust the total dollar value of net inventory change for the differences due to price changes in the value of the goods when they are placed into inventory compared with their value when they are withdrawn from inventory. This adjustment can be positive or negative, depending upon whether prices have decreased or increased over the given time period. (State estimates for this element were not made for the MRIO accounts.)

To maintain consistency between the state input-output tables and the interregional trade tables in the MRIO accounts, the inventory depletion component of net inventory change was estimated industry by industry for each region, subtracted from the corresponding elements of total GRP in column 82, and added as a row of positive numbers in the value added portion of each state input-output table (row 84). This adjustment in effect augmented all entries in column 82 for every industry with inventory depletions. It was required to account for all shipments of a given commodity, regardless of the year in which it was produced. Therefore, to the extent that an inventory depletion occurs for a given industry, the total GRP entry for that industry is larger than it would be if the inventory depletions had not been subtracted from it. To simplify the discussion, the resulting column of augmented figures will still be referred to as gross regional product, or GRP, in the remainder of the text. It must be stressed, however, that it is not the exact figure for GRP defined earlier.

After this subtraction of the inventory depletion elements, the row totals of the national control table for the MRIO accounts sum to the gross supply of goods shipped in the given year, but produced in any year, rather than to the more customary gross supply of goods produced in the given year.

Net foreign exports. In 1963, net foreign exports totaled $5,812 million, or 1 percent of the GNP. With two exceptions, each element in the net foreign exports column of the published 1963 national input-output table represents gross exports, rather than net exports, from the United States of a given good or service [269, p. 35]. The two exceptions are in the import rows in which negative entries appear. These two elements, which are the totals of all imports into the United States, are obtained by summing the elements in each respective row of imports in the input-output table.[9] Whereas these negative values appear in what would correspond to column 82 in the national table, for the MRIO accounts, they are placed in column 81 so that they can be distinguished from any import purchase by final users.

When all figures in the export column of the national table are totaled, the sum becomes net foreign exports, and it can be negative if gross foreign imports exceed gross foreign exports in a given year. It should be noted that for the MRIO accounts the terms *exports* and *imports* will be used to refer to foreign exports and imports, while *outflows* and *inflows* will be used for interregional shipments between regions of the United States.

The state export estimates were assembled using two different methodologies, depending upon whether they were estimated by place of production or port of exit. The methodologies are explained in detail in chapter 4. For the multiregional economic accounts, all final demands must be estimated in terms of their location of final consumption, but this location can be interpreted as being either at the place of production or at the port of exit. If a multiregional study is to be made, the particular set of export data used for an analysis will depend upon the nature of the model, the way in which the other data components (especially interregional trade flows) have been specified, and the type of study being conducted. It is possible, for example, that a research analyst would assemble transportation data to include only transportation of goods produced and consumed domestically. Goods produced domestically but destined for foreign consumption would not be included in the transportation statistics for such a study. In that case, foreign exports should be estimated separately and specified by place of production only. For the MRIO accounts, however, foreign exports must be specified by port of exit, because the transportation statistics include shipments of goods destined for consumption abroad.

Government sectors. The purchases of general government agencies are treated differently from those of government enterprises in the national and regional economic accounts. For the general government agencies, both capital and current account purchases of goods and services are included in the final demand sector of the national economic accounts. Public agencies are classified as government enterprises if they sell sufficient goods and services to the general public to cover over half of their current operating costs. For the government enterprises, the capital and current account purchases are separated, with the current account purchases being treated as intermediate purchases (comparable with those of private industry) and the capital account purchases being combined with the government agency purchases in the GNP column. The final demand purchases by the public sector of the economy, as defined above, are usually separated into two major subcomponents: state and local government purchases and federal government purchases.

For those purchases made on capital account by the public sector, it is usually possible to distinguish only the purchases of plant. As a rule, equipment purchases are not designated separately, because many state, local, and federal government agencies do not keep separate capital and current account records for equipment. Plant expenditures are generally so large that they appear as separate line items in the accounts, whereas most equipment purchases do not. For the national and the MRIO accounts, no attempt was made to obtain separate estimates of equipment purchases. It should be stressed, therefore, that the total of the government sector represents both current and capital account expenditures by the various government agencies, as well as capital account purchases by all government enterprises.

State and local government purchases. In 1963, state and local government net purchases of goods and services totaled $59,082 million, or 10 percent of the GNP. The estimation of these purchases was relatively straightforward. A distinction had to be made, however, between state and local government (SLG) expenditures and net purchases. Expenditures by the state and local governments include grants-in-aid, transfer payments, net interest, and the surplus or deficit of government enterprises, whereas net purchases include only the direct purchases of goods and services. The MRIO accounts follow the national convention of including only the latter (net purchases) figures in the final demand sector.

The data were compiled, however, from the Census publications, in which statistics are reported in terms of expenditures. The individual items listed above that had to be excluded to obtain net purchases figures were available from the "character and object" classification of the governmental finances reported by the Census and so could be subtracted from the expenditures figures for each state. The conversion is given in table 5-2 in the first volume of this series [181, p. 118]. The character and object classification of the Census includes data for current operation, capital outlay (for construction, equipment, land, and existing structures), assistance and subsidies, interest on debt, and insurance trust. After the conversion, the net purchases figures were assembled for the MRIO accounts using the functional rather than the character and object classification. The National Income and Product Accounts functional classification is given in table 5-1 in the first volume in this series [181, p. 116].

Federal government purchases. In 1963, federal government purchases of goods and services totaled $64,115 million, or 11 percent of the GNP. State-by-state figures for the capital purchases made by federal government enterprises could not be assembled. In *The Budget of the United States Government* [296], the capital account purchases made by these enterprises are frequently not even recorded separately at the national level, much less in state detail.

Many federal government purchases are recorded only on a main account in a central office in Washington, D.C., with no indication of the regions in which the goods and services were actually consumed. In a few cases, regional data are collected, and worksheets could be obtained directly from the government agency.

In addition, sometimes a particular method of recording the statistics is adopted for security reasons. Exports of military goods, for example, are often combined as one item in the export statistics. Furthermore, goods that are transported by special means, such as military transport, are not included in the Census of Transporation data. For the MRIO accounts, therefore, these data should be estimated separately and recorded as being purchased in the state where they are produced. If this is not done, the demand for, say, non-military transport of a good to the final place of consumption will be mis-specified. No information was available, however, to separate federal government purchases and private production into these two transport categories. Consequently, the lack of an appropriate and/or uniform method of recording federal government purchases frequently hindered efforts to assemble the state data.

Research and development data had been collected and recorded as a separate industry in the 1958 national input-output table. In the 1963 national table, IO-74, Research & development, was eliminated, and all federal government purchases of research and development (R&D) were combined with the individual industry purchases. As was mentioned earlier, in order to provide consistency in industry numbers from one input-output table to another, row and column 74 were retained in the table (but with zero entries). Only 10 percent of the total R&D is produced by the R&D industry (SIC 7391, Research, development, & testing laboratories), the other 90 percent being secondary products of other industries. The federal government purchases 97 percent of all R&D. When the federal government purchases an end product from an industry, it specifies the portion of the contract price that is to be used to defer the costs of R&D. Obviously, there is no feasible method for providing good accounting detail for this complex series of transactions; therefore, the 1963 national conventions were followed for the MRIO accounts.

In the 1963 national input-output table, Commodity Credit Corporation (CCC) inventory changes and donations are included in the federal government final demand, while the current account CCC expenses or gains are included in IO-78, Federal government enterprises. The inventory changes are purchases and sales of commodities stockpiled by the CCC; the inventory donations are gifts, such as the CCC school lunch programs. The expenses part of the CCC current account includes the costs of warehousing and transportation plus any other administrative costs, as well as any losses incurred in the disposal of commodities. The gains are those that resulted from the disposal of the commodities. (Commodities may be disposed of through nonrecourse loans, domestic sales, or overseas donations and sales.) For implementation of the MRIO model, the figures on the CCC expenses and gains must be subtracted from IO-78 and added to the CCC portion of federal government final demand. This will place the data on CCC purchases, sales, and donations in current market prices.

The data sources and estimation procedures used to make the state estimates of final demand are explained in chapter 4.

Column 83, Secondary Transfers-Out. The entries in column 83 represent the value of the secondary products of the industry indicated by the row of the table. Each entry contains the value of a heterogeneous mix of products, none of which is the major product of the industry. To make the accounts balance, the value of these secondary products is transferred out of the industry producing them and into the industry with the appropriate SIC classification, hence the term *secondary transfers-out,* or STRO.

Column 84. Zero entries are recorded in column 84 to maintain a square table.

Column 85, Scrap. The only entries in column 85 are in row 81, Transferred imports, and rows 65 and 69, representing transportation and trade margins on those imports. The remaining scrap production entries are given in row 85, Scrap production. Because the three import-related scrap entries would have had to be combined and included as an offset to the gross foreign export component in column 82 of row 85, they would have been obscured in the accounts. For that reason, they were left as separate entries in their original rows and column since this did not affect the use of the basic accounting structure for later studies.

Column 86. Zero entries are recorded in column 86 to maintain a square table.

Column 87, Gross Regional Consumption. The entries in column 87 represent total purchases by intermediate and final users in the region in a given year regardless of where the good or service was produced, where the income was earned, or where the purchaser lived. In addition to total purchases by intermediate and final users, the entries in column 87 include the value of secondary production of the particular industry; thus each entry represents the total consumption of a particular good or service in the state plus the value of secondary products that industry produced.

Special note should be made that in the MRIO accounting system, the sum of the rows of each of the input-output tables, which is called *Gross Regional Consumption,* has a different interpretation from that of the sum of the rows of the national input-output table. For the MRIO accounts, the gross regional consumption need not equal the gross regional output; therefore, the corresponding row and column sums in a regional table need not be equal, because shipments in and shipments out are not shown in the regional input-output table, but are accounted for in the interregional trade tables discussed later. For each industry in the national accounts, however, the corresponding row and column sums are equal.

Quadrants III and IV, Value Added. The entries in rows 80 through 86 in the rectangle at the bottom of each input-output table, Quadrants III and IV, represent mainly payments to the primary factors of production, but two import rows as well as some rows to make the accounts balance are also included. As in the case of final demand, two conventions exist, with the term *value added* being used either to identify all exogenous rows in the table or to designate only those entries comprising gross regional income. Also, as noted earlier, the value added term used in the income accounts is a net concept whereas that used by the Census is a gross concept.

Negative elements occur in several rows in the exogenous part of the table.

All of the elements in row 85, Scrap production, are negative. The negative elements in column 81 of rows 80 and 81 represent the negative of each row total and are inserted in that column rather than column 82 in order to keep the positive and negative values of directly allocated imports separate. The values need to be combined, however, to put foreign exports on a net base for the GRP. The fact that this convention also makes the row sums for each of the imports zero may seem somewhat strange at the regional level, where the sum of each row represents gross regional consumption—a perfectly acceptable value to have for imports. The subtraction was done, however, so that the appropriate value for net foreign exports could be obtained.

An important aspect of the value added portion of the input-output table must be noted. In general, national economic accounts are constructed to make gross national product (GNP) equal gross national income (GNI). This was also shown to be the case for the IRIO accounts, that is, those accounts are constructed to make gross regional product (GRP) equal gross regional income (GRI). But the regional value added in the MRIO accounts, at this point, represents all payments to factors of production by industries in a given region regardless of the location of the factors of production. There is no inherent reason why all the income payments made by industries in a given region should be paid only to factors of production located in the same region; some of the income may be paid to factors of production located in other regions, just as some of the expenditures on final goods and services in a region may be from income earned in other regions. Thus, to make GRP equal GRI in the MRIO accounts, some interregional balance-of-payments adjustments should be added in Quadrant IV of each input-output table. If these adjustments are not made, the GRI in the MRIO accounts will, first, include some regional income of factors of production located in other regions and, second, exclude some of the payments made to factors of production located in the given region. These adjustments were not made for the MRIO accounts because of lack of information. However, it should be noted that the regional value added components in the present accounts when summed for the nation do result in GNP being equal to GNI.

Each row of the value added portion of the table will now be described.

Row 80, Directly Allocated Imports.
Row 81, Transferred Imports. The U.S. foreign imports are separated in the national economic accounts into two categories: directly allocated and transferred. Prior to the 1958 national input-output table, these were referred to as noncompetitive and competitive imports, respectively, although there are some slight definitional differences in the new terms. In general, an import is classified as directly allocated (noncompetitive) if a final user purchases the import in a substantially unaltered form, or if there is no domestic production

of the good or service, or, at least, no close substitute. The OBE provides the following definition:

> Substitutability was determined on a judgmental basis using the following guide: the import should be interchangeable with a domestically produced item without any change in the technology of the consuming industry or the resultant product. [269, p. 25]

In the U.S. input-output accounts, directly allocated imports are always handled as a row (row 80b), that is, they are recorded as inputs purchased by given industries; and the value of their output is distributed to other industries in the same manner as any other direct purchase, that is, as part of the total cost of materials of the industry represented by the column.[10] Each element in the directly allocated import row contains a heterogeneous mix of goods and services that the industry imported.

An import is classified as transferred (competitive) if the good or service is produced domestically and if the import is not directly consumed by a final user. In the national 1963 table, these imports are recorded as row 80b. The imported item must correspond with the SIC definition of the good or service produced by the industry represented by the column. In the accounts, these imports can be treated either as positive elements in a row of the table or as negative elements in a column of the table. In the first part of the following discussion, the transferred imports are assumed to have been recorded as a row.

When the national input-output table is constructed, the domestic port value of transferred imports is added to the value of the output of the domestic industry to provide a measure of the total supply of the good or service to the economy in a given year. The value of the transferred imports also is recorded as part of the intermediate input or final purchase for each respective industry [155, pp. 1-31, 1-32, 1-33]. Mainly because industries are not required by the Census to differentiate between purchases from domestic sources and those from foreign sources, the sum of the elements in each row of the national input-output table equals the total domestic plus the total foreign supply of the given good or service, the same total supply value as the output control mentioned earlier in the description of foreign exports. Thus, a national input-output table with both directly allocated and transferred imports recorded as rows in the table is sometimes referred to as a total-supply-base table—the sum of each row and column of the national table being equal to the total supply of the good or service, whether of domestic or foreign production.

If the transferred imports are treated as negative elements in a column of the final demand sector of the table, this treatment has the effect of subtracting from the total supply of the industry (the sum of each row in the national table) the amount that is supplied from foreign sources, leaving only the gross domestic output of the industry. A table constructed in this way is sometimes referred to as a domestic-output-base table. It should be noted that although the value of the total output of the economy is reduced to represent only domestically produced output, the value of the GNP (the sum of the columns of the six GNP components) remains unchanged, because the value of transferred foreign imports had already been subtracted from the row in the total-supply-base table. In the domestic-output-base table, that negative element becomes zero; but the sum of the final demand column remains unchanged, because the value is now subtracted from the column as individual elements rather than as a lump sum.

When the transferred imports are treated as a column of negative figures, they are sometimes combined, element by element, with the positive gross export figures. In this case, any individual element in the combined column can be either negative or positive, depending upon whether the value of the imports is greater or less than the value of the exports for the particular industry.

For the MRIO accounts, row 80 contains directly allocated imports and row 81 contains transferred imports. Each element in the directly allocated import row represents purchases by an industry of a heterogeneous mix of products consisting of imported goods and services for which there are no domestic substitutes. For the assembly of the MRIO data, these imports are usually obtained as part of the calculation procedure established for the other inputs into the industry, as explained in chapter 5. Thus, the elements in row 80 represent a mix of imported products used by the industry in a particular region and are therefore specified at the location in which they are consumed, rather than at the port of entry. On the other hand, each element in the transferred import row of the MRIO accounts represents a homogeneous group of products, consisting of imported goods or services identical to those produced by the corresponding domestic firms. In the MRIO accounts, transferred imports are recorded at the port of entry, then allocated to the consuming state through the interregional shipment distributions.

Row 82, Gross Regional Income. Each entry in row 82 represents the total payment made to primary factors of production (labor, land, and capital) by the industry or final user represented by the column. The specific components are wages and salaries (including fringe benefits), rent, profits, depreciation, interest, dividends, indirect business taxes, and subsidies. As in the national input-output accounts, all of these payments are combined and referred to as either gross regional income or value added.

As explained in chapter 4, separate estimates were made for the labor component of value added, but the payroll estimates were not reconciled with the total value added figures in row 82 and should therefore be used with extreme caution. Before using the payroll data in the MRIO accounts, checks should be made, for example, to be certain that for each industry or final user the payroll figure is less than or equal to the total value added figure for the corresponding industry or final user.

Row 83, Secondary Transfers-In. Each entry in row 83 represents the value of the outputs other industries have produced that are classified in the SIC code of the industry indicated by the column of the table. Each entry is therefore composed of a homogeneous set of goods or services not produced by the industry itself but transferred in from other industries to make the accounts balance, hence the term *secondary transfers-in,* or STRI. The description of the estimation method used for the state data is given in chapter 5.

Row 84, Inventory Depletions. In the 1963 national input-output table, inventory depletions and inventory additions are not given separately. Only a net inventory change figure is published for each industry, and even unpublished worksheet information apparently is not available for those two components. Because of this lack of data, the national inventory depletions were approximated by aggregating the negative inventory elements in the 1963 OBE national input-output table from the 370-order to the 80-order level. These negative values were then distributed to states in proportion to total state commodity output for the respective industry. (Commodity output equals total regional output minus STRO plus STRI for each respective industry.)

Each negative state element was subtracted from the corresponding element in the total final demand column, column 82, (which in effect augmented total GRP) and was placed as a positive element in the corresponding column of row 84 of each respective state input-output table. By making this adjustment, a measure of the total supply of the products of each industry in a given year is obtained. This adjustment also has the effect of maintaining the accounting balance between the row and column sums in the national control table (which were equal to one another), because each corresponding row and column sum is augmented by the same amount.

Row 85, Scrap Production.
Row 86, Scrap Purchases. In the 1963 national input-output table, the amount of scrap produced by a particular industry is "sold" to IO-83, Scrap, used, & secondhand goods, and appears as a single entry in column 83 in the row for that industry. On the other hand, the purchases of scrap made by each particular industry are given in row 83 of the national table and are accounted for in the same way as purchases of any other product. Each element in this row can be composed of heterogeneous items, such as rubber, paper, and steel scrap. To use the national table for economic impact analyses, the entries in column 83 are set equal to zero, and the value of each entry is added to the intraindustry cell (the diagonal elements in the table) of the appropriate industry. This procedure prevents an industry's demand for scrap from generating additional industry

output when the national input-output model is implemented. But entirely dissimilar purchases are combined within the intraindustry flows, and the balance between the row and column sums of the national table are altered unless the scrap production values are also added as a negative row to exactly offset the entries added to the diagonal.

For the MRIO accounts, a convention slightly different from the national one was introduced to handle the production of scrap. Both the national production and national consumption of scrap were allocated to states using state establishment outputs as distribution factors, because actual state estimates were not available. The positive elements for scrap production were then transferred from the scrap column (column 83) and inserted as negative elements in row 85. Column 83 was used for secondary transfers-out.

Three points should be noted. First, both column 83 and row 83 in the national table are called Scrap, used, & second-hand goods. For the MRIO accounts, row 85 (national column 83) had to be distinguished from row 86; therefore, row 85 is called Scrap production and row 86 is called Scrap purchases.

Second, as a result of the scrap-production adjustment, both the column and row totals for each scrap-producing industry in the national control table are less than the corresponding totals in the 1963 OBE national input-output table by the amount of scrap the industry produces. The effect is the same as with the national method, that is, no scrap production is generated when the MRIO model is implemented. By using this accounting procedure, scrap production can be estimated in a separate calculation under the assumption that the ratio of scrap produced to total production of an industry remains unchanged over time, or the ratio can be altered to reflect changes known to have occurred.

Third, when scrap production is treated as a negative set of figures in the state input-output tables, the control totals used for the adjustment of the interregional trade tables do not include figures for the amount of scrap the industry produced and shipped. This seems to be an acceptable procedure, but a separate interregional trade table should be constructed for the shipment of scrap. An attempt was made to do this for the MRIO accounts, but sufficient data could not be found to complete the trade estimates for scrap.

Scrap purchases were estimated and included as row 86 in the state input-output tables.

Row 87, Gross Regional Output. The figures in row 87 are obtained by adding the elements in the corresponding columns. Each element represents the total value of output (both primary and secondary) of the establishments classified in the particular input-output industry plus the value of the secondary output produced by other establishments that corresponds to the output of that industry. Secondary products are therefore double-counted in the output figures.

Commodity Trade-Flow Tables

The basic structure of the interregional commodity trade-flow tables was described earlier in relationship to figure 2–2. For the MRIO accounts, these tables were constructed using data on commodity shipments, whereas the input-output tables contain data on establishment outputs. The consistency that must be maintained in the accounts between the data in the input-output tables and the data in the interregional trade tables was obtained by adjusting the estimates in the commodity-flow tables, using an adjustment procedure explained in chapter 6. Only the interregional trade figures were adjusted in the MRIO accounts to obtain this consistency. There were three reasons for restricting the adjustments to these figures.

First, at this stage, the figures in the state input-output tables had already been adjusted to be consistent with the data in the 1963 national input-output table. Any additional adjustments to the input-output tables would have altered that balance. Second, it was assumed that the data in the trade-flow tables were not as accurate as those in the input-output tables; therefore, some of the adjustments to them might even have improved their accuracy. Third, adjusting the data in both sets of tables would have complicated the procedure described below, creating problems that would not have been offset by any advantages to be gained.

After the commodity shipments in the interregional trade tables had been adjusted, state transfers-out for each particular commodity were added as column and row 52 in the table, thus maintaining the double-counting of secondary products required in the input-output accounts. For the implementation of the MRIO model, described in chapter 3, the double-counting of the secondary products was isolated in the diagonal of the interregional trade tables, that is, each secondary element in row and column *h* was eliminated in that row and column and added to the diagonal element, x_{io}^{hh}. The row and column sums of the interregional trade tables remain the same regardless of which of the two methods of treating secondary products is used.

To adjust the data in the trade-flow tables, the estimates for each commodity were forced to add to the total output and consumption figures for that industry taken from the state input-output tables. These consistency calculations were made using a distribute-the-undistributed (DUD) program, which is described in detail in chapter 6. They had to be done with the greatest possible accuracy since rounding errors would have had serious effects on the trade-flow estimates. A nine-step procedure was used to obtain a set of trade flows that were consistent with figures in the state input-output tables. Steps 1–4 were required to prepare the trade-flow data for the DUD program; steps 5–7 were needed to complete the DUD calculations; steps 8–9 were required for the final arrangement of the trade-flow estimates in the tables. The nine steps are specified here.

Step 1–Obtain gross regional consumption and output. Sum each row and column of the state input-output tables to obtain gross regional consumption and output, respectively, in each state, with secondary products double-counted. These are shown as column and row 87 in figure 2-5. Gross regional consumption, column 87, represents the amount of intermediate and final consumption of each good or service in the state plus the value of the secondary products produced by industries in that state. Gross regional output, row 87, represents the total value of output (both primary and secondary) of the establishments classified in the particular input-output industry plus the value of secondary output produced by other establishments that corresponds to the output of the input-output industry.

Step 2–Adjust for nontransported goods and services. Subtract each figure in the STRI row (row 83) in the state input-output tables from the corresponding state output figures in row 87 to obtain the total primary and secondary output of each establishment. Subtract each element in the column of totals in the interregional trade table, referred to as Commodity Output in figure 2-5, from the corresponding total establishment output figure and add the difference, if positive, onto the corresponding diagonal element of the interregional trade tables. (This step in the calculations is not shown in the figure.) This adjustment is required to account for nontransported goods and services produced by an establishment; it includes rents, royalties, intraplant shipments, etc.

Step 3–Obtain consumption and output control totals. Eliminate the double-counting of secondary products by subtracting the figures in the STRO column (column 83) in the state input-output tables from both the consumption and output totals (column and row 87) for each state input-output table. From this calculation, a column of figures referred to as Consumption Control Total in figure 2-5 is obtained. This column contains elements representing the total state consumption figure for each industry's product. A row of figures is also obtained and is referred to as Output Control Total in the figure. The elements in this row represent the total amount of an industry's output produced in a state, regardless of which establishment produced it.

Step 4–Adjust for undercoverage of intraregional shipments. Subtract the figures in the column in the interregional trade table referred to as Commodity Output in figure 2-5 from the corresponding figures in the Output Control Total row of the state input-output tables and add the difference, if positive, onto the corresponding diagonal element of the interregional trade tables. This difference is assumed to represent the undercoverage (discussed in chapter 6) of intraregional shipments in the Census of Transportation and other statistical sources. Note that this adjustment differs from the adjustment made in step 2 in that now the state output figure used is the commodity output control rather than the establishment output figure.

At this point, the commodity output data are in balance with the output control totals, but the commodity consumption data are not necessarily in

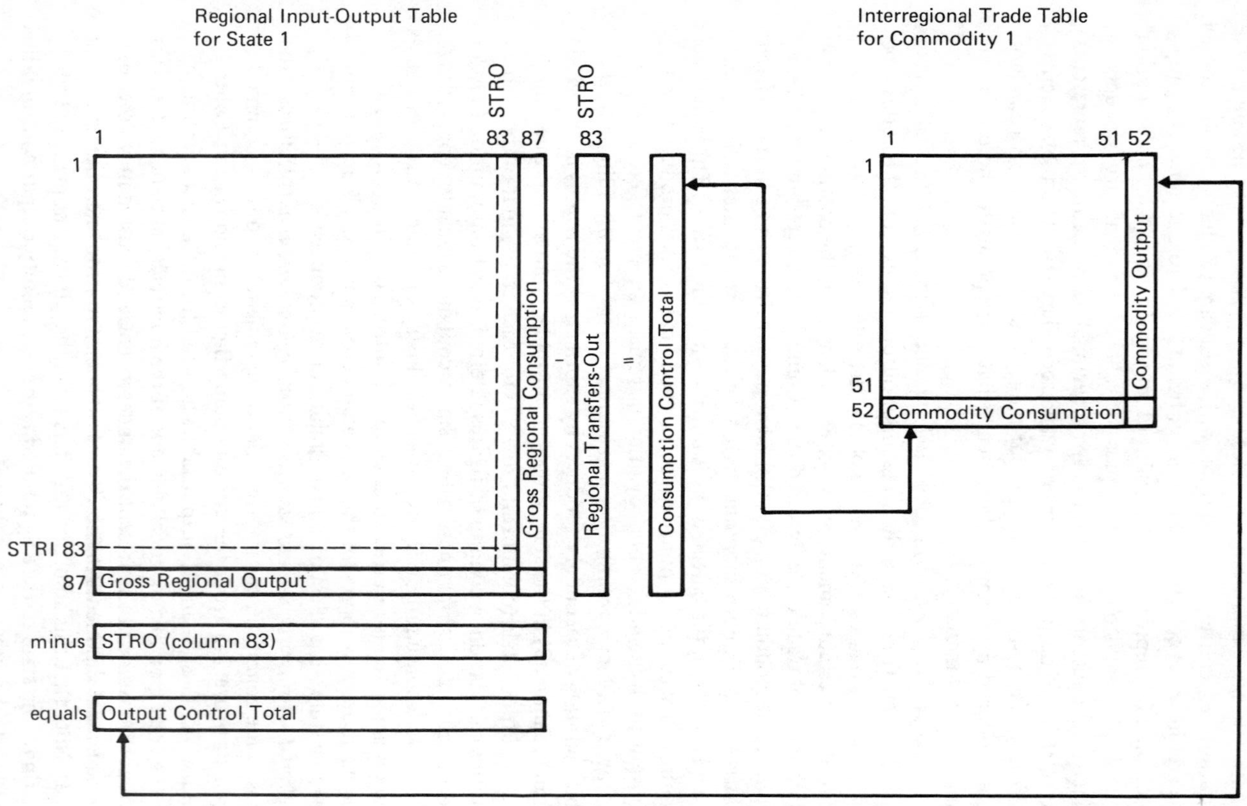

Figure 2–5. Establishment of Balance Between the State Input–Output Data and the Interregional Trade Flows

balance with the consumption control totals. Balances for both sets of figures could be obtained through use of the DUD program, as indicated in the next three steps.

Step 5–Force commodity consumption to equal commodity output. Obtain two sums, one by adding the elements from the state input-output tables that are used as controls for commodity consumption, the other by adding the elements used as controls for commodity output. The two sums are forced to add to the same total. This is done by distributing the commodity output control total in proportion to the original commodity consumption control figures, because the state output figures for an industry are assumed to have been more accurately estimated in the state input-output tables than were the state consumption figures. Although there had been no way of assuring that these totals were consistent as the state input-output tables were being constructed, the successive iterations of the DUD program would not have converged if the sums had been inconsistent.

Step 6–Obtain the undistributed figures. Subtract the elements in the row entitled Commodity Consumption and the column entitled Commodity Output of the interregional trade tables from the respective state input-output table elements in the column entitled Consumption Control Total and the row entitled Output Control Total. This calculation provides the undistributed figures that must be allocated to the cells of the trade tables.

Step 7–Distribute the undistributed. Use the DUD program to allocate the discrepancy that results from step 6. All undistributed figures are allocated alternately to the elements in the columns and rows of the interregional trade tables until the control totals are approximated to within a 1 percent range. For some industries, this requires thirty or more complete (first column, then row) iterations. At least five iterations are made for each commodity. After this series of iterations, if a discrepancy is still present between either set of control figures and the sums of the rows or columns of the trade tables, end the DUD run with the consumption totals in balance and the production totals out of balance. This decision was based upon the later use of these data in the column-coefficient trade model, described in chapter 3. The figures in the interregional trade tables should now be consistent with those in the state input-output tables.

Step 8–Add the secondary transfers-out. Add the STRO elements back onto the row and column controls for the state input-output tables. To maintain the balance between the input-output and trade-flow tables, add the STRO elements onto the respective control totals of the interregional trade tables. The addition to the trade-flow tables can be done in either of two ways: by adding a separate row and column of figures (row and column 52) or by adding a single element to each diagonal element (the intraregional shipments figures), which effectively adds the STRO value simultaneously to the row and column total. Both methods were used for the MRIO accounts.

For the implementation of the MRIO model (discussed in chapter 3), the double-counting of the secondary products was isolated in the diagonal of the interregional table by adding the STRO value to each respective intraregional shipments figure. This addition to the diagonal is portrayed by a dot in figure 2-6. For the printing and storing of the trade-flow tables, the STRO values were removed from the diagonal element and placed in row and column 52 of each trade-flow table, as shown in figure 2-7. This adjustment eliminates the double-counting from the intraregional trade flows in the table but maintains the commodity consumption and production balances with the state input-output tables obtained in step 7. The separate row and column isolate the double-counting of the secondary products from the actual commodity flows of the goods.

Step 9–Obtain a summation table. Add the 79 interregional trade tables element by element to obtain a summation table for all trade flows. The computer tapes contain trade flows only for the 61 input-output industries that transport goods, although trade-flow estimates were subsequently made for some of the service industries, namely, IO-65 through IO-79. Because the computer tapes do not contain trade data for IO-4, Agricultural, forestry, & fishery services, IO-11, New construction, and IO-12, Maintenance & repair construction, the sequential numbers of these trade data must be adjusted to place them with the appropriate input-output industry numbers listed in table A-1 in the appendix. It should be noted that trade data are provided on the computer tapes

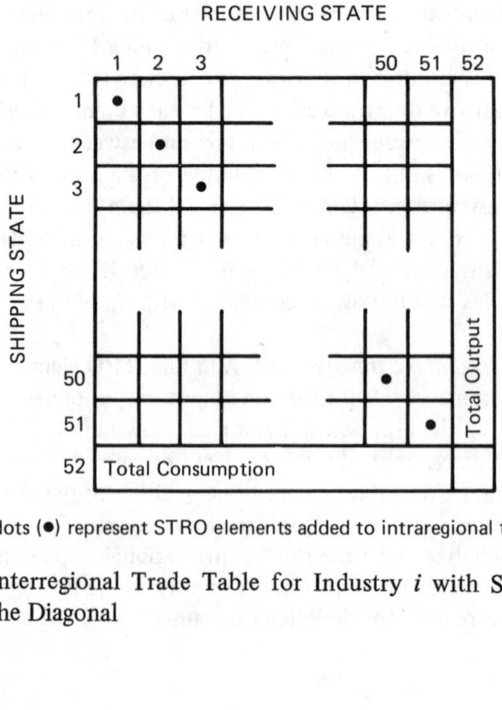

dots (•) represent STRO elements added to intraregional trade flows

Figure 2-6. Interregional Trade Table for Industry *i* with STRO Elements on the Diagonal

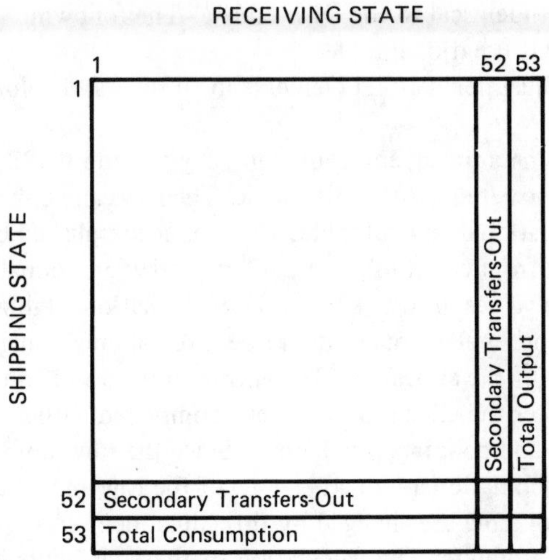

Figure 2-7. Interregional Trade Table for Industry *i* with STRO Elements in Row and Column 52

for IO-3, Forestry & fishery products, although elements appear only on the diagonal. The estimation of the NTB entries described earlier was done for this industry since commodity production did not equal commodity consumption in all regions. It was noted earlier that trade flows could not be assembled for IO-83, Scrap, used & secondhand goods, because of the lack of data. The industry is treated exogenously in the MRIO model described in chapter 3.

All trade flows were assembled in terms of tonnage units and were compiled for six modes of transportation (rail, truck, air, water, unknown, and other). The consistency checks and adjustments described in this section, however, were made only to the total interregional trade-flow data after they had been converted into value units. The trade flows before adjustment are referred to as PREDUD flows, while those after adjustment are referred to as POSTDUD flows. Details on the assembly of the estimates for the six modes of transport are provided in chapter 6.

The construction of the national input-output control table is now discussed.

National Control Table

A national control table was constructed from the 1963 national input-output table to use as a check for the state input-output estimates. Because of differences between the multiregional and national accounting definitions, the control table is not identical to the OBE table.[11] The following adjustments were made to the OBE national table.

Two of the adjustments affect elements in all rows and columns of the table. They are:

1. IO-81, Business travel, entertainment, & gifts, and IO-82, Office supplies, were specially constructed for the OBE table. The rows and columns were eliminated in the national control table. This was accomplished by calculating coefficient vectors from columns 81 and 82 in the 1963 national transfer (secondary) table. The values in rows 81 and 82 of the national table were then distributed to the other elements in the respective columns using the relevant coefficient vector for the allocation. The entries in rows and columns 81 and 82 were set to zero after the allocation had been completed. Other data were placed in the rows and columns (see below). Since the row sum is equal to the column sum for each national industry, none of the row and column sums of the national control table are changed by this adjustment.

2. Secondary products: The calculation of these elements is explained in chapter 5. It should be noted here, however, that in the national accounts, the elements in the table of secondary products are added cell by cell to those in the table of primary products, while for the MRIO accounts, the sums of the columns and rows of the 1963 national secondary table are inserted as a single row and column into the national control table. Each cell of the national control table is therefore less than the corresponding cell of the 1963 national transactions table to the extent that a secondary product is accounted for in that cell of the national transactions table.

Seven comments apply to the final demand sector (columns 80 through 86) of the national control table.

1. Column 80 contains no entries in the national control table.

2. Column 81 at the state level contains values of the net trade balance (NTB) for rows 3, 4, 11, and 12 only. For the industries represented by those rows, the difference between total output in a given region and total consumption in the same region was placed in the appropriate row of the state input-output table. This adjustment forces the row sums (total consumption) to equal the column sums (total output) in each region. Although the sum of the NTB for the 51 regions should equal zero (the residuals should cancel one another at the national level), extremely small values do occur in column 81 of the national control table because of rounding errors. In addition, the sums of row 80 (directly allocated imports) and row 81 (transferred imports) were placed as negative entries in the respective rows of this column.

3. Column 82 contains GNP entries. The following should be noted:

a. The entries for IO-82, Office supplies, were redistributed in the manner described above. (No GNP entries are listed in the OBE national table for IO-81, Business travel, entertainment, & gifts, so no adjustment was required.)

b. The Commodity Credit Corporation figures were subtracted from IO-78, Federal government enterprises, and added to the corresponding GNP figures. (These data are provided as separate figures on the computer tapes in case they are required for other calculations.)

c. The inventory depletion component of net inventory change was subtracted from the total GNP figures and added as a row of positive figures in the value added sector.

4. Column 83 contains the secondary transfers-out (row sums of the national secondary table).

5. Column 84 contains no entries.

6. Column 85 contains values for the competitive import of scrap, placed in row 81, and the margins on these imports, placed in rows 65 and 69.

7. Column 86 contains no entries.

Seven comments apply to the value added sector (rows 80 through 86) of the national control table.

1. Row 80 contains directly allocated imports. These entries are the same as those in row 80a of the 1963 national input-output table. The sum of row 80 was placed as a negative figure in column 81. The sum of row 80 then becomes zero, representing the fact that goods imported are not produced in this country.

2. Row 81 contains transferred imports. These entries are the same as those in row 80b of the 1963 national input-output table. The sum of row 81 was placed as a negative figure in column 81. The sum of row 81 then becomes zero, representing the fact that goods imported are not produced in this country. This sum in the national control table is $21 million less than the corresponding sum in the 1963 national input-output table. This difference represents the value that had not been allocated to the states in the net inventory change tables.

3. Row 82 contains value added, that is, payments to the primary factors of production. The values in the national control table are the same as those in the OBE table except for the value in column 82. The national control table value is $52,840 million, while the sum of the elements in the final demand columns of rows 84, 85, 86, and 87 in the national OBE table is $61,002 million. The difference of $8,162 million represents items that had not been allocated to states in the net inventory change (-$502 million), net foreign exports ($6,208 million), and federal government ($2,456 million) tables. These tables are provided in the first volume of this series [181, pp. 316–327, 364–375, 436–447].

4. Row 83 contains secondary transfers-in (column sums of the 1963 national secondary transfers table).

5. Row 84 contains inventory depletions (as positive figures). Because no data were available to separate inventory additions from inventory depletions in the national input-output table, the negative elements in the 370-order 1963

national input-output table were aggregated to the 80-order level and were transposed from a column of negative figures to a row of positive figures. For those industries with inventory depletions, this adjustment has the effect of augmenting the row and column sums of the national control table by identical amounts.

6. Row 85 contains values for the amount of scrap produced by the particular industry. For the national control table, the values in column 83 of the 1963 national table were transposed and placed as negative figures in row 85 of the table. This adjustment has the effect of reducing the row and column totals of the national control table for those industries that produce scrap.

7. Row 86 contains entries for scrap purchased by each industry. These entries correspond to those in row 83 of the 1963 national input-output table, except for the entry in column 82. The national control table value of final demand for purchases of scrap in row 86 is -$439 million, while the corresponding sum in row 83 of the 1963 national OBE table is -$334 million. The difference of $105 million represents an amount that was not allocated to states in the net inventory change tables.

The sums of the rows and columns of the national control table represent the following:

Column 87 contains the total amount of output purchased by intermediate and final users plus the total amount of output classified as secondary products of the establishment represented by the particular row of the table. Secondary products are double-counted in the total.

Row 87 contains the total amount paid for goods and services, including the payments to the primary factors of production and the payments for imports, plus the value of the secondary output produced by other establishments that corresponds to the output of the industry represented by the column. Secondary products are double-counted in the total.

Data Assembly Methodologies and Data Sources

In constructing the MRIO accounts, there were no previous methodologies to follow except for cases in which the required data were exactly the same as those used in the national economic accounts. Even in those cases, the national methodologies and the compositions and definitions of the national aggregates usually were not specified in sufficient detail or were outdated. Few or no definitions of the data were provided with either national or regional sources of data. A tremendous amount of time and effort was therefore required to develop reasonable definitions of the data and to determine the best methodologies to use for constructing the regional accounts.

Although many different data sources and various methodologies were used to assemble the figures, the basic procedure for all except the interregional trade flows was to find any available state data that could be used to make consistent sets of state estimates and then, if possible, to establish a general methodology for assembly of the data for all the components or, if that was not possible, to determine a separate methodology for each component. No national estimates of interregional trade flows for commodities existed, so, as a first step, state-to-state tonnage data were assembled for each commodity. These tonnage data were then converted into value (dollar) units and finally were adjusted to be consistent with the state input-output table controls for that commodity. For services, the transfers from region to region were approximated using sundry data sources, and the state-to-state transfers were adjusted to be consistent with the state input-output table controls for each service industry.

Criteria for Data Selection and Assembly

The lack of previous methodologies for constructing a set of multiregional accounts made it imperative that certain criteria be established for data selection and assembly. For each component of the 1963 MRIO accounts, a set of "ideal" data would have met the following requirements:

1. They would have been for 1963.
2. They would have been for all of the 51 regions.
3. They would have been specified for the exact number of producing industries, final demand sectors, purchasing industries, and value added sectors required for the 80-order industry classification.
4. They would have been specifically defined and would have either conformed with or have been capable of being accurately adjusted to conform with the conceptual framework and accounting definitions used for the MRIO table.
5. They would have been from the same statistical source.

Generally, several sets of data were available, but none of them met all the requirements. The three possibilities described below illustrate the types of decisions that had to be made.

First, two sets of data were available, one a reasonably accurate and well-defined distribution series but for a year other than the one desired, and the second a less accurate and less well-defined set of data but for the desired year. A decision had to be made as to how reasonable it was to assume that the state distributions did not vary between the two years and that the data for the first year could therefore be used as allocation factors for the national data for the desired year.

Second, data were available only for aggregate regions or for the nation rather than for states. A decision had to be made as to whether an accurate set of state estimates could be constructed by weighting the regional or national data by a series of aggregate state figures, or whether some proxy should be employed to make the state allocations.

Third, only very sparse regional data or none at all were available. A decision had to be made as to an appropriate distribution series that could be used to allocate the national figures to the states. Employment, payroll, or output figures were often used as the state allocation factors.

The data were assembled using five criteria:

Criterion 1. All state data for a particular component of the accounting framework are obtained from the same basic source or sources. Data obtained from diverse sources are less desirable because time and budget limitations restrict the number of data that can be compiled item by item from different sources. Judgments about which particular set of data is the best to use generally must be intuitive, of course, as there is no actual set of data against which the various estimates can be compared. Another factor is that statistics from different sources are usually not comparable in terms of data composition, extent of coverage, year, etc. To improve their comparability, extensive adjustments are required if data from different sources are used, but the precise nature of the noncomparabilities is difficult to determine because of the frequent lack of or limited documentation. In addition, because of a need to cross-check and revise data at later stages of the data-assembly process, it is strongly advisable to use the same data sources for estimates for each state.

This first criterion was applied even for cases, such as the state of Washington, where a state input-output table was available for the same year as the MRIO table–1963. Although it was believed that the MRIO estimates were less reliable than the Washington state estimates, data from that table could not have been directly integrated into the MRIO accounts because of differences in industrial classifications and accounting methodologies and because of the limited written documentation on the procedures used to construct them. To determine definitions, establish methodologies, and locate data sources for all data available directly from individual state sources would have required far too much time and money and might well have increased the already existing difficulty of determining overall accuracy of the MRIO accounts.

Criterion 2. Data specific to the item being referred to (input technology or final demands, for example) for any year and at any level of detail (regional, producing industry, final demand sector, consuming industry, or value added sector) are preferred to any intermediate (proxy) data that might be introduced, even though the intermediate data are for a year closer to 1963 or are at a better level of regional or industrial aggregation. All of this is subject to the constraints of criterion 1.

Criterion 3. Data for 1963 are preferred to those for any other year, because all results must be made consistent with the 1963 national input-output table. Even if data for some other year are considered to be slightly superior in accuracy to data for 1963, the 1963 data are still used. This criterion is subject to the constraints of criterion 2 and can sometimes be applied only at the national level—as when, for instance, the second decision mentioned above must be made as to an appropriate proxy series, and the proxy is for a year other than 1963.

Criterion 4. Data for 51 regions are preferred to more aggregate regional data, subject to constraints of criterion 3, and any regional data for a particular component are preferred to national data for that component. Thus, 1963 data for the nine census regions, which are consistent with the 1963 national input-output data, might be allocated to the states using, say, 1960 state figures as allocation factors; but the 1963 adjusted census region totals must be preserved in the process.

Criterion 5. Data for a specific industry or sector (both by producing and consuming industry or sector), being more stable over time than over geographic area, are preferred to more aggregated industry or sector data. This is subject to constraints of criteria 3 and 4. The input-output relationships from the 1963 table for the state of Washington, for example, were not used to approximate those for the states of Oregon and California; rather, individual series of specific data for those states, frequently for years other than 1963, were used.

The application of these basic criteria resulted in a set of MRIO accounts that are relatively comparable from state to state for any particular data component in terms of accuracy of the estimates and consistency with the 1963 national input-output table. In addition, the accounts reflect differential relationships from state to state and from component to component and incorporate the most relevant regional statistics available at the time they were assembled.

The theoretical model constructed for the present study is described in the next chapter; details of the data assembly, methodologies, and data sources are given in chapters 4 through 7.

Notes

1. All of the data sources and estimation procedures are summarized in chapters 4-7; the details are provided in the previous five volumes of the present series [181; 182; 191; 192; 198].

2. In a few cases, a different state-numbering scheme was used on the worksheets. Those cases are documented in the previous five volumes of this series, and the different schemes are provided there.

3. As far as is known, the only construction of an IRIO set of accounts

is that done by the Ministry of International Trade and Industry in Japan [139; 140; 141].

4. The differences in the definition of value added used in the national and regional economic accounts and that used by the Bureau of the Census are given in chapter 4. The term *regional value added* is referred to as *gross regional product originating* by the Bureau of Economic Analysis, but is usually referred to as *gross regional income* in this text.

5. This lack of detailed data may be partially overcome in the future. For the 1977 Census of Transporation, for example, data were collected, though only for manufacturing industries, on the industry and region of both the manufacturer and the receiver of each commodity [215, p. 718].

6. Originally, this assumption was made for all industries in the service sector as well, that is, IO-65 through IO-79, and the difference between regional consumption and regional output was called the *service industry residual* (SIR). Later, interregional transfers were estimated for those industries, and the SIR entries were eliminated. It was then decided that a more general term, *net trade balance,* should be given to the residuals for the remaining four industries as some of them are not service industries.

7. It should be noted that these expenditures are treated differently by the Bureau of Labor Statistics and the OBE. Information on the method used by the BLS is given in chapter 7.

8. Capital-flow tables can also be constructed in physical units. For this study, however, all capital flows referred to are in dollar values, unless otherwise designated.

9. Although some input-output tables contain only one import row, the discussion in this section will pertain to the methodology used for the national 80-order tables, which contain two.

10. Because directly allocated imports are not produced in the United States, they are recorded only in the appropriate import row; but the value, of course, is also incorporated as part of the final output value of the product of the industry.

11. The discussion above in the "Input-Output Tables" section, concerning the general procedure used in constructing the MRIO accounts in relationship to the three industries specially constructed in the OBE accounts (IO-74, IO-81, and IO-82), the three margin industries (transportation, trade, and insurance), and secondary products applies to this section as well and will not be repeated here.

3 Multiregional Input-Output Models

One purpose of the present study was to construct a comprehensive set of multiregional accounts, described in chapter 2. Another purpose was to formulate and implement a multiregional input-output (MRIO) model that can be used for various regional economic policy analyses. The theoretical structure of that model is described in this chapter. First, however, the major theoretical literature on regional analyses will be briefly reviewed, with special emphasis on the literature most relevant to the MRIO model. The review is a considerably expanded and modified version of a paper given in 1978 by the author at a regional conference in Siegen, Germany [178].

Review of Regional and Multiregional Modeling Literature

A great many methodologies have been developed for conducting national economic analyses, but only a few have been developed specifically for regional or multiregional analyses. A considerable number of the national methodologies, however, have been adapted for regional and multiregional studies. Among those frequently employed for regional and multiregional studies are input-output, regression (hereafter called econometric), linear programming, microanalytic, benefit-cost, shift-share, and economic base; new approaches, such as systems dynamics, are also being tried.

Although certain analysts tend to be committed to one and only one approach, increasing numbers of studies are being undertaken for which two or more methodologies are employed. An interesting and informative book entitled *Models in the Policy Process* [65] has recently been published. In it, Greenberger, Crenson, and Crissey review the development of nine methodologies and discuss the national policy analyses that have been conducted using them. Although the book contains only occasional references to regional and multiregional studies, it is especially recommended for those who want an in-depth view of national econometric and systems dynamics models. Much of the authors' discussion of these national models is also relevant for the corresponding regional and multiregional models.

The focus of the first part of this review will be on the analytic models that have been developed for regional and multiregional analyses of macroeconomic activity in the United States. Thus, models that are relevant for the examination of only one particular component of regional activity, such as population forecasting or network-flow models, will be excluded from the review. Those specialized models, of course, are often incorporated as subcomponents of overall macroeconomic models. Although considerable research on regional and multiregional modeling is being done in other countries, the discussion here will be restricted to research being conducted in the United States.

Some of the regional and multiregional economic accounting literature reviewed in chapter 1 dealt with models as well. The useful surveys written by Meyer [133], Kerr and Williamson [99], and Richardson [185] covered both regional and multiregional models and analyses. In 1963, Meyer summed up his review by calling for a redirection of effort away from economic accounts toward the formulation and testing of hypotheses on the behavior and role of financial organizations, market structures, entrepreneurship, private and public investment decisions, fiscal policies, and so on. He also suggested that regional studies should incorporate the basic ideas from modern statistical decision theory to evaluate the costs and benefits of using models and other tools to improve the decision-making process at the regional level. The major contribution thus far of regional economics, as Meyer saw it, was the provision of the broad measures and framework required to evaluate and organize economic activity. In his review, he provided examples from location theories, input-output and economic base studies, and mathematical programming techniques.

Kerr and Williamson in 1970 and Richardson in 1978 reviewed some of the main regional and multiregional economic theories, models, and techniques being employed for analyses and policy decisions. Included in their surveys were location, regional growth, and spatial price theories; economic base, input-output, econometric, and gravity models; and the shift-share technique. A review of regional growth theory is available in a 1974 article by Borts [9], and a discussion of the relevance of regional science is given in a 1976 article by Miernyk [136]. In his survey article referred to above, Richardson reviewed some econometric models [185], but the most valuable documentation of a large number of regional econometric models is that provided by Glickman in his 1974 article [58] and 1977 book [59]. An extensive discussion of input-output, econometric, and systems dynamics models, as well as a more limited discussion of microanalytic and linear programming models, is contained in a 1978 article by Polenske [178].

Survey articles restricted to input-output models and analyses have been written by Tiebout in 1957 [213], Miernyk in 1972 [135], and Riefler in 1973 [186], while Richardson in his 1972 book reviewed issues related to regional and multiregional input-output models with a long discussion of their use in combination with linear programming models [184]. Other less extensive reviews and discussions of input-output models are available in articles or books by Isard and Cumberland [93], Kuenne [109], the National Planning Association [202], Stevens [203], and Wilson [301].

Bibliographies specific to regional and multiregional input-output models and analyses have been published by Bourque and Hansen [11]; Bourque and Cox [10]; Giarratani, Maddy, and Socher [55]; and Hewings [77]. These supplement the regional literature on modeling listed in the general input-output bibliographies [189; 219-222]. As far as is known, no bibliography of the many other types of regional and multiregional models is available except in the references listed at the end of each of the surveys already mentioned. However, one other reference valuable to analysts working with all types of regional and multiregional models is a short article by Kendrick entitled "Mathematical Models for Regional Planning" [97].

In 1971, a survey article by Milliman was published, in which he reviewed the following seven regional projection models: (1) The New York Metropolitan Region Study by the Graduate School of Public Administration, Harvard University, for the Regional Plan Association; (2) The Upper Midwest Economic Study jointly undertaken by the Upper Midwest Research and Development Council and The University of Minnesota; (3) The Ohio River Basin Study by Arthur D. Little for the Corps of Engineers; (4) The California Development model for the state of California; (5) The Oahu, Hawaii, model for the state of Hawaii; (6) The Lehigh Basin simulation model by the Harvard Water Program; and (7) The Susquehanna Basin simulation model by the Battelle Memorial Institute [96, pp. 314-315]. Milliman listed, but did not review, five other major regional models. At that time (1971), only the Upper Midwest Economic Study analysts used a framework that included data for the entire United States; now, as indicated below, at least nineteen models are so designed. Milliman said that his most important conclusion was "the need to have further appraisal and postauditing of large-scale regional models" [96, p. 349]. He also concluded that "A major rationale for keeping models operative is internal model validation" [96, p. 350]. As he stressed, all of this, of course, depends upon having appropriate research budgeting for the development, implementation, and validation, as well as for later revision and improvement in the model structure based upon the initial experience in using the models.

During the past ten years, a large number of multiregional models have been formulated, some of which are being used for policy decisions. A list of the nineteen econometric, input-output, and linear programming multiregional economic models currently in operation or under development in the United States as of the spring of 1979 is provided in table 3-1. Only multiregional models that have both industrial and regional detail and that can be used for general macroeconomic analyses are included in the summary. Thus, although many multiregional economic models have been developed for the analysis of only one industry or sector of the economy, such as grains or transportation, these were excluded, as were transportation network-flow models. The summary is subject to constant revision, because new models are appearing every year and significant changes are being made to those already developed.

Table 3-1
Summary of Multiregional Models for the United States

Title of Model	*Acronym*	*Developed by*	*Number of Industries*	*Number of Regions*	*Purpose*
		Econometric Models			
Multiregional Forecasting and Simulation Model	MULTI-REGION	Richard J. Olsen Oak Ridge National Laboratory Now David Bjornstad (Olsen now at Charles River Associates, Inc.)	37	173	Used as a model of regional and interregional socioeconomic development that interprets the economy of each BEA economic area as a labor market and simulates or forecasts the demands and supplies of labor in all areas.
Multiregional Multi-Industry Forecasting Model	MRMI	Curtis C. Harris, Jr. University of Maryland	99	3,111 or 173	Used to make long-run regional forecasts of industrial output and employment for all counties in the United States. A recursive econometric model with regional variables linked to a national model and with a linear programming submodel.
Multiregional Policy Analysis Model	–	George Treyz University of Massachusetts, Amherst	25	51	Used to generate forecasts of employment, population, state and local government spending, and other regional economic variables, conditional on alternative values for government policy instruments.
National-Regional Impact Evaluation System	NRIES	Kenneth P. Ballard and Robert M. Wendling Regional Economic Analysis Division, Bureau of Economic Analysis, U.S. Department of Commerce	1-digit SIC	51	Used for policy impact analyses in examining effects of regional or national economic and demographic events upon regional activity in the United States. Also will be used for 6- to 10-year forecasts of regional economic and demographic activity.

Bureau of Economic Analysis Regional Projections (formerly Office of Business Economics and Economic Research Service Regional Projections)	OBERS	Kenneth P. Johnson Regional Economic Analysis Division, Bureau of Economic Analysis, U.S. Department of Commerce	58	585	Used to project employment, earnings, personal income, and population to 1980, 1985, 1990, 1995, 2000, 2010, 2020, and 2030 for 585 state and substate groups. Projections are based upon benchmark regional data obtained at the state and county level.
Regional Economic Projection Series	REPS	Timothy B. Sivia and David M. Levy National Planning Association	1-digit SIC	3,098	Used to forecast county earnings, employment, and population for 1976 to 1990, one region at a time. Projections are consistent with national forecasts. Model used is basically recursive.
Regional Energy, Activity, and Demographic Model	READ	William A. Donnelly, Frank Hopkins, and Terry Morlan Energy Information Administration, U.S. Department of Energy	48	3,112	Used to forecast regional shifts in energy demand that result from specific energy policies and exogenous changes. Also used to determine the effect of these shifts on industry and population locations, state and local government activities, and the environment. A simultaneous econometric model with a linear programming submodel.
Regional Forecasting Network	RFN	Dennis Paranzino Chase Econometric Associates, Inc. (CEAI)	20	51 and 104	Used to forecast population, employment, income, finance, and consumer variables for all regions, as well as 2-digit industry output and employment. Policy capability is provided by alternative forecasts.
State and Area Forecasting Service	SAFS	Staff Data Resources, Inc. (DRI)	2	50	Used to forecast employment, income, housing starts, and some financial variables for all 50 state economies and selected SMSA economies, to 1981. State and area models containing over 500 equations are linked with a national model.

Table 3–1 continued

Title of Model	*Acronym*	*Developed by*	*Number of Industries*	*Number of Regions*	*Purpose*
Wharton Annual Regional Model	WARM	Wharton Econometric Forecasting Associates, Inc.	12	16	Used to forecast regional economic growth and energy consumption, determining regional output, employment, and investment by industry and retail sales, employment, unemployment, wages, and population by demographic group. Model is comprised of a system of regional econometric labor-market models that are linked with a national model.
Multiregion Econometric Model of the United States	–	William J. Milne, Norman J. Glickman, and F. Gerard Adams University of Pennsylvania	9	6	Used to forecast regional output, employment, personal income, population, energy, and other variables. Regional output, employment, and wage rates are determined for six industrial sectors.
		Input-Output Models			
Battelle PREVIEWS Multiregional Input-Output Model	PREVIEWS	W. Halder Fisher Battelle-Columbus	127	50	Used for analyzing regional economic impacts of federal policies and of changes in industry locations.
Income Determination Input-Output Model	IDIOM	Stephen P. Dresch Institute for Demographic and Economic Studies	86	51	Used to evaluate regional economic effects arising from large-scale changes in fiscal structure and in other exogenous economic developments.
Multiregional Input-Output Model	MRIO	Karen R. Polenske Harvard Economic Research Project Now Massachusetts Institute of Technology	79	51	Used to specify consistent interindustry interregional flows; to analyze employment, transportation, energy, environmental, water resource, tax and expenditure, and other policies; and to project regional outputs, interregional trade flows, and relative regional prices.

Poverty Institute Regional and Distributional Model	–	Frederick L. Golladay and Robert H. Haveman Institute for Research on Poverty, University of Wisconsin	79	51	Used to estimate regional, occupational, industrial, and income distributional effects of changes in tax-transfer and public employment policies.
Multi-Regional Model of the Economy and Energy Demand	MREED	T.R. Lakshmanan Boston University	37	182	Used as a system of regional econometric models to provide (at the BEA economic area level) estimates of output by sector, wages, income, consumption, taxes, employment, pollution-abatement costs, and energy demand by land-use and fuel type.
Regional Earnings Impact System	REIS	A. David Sandoval, Robert M. Schnapp, and Robert S. Wenger U.S. Department of Energy	37	51	Used to project growth in state earnings given different assumptions about national economic and energy futures. Model is based upon macro model and an energy disaggregated version of the Bureau of Labor Statistics Input-Output (EDIO) model.
Regional Industrial Multiplier System	RIMS	Joseph V. Cartwright Regional Economic Analysis Division, Bureau of Economic Analysis, U.S. Department of Commerce	478	3,133	Used as a regional impact analysis tool to estimate industry-specific input-output type multipliers for regions composed of counties or groups of counties.
		Linear Programming Model			
Unconstrained and Constrained Dynamic Input-Output Models	–	Se-Hark Park and A. David Sandoval U.S. Department of Energy	16	9	Used to investigate intertemporal impacts of anticipated changes in energy policies on regional economic activity in terms of sectoral outputs, employment, income, exports, and investment and to identify optimal public and private responses to the energy shortages anticipated in the coming decade. Model includes unconstrained and constrained versions of dynamic regional input-output models.

The models are grouped under three main headings, according to whether they have primarily an econometric, input-output, or linear programming basis. Because econometric models can be constructed more rapidly and easily than input-output or linear programming models, it is not surprising that the largest of these groups is the econometric models, comprised of eleven models. Input-output models are the next largest classification, comprised of seven models. The popularity of input-output models, despite their extensive data requirements, stems from their wide applicability to multiregional analyses. Unlike other multiregional models, they simultaneously provide three tools: an accounting framework, a means of policy analysis, and a method of forecasting (planning).

Linear programming models have been the least used in multiregional macroeconomic analyses, with only one currently operational or under development. Cross-hauling, that is, the simultaneous shipment in both directions between any two regions of a supposedly homogeneous good, is difficult to incorporate into a linear programming model. This fact combined with the extensive data requirements similar to those for input-output models means that probably few analysts will use the linear programming technique alone in a multiregional model. Another important reason for the lack of development of the technique is no doubt the traditionally positive approach of multiregional analyses. Normative goals, such as profit maximization or cost minimization, are easily treated in a linear programming submodel linked with econometric or input-output models. This linkage approach is used in the Multiregional Multi-Industry Forecasting Model and the Regional Energy, Activity, and Demographic Model. Although this combination of modeling structures appears to hold great promise, it has not yet yielded significant improvements over the use of a single model.

Across model types, the number of industries varies from the approximate 1-digit to the 4-digit standard industrial classification (SIC) level, and the number of regions varies from the 9-census-region level to the 3,133-county level. The region numbers 50 and 51 refer to states; 173–182 to various levels of functional economic areas established by the Bureau of Economic Analysis (BEA) of the U.S. Department of Commerce; 3,098–3,133 to county or county-type units; 104 to the standard metropolitan statistical areas (SMSA); and 585 to state and substate groups. As most of the models listed are still being revised and extended, the number of industries and regions should be taken only as a rough approximation of the size of the model.

Special mention should be made of some of the multiregional econometric models listed in table 3–1. Many of the econometric models implemented to date (the summer of 1980) are for single regions, states, or cities. In 1968, Klein proposed the development of a multiregional econometric model [104], and a small-scale version has now been set up by Ballard and Wendling for the BEA [6]. The Wharton Annual Regional Model and the Multiregional Econometric Model of the United States are being developed at the University of Pennsylvania.

An econometric model originally developed by Friedlaender, Treyz, and Tresch [53] for Massachusetts has since been considerably refined and improved by Treyz [216], and work has been commenced on an extension of it to a multiregional basis, initially for the New England region and eventually for nine or more regions encompassing the entire United States. It is a policy-simulation model, and the results obtained from it are currently being used by a number of Massachusetts state agencies. In its revised form, the model has some important structural features that can ultimately be used to link it directly with an input-output model. Ways are currently being examined for linking it and the MRIO model. Although at present the equations in the econometric model are linked to national variables through the Data Resources, Inc. (DRI) model, this national link is not as critical as in Klein's theoretical structure of a multiregional system (in which each region is viewed as a satellite of a national model, and the regional model is "*driven*" by the national variables [34]).

Another important econometric model, linking regression and input-output models, was developed by Harris [70; 71]. In his model, the Interindustry Forecasting Model (INFORUM) instead of the DRI model is used to form the national link. The INFORUM model is a national dynamic input-output system developed by Almon and used by him and others at the University of Maryland [4]. Harris bases the input-output part of his model on the national projections obtained from INFORUM, then estimates the regional (county) "shares" using regression equations. Thus, his regional forecasts of industrial output are controlled by the national forecasts. His model is recursive. He uses the industry location equations to explain changes in regional outputs. In its latest version, his model has 99 industries and 3,111 regions (county-type units). Harris has used the model to evaluate five alternative highway systems; to study the onshore impact of offshore oil and gas development and the economic repercussions of opening new coal mines in Montana and Maryland; and to analyze other regional problems related to employment, agriculture, energy, and automobiles [72].

The theoretical foundations of the MRIO model are many, with the most important for analytical purposes being interindustry linkages, international trade theory, multiplier analysis, and price theory. Many methods of making such analyses have been developed and used at the regional level. For example, industrial complex analyses, comparative cost analyses, location theory, and linear programming approaches have been used to look at production technology and its location and changes over time and space. International trade theory is the forerunner of interregional trade models. These have been expanded from models for individual commodities to those for global economies, such as the World Bank global model [69] and the Carter-Leontief-Petri model of the world economy [127]. National multiplier analyses date back to Kahn's 1931 article that showed how much employment could be generated in the consumption-goods industries by increased government expenditures in investment-goods industries [95]. Regional multipliers are now constructed periodically by the BEA at various levels of regional detail under what is referred to as the Regional Impact Multiplier System, or RIMS [263]. Price theory is of growing concern as the high inflation rates in the U.S. economy continue year after year. Richardson reviews spatial price theory [185]. Only recently has significant progress been made in developing regional and multiregional input-output price models. All of these theoretical foundations of the MRIO model will be reviewed in greater depth in the next section.

Regional and Multiregional Input-Output Literature Review

It was not until almost fifteen years after Leontief's first input-output article had been published that the theory of the interdependence of outputs, incomes, and prices in different sectors of the economy was extended to include space. The spatial studies expanded rapidly. By 1955, 22 theoretical and 24 empirical regional and multiregional input-output studies had been published, most of them between 1951 and 1954 and nearly all of them for regions in the United States. Not surprisingly, Isard contributed half of the theoretical publications [189]. Only twelve years later, a total of 164 regional and multiregional studies had been completed in a comparable four-year period, 1963 through 1966, and by then, analyses were being made for regions throughout the world [221].

There are essentially four ways in which space is dealt with in input-output models. They are distinguished by the specific combinations of technology and trade structures used in the models. The four models will be referred to as regional, intranational, multiregional, and interregional. (They will be defined in the next section.) All four of the theoretical structures were specified in the early 1950s. Both the regional and interregional structures were set forth by Isard in 1951 [89]. Although other studies of single regions were made in the early 1950s, Isard's study of New England [89], Cumberland's of Maryland [23], and Moore and Peterson's of Utah [147], which were among the first attempts to use an input-output model for empirical studies at the regional level, have received the most attention. An empirical specification of the interregional model was long in coming. As far as is known to this writer, the first published data for an interregional system of accounts were the 1960, 1965, and 1970 Japanese interregional tables [139; 140; 141].

The theoretical structure and empirical implementation of the intranational model were discussed in articles by Leontief and Isard in 1953 [123; 90]. A major policy analysis using the intranational model concerned the impact of a 20 percent cutback in military expenditures in Vietnam. A paper on this research by Leontief and others was published in 1965 [126]. The staff working on that study were dissatisfied with the model and with the data available to implement it. Two years later (1967) funds were found to assemble data and formulate an improved multiregional model, now known as the MRIO model. The intranational framework is still being used by some regional analysts, such as Dresch, who by 1972 had developed the Income Determination Input-Output Model (IDIOM) [30].

For the multiregional theoretical framework, the principal early studies were the theoretical and empirical work by Moses for an 11-industry, 3-region, model of the United States [150], based upon his Ph.D. dissertation [149], and by Chenery, who implemented a 22-industry, 2-region, study for Italy in collaboration with Clark and Cao-Pinna [19]. This Chenery-Moses model became the basic theoretical structure used by Polenske to develop the large-scale (79-industry, 51-region) MRIO model for the United States being described in this text.

In the first regional and multiregional input-output models, it was customary to approximate the regional technology by adjusting the national coefficients. Moore and Peterson, for example, based their 1947 technologies for Utah on the 1947 national 190-industry direct input coefficients, adjusted to reflect production-technique, marketing-practice, or product-mix differences in the state [147]. The multiregional models by Moses [148; 150] and Leontief et al. [126] also used national technologies, because of the lack of regional data. It was largely due to the impetus given by the excellent survey-based studies conducted by Miernyk and Udis for the Colorado River Basin [134; 217], by Bourque and Tiebout for the state of Washington [12], and by Miernyk for the state of West Virginia [138] that more and more regional analysts have been taking surveys to obtain first-hand regional technology information. Short-cut methods are also being developed in an attempt to reduce the cost of data collection [130; 197], and the present study has provided a set of regional technology data, based on secondary data sources.

Until recently, by far the greatest part of the spatial input-output research in the United States and elsewhere has centered on single-region studies. The implementation of multiregional input-output models covering all regions of the United States has been rather limited, most of the studies having been done for states aggregated into 19 or fewer regions, with only a few major variations of the basic models described above having been used. The studies by Chenery, Isard, Leontief, Moses, and Polenske have already been mentioned. In addition, Greytak implemented the Chenery-Moses model for 19 regions, with Appalachia and the Ozarks specified in detail [66], and again for 8 regions, combining data for the 50 states [67]. The National Planning Association conducted a multiregional study concentrating on New York state, but also containing data for the rest of the regions of the United States [202].

Only a few multiregional input-output models have been developed for the United States as a whole. A larger number have been constructed for subareas of the United States for use in studies on topics ranging over a variety of economic issues from general economic development to particular topics, such as water resources, transportation, agriculture, and employment. Examples of general multiregional models that have been used for subarea analyses are those by Riefler and Tiebout for California and Washington [187]; Henderson and Krueger for the Upper Midwest [76]; Lee, Moore, and Lewis for three regions in Tennessee [114]; and Grubb for nine regions in Texas [68]. Examples of water-resource multiregional input-output models are those of Miernyk and Udis for the Colorado River Basin [134; 217]; Davis for the West [26]; the U.S. Army Corps of Engineers for the North Atlantic region [200]; and Kim, Park, and Kwak for the Arkansas River [101]. The use of multiregional input-output models for transportation is illustrated by the CONSAD study of the Northeast Corridor [21] and the study of Conrail conducted by Jack Faucett Associates, Inc. [39], while the Carter and Ireri study for California and Arizona [18] is an example of the use of a multiregional input-output model for agriculture, and the Rowan study of Massachusetts, New England, and the rest of the United States illustrates the use of the MRIO model for employment analyses [194].

Following a brief description of the general characteristics of the MRIO model, including some specific ways in which the model can be used, an extensive discussion of the input-output theory underlying the MRIO model will be presented.

General Characteristics of the MRIO Model

The MRIO model is a comprehensive, multipurpose tool that can be used for systematic studies of many regional economic policies. It provides a consistent framework for describing and analyzing not only the sales and purchases of all industries in every region of the economy, but also the shipments to and from all regions. The dual version of the model can be used for analyses of regional wages and prices. Because both industries and regions are strongly interdependent, the MRIO model provides a useful way of measuring the direct and indirect effects of variations in economic activities throughout the country. For example, it can be used to show how a purchase in one region generates a chain of transactions affecting industries in many regions. If the MRIO framework has been correctly specified, the outputs required from each region to fulfill the given demand and the resulting interregional shipments of all goods needed for the production of those outputs can be accurately measured.

There are eight distinguishing features of the MRIO data and model.

1. The data comprise a set of consistent multiregional accounts, established for 51 regions (50 states plus the District of Columbia) and 79 industries.

2. The data were assembled and the MRIO model was first implemented in its present form ten years ago, and since then, both the data and the model have been subjected to numerous validation tests.
3. The data and model are being used for policy decisions by federal and state governments, as well as for general research purposes by consulting firms and university research groups.
4. Direct and indirect economic (output, employment, income, trade, and price) repercussions of the policies can be measured.
5. All analyses made provide considerable industrial and regional detail while maintaining an internal consistency of all calculations.
6. The MRIO framework can be used to analyze the industrial and regional impact of economic policy decisions for the nation as a whole, and, at the same time, economic analysts in each region or group of regions can use the basic results of the calculations to provide controls for their own investigations of economic problems peculiar to the region or group of regions under study.
7. The model is one of the only multiregional macroeconomic models that can be used to determine gross interregional shipments among regions. Gross, rather than just net, shipments of commodities to and from each region can be estimated.
8. A dual and a primal version of the model are now being used, so policy analyses can be conducted for issues relating to output, employment, income, energy, and transportation, as well as prices and wages.

Because of the wide variation in needs of users, the data and model were specifically designed for adaptability to different policy studies. Complete methodologies of data assembly and information on the data sources used are readily available in published form [181; 182; 191; 192; 198], as are the computer tapes containing the data [176]. The present volume provides a guide to assist analysts in understanding the mathematical structure of the MRIO model and in using the data to implement the model. Additional information on the mathematical properties of the model is contained in Ph.D. theses by Bon [8] and Shalizi [201], while some difficulties in adjusting the interregional trade flows to be consistent with the regional input-output tables are investigated by Möhr in his Ph.D. thesis [145].

The MRIO model is an accounting tool, a policy analysis tool, and a planning (forecasting) tool. Each of these uses will now be discussed.

Accounting Tool

The structure of the MRIO accounts is discussed in chapter 2. As was stressed there, a tremendous advantage of an input-output accounting framework over other means of assembling data is the way in which the various components of the accounts must balance. The consistencies in the MRIO data were validated in three ways.

1. The state data were summed and checked against the national input-output figures for each component and industry.
2. The state estimates were checked against other estimates that were considered reliable to determine their relative accuracy and were further checked for internal consistency. In relation to the latter point, for example, sums of the matrices for interregional transportation shipments were compared with the appropriate regional production and consumption estimates from the state input-output tables.
3. The data were used in the base-year MRIO model to determine whether or not the base-year (1963) regional outputs could be reproduced. Backcast estimates for 1947 and 1958 were also made to see how accurately the regional outputs in a past year could be determined.

The consistency properties of the MRIO accounts are emerging as one of the strongest aids to planners. The model has been used since 1970 for a variety of policy analyses, which will be discussed below. In a number of cases, either through lack of information on particular entries in the accounts or because of a time limit for completing a study, errors were present in the data; also, in a few cases, the initial conceptual framework was misspecified. The errors, which have immediately emerged as the accounts were used in the MRIO model, were usually discovered in one of the three consistency checks just mentioned.

Policy Analysis and Planning Tool

Numerous groups–including people working for federal and state government agencies, private consulting firms, and academic institutions–have used the MRIO data and model for a variety of regional and multiregional policy analyses and forecasts. A partial listing of these groups is given in table 3-2. Of the studies conducted by other groups, some of the most interesting are the application of the MRIO model at the University of Wisconsin by Golladay and Haveman to evaluate the regional output, employment, and redistributional effects of a proposed federal income transfer policy [63]; the employment analysis conducted for the Conrail Final System Plan by the staff at Jack Faucett Associates, Inc. [39]; and the water-resource and employment analysis made for the Arkansas River Project by Kim, Park, and Kwak [101]. At the MRIO research project at the Massachusetts Institute of Technology, the model has been used for many different studies, among these, studies by Pucher to project rail freight shipments for five Midwest railroads [183]; by Rowan to make state

Table 3–2
Users of the MRIO Model and Data (as of January 1978)

Federal and State Government Agencies

BUREAU OF ECONOMIC ANALYSIS, U.S. Department of Commerce, has evaluated the MRIO model that was submitted to the EDA and worked closely with the MRIO staff at the Institute, giving helpful advice on the 1972 revisions that were made to the model.

FEDERAL PREPAREDNESS AGENCY, General Services Administration (formerly part of the Office of Emergency Preparedness, Office of the President), has set up a fully operational version of the MRIO model on the UNIVAC 1108 as the Regional Impact Analysis System (RIAS). This system has been used for an analysis of the SST cut-back of 1971 and a study of the impact of the 1974 coal strike.

BROOKHAVEN NATIONAL LABORATORY, Associated Universities, Inc., Upton, New York, intends to integrate the MRIO model with a multiregional energy model to study the energy, economic, and environmental implications of alternative energy and energy-related policies.

CORPS OF ENGINEERS, Institute for Water Resources, Department of the Army, has adapted the model to assess the employment and income impact of construction of the McClellan-Kerr Arkansas River Project.

DEPARTMENT OF BUSINESS DEVELOPMENT, State of Wisconsin, Madison, Wisconsin, has used the MRIO data in conjunction with a benefit-cost analysis to evaluate total economic and social benefits in relation to costs of alternative state investments and programs and development opportunities. The input-output model was used to make projections for investment planning in the business community.

DEPARTMENT OF COMMERCE, State of Michigan, Lansing, Michigan, has used the model and data base for a study of the automobile industry in Michigan.

DIVISION OF TRANSPORTATION AND DEVELOPMENT, Maryland Department of Transportation, Baltimore, Maryland, has developed a way to utilize the MRIO model for multimodal transportation impact analyses and showed how the model could be employed to measure direct and indirect impacts of expenditures at the regional level. Under another study, the results of measuring the regional impacts of interstate highway system expenditures are converted into population and travel estimates.

ECONOMIC RESEARCH SERVICE, Agricultural Extension Service, University of California, Berkeley, California, has used the MRIO data as cross-checks for data in local input-output models.

ECONOMIC RESEARCH SERVICE, Department of Agriculture, Lansing, Michigan, has used the MRIO table for Ohio for an impact study of agriculture.

ECONOMIC RESEARCH SERVICE, Economic Development Division, U.S. Department of Agriculture, Washington, D.C., has used the data to obtain regional multipliers. The model will be used to investigate a problem relating rural nonfarm economic growth to changes in the availability of energy. Some of the MRIO data have been supplied to various land-grant colleges, including Cornell, Virginia Polytech, Delaware, and Oklahoma State.

FOREST SERVICE, Department of Agriculture, Upper Darby, Pennsylvania, has used the trade-flow and state input-output data for a regional model with emphasis on Oregon, Washington, and Idaho.

Consulting Firms

BATTELLE NORTHWEST, Richland, Washington, has aggregated the 51-region MRIO data to 5 regions and also to 2 regions for use in economic impact analyses in 4 states: Washington, Idaho, Montana, and Oregon.

THE CENTER FOR THE ENVIRONMENT & MAN, INC., Hartford, Connecticut, has used the state input-output tables in the CEM regional activities analysis model, which

Table 3–2 continued

has been used to analyze the industrialization of Westover Air Force Base in the Springfield-Chicopee-Holyoke SMSA in Massachusetts.

DAVID BRADWELL ASSOCIATES, San Francisco, California, has used the state MRIO table for Oregon to compare with their estimated state table for Oregon. They are using a regional input-output model to study waterborne and airborne pollutants in the state.

JACK FAUCETT ASSOCIATES, INC., Chevy Chase, Maryland, has used the model for a study of the employment impacts of the Final System Plan (Conrail) for the U.S. Rail Administration.

HARBRIDGE HOUSE, Boston, Massachusetts, has used the MRIO model to assist in analyzing the impact of the Boston and Maine railroad on the New England economy. They have used the same approach to analyze the economic impact of all railroads serving New England.

LOUIS BERGER & ASSOCIATES, INC., East Orange, New Jersey, has used the model for a socio-economic study of the Lower Delaware River Basin (sponsored by the National Commission on Water Quality), and are engaging in two other studies, one in northeast New Jersey, to analyze the costs and benefits of the implementation of the Clean Water Act Amendments, the other in southeast Pennsylvania to predict the employment and production impacts of compliance with the Federal Water Pollution Control Act Amendments of 1972.

PARSONS, BRINCKERHOFF, QUADE, & DOUGLAS, New York, New York, has used the interregional trade-flow portion of the MRIO data for an in-depth analysis of commodity shipments through the East-West gateway in St. Louis.

PEAT, MARWICK, & MITCHELL, Washington, D.C., has used the state-to-state commodity flows to analyze potential rail-truck networks.

RESOURCE PLANNING ASSOCIATES, INC., Cambridge, Massachusetts, has employed the input-output and interstate trade data to construct a forecasting model to determine economic impacts of new industries in the state of Maine.

ROBERT REEBIE & ASSOCIATES, Greenwich, Connecticut, has used the model for an intermodal freight system study for the U.S. Rail Administration.

TEMPLE, BARKER, & SLOANE, INC., Boston, Massachusetts, has used the initial interregional trade flows from the MRIO model to help in making long-range forecasts of commodities transported by the Penn-Central railroad.

Universities

DEPARTMENT OF CITY AND REGIONAL PLANNING, Ohio State University, Columbus, Ohio, has used the MRIO state input-output tables to develop interindustry linkage indices for the purposes of testing the unbalanced growth hypothesis of regional development. The indices together with estimates of gross state product growth were used in estimating the analytical model.

DEPARTMENT OF COMMUNITY DEVELOPMENT, Rutgers State University, New Brunswick, New Jersey, is using the MRIO model for teaching a graduate course on planning of urban economies. The model has also been used by students working for consulting firms to forecast the economic impact of the Water Pollution Control Act on New Jersey and the implications of industrial water pollution control in Northeastern New Jersey.

DEPARTMENT OF ECONOMICS, Northeastern University, Boston, Massachusetts, has used the MRIO model for teaching and research.

DEPARTMENT OF ECONOMICS, University of Cincinnati, Cincinnati, Ohio, has used the MRIO data to update value added for Cincinnati and in the development of employment studies.

Table 3-2 continued

DEPARTMENT OF ECONOMICS, University of North Carolina, Chapel Hill, North Carolina, will use the MRIO model for the construction and simulation of two econometric models, one for the state of North Carolina, and another for the South. They plan to chart the trends in product composition and technology for those two regions.

DEPARTMENT OF MATHEMATICS, North Dakota State University, Fargo, North Dakota, is using the MRIO data to analyze economic impacts associated with changes in the natural gas industry.

ECONOMICS DEPARTMENT, Middlebury College, Middlebury, Vermont, has used the MRIO model to make impact studies related to transportation rates and energy costs.

INSTITUTE FOR RESEARCH ON POVERTY, The University of Wisconsin, Madison, Wisconsin, has used the model to evaluate the regional output, employment, and redistribution effects of a proposed federal income transfer policy. Work on the model is now continuing at the U.S. Department of Health, Education, and Welfare.

MATHEMATICS AND COMPUTING GROUP, Lawrence Berkeley Laboratory, Berkeley, California, has set up a fully operational version of the MRIO model for use in various regional analyses. This group has already used the MRIO data, along with more detailed information, to study water, waste, and general economic projections of growth in California and Nevada. They have developed income and employment multipliers and have used the model to determine the economic impact of a nationwide coal strike.

PEACE SCIENCE DEPARTMENT, University of Pennsylvania, Philadelphia, Pennsylvania, is using a modified version of the MRIO model for studying regional and national energy policies.

REGIONAL RESEARCH INSTITUTE, West Virginia University, Morgantown, West Virginia, has made comparisons of the MRIO data for West Virginia and Kansas against the state input-output tables for those states.

Other Countries

SETTLEMENT STUDY CENTRE, Rehovot, Israel, has used the MRIO framework for simulating regional development in Israel.

INSTITUTE OF SOCIO ECONOMIC PLANNING, University of Tsukuba, Tsukuba, Japan, will use MRIO publications extensively in their forthcoming project on interregional population movement and regional growth.

INSTITUTE OF ECONOMICS AND ORGANIZATION OF INDUSTRIAL PRODUCTION, Siberian Branch, USSR Academy of Sciences, has used the MRIO framework for comparison with USSR multiregional studies.

---

employment projections for Massachusetts [194]; by DiPasquale and Polenske to determine output, employment, and income multipliers for three regions in the United States [29]; and by other MRIO staff members for many studies relating to U.S. energy, transportation, employment, and income policies. All of these studies were made using the primal form of the model. In current research, the model has been reformulated as a dual model to examine changes in regional prices. Four studies using the dual form of the MRIO model have been conducted by the MRIO research staff. One by Young is a study of the industrial and regional effects of changes in transportation prices [302]; a related study by Polenske contains estimates of the industrial and regional price impacts resulting from changes in coal prices [177]. An initial study by Del Duca of the industrial and regional price impacts of imposing the 1974 Clean Air Standards [27] has been significantly extended by Pai in a valuable use of input-output price theory [168]. Because of the wide variation in the needs of users, the data and both forms of the model were specifically designed for adaptability to different policy studies.

The types of policy analyses for which the MRIO data and model have so far proven to be extremely valuable can be summarized as follows:

Multiregional output, employment, and income multipliers

Water-resource studies

Energy demand and price analyses

Transportation flow and price analyses

Price, output, and transportation impacts of imposing environmental regulations

Tax-transfer policy studies

As a forecasting technique, the MRIO model has also been used to assist planners in several ways, including

Employment and output projections for individual states

Freight projections of individual commodities for specific railroads

Relative price projections

Restrictions on resource availability

The flexibility of the MRIO model for use in various policy studies is one of its many advantages. In order to appreciate its usefulness as a policy tool, its theoretical base must be understood. A discussion of the economic theory used in input-output analyses and four types of spatial models is provided in the next section.

Input-Output Theory

The basic economic theory underlying input-output models concerns the production relations in the economy, that is, the technological structure of industries. For advanced industrialized countries, such as the United States, technologies have been shown to change very slowly over time for most industries, but changes do occur. Dynamic versions of input-output models have been formulated and have now been used for a number of years, partly in an attempt to account for technological change. The transformation from a static input-output model to a dynamic one is accomplished by allowing for changes in the direct input coefficients and by adding sets of capital-flow coefficients to the usual input-output framework. For the present study, the input-output model was restricted to a primal and a dual version of the static model, with the technical input coefficients forming the core of each version. Both versions will be described in detail later in the chapter.

While national input-output coefficients for industrialized countries do remain relatively constant in the short term, technology coefficients vary considerably from region to region. Variations in the regional technology of an industry may occur because of differences among regions in the technique of producing a good or service, in the commodity prices, and/or in the product mixes.

Variations in the regional techniques of production may arise as a result of internal or external economies of scale. As the quantity of output a firm produces varies, internal economies (or diseconomies) of scale may occur. Thus, firms producing varying quantities of output are located at different positions on the long-run average cost curve and therefore may have different direct input costs. These differences in costs are said to be caused by internal economies (or diseconomies) of scale: as a firm expands in size, it is generally able to reduce the cost of production per unit of output by varying the combination of inputs. Thus, the direct input costs of a firm producing 1,000 widgets in Alabama will usually vary from the corresponding costs of the widget producer in California manufacturing 15,000 widgets.

Rather than shifts along the cost curve for a given industry, shifts in the cost curve for the industry also occur, these from external economies or diseconomies of scale, some of which may be attributed at the regional level to localization or agglomeration economies. Hoover classifies the agglomeration (deglomeration) factors as follows:

> 1. *Large-scale economies* within a firm, consequent upon the enlargement of the firm's scale of production at one point.
> 2. *Localization economies* for all firms in a single industry at a single location, consequent upon the enlargement of the total output of that industry at that location.
> 3. *Urbanization economies* for all firms in all industries at a single location, consequent upon the enlargement of the total economic size (population, income, output, or wealth) of that location, for all industries taken together. [91, p. 172]

As will be discussed later in the chapter, input-output models in the United States must be constructed using input coefficients derived from dollar flows rather than physical inputs; therefore, variations in the price of the same physical input from region to region may result in different "technology" structures being shown in the regional direct input coefficients for any two regions even if the actual physical inputs are the same. Of course, in a perfectly competitive economy, any large variation in prices would disappear over time, as the factors of production would be shifted from one region to another until the regional price differentials were eliminated. In practice, however, many obstacles exist that prevent this shift.

A final factor that may result in varying regional technologies for the same industry is the different product mixes that occur from region to region. Thus, while the technology of producing steel bars may not vary from one region to another in a given year, the steel-bar industry is generally treated only as a subcomponent of the steel manufacturing industry, and each steel subindustry may need a different combination of inputs. The technology of the aggregate steel industry may therefore vary as a result of different product mixes among its subcomponents in each region.

Four Types of Spatial Models

Specifics of the regional technologies and interregional trade are important considerations in regional and multiregional studies. Because a regional economy is usually far more open than a national economy, the trade between regions is an especially important consideration. Economic analysts have developed four models that show alternative formulations of either regional or multiregional input-output systems. Interregional trade relationships are handled in distinct ways in each of the four models, while only two ways are used to handle the regional technology structure. The four models will be referred to as the regional, intranational, multiregional, and interregional input-output models. The specific characteristics of their technology and trade structures can be summarized as follows:

Regional–A Model of a Single Region. Each cell in the interindustry transactions table shows the amount that an industry in the given region purchases from itself or from other industries in the same region. Trade between regions is usually dealt with only in terms of total inflows and total outflows, which are not differentiated by region of origin and destination. Data required to implement the model are regional interindustry flows for a base year and regional final demands for a given year, for the particular region only. Examples of input-output models for a single region are those for the states of Washington [12] and West Virginia [138].

Intranational–A Model of Two or More Regions. This model is often referred to as the Leontief balanced model. Each cell in the interindustry transactions table shows the amount that an industry in the given region purchases from itself or from other industries regardless of the location of the producing industry. Trade between regions is dealt with only in terms of net exports or net imports from or to each of the regions. Data required to implement the model are interindustry flows for a base year, differentiated by region,[1] and regional final demands for a given year, with the regional final demands being specified for each region only for the so-called "local" industries. For the "national" industries, only national final demands are required. Production and consumption are balanced at the regional level for the local industries, but only at the national level for the national industries. Examples of input-output models using the intranational formulation of technology and trade are the ones by Leontief [123], Leontief et al. [126], and Dresch [30].

Multiregional–A Model of Two or More Regions. Each cell in the interindustry transactions table shows the amount that an industry in a given region purchases from itself or from other industries regardless of the location of the producing industry. Trade between regions is specified in terms of both the industry and the region shipping the commodity, but only in terms of the region receiving the commodity. To implement the model, data required for each region are interindustry flows for a base year, differentiated by industry; interregional flows for a base year, differentiated by region; and final demands for the given year for each industry. The model has been implemented using a point-estimate [19; 125; 150; 173], a gravity [125; 173], and a linear programming [148] formulation of the trading relationships.[2] Leontief and Strout formulated three versions of the gravity-trade model that do not require actual base-year interregional trade flows for the implementation and a fourth version that does require them. All four versions are described in their 1963 article [125]. A variant of the Chenery-Moses point-estimate formulation is the model by Riefler and Tiebout, which requires the actual amount of input to a particular industry in a given region supplied by the region itself [187].

Interregional–A Model of Two or More Regions. Each cell in the interindustry transactions table shows the amount that an industry in the given region purchases from itself or from other industries in the same region. Trade between regions is specified in terms of the industry and region of production and the industry and region of consumption. Implementation of the model requires a complete interindustry, interregional, table of transactions, providing industry and region of production and industry and region of consumption for a base year, and regional final demands for each industry for a given year. As far as is known to this writer, the only case in which this formulation has been used is for the work by the Ministry of International Trade and Industry (MITI) in Japan [139; 140; 141].

As has just been illustrated, one form of specification of industry technology is used for the regional and interregional models, namely, the input coefficient is defined both in terms of the industry and region of origin of the input and the industry and region of destination of the output. Another form of specification of industry technology is used for the intranational and multiregional models, namely, the input coefficient is defined, as before, in terms of the industry and region of destination of the output but now only in terms of the industry of origin of the input. The location where the input originates is not considered in defining the regional technology for the industry in the latter case. This is the specification selected for the present study, as it is more of an engineering definition, with importance being attached to the types and amounts of inputs required to produce a given output rather than to the exact location of their origin as well.

In each of the four models, the handling of the trade relationships between regions differs. In general, all of the models are more open with respect to trade than are national input-output models, meaning that far more of the goods consumed in a given regional economy are imported and far more of the goods produced are exported than is the usual case for a national economy. In the regional and intranational models, only the aggregate (or net) interregional trade is usually determined. In the regional model, the total exports and imports are specified for each commodity, but generally the regional destination and origin of this trade are not determined. For the intranational model, only the net trade between any two regions can be determined; thus, gross export and import figures are not obtainable from this model. Trade relations in the multiregional and interregional models are provided in considerably more detail and become integral parts of each model. Separate technology and trade relationships are specified as two sets of coefficient matrices in the multiregional system, while the two relationships are both specified by the one very detailed coefficient matrix in the interregional model.

Selection of a Model

A number of spatially differentiated, general equilibrium models have been specified in the literature, only some of which can be used to obtain simultaneous estimations of regional outputs and interregional trade for an economy. The main types of models considered for the present study were econometric, linear programming, and input-output. Other multiregional models, such as microanalytic and systems dynamics, were not considered at all for the study. Actually, very little consideration was given to econometric (regression) models, because in the mid-1960s it would have been virtually impossible to implement a multiregional version of such a model. Many difficulties would have been encountered in specifying accurate time-series or cross-section data with which to fit the regression equations for 51 regions. Another important consideration, which is still pertinent today, was that it was desirable to have a multiregional model designed to be more than a forecasting model. Relative to input-output models, econometric models are inexpensive to implement to obtain forecasts if data are available. But econometric models cannot be used as accounting tools, nor do they provide as detailed and consistent sets of output, employment, and income multipliers as are readily obtainable from input-output models.

Linear programming (LP) versions of multiregional models were eliminated from consideration for three reasons. First, one of the main problems with LP models is that they cannot be used to obtain accurate estimates of interregional commodity shipments in cases where considerable cross-hauling occurs between regions. Cross-hauling is defined as the simultaneous shipment of the *same* good from region g to region h and from region h to region g. In most statistics, shipments data usually are aggregated by commodity, by region, and by season. Such aggregations result in the cross-hauling of what appear to be homogeneous commodities. Thus, aggregation by commodity is one cause of cross-hauling. One commodity may include many different grades or qualities of a single product, each being manufactured in a different region, and cross-hauling will occur.

Aggregation by region is a second cause of cross-hauling. If a transportation model is to be formulated to estimate shipments for all commodities, regional aggregation generally is unavoidable because of the massive number of estimates to be determined. Usually, the distributing and receiving areas can be specified as single points, or, at least, be separated into numerous geographic regions, only when the transportation shipments are being determined for a single commodity. Again, cross-hauling will occur if sending and receiving points are aggregated.

Finally, aggregation by season is a third cause of cross-hauling. Some goods, especially agricultural products, are produced only during certain seasons of the year in some regions of the country. In the winter months, some fresh fruits and vegetables, for example, are shipped into the North from the South, while in the summer the same types of fresh fruits and vegetables not only are produced and consumed in the North, but also large quantities are shipped to the South. It has been shown that even for homogeneous commodities, such as potatoes, more than 2 percent of all shipments were cross-hauled between 50 regions in 1960, 1962, and 1964. For total fruits and vegetables, of which potatoes is a subcomponent, the cross-haul percentage was even higher—over 5, while for those fruits and vegetables shipped by truck the percentage rose to over 11 [170, pp. 40–41]. In the MRIO industry classification, however, even fruits and vegatables is only one subcomponent of IO-2, Other agricultural products; thus, the cross-hauls for the total industry would undoubtedly be even larger. The extent of cross-hauling becomes substantial when the figures used involve all three apparent reasons for cross-hauls: conglomerate commodities, large regions, and seasonal shipments.

A major difficulty arises in trying to specify an LP model to account for these cross-hauls. The transportation LP model has the important characteristic that the total supply of all regions must exactly equal the total requirements of those regions. If there are n origins and n destinations, each of the $2n - 1$ effective constraints determines a shipment between two regions, which means that only $2n - 1$ interregional shipments are specified. The shipments between the other $n^2 - 2n + 1$ regions must be zero, unless additional constraints are added, but more information is required if these constraints are to be specified. Given the aggregate nature of the multiregional data, not all interregional shipments could be adequately determined from an LP model.

The second factor that negated the use of an LP model was the lack of transportation cost information on a state-by-state basis for all the commodities. The third factor was that the interregional transfer of services could not be easily estimated with the use of an LP model, given that no measures of the transfer costs of services were available. For all these reasons, LP versions of multiregional economic models were rejected for use in the present study.

The final choice of the model to be used was narrowed to three versions of fixed-trade-coefficient models: the column-coefficient, row-coefficient, and point-estimate gravity. When the row-coefficient model was implemented using the Japanese multiregional input-output data, many negative elements occurred in the inverse matrix [173]. Since then, as noted earlier, the row-coefficient model was found by Bon to be incompatible mathematically with the input-output model [8]. Negative elements also occurred in the inverse matrix of the point-estimate gravity-trade model; however, since that model had been specified by Leontief and Strout in incremental terms, consideration was given to using it for the MRIO model. An attempt was made to implement it for 79 U.S. industries and 44 regions, using an iterative procedure, but the iterations would not converge, probably for the same reasons of mathematical inconsistency determined by Bon for the row-coefficient model, since the gravity-trade coefficients are weighted combinations of the row and column coefficients. The current versions of the MRIO model are therefore based upon the Chenery-Moses column-coefficient model. Interregional trade and regional input-output data could be assembled for the column-coefficient model, the model is structurally sound, and testing of the three fixed-coefficient models showed there to be "no discernible difference in the overall predictive ability of the column-coefficient and point-estimate gravity trade models" [173, p. 82].

Before the primal and dual structures of the MRIO model are presented, the basic assumptions of the model will be briefly reviewed.

Assumptions of the MRIO Model

The three basic assumptions usually made explicitly in static, open input-output models are: constant returns to scale, homogeneous products with no joint production, and fixed direct input (technology) coefficients.[3] To these three assumptions can be added numerous others, such as that there are no induced consumption or investment accelerator effects, no substitution of one input for another, and no production-capacity constraints. Much of the criticism of input-output models has centered on these seemingly unrealistic assumptions. Yet, most of them can be relaxed from one study to another, largely depending upon the availability of the necessary data. Many input-output analyses, for example, are now made using models partially closed, with respect to households, to allow for responses to induced consumption.

The assumption of constant returns to scale eliminates the possibility for external economies or diseconomies of scale to occur. The second assumption implies that each industry produces output that is identical from product to product and that each commodity is supplied by a single industry. The most frequently raised criticism of input-output models has to do with the third assumption, that of fixed technologies. As discussed earlier, changes in technologies over time or between regions are caused by variations in product mix, relative prices, and methods used to produce the goods, with the last partially occurring in response to changes in the composition of final demand. The 1958 recession and the 1973 oil crisis in the United States highlight the concern about the fixed technology assumption. A quick check of the input-output coefficients in the 1958 and 1963 input-output tables [278; 269] shows that there were discernible, though relatively minor, differences in the technologies of the two years. How many of the differences are attributable to the recession is impossible to determine, but the fact that the differences are small lessens the concern. Also, Carter has verified through empirical tests using U.S. data from the 1939, 1947, 1958, and 1961 national input-output tables that the national input coefficients are relatively stable in the short run [16]. The energy crisis may have created an exception to the rule, but empirical testing of the impact on technologies of that crisis will have to await the publication of the 1977 national input-output table.

In a large and highly industrialized country like the United States, technology does not change rapidly, as was mentioned earlier. (Exceptions would be times of crises caused by wars, severe resource shortages, revolutions, and so on.) Thus, the assumption of fixed technology is usually not untenable for studies covering periods of ten to fifteen years. Still, because some technology changes do occur even in the short run, it would be ideal to be able to account for them. As more and more data become available, models are being structured so as to allow technologies to change both over time and between regions. Dynamic national and regional input-output models that take account of changing technologies have been developed and used for more than a decade now.

The present versions of the fixed supply form of the static MRIO model are based upon the assumptions already discussed for the input-output portion of the model. In addition, three assumptions are made concerning the trade portion of the model. The first is an assumption of constant trade coefficients. No substitution among supplying regions is allowed to occur. Thus, a region is assumed to continue supplying a given fraction of the consumption of another region over time. No empirical verification of this assumption has been possible because of the lack of data. The second is an assumption of uniform industrial shares. Each industry in a given region is assumed to have the same import pattern as the average for the region as a whole [150, p. 810]. By incorporating this assumption, the number of data required to implement the model is drastically reduced. The third is an assumption of full capacity (ex ante). In the static version of the model, all transportation, as well as all production, facilities are assumed, ex ante, to be operating at less than full capacity.

As the MRIO model is refined and as more data become available, many of the assumptions just discussed can be relaxed. (A method of accounting for responses to induced consumption, for example, is discussed later in this chapter.) Several versions of the MRIO model have been implemented using these assumptions; they include the primal, the dual, and a truncated dual.[4] Each of these three versions will be described in the following section.

Theoretical Structure of the MRIO Model

The primal version of the national input-output model was the first to be implemented in the United States using empirical data; then, the dual version was implemented. This was also true for the MRIO model. In the case of the national model, the major concern during the early 1940s was with the effect the war would have on output and employment; later, the concern was with the effect its ending would have on these variables. Both effects could be readily determined in considerable industrial detail using the primal version of the national input-output model. As the war ended, other problems came to the forefront. Inflation was one of them. Accordingly, the dual version of the national input-output model was implemented to investigate the industrial ramifications of the wage and price increases. Both versions of the national input-output model have been extended in the present study to the multiregional level.

Before describing the equation systems, definitions are provided of the notations. These are presented in a general form for m industries or commodities, n regions, k final users, and s value added components. Since it is assumed that each industry produces a single type of homogeneous commodity and that each commodity is produced by only one industry, unless otherwise indicated the terms *industry* and *commodity* will be used interchangeably in this portion of the text to simplify the discussion. Also, for the same reason, the term *commodity* will include goods and services. The notations are defined as follows:

m designates the number of industries, with subscripts i indicating the producing industry and j the purchasing industry.

n designates the number of regions, with superscripts g indicating the shipping region and h the receiving region.

p designates the number of final users, with the subscript k indicating the specific purchaser.

q designates the number of components of value added, with the subscript s indicating the specific component.

o as a subscript, indicates a summation over all industries (or final users or value added components); as a superscript, indicates a summation over all regions.

$\hat{}$ indicates a block diagonal matrix.

t as a superscript, indicates a transposed matrix.

-1 as a superscript, indicates the inverse of a matrix.

X = vector, $mn \times 1$, of commodity outputs. Each element, x_{oj}^{go}, describes the total output of commodity j produced in region g.

Y = vector, $mn \times p$, of final demands. Each element, y_{ik}^{oh}, describes the amount of commodity i purchased by the final user k in region h regardless of where the good was produced.

A = block diagonal square matrix, $mn \times mn$, of technical input coefficients for each region, with the direct input coefficients for each region appearing as n square matrices, $m \times m$, on the diagonal blocks of the large matrix and with zeros appearing in all off-diagonal blocks. Each technical coefficient, $a_{ij}^{oh} = x_{ij}^{oh} / x_{oj}^{go}$, describes the amount of commodity i purchased by industry j in region h, x_{ij}^{oh}, per dollar of industry j's output in that region.

C = square matrix, $mn \times mn$, of expanded trade-coefficient matrices, with the trade coefficients arrayed along the principal diagonal of each of the n^2 blocks and zeros for the off-diagonal elements. Each block in the expanded matrix has an $m \times m$ dimension. Each trade coefficient, $c_{io}^{gh} = x_{io}^{gh} / x_{io}^{oh}$, describes the amount of commodity i shipped from region g to region h, x_{io}^{gh}, per dollar of region g's consumption of commodity i.

U = vector, $mn \times 1$, of value-added-per-unit-of-output coefficients. Each element, $u_{sj}^{oh} = v_{sj}^{oh} / x_{oj}^{oh}$, describes the amount of value added component s purchased by industry j in region h, v_{sj}^{oh}, to produce one unit of industry j's output in that region.

$\widetilde{P}$ = vector, $mn \times 1$, of relative commodity prices. Each element, $\widetilde{p}_{oj}^{go}$, describes the relative price of commodity j in region g per unit of output of commodity j in that region.

These notations can be specified in terms of matrices as shown; subscripts refer to producing and purchasing industries and superscripts refer to shipping and receiving regions for m industries and n regions. A summation over all industries or all regions is denoted by the use of a subscript o or a superscript o, respectively.

$$X = \begin{bmatrix} x_1^1 \\ x_2^1 \\ \vdots \\ x_m^1 \\ x_1^2 \\ x_2^2 \\ \vdots \\ x_m^2 \\ \vdots \\ x_1^n \\ x_2^n \\ \vdots \\ x_m^n \end{bmatrix} \quad Y = \begin{bmatrix} y_1^1 \\ y_2^1 \\ \vdots \\ y_m^1 \\ y_1^2 \\ y_2^2 \\ \vdots \\ y_m^2 \\ \vdots \\ y_1^n \\ y_2^n \\ \vdots \\ y_m^n \end{bmatrix} \quad U = \begin{bmatrix} u_1^1 \\ u_2^1 \\ \vdots \\ u_m^1 \\ u_1^2 \\ u_2^2 \\ \vdots \\ u_m^2 \\ \vdots \\ u_1^n \\ u_2^n \\ \vdots \\ u_m^n \end{bmatrix} \quad \widetilde{P} = \begin{bmatrix} \widetilde{p}_1^1 \\ \widetilde{p}_2^1 \\ \vdots \\ \widetilde{p}_m^1 \\ \widetilde{p}_1^2 \\ \widetilde{p}_2^2 \\ \vdots \\ \widetilde{p}_m^2 \\ \vdots \\ \widetilde{p}_1^n \\ \widetilde{p}_2^n \\ \vdots \\ \widetilde{p}_m^n \end{bmatrix}$$

$$\hat{A} = \begin{bmatrix}
a_{11}^{o1} & a_{12}^{o1} & \cdots & a_{1m}^{o1} & 0 & 0 & \cdots & 0 & \cdots & 0 & 0 & \cdots & 0 \\
a_{21}^{o1} & a_{22}^{o1} & \cdots & a_{2m}^{o1} & 0 & 0 & \cdots & 0 & \cdots & 0 & 0 & \cdots & 0 \\
\vdots & \vdots & \ddots & \vdots & \vdots & \vdots & \ddots & \vdots & \cdots & \vdots & \vdots & \ddots & \vdots \\
a_{m1}^{o1} & a_{m2}^{o1} & \cdots & a_{mm}^{o1} & 0 & 0 & \cdots & 0 & \cdots & 0 & 0 & \cdots & 0 \\
0 & 0 & \cdots & 0 & a_{11}^{o2} & a_{12}^{o2} & \cdots & a_{1m}^{o2} & \cdots & 0 & 0 & \cdots & 0 \\
0 & 0 & \cdots & 0 & a_{21}^{o2} & a_{22}^{o2} & \cdots & a_{2m}^{o2} & \cdots & 0 & 0 & \cdots & 0 \\
\vdots & \vdots & \ddots & \vdots & \vdots & \vdots & \ddots & \vdots & \cdots & \vdots & \vdots & \ddots & \vdots \\
0 & 0 & \cdots & 0 & a_{m1}^{o2} & a_{m2}^{o2} & \cdots & a_{mm}^{o2} & \cdots & 0 & 0 & \cdots & 0 \\
\vdots & \vdots & \ddots & \vdots & \vdots & \vdots & \ddots & \vdots & \ddots & \vdots & \vdots & \ddots & \vdots \\
0 & 0 & \cdots & 0 & 0 & 0 & \cdots & 0 & \cdots & a_{11}^{on} & a_{12}^{on} & \cdots & a_{1m}^{on} \\
0 & 0 & \cdots & 0 & 0 & 0 & \cdots & 0 & \cdots & a_{21}^{on} & a_{22}^{on} & \cdots & a_{2m}^{on} \\
\vdots & \vdots & \ddots & \vdots & \vdots & \vdots & \ddots & \vdots & \cdots & \vdots & \vdots & \ddots & \vdots \\
0 & 0 & \cdots & 0 & 0 & 0 & \cdots & 0 & \cdots & a_{m1}^{on} & a_{m2}^{on} & \cdots & a_{mm}^{on}
\end{bmatrix}$$

The large matrix $\hat{A}$ is formulated from the n technology coefficient matrices:

$$\begin{bmatrix}
a_{11}^{oh} & a_{12}^{oh} & \cdots & a_{1m}^{oh} \\
a_{21}^{oh} & a_{22}^{oh} & \cdots & a_{2m}^{oh} \\
\vdots & \vdots & \ddots & \vdots \\
a_{m1}^{oh} & a_{m2}^{oh} & \cdots & a_{mm}^{oh}
\end{bmatrix}$$

Each a_{ij}^{oh} term is obtained by dividing the amount of commodity i purchased by industry j located in region h, x_{ij}^{oh}, by the total output of commodity j in region h, x_{oj}^{oh}.

$$
C = \begin{bmatrix}
c_{o1}^{11} & 0 & \cdots & 0 & c_{o1}^{12} & 0 & \cdots & 0 & \cdots & c_{o1}^{1n} & 0 & \cdots & 0 \\
0 & c_{o2}^{11} & \cdots & 0 & 0 & c_{o2}^{12} & \cdots & 0 & \cdots & 0 & c_{o2}^{1n} & \cdots & 0 \\
\vdots & \vdots & \ddots & \vdots & \vdots & \vdots & \ddots & \vdots & \cdots & \vdots & \vdots & \ddots & \vdots \\
0 & 0 & \cdots & c_{om}^{11} & 0 & 0 & \cdots & c_{om}^{12} & \cdots & 0 & 0 & \cdots & c_{om}^{1n} \\
c_{o1}^{21} & 0 & \cdots & 0 & c_{o1}^{22} & 0 & \cdots & 0 & \cdots & c_{o1}^{2n} & 0 & \cdots & 0 \\
0 & c_{o2}^{21} & \cdots & 0 & 0 & c_{o2}^{22} & \cdots & 0 & \cdots & 0 & c_{o2}^{2n} & \cdots & 0 \\
\vdots & \vdots & \ddots & \vdots & \vdots & \vdots & \ddots & \vdots & \cdots & \vdots & \vdots & \ddots & \vdots \\
0 & 0 & \cdots & c_{om}^{21} & 0 & 0 & \cdots & c_{om}^{22} & \cdots & 0 & 0 & \cdots & c_{om}^{2n} \\
\vdots & \vdots & \ddots & \vdots & \vdots & \vdots & \ddots & \vdots & \ddots & \vdots & \vdots & \ddots & \vdots \\
c_{o1}^{n1} & 0 & \cdots & 0 & c_{o1}^{n2} & 0 & \cdots & 0 & \cdots & c_{o1}^{nn} & 0 & \cdots & 0 \\
0 & c_{o2}^{n1} & \cdots & 0 & 0 & c_{o2}^{n2} & \cdots & 0 & \cdots & 0 & c_{o2}^{nn} & \cdots & 0 \\
\vdots & \vdots & \ddots & \vdots & \vdots & \vdots & \ddots & \vdots & \cdots & \vdots & \vdots & \ddots & \vdots \\
0 & 0 & \cdots & c_{om}^{n1} & 0 & 0 & \cdots & c_{om}^{n2} & \cdots & 0 & 0 & \cdots & c_{om}^{nn}
\end{bmatrix}
$$

The large matrix C is formulated from the m commodity-trade coefficient matrices:

$$
\begin{bmatrix}
c_{oi}^{11} & c_{oi}^{12} & \cdots & c_{oi}^{1n} \\
c_{oi}^{21} & c_{oi}^{22} & \cdots & c_{oi}^{2n} \\
\vdots & \vdots & \ddots & \vdots \\
c_{oi}^{n1} & c_{oi}^{n2} & \cdots & c_{oi}^{nn}
\end{bmatrix}
$$

Each c_{oi}^{gh} term is obtained by dividing the trade flow for commodity i from region g to h, x_{oi}^{gh}, by the total consumption of commodity i in region h, x_{oi}^{oh}.

Using the notations just defined, the primal version of the MRIO model is discussed first, then the dual and truncated-dual versions.

Primal MRIO Model

The primal version of the MRIO model is used to project regional outputs and interregional shipments. It is a static open model. In this case, open refers to the number of outputs determined endogenously or exogenously, rather than as earlier, where the term referred to the extent a region trades with other regions. An input-output model is said to be an open model if all the final demand components are specified exogenously, that is, are initially known or given. As more and more of the final demands are determined endogenously, that is, are explained by the system, the model becomes increasingly closed. Thus, if the household portion of final demand is determined endogenously, the model is said to be partially closed with respect to households. Such a partially closed version of the primal model will be presented later, and the multipliers obtained from the open and partially closed versions will be compared. The first model to be described, however, will be the static version of the open MRIO model.

Although the MRIO model was implemented using data for 79 industries, 51 regions, and 1 total final demand, the systems of equations will be specified in general terms for m industries, n regions, and k final users. The demand for a commodity must equal the supply of the commodity at any given point in time. This balance condition for a national economy can be extended to the multiregional level. In the set of balance equations given in equation system (3.1), the supply of output of each industry in each region, x_{oj}^{go}, is equal to the amount of output demanded by all intermediate and final users in all regions,

$$x_{ij}^{gh} + y_{ik}^{gh} \qquad (i,j = 1, \ldots, m; h = 1, \ldots, n; k = 1, \ldots, p)$$

Because there are mn^2 - nmp variables, but only mn equations, the balance equations cannot be solved. A solution can be obtained, however, by calculating two sets of structural coefficients, technology and trade, for the system and then making two assumptions, namely, that both the technology and trade coefficients are constant over time. The first set of constants is the input-output coefficients for each region, constructed from the MRIO accounts. They show the structure of production in each region and can be used in the static model under the assumption that the amount of each good required by every industry in a region is strictly proportional to the output of the industry. The coefficient a_{81}^{o2} from the MRIO accounts will be used for illustration. (All numbers for industries and regions in the illustration refer to those listed in the industrial and regional classification given in the appendix as tables A-1 and A-2, respectively.) It is obtained by dividing the purchase of petroleum by the livestock

$$
\begin{array}{lllllllll}
x_{o1}^{1o} - x_{11}^{11} - x_{12}^{11} - \cdots - x_{1m}^{11} & - x_{11}^{12} - x_{12}^{12} - \cdots - x_{1m}^{12} - & \cdots & - x_{11}^{1n} - x_{12}^{1n} - \cdots - x_{1m}^{1n} & = & y_{1o}^{11} + y_{1o}^{12} + \cdots + y_{1o}^{1n} \\
x_{o2}^{1o} - x_{21}^{11} - x_{22}^{11} - \cdots - x_{2m}^{11} & - x_{21}^{12} - x_{22}^{12} - \cdots - x_{2m}^{12} - & \cdots & - x_{21}^{1n} - x_{22}^{1n} - \cdots - x_{2m}^{1n} & = & y_{2o}^{11} + y_{2o}^{12} + \cdots + y_{2o}^{1n} \\
\vdots \quad \vdots \quad \vdots \quad \ddots \quad \vdots & \vdots \quad \vdots \quad \ddots \quad \vdots & \cdots & \vdots \quad \vdots \quad \ddots \quad \vdots & \vdots & \vdots \quad \vdots \quad \ddots \quad \vdots \\
x_{om}^{1o} - x_{m1}^{11} - x_{m2}^{11} - \cdots - x_{mm}^{11} & - x_{m1}^{12} - x_{m2}^{12} - \cdots - x_{mm}^{12} - & \cdots & - x_{m1}^{1n} - x_{m2}^{1n} - \cdots - x_{mm}^{1n} & = & y_{mo}^{11} + y_{mo}^{12} + \ldots + y_{mo}^{1n} \\
x_{o1}^{2o} - x_{11}^{21} - x_{12}^{21} - \cdots - x_{1m}^{21} & - x_{11}^{22} - x_{12}^{22} - \cdots - x_{1m}^{22} - & \cdots & - x_{11}^{2n} - x_{12}^{2n} - \cdots - x_{1m}^{2n} & = & y_{1o}^{21} + y_{1o}^{22} + \cdots + y_{1o}^{2n} \\
x_{o2}^{2o} - x_{21}^{21} - x_{22}^{21} - \cdots - x_{2m}^{21} & - x_{21}^{22} - x_{22}^{22} - \cdots - x_{2m}^{22} - & \cdots & - x_{21}^{2n} - x_{22}^{2n} - \cdots - x_{2m}^{2n} & = & y_{2o}^{21} + y_{2o}^{22} + \cdots + y_{2o}^{2n} \\
\vdots \quad \vdots \quad \vdots \quad \ddots \quad \vdots & \vdots \quad \vdots \quad \ddots \quad \vdots & \cdots & \vdots \quad \vdots \quad \ddots \quad \vdots & \vdots & \vdots \quad \vdots \quad \ddots \quad \vdots \\
x_{om}^{2o} - x_{m1}^{21} - x_{m2}^{21} - \cdots - x_{mm}^{21} & - x_{m1}^{22} - x_{m2}^{22} - \cdots - x_{mm}^{22} - & \cdots & - x_{m1}^{2n} - x_{m2}^{2n} - \cdots - x_{mm}^{2n} & = & y_{mo}^{21} + y_{mo}^{22} + \cdots + y_{mo}^{2n} \\
\vdots \quad \vdots \quad \vdots \quad \ddots \quad \vdots & \vdots \quad \vdots \quad \ddots \quad \vdots & \cdots & \vdots \quad \vdots \quad \ddots \quad \vdots & & \vdots \quad \vdots \quad \ddots \quad \vdots \\
x_{o1}^{no} - x_{11}^{n1} - x_{12}^{n1} - \cdots - x_{1m}^{n1} & - x_{11}^{n2} - x_{12}^{n2} - \cdots - x_{1m}^{n2} - & \cdots & - x_{11}^{nn} - x_{12}^{nn} - \cdots - x_{1m}^{nn} & = & y_{1o}^{n1} + y_{1o}^{n2} + \cdots + y_{1o}^{nn} \\
x_{o2}^{no} - x_{21}^{n1} - x_{22}^{n1} - \cdots - x_{2m}^{n1} & - x_{21}^{n2} - x_{22}^{n2} - \cdots - x_{2m}^{n2} - & \cdots & - x_{21}^{nn} - x_{22}^{nn} - \cdots - x_{2m}^{nn} & = & y_{2o}^{n1} + y_{2o}^{n2} + \cdots + y_{2o}^{nn} \\
\vdots \quad \vdots \quad \vdots \quad \ddots \quad \vdots & \vdots \quad \vdots \quad \ddots \quad \vdots & \cdots & \vdots \quad \vdots \quad \ddots \quad \vdots & \vdots & \vdots \quad \vdots \quad \ddots \quad \vdots \\
x_{om}^{no} - x_{m1}^{n1} - x_{m2}^{n1} - \cdots - x_{mm}^{n1} & - x_{m1}^{n2} - x_{m2}^{n2} - \cdots - x_{mm}^{n2} - & \cdots & - x_{m1}^{nn} - x_{m2}^{nn} - \cdots - x_{mm}^{nn} & = & y_{mo}^{n1} + y_{mo}^{n2} + \cdots + y_{mo}^{nn}
\end{array}
$$

Equation System (3.1)

industry in Arizona, x_{81}^{o2}, by the total livestock output in Arizona, x_{o1}^{2o}, and will therefore indicate the amount of petroleum purchased by the livestock industry in Arizona per dollar of livestock produced in Arizona. Final results of the divisions are grouped for each region and form the n regional blocks, which are then placed along the principal diagonal of the $\hat{A}$ matrix shown earlier. The coefficients as calculated from the complete MRIO accounts table will sum to 1.0 for each column. However, because the value added components are dropped when the static open model is implemented, each column of coefficients will sum to less than 1.0 in the $\hat{A}$ matrix, unless, of course, the value added components are zero, which is almost never the case.

The second set of structural constants is the interregional trade coefficients. The coefficient c_{1o}^{23} will be used for illustration. It is obtained by dividing the shipment of livestock from Arizona to Arkansas, c_{1o}^{23}, by the total consumption of livestock in Arkansas, x_{1o}^{o3}, and will therefore relate the shipment of livestock between Arizona and Arkansas to the total regional consumption of the commodity in Arkansas. The final results of the divisions for all regions and commodities form m commodity-trade matrices, each dimensioned $n \times n$. If a particular commodity is not traded, as may be the case for certain service industries, the trade-coefficient matrix becomes a diagonal matrix with ones along the main diagonal and zeros for all the off-diagonal elements. The sum of each column of the commodity-trade-coefficient matrices will be 1.0, regardless of whether or not the commodity is traded. To implement the MRIO model, the trade coefficients must be rearranged from the individual matrices in order to conform with the regional and industrial organization of the technology matrices. The final result of the permutation is the large expanded matrix of trade coefficients, represented by matrix C in the earlier notations, ordered region by region.

It should be noted that because of lack of data, trade in the MRIO model is not specified in terms of the industry receiving the commodity; rather, it is assumed that a supply pool exists from which industries in each region draw their requirements. To implement the model, it is therefore necessary to assume that each industry within region h will consume the same fraction as imports, that is,

$$c_{io}^{gh} = c_{i1}^{gh} = c_{i2}^{gh} = \cdots = c_{im}^{gh}$$

This is the assumption of uniform industrial shares mentioned in the preceding section.

Using the two sets of structural constants just defined, the balance equations of the MRIO model can be rewritten as equation system (3.2). There are

$$
\begin{array}{lllllll}
x^{1o}_{o1} - b^{11}_{11}x^{1o}_{o1} - b^{11}_{12}x^{1o}_{o2} - \cdots - b^{11}_{1m}x^{1o}_{om} - & \cdots & - b^{1n}_{11}x^{no}_{o1} - b^{1n}_{12}x^{no}_{o2} - \cdots - b^{1n}_{1m}x^{no}_{om} & = & c^{11}_{1o}y^{o1}_{1o} + c^{12}_{1o}y^{o2}_{1o} + \cdots + c^{1n}_{1o}y^{on}_{1o} \\
x^{1o}_{o2} - b^{11}_{21}x^{1o}_{o1} - b^{11}_{22}x^{1o}_{o2} - \cdots - b^{11}_{2m}x^{1o}_{om} - & \cdots & - b^{1n}_{21}x^{no}_{o1} - b^{1n}_{22}x^{no}_{o2} - \cdots - b^{1n}_{2m}x^{no}_{om} & = & c^{11}_{2o}y^{o1}_{2o} + c^{12}_{2o}y^{o2}_{2o} + \cdots + c^{1n}_{2o}y^{on}_{2o} \\
\vdots \quad \vdots \quad \vdots \quad \ddots \quad \vdots & \cdots & \vdots \quad \vdots \quad \ddots \quad \vdots & \vdots & \vdots \quad \vdots \quad \ddots \quad \vdots \\
x^{1o}_{om} - b^{11}_{m1}x^{1o}_{o1} - b^{11}_{m2}x^{1o}_{o2} - \cdots - b^{11}_{mm}x^{1o}_{om} - & \cdots & - b^{1n}_{m1}x^{no}_{o1} - b^{1n}_{m2}x^{no}_{o2} - \cdots - b^{1n}_{mm}x^{no}_{om} & = & c^{11}_{mo}y^{o1}_{mo} + c^{12}_{mo}y^{o2}_{mo} + \cdots + c^{1n}_{mo}y^{on}_{mo} \\
x^{2o}_{o1} - b^{21}_{11}x^{1o}_{o1} - b^{21}_{12}x^{1o}_{o2} - \cdots - b^{21}_{1m}x^{1o}_{om} - & \cdots & - b^{2n}_{11}x^{no}_{o1} - b^{2n}_{12}x^{no}_{o2} - \cdots - b^{2n}_{1m}x^{no}_{om} & = & c^{21}_{1o}y^{o1}_{1o} + c^{22}_{1o}y^{o2}_{1o} + \cdots + c^{2n}_{1o}y^{on}_{1o} \\
x^{2o}_{o2} - b^{21}_{21}x^{1o}_{o1} - b^{21}_{22}x^{1o}_{o2} - \cdots - b^{21}_{2m}x^{1o}_{om} - & \cdots & - b^{2n}_{21}x^{no}_{o1} - b^{2n}_{22}x^{no}_{o2} - \cdots - b^{2n}_{2m}x^{no}_{om} & = & c^{21}_{2o}y^{o1}_{2o} + c^{22}_{2o}y^{o2}_{2o} + \cdots + c^{2n}_{2o}y^{on}_{2o} \\
\vdots \quad \vdots \quad \vdots \quad \ddots \quad \vdots & \cdots & \vdots \quad \vdots \quad \ddots \quad \vdots & \vdots & \vdots \quad \vdots \quad \ddots \quad \vdots \\
x^{2o}_{om} - b^{21}_{m1}x^{1o}_{o1} - b^{21}_{m2}x^{1o}_{o2} - \cdots - b^{21}_{mm}x^{1o}_{om} - & \cdots & - b^{2n}_{m1}x^{no}_{o1} - b^{2n}_{m2}x^{no}_{o2} - \cdots - b^{2n}_{mm}x^{no}_{om} & = & c^{21}_{mo}y^{o1}_{mo} + c^{22}_{mo}y^{o2}_{mo} + \cdots + c^{2n}_{mo}y^{on}_{mo} \\
\vdots \quad \vdots \quad \vdots \quad \ddots \quad \vdots & \cdots & \vdots \quad \vdots \quad \ddots \quad \vdots & \vdots & \vdots \quad \vdots \quad \ddots \quad \vdots \\
x^{no}_{o1} - b^{n1}_{11}x^{1o}_{o1} - b^{n1}_{12}x^{1o}_{o2} - \cdots - b^{n1}_{1m}x^{1o}_{om} - & \cdots & - b^{nn}_{11}x^{no}_{o1} - b^{nn}_{12}x^{no}_{o2} - \cdots - b^{nn}_{1m}x^{no}_{om} & = & c^{n1}_{1o}y^{o1}_{1o} + c^{n2}_{1o}y^{o2}_{1o} + \cdots + c^{nn}_{1o}y^{on}_{1o} \\
x^{no}_{o2} - b^{n1}_{21}x^{1o}_{o1} - b^{n1}_{22}x^{1o}_{o2} - \cdots - b^{n1}_{2m}x^{1o}_{om} - & \cdots & - b^{nn}_{21}x^{no}_{o1} - b^{nn}_{22}x^{no}_{o2} - \cdots - b^{nn}_{2m}x^{no}_{om} & = & c^{n1}_{2o}y^{o1}_{2o} + c^{n2}_{2o}y^{o2}_{2o} + \cdots + c^{nn}_{2o}y^{on}_{2o} \\
\vdots \quad \vdots \quad \vdots \quad \ddots \quad \vdots & \cdots & \vdots \quad \vdots \quad \ddots \quad \vdots & \vdots & \vdots \quad \vdots \quad \ddots \quad \vdots \\
x^{no}_{om} - b^{n1}_{m1}x^{1o}_{o1} - b^{n1}_{m2}x^{1o}_{o2} - \cdots - b^{n1}_{mm}x^{1o}_{om} - & \cdots & - b^{nn}_{m1}x^{no}_{o1} - b^{nn}_{m2}x^{no}_{o2} - \cdots - b^{nn}_{mm}x^{no}_{om} & = & c^{n1}_{mo}y^{o1}_{mo} + c^{n2}_{mo}y^{o2}_{mo} + \cdots + c^{nn}_{mo}y^{on}_{mo}
\end{array}
$$

Equation System (3.2)

mn such equations to be determined. The following notation, used by Moses, is introduced to simplify the presentation:

$$b_{ij}^{gh} = a_{ij}^{oh} c_{io}^{gh}$$

Only a limited number of data are needed to implement the primal open MRIO model. The basic data are technical coefficients, preferably a separate set for each region in the economy to reflect regional differences in technology; a set of final demands for each region, either separated by type of final user or given as a total; and a set of interregional trade coefficients for each commodity. Using the technology and trade coefficients for a base year and final demands for the given year, the regional outputs and interregional trade for the given year are determined. The solution of the equations in terms of matrix notations is provided to show the similarity to the national input-output model. The system of equations for the national input-output model is modified by the insertion of the matrix of trade coefficients, *C*, as follows:

$$X = (C\hat{A})X + CY$$

$$X - (C\hat{A})X = CY$$

$$(I - C\hat{A})X = CY$$

$$X = (I - C\hat{A})^{-1} CY \tag{3.3}$$

or

$$X = (C^{-1} - \hat{A})^{-1} Y \tag{3.3a}$$

Only the regional outputs are obtained from the calculations based upon the above system of equations. Another set of calculations, shown in equations (3.4), (3.5), (3.6), and (3.7), is required to determine the estimated interregional trade flows.

First, the regional technical coefficients are column multiplied, *cm,* by the transpose of the estimated outputs vector to determine the estimated level of intermediate demands, *D,* on an industry-by-industry basis:

$$D = \hat{A} cm X^t \tag{3.4}$$

Then, the elements in each row of the intermediate demand matrix are summed to obtain a vector of intermediate demands, D^*:

$$D^* = \sum_{j=1}^{m} d_{ij}^{oh} \tag{3.5}$$

Next, the intermediate demands vector is added element by element to the predetermined final demands vector to obtain a vector of estimated total consumption, G, in each region:

$$G = D^* + Y \tag{3.6}$$

Finally, the base-year trade coefficients are column multiplied by the transpose of the estimated regional consumption vector to determine the estimated interregional trade flows, T:

$$T = CcmG^t \tag{3.7}$$

The vector of regional outputs obtained from the equation system (3.3) and the matrices of interregional trade flows, both estimated for prespecified years, are ready for analysis.

The primal version of the open static MRIO model has been used in many ways, some of which were cited earlier in table 3-2. A 19-industry, 9-region, version of the 79-industry, 51-region, model is provided in appendix B, and the industrial and regional classifications are given in tables A-3 and A-2, respectively. It should be noted that industry 19 is electricity. The nine regional transactions tables are given in table B-1 and the corresponding direct input coefficients, A, in table B-2. For the 19 industries, the region-to-region trade flows are given in table B-3 and the trade coefficients, C, in table B-4. All of these are for 1963. The 1963, 1970, and 1980 final demands are shown in table B-5, and the outputs for the same years are given in table B-6. Finally, the projected 1980 trade flows are provided in table B-7.

Another major use of the primal version of the MRIO model—the derivation of output, employment, and income multipliers—will be discussed after a presentation is made of the dual and truncated-dual models.

Dual Model

Inflation has been one of the major economic concerns of the 1970s. Wage and price increases can have extremely large differential impacts on various economic units. As has become increasingly evident, extended inflation causes some people, some industries, and some regions to profit and others to lose in terms of their relative economic positions before, during, and after the period of inflation. The static input-output model is most useful for examinations of the impacts that increases or decreases in wages or prices have if they occur in a single industry or region. When inflation is more pervasive and affects all industries and regions year after year, significant substitution in inputs begins to take place, and this violates one of the basic input-output assumptions. In such cases, dynamic input-output models are especially valuable, because wide-spread inflation creates substantial structural changes, which can be evaluated in detail through the use of the input-output framework.

As mentioned earlier in this chapter, a dual version of the MRIO model has been implemented to analyze changes in transportation and energy prices. The model has also been used to investigate the regional and industrial differential price impacts of imposing specific environmental regulations. The set of MRIO price equations will be presented after the national input-output price model has been described.

National Price Model. Because the dual version of the national input-output model is not well known, and because some of the points relating to the dual system of equations can be best understood without the complex interpretations that must be provided when the regional dimension is incorporated, the national system of dual input-output equations will be presented first. The notations are defined as follows:

p_j = price of the commodity produced by industry j

p_w = price of the factors of production

q_{ij} = physical quantity of commodity i bought by industry j

q_j = total physical output of industry j

s_j = physical quantity of value added in industry j

f_{ij} = direct input coefficient for industries i and j (in physical units) = q_{ij}/q_j

w_i = value added per unit of output for industry $i = p_w s_j/q_j$.

The m balance equations for the national price model are given in equation system (3.8):

$$
\begin{array}{llllll}
p_1 q_1 & = p_1 q_{11} & + p_2 q_{21} & + \cdots + & p_m q_{m1} & + p_w s_1 \\
p_2 q_2 & = p_1 q_{12} & + p_2 q_{22} & + \cdots + & p_m q_{m2} & + p_w s_2 \\
\vdots & \vdots & \vdots & \ddots & \vdots & \vdots \\
p_m q_m & = p_1 q_{1m} & + p_2 q_{2m} & + \cdots + & p_m q_{mm} & + p_w s_m
\end{array}
\tag{3.8}
$$

Each equation shows the balance between the total value of outlays and the component values of purchases for a given industry. Thus, the first equation shows that the value of outlays of the first industry must equal the total value paid by that industry for all the intermediate goods and services plus the total value it pays for the services of the factors of production. As is the case with the primal model, the balance equations cannot be solved, because there are more variables than equations. To obtain a solution, a set of structural constants must be introduced, in this case the matrix of physical input coefficients, F. A particular physical input coefficient, f_{ij}, is interpreted as, say, the kilowatts of electricity required per ton of steel. By replacing each q_{ij} term on the right-hand side of equation system (3.8) with the corresponding $f_{ij}q_j$ term, equation system (3.9) results:

$$\begin{array}{llllll} p_1q_1 & = p_1f_{11}q_1 & + p_2f_{21}q_1 & + \cdots + & p_mf_{m1}q_1 & + p_ws_1 \\ p_2q_2 & = p_1f_{12}q_2 & + p_2f_{22}q_2 & + \cdots + & p_mf_{m2}q_2 & + p_ws_2 \\ \vdots & \vdots & \vdots & \ddots & \vdots & \vdots \\ p_mq_m & = p_1f_{1m}q_m & + p_2f_{2m}q_m & + \cdots + & p_mf_{mm}q_m & + p_ws_m \end{array} \tag{3.9}$$

The m prices for the commodities produced by the m industries can be obtained by dividing all the terms in each of the m equations in equation system (3.9) by the appropriate output, q_j. The result is equation system (3.10):

$$\begin{array}{llllll} p_1 & = p_1f_{11} & + p_2f_{21} & + \cdots + & p_mf_{m1} & + w_1 \\ p_2 & = p_1f_{12} & + p_2f_{22} & + \cdots + & p_mf_{m2} & + w_2 \\ \vdots & \vdots & \vdots & \ddots & \vdots & \vdots \\ p_m & = p_1f_{1m} & + p_2f_{2m} & + \cdots + & p_mf_{mm} & + w_m \end{array} \tag{3.10}$$

Thus, the price of each commodity equals the unit cost of production, which includes the costs of the inputs of intermediate goods and services as well as the value added costs.

Given the technical input coefficients for a base year and the value-added-per-unit-of-output ratios for a future year (all still in physical units), the prices per unit of output for the future year can be determined. The method of implementing the model is the same as that used for the primal model.

So far, the entire system has been specified in terms of the physical amount of output produced by each industry. National and regional input-output tables in the United States are never assembled using physical outputs, because of the limited availability of data in physical units for many industries; rather, all data are specified in dollar values. Before proceeding with the presentation of the dual version of the MRIO model, a comparison of the primal and dual versions of the national input-output systems of equations in physical and value units is presented. The physical-unit matrix equations are presented first for the primal in equation system (3.11a) and then for the dual in equation system (3.11b). The value-unit matrix equations are presented for the primal in equation system (3.12a) and then for the dual in equation system (3.12b).

	Primal Model		*Dual Model*	
Physical Units	$Q = FQ + Z$ $Q - FQ = Z$ $(I - F)Q = Z$ $Q = (I - F)^{-1}Z$	(3.11a)	$P = F^tP + W$ $P - F^tP = W$ $(I - F^t)P = W$ $P = (I - F^t)^{-1}W$	(3.11b)
Value Units	$X = AX + Y$ $X - AX = Y$ $(I - A)X = Y$ $X = (I - A)^{-1}Y$	(3.12a)	$\tilde{P} = A^t\tilde{P} + U$ $\tilde{P} - A^t\tilde{P} = U$ $(I - A^t)\tilde{P} = U$ $\tilde{P} = (I - A^t)^{-1}U$	(3.12b)

It should be noted that the direct input coefficients form the core of all four systems of equations, and that the direct input coefficient matrix F^t or A^t used in the dual version is the transpose of the corresponding matrix used in solving for outputs in the primal system.

For the dual model, it should be especially noted that both W and U are vectors of value-added-per-unit-of-output ratios, the first using physical units and the second monetary units. Thus, w_1 might be the number of person years required per 100 head of livestock produced (assuming labor is the only component of value added). It should also be noted that P represents a vector of actual prices, whereas $\tilde{P}$ represents a vector of relative prices that all equal 1.0 in the base year. When the model is implemented, the estimated values for $\tilde{P}$ can be used to show deviations of the prices from the base year. Thus, an estimated value for $\tilde{p}_1$ of 1.15 will indicate that prices of, say, livestock have increased by 15 percent from the base year, not that livestock is \$1.15 per head.

Given the particular set of information used, a solution for the value system of equations is directly obtainable through the fact that the entire system when specified in dollars (or other appropriate monetary unit) is normalized to 1.0. Each coefficient, a_{ij}, in the technical input matrix represents the dollar value of good i purchased by industry j to produce \$1.00 of good j. In the input-output accounting framework, the sum of the costs of all intermediate and primary factor inputs used to produce a unit of good j must be equal to the total value of output of one unit of good j. The technical input coefficient matrix provides a means of normalizing these costs in relation to \$1.00 of the commodity produced. In other words, the total cost of production for one unit of output for each industry is equal to \$1.00, and that is also the price of the unit of output produced by the industry, because in a competitive economy, the cost of production must equal the price of the good produced. One consistency test that can be run with a new set of value accounts, then, is to solve equation system (3.12b) to determine whether or not prices do equal \$1.00.

Now that the basic theory underlying the price input-output model has been explained, the MRIO version of the model will be presented.

MRIO Price Model. To form the MRIO price model, the system of equations (3.12b) is modified by the insertion of the matrix of trade coefficients, C, as follows:

$$\begin{aligned} \tilde{P} &= (C\hat{A})^t\tilde{P} + U \\ \tilde{P} - (C\hat{A})^t\tilde{P} &= U \\ [I - (C\hat{A})^t]\,\tilde{P} &= U \\ \tilde{P} &= [I - (C\hat{A})^t]^{-1}U \end{aligned} \tag{3.13}$$

where the notations are as defined earlier.

It is too cumbersome to write all the equations for equation system (3.13), but the first of the mn equations is presented here for illustration:

$$\begin{aligned} \tilde{p}_1^1 = {} & c_{1o}^{11}a_{11}^{o1}\tilde{p}_1^1 + c_{2o}^{11}a_{21}^{o1}\tilde{p}_2^1 + \cdots + c_{mo}^{11}a_{m1}^{o1}\tilde{p}_m^1 + c_{1o}^{21}a_{11}^{o1}\tilde{p}_1^2 + c_{2o}^{21}a_{21}^{o1}\tilde{p}_2^2 + \cdots \\ & + c_{mo}^{21}a_{m1}^{o1}\tilde{p}_m^2 + \cdots + c_{1o}^{n1}a_{11}^{o1}\tilde{p}_1^n + c_{2o}^{n1}a_{21}^{o1}\tilde{p}_2^n + \cdots + c_{mo}^{n1}a_{m1}^{o1}\tilde{p}_m^n + u_1^1 \end{aligned} \tag{3.14}$$

It should be noted that because of the assumption of the identical import patterns discussed earlier, the industry purchasing the output is not distinguished in the c_{io}^{gh} coefficient. Thus, the same c_{1o}^{11} coefficient will appear in the first term for each of the first m equations. Without the second assumption, the amount of trade data required would increase dramatically to $mn^2 - mn$ times the present requirements. For the U.S. model with 51 regions and 79 industries, for example, more than 200,000 additional trade-flow figures would be required.

The base-year data from the MRIO accounts can be used, as was the case with the primal model, to determine whether or not the data are accurate. If they are, and if the model has been appropriately set up on the computer, all the m industrial prices in each of the n regions will be \$1.00 in the base period when equation system (3.13) is solved.

The uses of the MRIO price model are many. As an example, if workers in one major industry, such as steel, win a wage increase, the price model can be used to see what impact it will have on the price of steel and on other industrial prices in each region of the country. In the short run, substitution among inputs is unlikely to occur, so it is assumed that the increase is passed directly on to other prices. Efforts should of course be made to determine whether or not the particular industry concerned will absorb some of the increase by lowering its profit margin, in which case total value added for that industry may change by a lesser amount than the original wage increase; it is the change in total value added that has been modeled in the present instance. It is also possible, however, to separate wages from other value added and to treat other value added endogenously.

There are many other ways of using the price model to investigate policy issues that arise in a period of inflation. One area of particular interest at the present time is to isolate the price changes occurring in a single industry, such as construction, energy, food, or agriculture, and to trace the short-run regional impact those price changes have on other industrial prices. To be used in this way, the model must be reformulated into a truncated version.

Truncated MRIO Price Model. The truncated version of the MRIO price model is formulated by exogenously determining the price of one or more commodities in one or more regions. The value added component becomes endogenous for each corresponding commodity for which the price is set exogenously, thus maintaining the appropriate number of endogenous variables. An example will be given for making the price of the first commodity in the first region, p_1^1, exogenous. A new vector is defined, the T^* vector, the elements of which correspond to all the inputs in the first industry in the first region (see page 126).

In other words, the T^* vector will consist of all terms in equation system (3.13) that contain the exogenously set prices, in this case all the terms containing p_1^1.

The new system of equations is defined in equation (3.15):

$$\tilde{P}^* = [I - (CA)^{t^*}]^{-1} [T^* + U^*] \tag{3.15}$$

The * indicates that the price equation or equations corresponding to the price(s) in the T^* vector have been removed from the original mn set of equations given in equation system (3.13).

As already mentioned, the truncated form of the MRIO model has been used by Young [302] to determine the industrial and regional impacts of a change in transportation prices and by Polenske [177] to examine the effects of the 1972-1976 changes in coal prices. One of the most valuable ways to use

$$T^* = \begin{bmatrix} c_{1o}^{11} a_{12}^{o1} p_1^1 \\ \vdots \\ c_{1o}^{11} a_{1m}^{o1} p_1^1 \\ c_{1o}^{12} a_{11}^{o2} p_1^1 \\ c_{1o}^{12} a_{12}^{o2} p_1^1 \\ \vdots \\ c_{1o}^{12} a_{1m}^{o2} p_1^1 \\ \vdots \\ c_{1o}^{1n} a_{11}^{on} p_1^1 \\ c_{1o}^{1n} a_{12}^{on} p_1^1 \\ \vdots \\ c_{1o}^{1n} a_{1m}^{on} p_1^1 \end{bmatrix}$$

the price (dual) version of the MRIO model is to combine it with the output (primal) version of the model, as was done by Pai in an examination of the industrial and regional repercussions of implementing the 1974 Clean Air Act [168]. A brief description of the combined use of the two models is presented here.

Combined Dual and Primal MRIO Models. Significant changes in the price of any commodity will have repercussions on other prices, but one of the final results will be that changes will occur in consumption, investment, and government expenditures. Such changes in the final demand for products can be examined to determine variations in output and employment. Thus, the initial use of the dual MRIO model leads to the later use of the primal MRIO model to determine the output and employment effects of a given price or wage policy on a region-by-region basis. This analysis can be carried out through the use of a set of four equations:

$$X = [I - C\hat{A}]^{-1} C[Y_{en} + Y_{ex}] \tag{3.16}$$

$$\theta = A_L X \tag{3.17}$$

$$Y_{en} = \hat{K}\tilde{P}^{\beta}_{en}\,\theta \tag{3.18}$$

$$\tilde{P} = [I - (C\hat{A})^t]^{-1} V \tag{3.19}$$

where Y_{en} = vector, $mn \times 1$, of final demand to be determined endogenously

Y_{ex} = vector, $mn \times 1$, of exogenous final demand = $Y - Y_{en}$

A_L = vector, $1 \times mn$, of labor input per unit of output

$\hat{K}$ = diagonal matrix, $mn \times mn$, of consumption coefficients obtained by dividing the vector of personal consumption expenditures by total personal income devoted to consumption

$\tilde{P}^{\beta}_{en}$ = vector, $mn \times n$, of price elasticities for good i

θ = vector, $n \times 1$, of total income in each region devoted to personal consumption.

All other terms have been defined earlier.

The income equation, (3.17), is calculated by multiplying the income received by labor per unit of output, A_L, by the amount of output produced. The result is θ, an $n \times 1$ vector of total income devoted to personal consumption in each of the n regions. The consumption equation has been formed so as to allow for nonunitary price elasticities, $\tilde{P}^{\beta}_{en}$, for consumer goods, an $mn \times n$ matrix. In an initial implementation of the model, the same national price elasticities were used for each of the n regions. Regional price elasticities can be calculated, but this requires considerable research. The k coefficients are obtained by dividing each element in the personal consumption expenditures vector by total income devoted to consumption. These coefficients are then arranged along the diagonal of the $mn \times mn$ matrix $\hat{K}$.

For solution of the model, the following equation is used:

$$X = (I - C\hat{A} - C\hat{K}\tilde{P}^{\beta}_{en} A_L)^{-1} CY_{ex} \tag{3.20}$$

This phase of the research only determines the impact of price changes as traced through changes in the cost of living for consumers. Other theoretical and empirical work is necessary to develop methods of examining the investment and government expenditures ramifications.

Another important area of research will be to formulate means of allowing for long-run substitution among inputs. As the price of, say, coal increases relative to the price of other fuels, industrial and other users of coal will switch from coal, and as the price of all fuels increases relative to other prices in the economy, means will be found to substitute labor, capital, or other inputs for the fuels. These price elasticities should be determined on a regional level and used to alter the input coefficients in the MRIO model. Initial exploration into making such analyses at the national level has been set forth in a recent paper by Almon [3].

While a general method of using the combined dual and primal models has been outlined here, the amount of empirical work involved in each of the steps is large and should not be underestimated. However, it should be stressed that the use of the MRIO accounting framework for such studies at the regional level is especially valuable because of the assurance that the estimates made are internally consistent from industry to industry and region to region. The MRIO accounting framework also assures that multipliers calculated at the regional level are consistent and are based upon structural differences in each industry and region. The various types of MRIO multipliers are now described.

Multiregional Multipliers

An important by-product of any input-output model is the set of multipliers that is an integral part of the system. The MRIO model is no exception. The MRIO multipliers can be used to answer a number of policy questions, such as: How much additional output will be produced in a given region as a result of particular federal or state expenditures? How much additional income will be generated and how many jobs will be created by those same expenditures? Which industries in the region will be affected most? How many jobs will be lost by a given slash in public spending necessitated by recently instituted reductions in tax contributions? Most multipliers can account not only for the effects of an increase or decrease in spending, but also for the subsequent rounds of increased or decreased spending generated by the initial round. The MRIO multipliers give regional specificity to these spending impacts.

Although Keynesian multiplier analysis has been used at the national level for policy studies for many years, it is only recently that emphasis has been placed on assessing economic impacts at the urban and regional levels using multipliers. One important attempt to construct regional multipliers was made by the BEA staff in 1977 when they prepared the Regional Impact Multiplier System (RIMS) for the U.S. Water Resources Council [263]. Many regional analysts are using those multipliers. The multipliers, which at present are available for 56 industries and 173 BEA economic areas, as well as all states, seem to fill an important need; but they must be used cautiously because of the basis used for their construction. Differences between regions in the size of multipliers should reflect variations in regional production structures and in interregional transportation networks. In an attempt to show these variations, the BEA has modified the detailed 370-order 1967 national input-output coefficients through the use of secondary regional data including location quotients. The revised methodology still has some severe limitations that the BEA is presently trying to modify [263, pp. 23-24].

Multipliers from the MRIO model are more refined than the BEA multipliers, because they reflect actual variations in regional production structures and in interregional transportation networks as a result of the use, whenever possible, of actual regional data when the MRIO accounts were assembled. A considerable amount of literature now exists on the MRIO multipliers and their applications. Examples are the publications of DiPasquale and Polenske [29], Faucett [39], Golladay and Haveman [63], Kim, Park, and Kwak [101], Rowan [194], Polenske and Rowan [179], and Shalizi [201]. A rigorous theoretical discussion of multiregional multipliers is given in the thesis by Shalizi. He also presents a new means of expanding the model to assess the effects of income formation. In the DiPasquale and Polenske article, the authors specified in detail the structure of the MRIO multipliers, providing

> explicit details on the calculation and interpretation of multiregional output, employment, and income multipliers in theory, substantiated with actual data for the United States. [29, p.2]

Following is a summary of the study reported in the article by DiPasquale and Polenske.

Both the open and partially closed versions of the static MRIO model can be used to determine multipliers. In the open version, all final demands are treated exogenously, that is, are predetermined or given, while in the partially closed version, one or more of the final demands and the corresponding part of value added are treated endogenously, that is, they become variables that are determined by solving the system of equations. In a model partially closed with respect to households, for example, the personal consumption expenditures part of final demand and the wages and salaries part of value added are treated as endogenous components of the model. The direct and indirect output requirements are determined using the inverse matrix of the open model and a set of final demands. In response to a given set of final demands, all industries produce some outputs that are used as direct inputs in the production of the outputs. But these inputs generate additional demands, and more outputs must be produced to fulfill these demand requirements, and this iterative process continues as it converges toward zero. The total (direct and indirect) requirements determined by this iterative process are assumed to be obtained within a selected year. Thus, each inverse coefficient in the MRIO model is an output multiplier.

The production of outputs to fulfill the given set of final demands also results in changes in income that, in turn, will lead to additional changes in final demand, say personal consumption expenditures, touching off yet another round of expenditures. The effect of these reactions on outputs, employment, and income are called *induced changes,* and they can be traced by partially closing the model. The direct, indirect, and induced output requirements, for example, are determined using the inverse matrix of the partially closed model and a given set of final demands. For the partially closed model, one or more of the final demands, say personal consumption expenditures, are treated endogenously. The corresponding part of value added, say wages and salaries, must also become endogenous, its level now being determined by changes in the remaining exogenous final demands whereas previously its level and composition were determined exogenously. Personal consumption expenditures and wages and salaries will now be referred to collectively as the household industry.

In the example just cited, personal consumption expenditures and wages and salaries become the $m + 1$ producing industry in each region, with a technology represented by the expenditures pattern given in the personal consumption expenditures column of the MRIO table; its output is distributed according to the amount of labor required by each industrial and final user in each region, as shown in the wages and salaries rows of the MRIO table. To complete the system, a set of interregional trade flows for the household industry is also needed. In the absence of actual data, a first approximation can be made by assuming that the trade flows for households are all intraregional, then the trade coefficient matrix for that "industry" has ones along the diagonal. All of this information for the technologies and trade flows must be rearranged into expanded A and C matrices. Then the inverse coefficients using the expanded matrices will reflect the direct, indirect, and induced output requirements. Depending upon the desired analysis, investment, foreign exports, or government expenditures–instead of households–could be treated endogenously.

The capabilities and usefulness of the Leontief matrix of direct and indirect coefficients, hereafter referred to as the Leontief inverse coefficients, are well known. Yet, in the growing amount of literature on input-output multipliers, most authors neglect the Leontief inverse coefficients in their role as individual multipliers and concentrate instead on summary measures of them. This neglect has led to confusion as to what a multiplier is; how output, employment, and income multipliers are related; and with what data they should be combined. It has also obscured the rich detail of information that is available for planning purposes. The value of the individual inverse coefficients will become evident later.

For the MRIO analyses, the multiregional output, employment, or income multipliers are always combined with projected changes in final demand to determine the corresponding output, employment, or income effects of those expenditures. However, in most early studies, such as those by Moore and Petersen [147], Hirsch [79], and Miernyk [137], the multipliers were divided by the direct income in the corresponding industry and region of demand, and the multipliers were then combined with projected changes in direct income. The multiplier must always be established on a base that is consistent with the data by which it is to be multiplied. The base to be used will be partly determined by the ease of obtaining projections of final demand or income or some other variable. Most regional analysts have used direct income, perhaps because for the early regional studies this measure was either already available or could be easily projected at the state level. Even today, estimates of gross regional product are unavailable for many regions; consequently, for some studies direct income still has to be used as the base. Schaffer is one of the analysts to specify regional multipliers (he obtained them for Georgia) in terms of changes in gross regional product, the same measure used in the MRIO model, rather than in terms of gross regional income [196, pp. 60-61]. The fact that multipliers specified in RIMS also are based on gross regional product suggests that this is becoming more commonly used as a base.

Many different multipliers are referred to in the literature. Detailed definitions are given in this chapter of output, employment, and income multipliers in open and partially closed static multiregional and national (regional) input-output models. Four types of multipliers will be defined: detailed, industry-specific, region-specific, and total.

Multiregional Output Multipliers. By definition, the multiregional detailed output multiplier for industries i and j and regions g and h is identical to the multiregional inverse coefficient for the same industries and regions. This multiplier is defined as

$$XM_{ij}^{gh} \equiv d_{ij}^{gh} \qquad (i,j = 1,\ldots,m; g,h = 1,\ldots,n) \tag{3.21}$$

where

XM_{ij}^{gh} is the output multiplier for final demand in region h for commodity j and output in region g of commodity i

d_{ij}^{gh} is the multiregional inverse coefficient for outputs, showing the amount of output generated by industry i located in region g to fulfill the final demand in region h for the products of industry j

all superscripts and subscripts are as defined earlier.

The term *detailed* will be used to refer to the fact that for national, regional, or multiregional multipliers, industrial detail is provided for both the producing industry and the industry where the demand is being generated; and, for the multiregional multiplier, the shipping and purchasing regions are also specified. When the detailed output multiplier is multiplied by the final demand (gross regional product) in region h for the output of industry j, the total amount of output generated by industry i located in region g to fulfill a $1 change in a particular final demand is determined. For m industries and n regions, there are $mn \times mn$ such multipliers.

For some analyses, the aggregate output of a specific industry generated by a change in final demand in a particular region may be of interest. This multiplier will be called the multiregional industry-specific output multiplier. It is defined as

$$XM_{ij}^{oh} = \sum_{g=1}^{n} d_{ij}^{gh} \quad (i,j = 1,\ldots,m; h = 1,\ldots,n) \tag{3.22}$$

where all elements are defined as in equation (3.21), and o represents a summation over all regions.

This multiplier is obtained by summing all elements in a column (for a specific industry and region) of the MRIO inverse that refer to a specific industry. When it is multiplied by the final demand in region h for the output of industry j, the total amount of output generated by industry i in all regions to fulfill that particular final demand is determined. Thus, the region in which the output is generated is not given, but the specific industry generating the output is known, hence the name industry-specific. In general, there will be $n \times m^2$ multiregional industry-specific multipliers. For these multipliers, one of the regional dimensions of the multiregional detailed output multiplier is withheld, namely the region in which the output is being produced. These multipliers are used when a policy analyst or planner needs to know how much output will be generated by each industry in the country per unit change in demand for the output of an industry in a specific region.

A related summary output multiplier measure is the multiregional region-specific output multiplier. In this case, one of the industry dimensions of the multiregional detailed output multiplier is withheld, namely the industry producing the output, but now the region in which the output is produced is known, hence the name region-specific. It is defined as

$$XM_{oj}^{gh} = \sum_{i=1}^{m} d_{ij}^{gh} \quad (j = 1,\ldots,m; g,h = 1,\ldots,n) \tag{3.23}$$

where all elements are defined as in equation (3.21), and o represents a summation over all industries.

The multiplier is obtained by summing all the elements in a column-block of the MRIO inverse matrix, where each column is blocked according to regions. When it is multiplied by the final demand in region h for the output of industry *j,* the total amount of output generated by all industries in a particular region to fulfill that particular final demand is determined. In general, there will be $m \times n^2$ multiregional region-specific multipliers. The industry-specific and region-specific summary multipliers may be especially useful to analysts and planners interested in the impacts on regional output of changes in the composition and level of gross regional product.

An even more aggregate summary measure of output multipliers can now be determined. For this multiplier, both the regional and industrial origin of output are withheld; only the region and industry where the demand originates are known. This will be called the multiregional total output multiplier. It is defined as

$$XM_j^h = \sum_{i=1}^{m} XM_{ij}^{oh} = \sum_{g=1}^{n} XM_{oj}^{gh} = \sum_{i=1}^{m} \sum_{g=1}^{n} d_{ij}^{gh} \qquad (j = 1,\ldots,m;\, h = 1,\ldots,n) \tag{3.24}$$

where all elements are as defined in equations (3.21), (3.22), and (3.23).

When this figure is multiplied by the final demand in region *h* for the output of industry *j,* the total amount of output generated by all industries in all regions to fulfill that particular final demand is determined. It is obtained by adding either the *m* industry-specific output multipliers, or the *n* region-specific output multipliers, or the *mn* detailed output multipliers for industry *j* in region *h.* In other words, it is the sum of the elements in a column of the inverse matrix of coefficients. For a total of *m* industries and *n* regions, there are *mn* multiregional total output multipliers. These multipliers are provided for each industry in each region where demand is originating, but no information is provided concerning either the industry or region producing the output, detail often of critical importance to planners.

From the above discussion, the immense amount of detail provided by multiregional output multipliers is evident. The four basic types of multiregional multipliers (detailed, industry-specific, region-specific, and total) all condense into a single number the several rounds of reactions that occur in output and income over a finite time period. In the static model, the total reaction to an increase or decrease of final demand is assumed to occur within the given year. As mentioned earlier, the resulting changes are reflected in the inverse coefficients for the partially closed model. Thus, each inverse coefficient (detailed multiplier) in the partially closed model will be as large as or larger than the corresponding coefficient in the open model. Each of the other three types of multipliers will likewise be at least as large for the partially closed model as for the open model.

In the partially closed model, the household industry is treated as the $m + 1$ endogenous industry. It should be noted that the detailed output multipliers for this industry are identical to the region-specific income multiplier for the same industry in the particular region. (Income multipliers will be defined in the next section.) The output multipliers have been described in considerable detail. Because the other frequently used multipliers—employment and income—are based upon the output multipliers, they can be easily explained.

Open Model Employment and Income Multipliers. Underlying all MRIO employment and income multiplier calculations are the production structures in and transportation networks among regions. Differences between industries and between regions in employment multipliers, for example, are then only partly the result of variations in employment-to-output ratios. Shifts in interindustry and interregional structures of production and transportation, respectively, will also affect the size of the multiplier. The same holds for income, energy, and other MRIO multipliers.

Corresponding to each of the multipliers specified above is an employment and income multiplier, each based upon the same set of inverse coefficient relationships. The inverse coefficients are now combined with either an employment-to-output ratio or an income-to-output ratio. The calculation is done as follows. According to the procedure now well established in the national employment estimations made by the U.S. Bureau of Labor Statistics [292], each element in a row of the inverse matrix is multiplied by the employment-to-output (income-to-output) ratio for the particular industry represented by the row. The same procedure is used at the multiregional level, with the industries now being differentiated by the region, as well as the industry, in which the output is produced.

For the income multipliers, an income-to-output ratio is used, and this happens to be already present in the matrix of direct coefficients as the household industry row for the wages and salaries paid to labor. This household coefficient in a particular column of the matrix is obtained by dividing the wages and salaries in industry i in region g by the corresponding output of industry i in region g.

In each case, there are detailed, industry-specific, region-specific, and total multipliers, but only the detailed and total multipliers will be defined here. The following notations are used:

XM = output multiplier

EM = employment multiplier

WM = income multiplier

e_{io}^{go} = total employment in industry i located in region g

x_{io}^{go} = total output of industry i located in region g

x_{wi}^{go} = total wages and salaries in industry i located in region g

all superscripts and subscripts are as defined earlier.

The multiregional detailed employment multiplier (open model) is defined as

$$EM_{ij}^{gh} = d_{ij}^{gh} \cdot \frac{e_{io}^{go}}{x_{io}^{go}} \equiv XM_{ij}^{gh} \cdot \frac{x_{wi}^{go}}{x_{io}^{go}} \qquad (i,j = 1,\ldots,m;\ g,h = 1,\ldots,n)$$

The multiregional total employment multiplier (open model) is defined as

$$EM_{oj}^{oh} = \sum_{i=1}^{m} EM_{ij}^{oh} = \sum_{g=1}^{n} EM_{oj}^{gh} = \sum_{i=1}^{m} \sum_{g=1}^{n} EM_{ij}^{gh} \qquad (j = 1,\ldots,m;\ h = 1,\ldots,n)$$

The multiregional detailed income multiplier (open model) is defined as

$$WM_{ij}^{gh} = d_{ij}^{gh} \cdot \frac{x_{wi}^{go}}{x_{io}^{go}} \equiv XM_{ij}^{gh} \cdot \frac{x_{wi}^{go}}{x_{io}^{go}} \qquad (i,j = 1,\ldots,m;\ g,h = 1,\ldots,n)$$

The multiregional total income multiplier (open model) is defined as

$$WM_{oj}^{oh} = \sum_{i=1}^{m} WM_{ij}^{oh} = \sum_{g=1}^{n} WM_{oj}^{gh} = \sum_{i=1}^{m} \sum_{g=1}^{n} WM_{ij}^{gh} \qquad (j = 1,\ldots,m;\ h = 1,\ldots,n)$$

From these definitions, it is evident that output multipliers form the base of both the employment and income multipliers and will, in fact, be the base of any other multipliers, such as exports, government, and so on. Variations in detailed employment and income multipliers will be a function of differences in industrial technology, interregional trade structures, and levels of employment or income, relative to the output for a particular industry and region. Any of these factors can cause the detailed multipliers to vary. Finally, as noted earlier, all multipliers in this chapter have been defined in terms of changes in final demand. The multipliers can be transformed in a number of ways, depending upon the needs of the analyst and the available data. If direct income projections, instead of projected final demand, are available, say for 1990 for a given region, the income multiplier should of course be transformed to this basis. The reader is referred to the paper by DiPasquale and Polenske [29] for a full specification of the four types of output, employment, and income multipliers in open and partially closed versions of the MRIO model, including actual 1963 multipliers for three regions and four industries in the United States.

Conclusion

Although the MRIO model is a flexible tool that can be used for a considerable number of policy studies, it must always be used with care given to the particular assumptions upon which it is based. It is an extremely large model. With plans being made in the second round of data assembly to increase the number of industries from 79 to more than 100, attention must be directed to improving the computation time involved in solving the system of equations. The large-scale 79-industry, 51-region model has not been inverted. Solutions have always been obtained through use of a modified Gauss-Jordan iteration FORTRAN program, written by Charles Cohen, a copy of which is included as Appendix B.3 in a report by Polenske, Anderson, and Shirley [180, pp. 112–114]. In the same report, a listing is given of a FORTRAN program designed by Harold Luft for obtaining the solution through a partitioned border inversion [129, pp. 115–119]. When the column-coefficient model was implemented at the Harvard Economic Research Project in 1970 for the 79-industry, 44-region, data and at the Massachusetts Institute of Technology from 1972 on for the 51-region, 79-industry data, the iterative technique was used to obtain a solution. The iterations are relatively inexpensive to do, compared with an inversion, and can therefore be rerun whenever corrections or changes are made to the input data.

The investigation into performing inversions indicated that the costs in 1969 of doing a pivot search and inversion of the 83-industry, 51-region matrix on the IBM 360/65 at Harvard would have ranged from a low of $18,306 to a high of $61,020 [129, p. 33]. This investigation should be reopened to determine present costs given the new computer technology and also to explore any new methodologies that have been developed for inverting large sparse matrices. Additional details on the partitioned border inversion are included in Luft's report, which is available through the National Technical Information Service [129].

Analysts using the MRIO model must be familiar with multiregional accounting practices, regional theory, especially input-output theory, computer techniques used to solve the systems of equations, and with data sources and methods used to assemble the accounts. The remaining chapters of this text are devoted to data sources and methodology.

Notes

1. If regional technology data are not available, the national technology data can be used for each of the regions.

2. The point-estimate version of the multiregional model is also referred to in this text as the Chenery-Moses or column-coefficient model.

3. In the literature, technical coefficients are also referred to as direct input coefficients. (Leontief often calls them "cooking recipes.")

4. The terms *primal* and *output* will be used interchangeably in the remainder of the text, as will the terms *dual* and *price.*

4 State Outputs, Employment, Payrolls, and Final Demands

The sets of data most commonly used at the regional level for all types of analytical and policy studies are outputs, employment, payrolls, and final demands. State outputs, for example, are frequently compiled as controls for state input-output tables, although the specific data sources and estimation procedures employed are not usually given in sufficient detail for state-to-state comparisons to be made. In the case of gross state product (state final demand) data, on the other hand, an increasing amount of literature is becoming available in terms of detailing estimation procedures, providing actual estimates, and/or comparing estimates from different studies. Some of the most recent studies include those by Garnick [54], L'Esperance [115], Kendrick and Jaycox [98], and Weber [300], to mention just a few.

The major effort in assembling the multiregional input-output (MRIO) accounts, in terms of both time and money, was devoted to the compilation of the output, employment, payroll, and final demand data. This was necessary for three reasons. First, given the lack of complete and consistent regional statistics, the establishment of some control totals for each type of regional activity seemed to be an important initial step in the collection of data for the construction of the input-output tables. Second, when particular regional data were unavailable, output, employment, or payroll data were frequently used as proxies to distribute national totals of the data to the regions. Third, because detailed descriptions of the industry compositions were available at the national level for output and final demand data, their estimation was viewed as a necessary step in helping to define industries. Regional estimates of outputs and final demand were made with information concerning the exact composition of the national aggregates being used to determine the types of data required for the regional figure; the methods of estimation were the same as those used for the national figures. To estimate the technology inputs and secondary products at the regional level, however, special methods had to be established, even though the exact composition of the national aggregate was known. For the interregional trade flows, no comparable set of information had been required at the national level.

For all these reasons, work on the output, employment, payroll, and final demand estimates was begun first. In each case, a second round of estimates (in some cases, a third and fourth round) was made during the second or third year of the study. Before providing a brief history of the data assembly and a summary of the data sources and estimation procedures employed, the definitions and uses of production measures will be given.

Definitions and Uses of Production Measures

Various types of production measures were used in constructing the MRIO accounts. In the literature, the terms for production measures are often confusing, partly because different terms are used for the same measure. All of the major measures of production, regardless of whether they were used in the MRIO accounts, will be defined now as an aid in understanding the methodology and data source descriptions presented later; then the uses of these and other measures will be specified.

Definitions of Production Measures

At least nine expressions are used for production measures. They are: industry value of shipments; product value of shipments; establishment output; gross regional output; commodity output; value added as defined by the U.S. Bureau of the Census (Census); value added as defined by the Bureau of Economic Analysis (BEA); gross product originating; and income originating.[1] A summary of the definitions of the nine terms is given in table 4-1, and a detailed description is given here.

Table 4-1
Summary of Definitions of Nine Production Measures

Production Measures	*Basis of Data*	*Definition*	*Comments*
Industry value of shipments	Establishments	Net selling value of all output establishment ships in a given year.	Excludes freight charges and excise taxes but includes both primary and secondary production of firm as well as goods shipped from inventory.
Product value of shipments	Products	Net selling value of all output of a given product shipped by domestic firms in a given year.	Excludes freight charges and excise taxes but includes goods shipped from inventory. No problem with secondary products.

Table 4-1 continued

Production Measures	*Basis of Data*	*Definition*	*Comments*
Establishment output	Establishments	Net selling value of all production of the establishment for a given year. (Shipments adjusted for inventory change.)	An MRIO term defined to exclude freight charges and excise taxes but include both primary and secondary production of firm as well as goods shipped from inventory. It is obtained by adjusting industry value of shipments for inventory change of goods in process and finished products.
Gross regional output	Establishments and miscellaneous values	Net selling value of production of the establishment plus value of products primary to the industry produced by other domestic firms and imports of the product.	An MRIO term defined to alter establishment output to include imports, primary products of firm produced by other firms, and inventory depletions. Should not be confused with gross regional product, which only represents output sales to final users.
Commodity output	Products	Value of output sold in a given year of a particular good, such as grains, including imports and miscellaneous receipts.	An MRIO term defined to exclude regional transfers-out from gross regional output.
Census value added	Establishments	Net selling value of all output establishment ships in a given year less the total cost of materials.	Obtained from establishments.
BEA value added	Establishments	Net selling value of all output establishment ships in a given year less the total cost of materials and the purchases of services.	Varies from the Census concept in that purchases of services are not included.
Gross product originating	Establishments	Net selling value of all output establishment ships in a given year less the total cost of materials and the purchases of services.	Same as BEA value added.
Income originating	Companies	Sum of all factor costs incurred by an industry in production.	Obtained from companies, not establishments. It is a *net* concept of value added rather than the gross concept used by the Census, excluding depreciation, state and local taxes, and other miscellaneous items included in the Census definition.

Industry Value of Shipments. The term *industry value of shipments* refers to data obtained from the official census publications, such as the Census of Manufactures and Census of Mineral Industries. Firms are requested by the Census "to report net selling values, f.o.b. [free on board] plant, after discounts and allowances and excluding freight charges and excise taxes" [234, p. 18]. In the case of multiunit companies, the output of each plant (establishment) is reported separately, and the value of interplant transfers for these companies must include, in addition to the cost of production, a proportion of the total company overhead and profits. The values of both the primary and secondary outputs of each establishment are included (refer to the section on secondary products in chapter 5 for a discussion of their meaning).

The total value of shipments of a particular standard industrial classification (SIC) establishment is therefore the value of all output it shipped, regardless of the year in which the output was produced or the type of output shipped. This value therefore includes goods taken from inventory but produced in a past year, but not goods produced in the current year and put into inventory, and secondary output produced by the establishment. Although accounting both for secondary products and miscellaneous receipts of an establishment poses measurement and other problems, this production measure is used in statistical series more frequently than the less difficult to determine product value of shipments (defined below) [234, p. 20].

Product Value of Shipments. A particular, say four-digit, SIC value-of-shipments figure for a product group will differ from the value-of-shipments figure for an industry, although both will be given in the census. The product-group value includes all output of a given product, regardless of which establishment produced it; thus, secondary outputs pose no difficulties. Miscellaneous receipts of an establishment are not included, because the product-group value is obtained by summing only the values of individual products shipped.

Establishment Output. For the MRIO accounts, *establishment output* is the term applied to the initial outputs assembled at Jack Faucett Associates, Inc. (JFA) for all the input-output industries, most of which (52 out of 79) were obtained directly from manufacturing value-of-shipments establishment data adjusted for inventory change; hence the term *establishment output.* This output value is distinguished from that of commodity output (defined later), in that the output value will represent the sum of the value of all outputs produced by an establishment or activity, regardless of the SIC product group to which the good belongs. Radios produced by the car industry, for example, are counted as establishment output of the car industry, not the radio industry, and drugs produced by the chemical industry are counted as output of the chemical industry rather than the drug industry, according to this definition of output.

The total output of the industry represents the production of all primary and secondary output of the establishment classified in an input-output industry in a given year. The value of output includes manufacturers' excise taxes, receipts for services provided to foreigners, rents and royalties received, and receipts for research and development performed by auxiliaries and central administrative offices.

Gross Regional Output. The sum of each column in a regional input-output table is called *gross regional output.* It is comparable with gross output in the national input-output tables. Special note should be made that it represents output sales from a given region to all intermediate and final consumers and should not be confused with the term *gross regional product,* which represents output sales in a given region only to final consumers.

Gross regional output in the MRIO accounts is obtained by adding the values of transferred imports, regional transfers-in (secondary products), and inventory depletions to each corresponding state establishment output figure. Directly allocated imports are assumed to be part of the establishment output figure; thus, only transferred imports need to be added here. The row of figures of transfers-in must be added to create a balanced national table. Inventory depletions are added to the corresponding output figures in the state of production on the assumption that inventories impose a demand for transportation in the current year, rather than the year in which they were produced. (All inventories are assumed to remain with the producer until used, rather than at an intermediate warehouse or in storage at the location of the purchaser.) Because only scanty data are available on interregional shipments of scrap, it is treated differently from the national accounts as a completely exogenous component of the MRIO production and transportation framework. Scrap purchases are added to and scrap production subtracted from the gross regional output figure for each industry.

Commodity Output. *Commodity output* is a term used in the MRIO accounts to define the value of output of a particular good, such as grains or livestock, shipped in a given year, regardless of the year in which it was produced. It can be obtained in the MRIO accounts indirectly by subtracting the respective secondary transfers-out of the industry from the gross regional output figure, which includes both the primary and secondary outputs of establishments. These figures are used as regional production control totals for the MRIO interregional shipments data.

Census Value Added. Value added as defined by the Census is a gross concept of value added, but a net concept of production. The total cost of materials (materials, supplies, fuels, electric energy, and cost of resales and the cost of miscellaneous receipts) is subtracted from value of shipments (including resales) and other receipts. The net changes in finished products and work-in-process inventories between the beginning and the end of the year are then subtracted from the resulting difference. According to the Census, it is "the best value measure now available for comparing the relative economic importance of manufacturing among industries and geographic areas" [234, p. 22]. This conclusion is reached because in comparison with the Census value-of-shipments figure, output values for establishments shipping materials and components are combined with values for those shipping finished products, thus accounting for the value of the material at least twice. The Census avoids this duplication in its value added measure.

BEA Value Added. The term *value added* is used by the BEA interchangeably with the term *gross product originating.* It can be obtained from the Census value added by subtracting the purchases of services (telephones, business services, and so on).

Gross Product Originating. Another term for BEA value added, just defined, is *gross product originating.* It is used mainly in some of the unpublished work-sheets and computer runs of the BEA.

Income Originating. The term *income originating* is a BEA concept that represents the "sum of factor costs incurred by an industry in production" [234, p. 22]. According to the Census, it is a more net concept of value added than Census value added, because it excludes

> depreciation charges, state and local taxes (other than corporate income taxes), allowance for bad debts, and purchases of services from nonmanufacturing enterprises, such as contract costs involved in maintenance and repair, services of development and research firms, services of engineering and management consultants, advertising, telephone and telegraph expense, insurance, royalties, patent fees, etc. [234, p. 23]

Because the Department of Commerce data are obtained from company—rather than establishment—data, the net value added of manufacturing establishments of nonmanufacturing companies is excluded, while the net value added of nonmanufacturing establishments of manufacturing companies is included. For some industries, especially the Petroleum and Coal Products major industry group, the income originating figure, although a net figure, exceeded the gross value added figure of the Census because of these difficulties in exclusions and inclusions.

Of the nine terms, gross regional output, commodity output, and establishment output were specifically defined and used as consistency checks for the

MRIO model. The establishment output measures constructed at JFA form the base for each of the other two measures. They were assembled from Census industry value-of-shipments data for 52 of the 79 input-output industries and from activity-based and commodity-based outputs for the remaining 27 industries.

Uses of Production and Other Measures

The nine production measures just defined are referred to frequently in the literature. In the present study, however, only a few of them were used, sometimes in combination with payroll and employment measures. The most significant uses of these data for the MRIO model, other than in their normal role as part of the MRIO accounting framework, were as follows:

1. When data were unavailable for certain components of the regional accounts, the 1963 regional establishment outputs or the 1963 regional employment or payroll data were used as allocation factors for the national totals. This was necessary, for example, for detailed subcomponents of final demands, technology inputs, and trade flows—refer to chapters 4, 5, and 6, respectively. (The 1947 and 1958 regional establishment outputs were used to distribute some detailed subcomponents of the respective 1947 and 1958 final demands.)

2. The 1963 regional establishment outputs were used for the distribution of some or all components of the following miscellaneous accounting components: regional transfers-out, scrap purchases, scrap production, transferred imports, directly allocated imports, and inventory depletions (refer to chapter 5).

3. The 1963 regional establishment outputs were combined with national input coefficients to obtain first-round estimates of 1963 regional intermediate consumption, which were then used as commodity consumption controls for the initial estimates of 1963 interregional trade flows. Row sums from the 1963 regional input-output tables were used as control totals in the second-round estimates, but these data had not yet been assembled when the first-round estimates were being prepared (refer to chapter 2).

4. The 1963 gross regional outputs, adjusted for consistency with the national input-output totals, were used as control totals for the column sums of each regional input-output table (refer to chapters 2 and 5).

5. The 1963 regional commodity outputs (production outputs minus transfers-out) were used as control totals for the interregional shipments flows (refer to chapter 2).

6. Detailed 3-digit and 4-digit SIC 1963 regional value-of-shipments (essentially, establishment outputs) estimates were used as weights with 1963 manufacturing and service industry national technologies to estimate 1963 regional technologies (refer to chapter 5).

7. The 1947, 1958, and 1963 regional establishment outputs were used to obtain regression coefficients for a rough estimation of 1970 and 1980 regional outputs. These output estimates were then used in conjunction with other data to determine 1970 and 1980 regional plant and equipment investment and net investment in inventories, as well as the 1980 projections of federal government purchases. The 1970 and 1980 regional output projections from the MRIO model were not available when these final demand projections were made (refer to chapter 7).

8. The 1963 gross regional outputs, adjusted from an establishment to an industry basis, were used to check the consistency of the 1963 data, the accuracy of the MRIO computer program, and the accuracy of the MRIO model in predicting 1963 outputs (refer to chapter 3 and to a report by Fencl and Ng [51]).

9. The 1947 and 1958 regional establishment outputs, adjusted to a regional production output basis [51, p. 19] were used as checks on 1947 and 1958 calculations to determine the sensitivity and accuracy of the MRIO model in predicting regional outputs for the two years (refer to chapter 3).

Establishment output data were used for most of the purposes outlined above. Because of their general usefulness, these data have been made available as information separate from the rest of the MRIO accounts both in printed form [182, pp. 474-509] and on computer tapes [176]. They are believed to be far more accurate than any of the other production measures used in this study, such as commodity outputs, the values of which are obtained by adding (or subtracting) rough estimates of other regional accounting data to (or from) the establishment outputs. In fact, almost all other production measures start with the establishment outputs as a base, and adjustments are made to them to obtain the new production measures. In the case of gross regional outputs, establishment outputs were adjusted to account for regional imports, scrap production, scrap purchases, secondary transfers-in, and net inventory change. All of these represent very rough estimates, and some of the entries had to be estimated using the regional establishment outputs as distribution factors, which may affect their total value. In the case of commodity outputs, they represent gross regional outputs minus secondary transfers-out. Their value may be affected by the rough estimates made of regional transfers-out, which, for lack of better information, were made by distributing national transfers-out to regions, using the regional establishment outputs as distribution factors. Because these establishment outputs had to be used throughout almost all the remaining estimation procedures to a greater or lesser extent, making it imperative that they be as accurate as possible, a considerable amount of time and money was spent on their estimation.

In the next section of this chapter, details are provided on the history of the output, employment, payroll, and final demand data assembly and on the data sources and estimation procedures employed.

Data-Assembly History, Data Sources, and Estimation Procedures

The accuracy of the results obtained from implementing the MRIO model is dependent upon the assumptions made, upon the procedures employed to assemble the regional data, and, of course, upon the accuracy of the data used. One of the primary objectives in constructing the MRIO accounts was to maintain as much comparability as possible among the estimates for 1947, 1958, and 1963. To achieve this objective, major adjustments had to be made to the 1947 data, because a completely revised classification of industrial establishments was published in the 1957 Census Manual [287]. Therefore, in estimating 1947 outputs, employment, payrolls, and final demands, 4-digit 1947 Census codes were split, where necessary, among 3-digit 1957 SIC codes, using conversion ratios developed at the Harvard Economic Research Project (HERP) [212]. The reclassified items were aggregated to 3-digit 1957 SIC codes and then to input-output industry totals.

Because of their importance, the major data sources and estimation procedures used to determine the state output, employment, payroll, and final demand estimates for 1947, 1958, and 1963 are summarized in this section. Considerably more detail is provided in *State Estimates of Outputs, Employment, and Payrolls, 1947, 1958, 1963* [191] and *State Estimates of the Gross National Product, 1947, 1958, 1963* [181]. The actual state estimates of the various data for the three years are given in the appendices to the two volumes.

The construction of output, employment, payroll, and final demand estimates was completed in several phases, depending upon the particular data component, with modifications being made if new data became available or if discrepancies were discovered in the original estimates as these data were incorporated into the total MRIO accounting framework. A detailed explanation of the first round of estimation will be given only in the case of personal consumption expenditures, where it is important for an understanding of the accuracy of the final estimates. As indicated previously, all the MRIO data were assembled in terms of the 79-industry classification given in the appendix, table A-1.

State Establishment Outputs

State establishment outputs were intitially estimated for 1947, 1958, and 1963 by the JFA staff for the 79-industry classification only, which represented 2-digit and 3-digit SIC industries. As the work proceeded and needs arose for more detailed sets of estimates, 3-digit and 4-digit estimates were prepared by members of the JFA staff for 152 manufacturing and service industries. During the first phase of estimation, the detailed 152-industry value-of-shipments state data were aggregated to the 79-industry level before reconciling the aggregated figures with the Office of Business Economics (OBE) national data. In the second phase, the reconcilation was made at the 3-digit and 4-digit SIC level, using the respective national 1947, 1958, or 1963 outputs as control totals; the reconciled state data were then aggregated to the 79-industry level. In addition to this new reconciliation process, review of the initial estimates, comparison of the initial estimates with the set of 1963 national OBE output data that had recently been published, and comparison of the initial state output estimates for all three years with the corresponding state employment and payroll estimates revealed some major discrepancies in the estimates. Adjustments were made by the JFA staff during 1969–1970 to the original estimates to correct for discrepancies and by members of the HERP staff late in 1970 to make the state 1947, 1958, and 1963 establishment output estimates consistent with the national input-output data for each of the three respective years.[2]

The value of output of an industry includes both the primary and secondary products of each establishment shipped during a given year. The state establishment outputs were assembled from value-of-shipments data for 3-digit and selected 4-digit manufacturing and mining industries and for certain service industries. For the remainder of the nonmanufacturing industries, the state data were assembled from value-of-production or establishment-receipts data, or, in certain cases, approximated using allocation factors, such as state employment or payrolls. Although value of shipments constitutes the major portion of value of production, as defined for an input-output industry, some minor items, such as work-in-process and finished-goods inventory changes, excise taxes, and rents and royalties, are excluded. The full definition of establishment outputs was provided earlier in the chapter, but it should be especially noted that the value of secondary products is not double-counted in the establishment output measure while it is in the gross regional output measure.

The 1947, 1958, and 1963 establishment output estimates prepared for the MRIO accounts were revised from four previous studies that had been made by members of the staff at JFA and published in 1967 and 1968. The four studies were: (1) detailed 1947 and 1958 output data by transporation mode, prepared for the Office of Transportation, U.S. Department of Transportation [40]; (2) detailed county, standard metropolitan statistical area, and state 1963 manufacturing industry value-of-shipments estimates, prepared for the Office of Civil Defense [44]; (3) detailed 1963 standard metropolitan statistical area and nonmetropolitan state area estimates of output measures by input-output industry, prepared for the Institute of Defense Analyses [46]; and (4) 1963 estimates of mineral outputs, prepared for the Bureau of Mines, U.S. Department of the Interior [49].

The different data sources and estimation procedures used to construct outputs for the nonmanufacturing and manufacturing industries will be summarized here. A more detailed account of the data sources and estimation procedures is given in *State Estimates of Outputs, Employment, and Payrolls, 1947, 1958, 1963* [191].

Nonmanufacturing Outputs. Various data sources and estimation procedures were used to estimate the 1947, 1958, and 1963 outputs for the nonmanufacturing industries. The general procedure was as follows: (1) The major components of industry output, using the national output data and documentation for each of the three years, were determined in value and percentage terms. (2) State sources for the major components were found. (3) If state data were not available, suitable allocation factors to distribute the national values to the states were determined. (4) The state data were tabulated. (5) The national values—for each component, where possible—were distributed to the states using the tabulated state data as distribution factors. (6) The state values for the individual components were summed, state by state, to obtain a total industry figure for each state. (7) Any residual output for unspecified components was distributed using these total state figures for the industry as allocation factors. This residual portion represented either minor errors in estimating the components of output or portions of output not specified in the input-output industry description [267].

To determine the major components of output of each industry, the definition of output used in the national input-output table was obtained for each component from the OBE publication "Industry Description Appendix I to Input-Output Study, 1958" [267, pp. 2-26]. The same definitions used for the 1958 table [278] applied to the 1963 table [269], as well as to the revised 1947 table [268]. Additional information on components of output was obtained from the detailed 1963 transactions table [270]. The value and percentage composition of the components of output for each industry were determined at the national level, using the detailed 1963 transactions table and other available information.

The adjustment of state values to the national input-output totals was necessary even in cases where state sources for the specific component were available on a basis comparable with the national source because of discrepancies between the sums of the tabulated state data and the national values obtained from the OBE. Although this adjustment was originally made at the 79-industry level, the final output estimates, published in appendix D to the fourth volume of this series [182, pp. 474–509], were adjusted using the individual 3-digit and 4-digit SIC industries that comprised each of the 79 industries, rather than the less-detailed information.

In chapters 3 through 6 of the second volume of this series, the major data source(s) and estimation procedure(s) used for each nonmanufacturing industry are given in detail [191].

Manufacturing Outputs. Manufacturing outputs are specified on an establishment, rather than a commodity, basis and are tabulated from the industry value of shipments tables in the *Census of Manufactures, 1947* [232], *1958* [233], and *1963* [234], supplemented with data from special Census tabulations [37]. The general procedure used was analogous to that used for the nonmanufacturing outputs, with two major differences. All data were available from the major sources cited above, and when state data were not available, one specific procedure was used in each year to obtain the missing values.

In each year, some data were withheld by the Census to prevent disclosure of individual establishment outputs for a state. For 1947, the undisclosed data were estimated by using as allocation factors the number and employment of state 4-digit SIC establishments, determined from footnotes in the *Census of Manufactures, 1947* [232]. For 1958 and 1963, the Census excluded even this information from the publications. The nondisclosed data were approximated using average shipments per employee, combined with state industry employment estimates. These estimates were obtained as an average of state industry employment calculated from frequency distributions of plants, stratified by employment-size class, obtained from *Location of Manufacturing Plants, 1958* [247] and *1963* [248], and 1963 state industry employment data, obtained from *County Business Patterns, 1959* [242] and *1964* [243]. An average was used, because a previous analysis had shown that data estimated from the average of the two were more accurate than data obtained from either individually [191].

After the 1947, 1958, and 1963 state establishment outputs for each of the 79 industries had been assembled, the 1963 outputs were adjusted to a gross regional output base for use in the MRIO accounts.

Estimation of State Employment and Payrolls

State employment and payroll data were estimated at JFA for 1947, 1958, and 1963 for 81 input-output industries. The industries comprised the 79 endogenous industries, as well as the household and government industries (the latter two representing either employment of or wage payments to household workers and government employees, respectively). As the output, employment, and payroll data for each industry in each state were reviewed and compared, the original estimates were adjusted by the JFA staff to correct for discrepancies before final reconciliations were made by the MRIO staff. It should be noted that time did not permit incorporation of the payroll estimates into the regional input-output tables as a separate row nor a reconciliation of the payroll and value added estimates for corresponding states and industries. A comparison of the two estimates was made as part of the general evaluation of the MRIO data by members of the OBE staff. That comparison is discussed in their evaluation report of the preliminary set of MRIO estimates distributed in 1970 [259, pp. 114–128].

Employment and payrolls were tabulated on an establishment basis, with the employment estimates being adjusted to include self-employed workers. There are many data sources for employment and payrolls, but to maintain comparability with other data assembled for this project, the same data source used to estimate outputs for a given year was used for the employment and payroll estimates whenever possible. When this was not possible, an alternative source was used. As a rule, this was *County Business Patterns, 1959* [242] or *1964* [243], which contain Social Security Administration data published by the Census.

The number of employees and the number of self-employed individuals were combined to obtain the total number of employees in each industry, with full-time and part-time employees being given equal weight in the tabulations. When the County Business Patterns publication was used, first-quarter employment statistics were adjusted to remove seasonal variations. This was done by calculating the ratio of employment reported in the National Income and Product Accounts (NIPA) to the national value of first-quarter employment. State first-quarter employment data were then multiplied by this ratio to estimate state annual employment. For the construction, transportation, finance, and real estate industries, the employment first-quarter data were altered using state correction factors developed from OBE Regional Economics Division state wage data. The self-employment estimates were made by calculating the national ratio of self-employed persons to total employees and using this ratio to scale individual state estimates of employment by industry to obtain state self-employment by industry.

To establish estimates for the cost of labor, industrial payroll data were used. Because wages and salaries of the self-employed cannot be distinguished from other components of their incomes, such as interest, dividends, and profits, no payroll estimates were included for these persons. First-quarter payrolls reported in the County Business Patterns publication were adjusted to an annual level by calculating the ratio of payrolls reported in the NIPA to the national value of first-quarter payrolls. State first-quarter payrolls were then multiplied by this ratio to estimate state annual payrolls.

The specific sources used for each year and each input-output industry are given in tables 7-3 and 7-2 in the second volume of this series for employment and payrolls, respectively [191, pp. 108–110]. As shown in the tables, a number of major data sources and estimation procedures had to be used for the nonmanufacturing estimates, while only one major data source was used for the manufacturing estimates.

Nonmanufacturing Employment and Payrolls. Employment and payrolls were tabulated from many major data sources, as shown in the tables referenced above. When none of the usual sources contained the appropriate data for nonmanufacturing industries, the 1958 and 1963 data were estimated from *County Business Patterns, 1959* [242] and *1964* [243], respectively. These data were used for a number of the service industries. To use the data in this way, the first-quarter payroll data were expanded to an annual value by multiplying state statistics by the national ratio of NIPA annual wage and salary statistics to the first-quarter payrolls. The employment statistics were adjusted to remove seasonal variations, either by using state correction factors calculated from OBE Regional Economic Division state wage and salary data or by using national coefficients from the NIPA statistics.

For other estimates, ratios were used. National employment-to-output and payroll-to-output ratios had to be used to estimate 1947, 1958, and 1963 regional employment and payrolls, respectively, for IO-3, Forestry & fishery products, and IO-4, Agricultural, forestry, fishery services. State employment-to-output and payroll-to-output ratios for 1958 had to be used to estimate 1947 employment and payrolls, respectively, for all mining industries except IO-7, Coal mining, and for four of the service industries. The estimates were then reconciled to NIPA totals.

Manufacturing Employment and Payrolls. The *Census of Manufactures, 1947* [232], *1958* [233], and *1963* [234] were the principal sources used for the 1947, 1958, and 1963 manufacturing employment and payroll data.

For 1947, the estimates were tabulated for 3-digit and 4-digit SIC industries, aggregated to the MRIO industry classification, and then transformed from the 1947 Census coding scheme to a 1957 Census coding scheme, using the HERP industrial conversion percentages [212]. The data were then adjusted to add to the national 1947 totals.

For 1958 and 1963, data were tabulated for 3-digit and selected 4-digit SIC industries, aggregated to the MRIO industry classification, and then adjusted to add to the national totals for the two respective years.

The manufacturing data were supplemented with estimates made for withheld data, self-employed persons, and central administrative offices. No effort was made to obtain information for industry splits, imputed data, or suboffices of central administrative offices. The lack of adjustment for the last three factors is believed not to have caused any serious errors or biases in the estimates. A detailed description of all data sources and estimation procedures used is provided in *State Estimates of Outputs, Employment, and Payrolls, 1947, 1958, 1963* [191].

The estimation of state final demands is summarized in the next section of this chapter.

State Final Demands

During 1966–1970, estimates of gross regional product (regional final demand) were made at HERP for each of the six major components: personal consumption expenditures, gross private fixed capital formation, net inventory change, net foreign exports, state and local government purchases, and federal government purchases. The first round of estimates was completed by 1968; second-, third-, and fourth-round revisions were completed during 1969–1970. The history of the research, data sources, and estimation procedures for each of the major final demand components will be discussed separately.

Each of the six major components of the gross regional product was assembled using different data sources and different estimation procedures. For each component, data were assembled for 87 industries in each of 51 regions for 1947, 1958, and 1963, the three years for which comparable national input-output tables were available from the OBE. These state final demand estimates, combined with the 1970 and 1980 state projections of final demand, provide comparable state gross regional product estimates for five years in all. For final demands in all years, the MRIO data were assembled and published for 87 industries, rather than 79, to maintain comparability with the national data. The OBE national input-output industries 80 through 87 are not directly comparable with the MRIO industries 80 through 87; therefore, the assembled state data were rearranged before using them in the MRIO accounts.

A summary of the major data sources and estimation procedures used to construct the base-year data is provided here; more detail is given in *State Estimates of the Gross National Product, 1947, 1958, 1963* [181]. Each section is preceded by a brief historical sketch of the various sets of estimates.

Personal Consumption Expenditures. When work on the personal consumption expenditures (PCE) was begun at HERP in 1966, only the 1960–1961 Bureau of Labor Statistics consumer expenditures survey (CES) data in aggregated form (22 major consumer categories) were available. A general methodology and transformation matrices developed by H. Albert Green of the U.S. Department of Agriculture were used to construct an initial set of PCE estimates for the MRIO accounts [64]. When more detailed 126-category CES data became available late in 1967, a new procedure was devised for making the state estimates, using the 126 CES average consumption data and original state population estimates. During 1968–1969, these estimates were reviewed. It was found that there were some substantial omissions in the CES coverage, and these were corrected. In addition, a method developed by Ono of the Census to convert population enumeration by income groups from a before-tax to an after-tax basis [167] had been modified by the JFA staff for making the 1970 and 1980 projections of the personal consumption expenditures. This method, described in Scheppach [198, pp. 12–14] and Polenske et al. [181, pp. 22–30], was used to obtain new 1947, 1958, and 1963 state estimates of population by after-tax income distribution group and by family type and place of residence. These estimates were then used to weight the revised 126-category CES data.

Thus, in all, three major rounds of estimates were made of personal consumption expenditures.[3] For the first round, the 22 CES consumption category data were weighted by an initial set of state population estimates. For the second round, the 126 CES consumption expenditures categories were used with the unmodified population estimates of the first round. For the third round, an adjusted set of 126 CES consumption expenditures was used with revised state population estimates.

As just explained, three major sets of state consumption estimates were made, each representing an improvement over the preceding one. The first set was estimated using the 22-commodity CES average consumption expenditures data, weighted by an initial set of state population figures. The basic procedure and two of the ratio (transformation) matrices were adapted from those developed by H. Albert Green for consumption estimates for a ten-county area in North Carolina [64].

The procedure was as follows: The 22-commodity CES average consumption data for each of four regions were aggregated from 60 to 32 groupings of consumers to make the groupings identical with state population data available from the Census [181, p. 35]. The 22 CES commodity categories were first converted into the corresponding 65 National Income Personal Consumption Expenditures (NIPCE) categories, using a modification of a ratio matrix developed by Green. The NIPCE categories were then converted to an input-output grouping, by means of modification of a second ratio matrix developed by Green. These adjusted average consumption data were multiplied by state population estimates to obtain total rather than average expenditures, and the state estimates of total consumption were transformed from purchaser to producer prices. The major problem with the estimates first obtained compared with the revised estimates explained later was the need to begin with only 22 consumption categories, rather than 126, and the use of an unrefined set of population estimates. The use of the 22 categories did not provide adequate differentiation of consumption expenditures for the 79 input-output industries but was required because of the unavailability of the 126-category data that were published later. An improved methodology for estimating state population was also developed after the first round of estimates had been completed.

For the second set of estimates, the 126-commodity CES average consumption expenditures data were used with the unmodified population estimates from the first round.

For the third set of estimates, major adjustments were made to the 126-

commodity CES average consumption data, which were then weighted with revised state population data to obtain state total consumption estimates for each input-output industry. The major data sources used to make these estimates are given in the first volume of this series [181, pp. 22-30].

The procedure was as follows: The average consumption expenditures classification for each of the 126 CES categories was aligned with the appropriate input-output industry number, using an aligment scheme specifically prepared for the MRIO accounts [181, pp. 173-211]. For each of four regions of the United States (Northeast, North Central, South, and West), the CES data were at the same time aggregated from 60 divisions to 32, yielding eight income distribution groups, for two places of residence (rural and urban), and two types of family (unrelated individuals and families of two or more persons). This aggregation was necessary to make the consumption data comparable with the population data with which they were to be weighted. The 1960–1961 CES data were used for the consumption estimates for all five years (1947, 1958, 1963, 1970, and 1980) because of the lack of comprehensive and detailed estimates for any other year.[4] In the 1960 survey, data were given for 379 items, many of which represented subclassifications of a specific expenditures category; thus, the 126 items used for this study represented a full coverage of all expenditures included in the survey.

Five special adjustments were then made to the 87 input-output consumption estimates for each state.

1. To represent purchases of domestic goods only (by subtracting imports from total consumer purchases), since no distinction was made in the CES between consumption items domestically produced and those imported.
2. To account for purchases out-of-the-home city, because the MRIO state final demand data had to be constructed to account for purchases where they were made, rather than where the consumer lived, which is the information recorded by the CES.
3. To account for incomplete CES data, especially for rural farm individuals in Region 1, Northeast, and Region 4, West, and for several income groups in the remaining data for which no average consumption data were recorded. In each case, the national average for the respective income group was used. A few adjustments were also made for what appeared to be unrealistic estimates resulting from the limited coverage of the survey.
4. To account for expenditures made by foreigners, which is recorded as a purchase from IO-85, Rest of the world industry, in the 1963 national input-output industrial classification.
5. To make imputations for four expenditures items: services furnished without payment by financial intermediaries; food consumed on farms; rental value of owner-occupied dwellings; and food, clothing, and housing in

kind. Separate estimation procedures were used for each of the imputations, as shown in table 2-13 of the first volume of this series [181, p. 45]. At the national level, the amount of imputations was $1.8 billion in 1947, $10.7 billion in 1958, and $19.6 billion in 1963, representing 1.1 percent, 3.7 percent, and 5.2 percent, respectively, of total personal consumption expenditures in each year. While the aggregate percentage is small, the percentage for the imputed space rental value of owner-occupied housing (including farms) and institutional buildings represented 74 percent of the total IO-71, Real estate & rentals, purchases in 1963.

The last two adjustments were made after the data had been transformed from purchaser to producer prices. National transporation, trade, and insurance margins for each of the three years were used for the conversion to producer prices [181, pp. 40–41]. All of the adjustments are explained in detail in the first volume of this series [181, pp. 34–46].

Because the CES population data were available only for regions of the United States, 1950 and 1960 state population data, obtained from table 66 of the *U.S. Census of Population, 1960* [238], were adjusted and used in the calculations. Three basic adjustments were made to the population data.

1. To make the Census of Population (CP) data compatible with the CES data, the CP data were adjusted from a before-tax to an after-tax base. The 1950 and 1960 CES population data [237; 238] were used to determine the relationship between the two classifications, because these data give an average after-tax income and an average before-tax income for each income group. The average for a region was used to determine the respective state CP adjustment for population within each income group in a particular region.
2. To distribute 1950 undistributed CP data, the residual number of families not included in any income distribution class was allocated in proportion to the number of families enumerated in the established income classes for the respective state and family type.
3. To determine 1963 population data for Alaska and Hawaii, the 1960 CP data for all income groups in the respective states were adjusted from before-tax to after-tax income groups, using proportions developed for Region 4, West, and were augmented to 1963 values, using the state rate of growth for the total population between 1960 and 1963 for each income group.

No adjustments could be made to account for other inconsistencies between the CES and the CP definitions of population, because the nature of the discrepancies could only be approximated. More details on the possible nature of these discrepancies are provided in the first volume of this series [181, pp. 29–31].

To make the consumption estimates, the basic assumption had to be made that the average consumption expenditures of families within an income group for specific consumer goods do not vary over time nor among states within a given region. All variations in consumption expenditures from year to year were therefore assumed to occur from changes in the number of families within the different income groups. The adjusted 1960–1961 average consumption expenditures figure for each of the 87 input-output industries for a particular income distribution group, place of residence, and type of family was then weighted by the respective modified 1947, 1958, or 1963 state population figure to obtain the respective 1947, 1958, or 1963 estimates of total consumption. The national input-output PCE totals for each industry in each year were then distributed using the state total consumption estimates for the corresponding industry as the allocation factors. All of the adjustments and calculations are explained in detail in the first volume of this series [181, ch. 1].

Gross Private Fixed Capital Formation. The state estimates for gross private fixed capital formation were developed using the national capital-flow matrix for each of the three years (1947, 1958, and 1963), combined with state plant and equipment expenditures data for the corresponding year. The initial equipment estimates were not altered and were used in subsequent rounds, but new estimates of construction were prepared. In the first phase, the construction estimates were obtained by taking total regional construction for six components only and developing the estimates of gross private capital purchases of construction, using a product-mix procedure explained in chapter 5. In the second phase, the new construction industry was separated into twenty-four components, and state output estimates prepared for the state technology research were used to obtain the final demand estimates for private and public construction. In the final phase, the state private construction output figures for 1947, 1958, and 1963 were adjusted to sum to the corresponding national values of gross private fixed capital formation.

Available state data on fixed capital formation are limited to figures on total expenditures by industry on plant and equipment. Therefore, to approximate the specific kinds of plant and equipment purchased on capital account by particular private industries in each state, it was necessary to combine data from national capital-flow matrices for 1947, 1958, and 1963 with state capital expenditures for the corresponding year. The basic assumption had to be made that the capital technology for each state is the same as the average capital technology for the nation, industry by industry.

The procedure for constructing the state vectors of gross private fixed capital formation was as follows: A national 1947 capital-flow matrix, estimated specifically for this study [181, pp. 62–65]; the national 1958 capital-flow matrix, published by the Bureau of Labor Statistics [284]; and a 1963 unpublished table, prepared by the staff at JFA [38], were adjusted by deleting row 11, representing new construction expenditures. Elements in each-column were then divided by the sum of the column to obtain a distribution of equipment expenditures for each industry. State capital equipment expenditures data, representing total capital equipment purchases by industry, were compiled from various publications of the Census, using the data sources and estimation procedures given in the first volume of this series [181, pp. 66–76]. When no state expenditures data were available for a given industry, national data were allocated to states, based upon the percentage distribution of state establishment outputs [182, pp. 474–509]. For each state, the 1947, 1958, or 1963 national capital-flow distributions were multiplied by the relevant state capital equipment expenditures total to approximate state capital-flow matrices for equipment. The element in the rows of these state matrices were summed to obtain a vector of gross private capital equipment formation for each state.

State construction data were originally estimated for six construction components, and the private construction component was inserted into row 11 of the corresponding state vector of gross private capital equipment formation. For the final MRIO accounts, however, the 24-subindustry output estimates compiled for the state construction technology estimates were used. The procedure for making those estimates is explained in the construction technologies section in chapter 5.

Finally, the OBE national gross private fixed capital formation data for each industry in each year were distributed using the state gross private fixed capital formation estimates for the corresponding industry as the allocation factors.

Net Inventory Change. For IO-1, Livestock & livestock products, and IO-2, Other agricultural products, state net inventory change figures for 1947, 1958, and 1963 were provided by the U.S. Department of Agriculture [255]. The national net inventory change data for all other industries were distributed in proportion to the state output of the respective industry. In later phases, the net inventory data for all industries except the first two were therefore adjusted each time new state output data were calculated.

To obtain net inventory change state figures for IO-1, Livestock & livestock products, and IO-2, Other agricultural products, actual state data were obtained directly from U.S. Department of Agriculture worksheets [255]. These data were used as allocation factors to distribute the national OBE totals for the two industries. For the remaining industries, percentage distributions of gross state establishment outputs were used to allocate the national totals for the respective industries [182, pp. 474–509]. These state estimates were therefore altered each time a new set of outputs was determined.

For 1963 only, the net inventory change figures were separated into gross additions and gross depletions for use in the MRIO accounts. This separation was made, for lack of better information, by taking the detailed 370-order OBE 1963 net inventory change data and placing all negative values into a gross depletion vector and all positive values into a gross addition vector. State estimates for both were obtained by aggregating the national 370-order data and distributing them to states, using the detailed state establishment outputs as distribution factors. The state data were then aggregated to the national input-output 87-industry level and converted to the MRIO 87-industry classification.

Net Foreign Exports. Net foreign exports comprises gross foreign exports minus gross foreign imports. In the first phase, gross foreign exports for 1947, 1958, and 1963 were available only on a place-of-production basis. By 1970, a new publication, *Highlights of U.S. Exports and Imports* [246], had become available. This publication provides very detailed 1963 gross export data by port of exit. Data for 1947 and 1958 are still available only on a place-of-production basis. The first set of gross export estimates, made in the summer of 1968, were for 1947, 1958, and 1963 gross exports by place of production only. It was supplemented by a second set, completed in the summer of 1970, for 1963 estimates by port of exit. Estimation methodologies for both sets of estimates are explained here.

Gross foreign imports is comprised of directly allocated imports and transferred imports. Because directly allocated imports were estimated as part of the technology input of each industry, the initial sets of estimates made in 1970 were redone with the second round of technology inputs made in 1972. The two rounds of directly allocated import estimates therefore vary to the extent that the state output weights varied (refer to chapter 5). In the first round of estimates for transferred imports, data were compiled for only 44 regions and for only primary and manufactured commodities. For the second round of estimates, completed in 1973, the transferred import data were compiled for 51 regions and for the 3 margin industries (IO-65, IO-69, and IO-70) in addition to the primary and manufacturing industries.

Foreign Exports by Place of Production. For all nonmanufacturing exports and for 1947 manufacturing exports, the national gross foreign export data were allocated to states according to the state establishment output data [182, pp. 474–509]. For the manufacturing exports, state estimates for all three years were made for exports by place of production using only 1958 and 1963 data. The data sources and estimation procedures are given in the first volume of this series [181, pp. 78–107]. The OBE gross foreign export totals for each industry in each year were then distributed using the state gross export estimates for the corresponding industry as the allocation factors.

Foreign Exports by Port of Exit. As mentioned above, gross foreign exports by port of exit could be assembled only for 1963. Estimates for the agriculture, mining, manufacturing, and scrap industries were calculated by combining 1967 commodity export data for customs regions with 1963 estimates of U.S. gross exports. The 1967 data were obtained from table E–5 of the Census publication *Highlights of U.S. Exports and Imports* [246]. Although data by port of exit were available for 1963 in the publication *Export Tabulations,*[5] they were far too detailed for use in this study, and limited research funds precluded the conversion from the product classification used there to the input-output classification used for the MRIO accounts. The conversion of the 1967 customs regions data into 1963 gross export data by state of exit was accomplished in three major steps: (1) conversion of the product classification to the 79-industry input-output classification; (2) conversion of the customs regions into states; and (3) adjustment from 1967 to 1963 estimates.

For the estimation for the construction and service industries, the state of exit was considered to be the state of production, so the state-of-production estimates were used with the following exceptions:

IO-13, Ordnance & accessories. It was assumed that all IO-13 exports left from ocean ports and that exports produced in states with ocean ports left from these ports; therefore, all exports from states without ocean ports were distributed to states having ocean ports in proportion to the estimated export production in the state.

IO-65, Transportation & warehousing. The estimates of exports by state of exit were used to calculate transportation margins (1963 national transportation margins were used for each state). The margin estimates were added to the original set of directly purchased estimates (from the state-of-production estimates) to obtain a state distribution of total transportation exports.

IO-69, Wholesale & retail trade. It was assumed that the exports of this industry consisted entirely of wholesale trade margins. The U.S. total was distributed to states based upon the total value of 1963 nonservice exports leaving each state.

Gross Imports–Directly Allocated. As noted in chapter 2, each element in the directly allocated import row represents a heterogeneous mix of products consisting of imported goods and services for which there are no domestic substitutes purchased by an industry. The state estimates for these imports were obtained by weighting the national import coefficient by the state outputs (refer to chapter 5). Given the method of estimation, the elements in this import row (row 80 of the MRIO accounts) represent a mix of imported products at the location of consumption, rather than at the port of entry.

Gross Imports–Transferred. Each element in the transferred import row of the MRIO accounts (row 81), on the other hand, represents a homogeneous group of products largely consisting of imported goods or services for which domestic substitutes exist. These imports were allocated to the port of entry, using data from the Census publication *Highlights of U.S. Exports and Imports* [246]. Special state estimates were made for IO-65, Transportation & warehousing; IO-68, Electric, gas, water, & sanitary services; IO-70, Finance & insurance; and IO-83, Scrap, used, & secondhand goods. The detailed description of those estimates is provided in the fourth volume of this series [182, pp. 32-34].

State and Local Government Purchases. The 1947, 1958, and 1963 state estimates made during the first phase for state and local government purchases were prepared in the summer of 1968. A review of these initial estimates in 1969 indicated two revisions that should be made: (1) the inclusion of the capital expenditures of state and local enterprises in the state and local government final demand estimates and (2) the incorporation of a revised set of state construction estimates. These and other minor revisions were made in the spring and summer of 1970.

The state and local government (SLG) final demand estimates include the purchases of state and local governments on both current and capital account for general governmental activities plus the capital account purchases of SLG enterprises. (All current account purchases of SLG enterprises are classified in IO-79.)

The state data were estimated on a functional basis to be consistent with the NIPA estimates [272]. The 1958 national functional distribution for the 15 functions was used for both 1947 and 1958 because no functional breakdown of 1947 SLG net purchases exists [275]. The 1963 detailed 370-order distribution for four functions was used for 1963 [270]. To obtain state estimates, it was assumed that the national composition of industrial purchases for a particular function remained constant from state to state, but that the functional mix varied from state to state and over time. Total state net purchases by function were used to weight the national functional coefficients.

State expenditures data by function were assembled from the *Compendium of State Government Finances in 1947* [240], *Census of Governments, 1957* [229, t. 31], and *1962* [230, t. 35] for 1947, 1958, and 1963, respectively. Because the 1947 sources provided only state, not local, government data, an estimated set of local government expenditures was obtained by linearly interpolating from the 1942 and 1957 local government figures, obtained from the *Census of Governments, 1942* [225; 226; 227; 228] and *1957* [229], respectively.

The NIPA calendar-year data were obtained as strict arithmetic averages for the straddling fiscal years, so the fiscal-year state data were merely forced to sum to the NIPA calendar-year national total for each function in the respective year. Special adjustments were made for assistance and subsidies, insurance trust, interest on debt, government enterprises, and state toll highways.

After the state functional expenditures data for each year had been tabulated from the census publications, they were used as follows:

Step 1. The special adjustments mentioned above were made to the data obtained from the Census publications.

Step 2. All fiscal-year expenditures data were adjusted to a calendar-year purchase concept by allocating the NIPA national functional totals, using the state data as distribution factors.

Step 3. Each element of the national functional input-output data was divided by the total to obtain percentage distributions.

Step 4. The industry-by-function national matrix was multiplied by the respective 1947, 1958, or 1963 total net purchases function-by-state matrix to obtain a total SLG net purchases industry-by-state matrix for each year.

Step 5. The OBE final demands for total SLG net purchases for each industry were distributed in proportion to the original entries in each row to obtain an industry-by-state matrix that was consistent with the national input-output totals.

This completed the estimation for the state and local government purchases.

Federal Government Purchases. The initial round of 1947, 1958, and 1963 estimates of federal government purchases was made in the summer of 1968. A review of these data in 1970 indicated that certain components, such as research and development and federal construction, should be treated in a different manner. A new set of estimates was therefore prepared, and an extensive modification of the methodology description was completed in the summer and fall of 1970.

Federal government purchases include general operations purchases made on current and capital account by all military and nonmilitary government agencies plus the capital account purchases of federal government enterprises. The military category includes the Department of Defense (DOD), the National Aeronautics and Space Administration (NASA), and the Atomic Energy Commission (AEC); the nonmilitary category includes data for all other federal agencies except the current account purchases of federal enterprises, which are classified in IO-78.

For 1958 and 1963, government purchases were divided into military and nonmilitary components, and separate state estimates were made wherever possible, while for 1947, because only total federal purchases were available, state estimates were made just for the total, not the two components, of federal purchases. The basic procedure was to adjust the federal government figures for the expenditures on research and development (R&D) and the purchases of the Commodity Credit Corporation (CCC); separate the national data into military and nonmilitary components; determine the basic composition of federal purchases for each component for each industry; and then find an appropriate state allocation factor. The special data sources and allocation factors used are given in the first volume of this series [181, pp. 131–163].

Only the 1947 and 1958 input-output tables had a separate research and development industry (IO-74). For the 1963 input-output table, the industry was eliminated (the number is still assigned to the industry, but all entries in the row and column are zero), and all federal purchases of R&D (representing

97 percent of total R&D) were combined with the appropriate industry purchase. Thus, to make the 1947 and 1958 data comparable with those for 1963, all R&D purchases were transferred from IO-74, Research and development, to the industry where the research was actually done. Purchases of R&D from the aircraft industry, for example, had to be reallocated from IO-74 to IO-60, Aircraft & parts. All 1947 [268] and 1958 [278] R&D figures, except those for IO-77, Medical, educational services, & nonprofit organizations, were distributed using state establishment outputs [182, pp. 474–509] as the allocation factors. For IO-77, the total was distributed using special state data obtained from the National Science Foundation [165].

The Commodity Credit Corporation expenses (costs of warehousing, transportation, and administration, plus losses incurred in the disposal of commodities) or gains on current account had to be subtracted from IO-78, Federal government enterprises, and added to the CCC inventory changes and donations already included in the federal government purchases data.

Additional details on the data sources and estimation procedures used are provided in the first volume of this series [181, pp. 131–163].

It should be noted that although each of the six components of final demand was estimated separately, the figures were combined into a total final demand column for implementation of the MRIO model. The state estimates for 1947, 1958, and 1963 for the six components are provided in appendix C of the first volume of this series [181, pp. 220–447].

Deflators

To conduct comparative analyses of the output, payroll, and final demand data for 1947, 1958, and 1963, all the data must be converted to constant dollars. Two types of deflators were constructed for this purpose: output and final demand. (The final demand deflators are used to deflate both the payroll and final demand data.) Because of time and budget limitations, only national deflators could be constructed. Thus, an assumption must be made that price changes in a given industry over time are uniform across all states.

Output Deflators. Four sets of output deflators were prepared: (1) 1947 deflators (1958 dollars), (2) 1947 deflators (1963 dollars), (3) 1958 deflators (1963 dollars), and (4) 1963 deflators (1958 dollars). For 1947, the 1947 (1958 dollars) deflators were computed as weighted averages of HERP 1947 deflators for 450 industries. The 1947 (1963 dollars) deflators were obtained as the product of the corresponding 1947 (1958 dollars) deflators and OBE 1958 (1963 dollars) deflators.

For 1958, the reciprocal of the 1963 (1958 dollars) OBE gross product originating (that is, total contribution of primary factors of production to industry output) deflators were used.

For 1963, the OBE deflators (1958 dollars) were used directly. Additional details on the construction of these deflators and the actual 80-order industry deflators for each of the four sets are provided in the second volume of this series [191, pp. 12-19].

Final Demand Deflators. Two sets of final demand deflators were specified: (1) 1947 (1958 dollars) for total final demand only and (2) 1958 (1963 dollars) for the six final demand components. The deflators for 1947 were obtained from the OBE, while those for 1958 were constructed by the JFA staff as part of the final demand projection project. Both sets are given in the third volume of this series [198, pp. 108-110].

Conclusion

As indicated throughout this chapter, considerable detail was maintained in estimating each of the four basic components of the MRIO accounts: outputs, employment, payrolls, and final demands. A comprehensive set of worksheets was used to provide the documentation summarized in this chapter. All the documentation is provided in more detail in previous volumes of this series; however, some of the original data estimates were altered after the original set of estimates had been established, the modifications being based upon inconsistencies that were found as the MRIO model was implemented for different studies. Additional time and money should now be allocated to improving the data and estimation procedures used in the construction of the four components of the state economic accounts discussed in this chapter.

Notes

1. In addition, some of the BEA 80-order output figures are estimated on a commodity basis (raw furs, standing timber, Christmas trees, tree seeds, and so on). Many are estimated on an activity basis (cotton ginning, fruit picking, forestry services, new construction, hotels, direct mail advertising, and so on); and at least two are estimated on a modified-activity basis (transportation and trade). Specific definitions of each input-output industry are provided in *State Estimates of Outputs, Employment, and Payrolls, 1947, 1958, 1963* [191, pp. 21-100].

2. Errors are present in the output data published in *State Estimates of Outputs, Employment, and Payrolls, 1947, 1958, 1963* [191, pp. 134-169]. Corrected output figures are published as appendix D in *State Estimates of Technology, 1963* [182, pp. 474-509].

3. In the MRIO reports provided to the Economic Development Adminis-

tration, the first round of estimates was referred to as Scheme I and the second round as Scheme II. The third round was published in *State Estimates of the Gross National Product, 1947, 1958, 1963* [181, pp. 220-255].

4. At the time of the study, the only other recent consumer survey data were for 1950, but those data were available for only about 40 items, rather than the 379 items given in the 1960-1961 survey, and farm consumer units were excluded from the 1950 survey.

5. U.S. Bureau of the Census, EA-663, EA-664, GPO, 1963.

5 Estimation of Regional Technologies

Technology is defined here in terms of the specific inputs required per unit of output, which is the definition used in input-output literature. The study of input structures at the regional level is concerned both with differences in technologies between regions and with changes in technologies over time within one region. For the multiregional input-output (MRIO) accounts, technology data were assembled for 79 industries and for 51 regions (50 states plus the District of Columbia). The industrial and regional classifications are given in the appendix, tables A-1 and A-2, respectively.

Previous important work on technology has been done at the national level. Wassily Leontief, for example, in his book *The Structure of American Economy, 1919–1939,* discusses difficulties in measuring changes in technology [122, pp. 106-136]. Using data from the 1939, 1947, 1958, and 1962 input-output tables, Anne P. Carter attempted such measurements as she conducted an extensive historical analysis of structural changes. Carter documented two important features of technological change. The first was that although changes in technology do occur in the United States, the infusion of new technologies occurs slowly for most industries, exceptions being aircraft, instruments, and coal mining during the period 1939 to 1962. The second was that a dominant feature of the change in input requirements has been the across-the-board decrease in labor inputs. Detailed results of her study are reported in the book *Structural Change in the American Economy* [16] and in articles in *The Review of Economics and Statistics* [15] and *Scientific American* [14]. Beatrice N. Vaccara has supplemented Carter's study by an analysis of variations that occurred between 1947 and 1958 [297]. An up-date of these two large-scale empirical studies should be made to determine whether the same national trends exist today.

National input coefficients are now routinely projected by the staff of the Interagency Growth Project at the Bureau of Labor Statistics (BLS), using methodologies similar to those developed for their projections to 1970 [290]. Projections are now available for 1975, 1980, and 1985 [291; 292]. Clopper Almon has been the leader in the development of operational dynamic national input-output models that include projected technical coefficients. In the book by Almon et al. entitled *1985: Interindustry Forecasts of the American Economy,* a discussion is provided of the forecasting of input coefficients [4, pp. 157-165].

While estimation of national technologies is now done on a routine basis for each major census year, regional technologies are usually available in a given year only for a few regions. Prior to the assembly of the MRIO technology data, most regional studies have been conducted either using national technical coefficients, or, at best, by adjusting the national data to approximate regional technologies, the assumption being that national and regional technologies are virtually the same. Any variations observed in regional technologies have usually been assumed to be a direct result of the level of industrial aggregation used for the analysis, and national coefficients have been altered (using what is called a product-mix method) to try to account for the differences that occur when the mix of industries varies from region to region. Miernyk provides a comprehensive discussion of the construction and use of regional input-output coefficients in an article entitled "Regional and Interregional Input-Output Models: A Reappraisal" [135]. As noted in chapter 3, the first attempt to alter national coefficients was made by Moore and Peterson in their study of the Utah economy, published in 1955 [147]. They adjusted the national input coefficients using information on the differences between Utah and the United States in production techniques, marketing distributions, and product mix. In a later regional study of the St. Louis economy by Hirsch, published in 1959, a survey was taken to obtain regional coefficients with officials in medium-size and large-size firms in the city being asked to provide data on input requirements [79]. The survey technique was also used for a number of the early regional input-output tables, including those for the state of Washington by Tiebout, as reported by Bourque et al. [12]; for the Colorado River Basin by Miernyk and Udis [134; 217]; and for the state of Virginia by Miernyk et al. [138]. Now, many regional (mainly state) input-output tables are being constructed based upon sample surveys, with national data being interspersed when local data are unavailable.

Miernyk, who is the most vocal advocate of survey-based studies, was involved early in his career in conducting three impressive studies: one for the Colorado River Basin [134], another for Boulder, Colorado [137], and the third for West Virginia [138]. For these studies, he has worked with regions that comprise parts of states, an entire city, and an entire state. He also has assisted many regional groups attempting to conduct their own surveys. Compared with the adjustment of national coefficients, the assembly of technology data from survey-based studies is very costly. It is not surprising, therefore, that ways are being sought to reduce the cost. These include short-cut methods that are being developed for conducting the surveys, such as the use of small-sample survey techniques [130; 197].

Attempts are also being made to improve the methods used to adjust the national input coefficients, to the point where surveys can be eliminated entirely. At least three separate studies have been made, for example, in which the regional input coefficients for the state of Washington were compared with a set of input coefficients obtained for the same state by adjusting the national coefficients. The results differed. Czamanski and Malizia [25] and Schaffer and Chu [197] found that the two sets of estimates had wide variations. On the other hand, Walderhaug made a third set of estimates, adjusting the national coefficients substantially. The adjustments were made using information on the national data that was available to him from his work at the Bureau of Economic Analysis (BEA). He found his estimates to be reasonably comparable with those constructed from the survey-based study [298]. Given the fact that few analysts have Walderhaug's experience in working on the national input-output data and that most analysts do not have such ready access to all the unpublished material of the BEA, the conclusion at the present time must be that regional coefficients obtained by adjusting national data will not be very accurate.

For the projection of regional coefficients, many techniques are used. Among these is one developed by Miernyk, which he refers to as the "best-practice" technique. According to him,

> The method is quite simple, provided appropriate data have been collected for the construction of the regional table. It consists of the selection of a subsample of "best-practice" establishments in each sector. The assumption is that these establishments are more technologically advanced than the average establishment in each sector, and that their input structures will represent those of average establishments at some future time. [138, p. 21]

Even with all the current developments in establishing less costly means of conducting surveys, the regional analyst must use secondary data sources when technology data are needed for regions on a consistent base for a given year. The technology data compiled for the 51 regions in the MRIO accounts provide a rich data base for beginning technology-change studies to determine the extent of variation in regional input structures.

For the MRIO accounts, industries were separated into two types: those for which it could be assumed that regional technologies varied considerably from region to region, mainly resource-based industries and the construction industry, and those for which it could be assumed that technologies varied from region to region only to the extent that the composition (product-mix) of the industry varied. Separate regional input data were found for the first set of industries, while the national input coefficients were weighted with regional outputs for the second set. Details on the data sources and estimation procedures used will be presented in the remainder of this chapter. The discussion is a summary of the material given in *State Estimates of Technology, 1963* [182], with supplemental information provided to indicate more clearly the relationship of the technology data estimates to the entire structure of the MRIO accounts.

History of the Technology Data Assembly

The technology data for the multiregional input-output accounts were assembled and reviewed in three phases, the first being the initial set of estimates prepared prior to December 1970, the second being a review and comparisons made during 1971, and the third being a series of methodology and data revisions made in 1971-1972.

Initial Data Assembly

The initial data assembly of technologies was based upon the detailed 370-order 1963 national input-output technologies that became available from the Office of Business Economics (OBE) late in 1969 [270]. All inputs were reconciled to be consistent with those data. The regional output data had already been revised once, and the revised estimates were used both as regional weights for the industrial product-mix calculation for the manufacturing and service industries and as regional distribution factors for the manufacturing and service industries when proxies were necessary to allocate inputs to regions. (Regional output, employment, or payroll distributions were used only when actual data were not available and the proxy was deemed to be a suitable allocation factor or when a more appropriate factor could not be found.)

Review of Technology Data Assembly

During 1971, two extensive reviews of all the assembled data and of the MRIO model were made simultaneously. One was made by members of the staff at the Harvard Economic Research Project (HERP), the other by members of the staff at the OBE. The latter review was made at the request of the Economic Development Administration, the Department of Commerce agency that provided the initial funds for the MRIO research. A report on the OBE review is available from the National Technical Information Service [259]. It should be noted, however, that a considerable number of the difficulties and errors mentioned in that report were overcome or corrected during the 1971-1972 revisions made at HERP.

Revision of Technology Data

Four revisions were made at HERP during 1971-1972 to the first set of technology estimates, because major inconsistencies had been discovered in the initial estimates of the outputs, secondary products, value added, and imports, these being some of the components of the MRIO accounts used in establishing the technology inputs. The MRIO model, in the meantime, had been set up and implemented at the Federal Preparedness Agency (FPA). The new technology estimates were therefore sent to the FPA for testing and double-checking before being incorporated into the MRIO model. With the exception of the import data revisions, the technology data revisions that were made when the interregional trade data were expanded from 44 to 51 regions would have had to be made even if the model had originally been implemented for 51, rather than 44, regions. All data, except the interregional trade-flow and import data, had been initially assembled for 51 regions, then aggregated to 44 regions to maintain comparability with the regional grouping required for the interregional trade data. (Additional details on the 44-region estimates are provided in chapter 6.)

The four major adjustments that were made to the 51-region, but not to the 44-region, technology data are:

1. The technologies were recalculated for the 152 manufacturing and service industries, using revised output estimates.
2. A new method for estimating secondary products was established, and the new estimates were made and incorporated into the technology tables.
3. The value added figure was adjusted to obtain a larger value for those industries for which the initial estimate was less than 5 percent of the respective state establishment output.
4. Imports were estimated for 51, rather than just 44, regions.

Additional details on all four adjustments are provided later in this chapter.

Technology Data Sources and Estimation Procedures

Different data sources and estimation procedures were used to compile the state technology estimates for each of four major sectors: agriculture, mining, construction, and manufacturing. The same data sources and estimation procedures were used for the manufacturing and service sectors. For the agriculture, mining, and construction sectors, two major assumptions were made. The first was that technologies differ from the national average for a given industry, which allows for region-to-region variations in input requirements. The second was that technical coefficients for industries in each sector are relatively more stable over time than over geographic area. The first assumption was dropped for the manufacturing and service sectors. For industries in these sectors, product-mix variations were considered far more likely to be the cause of variations in regional input requirements than were actual differences in industry technologies; therefore, national technology data were used for 152 manufacturing and service industries, rather than for the 69 such industries eventually retained in the 51 regional tables. For agriculture, specific state-to-state variations were determined for each of 17 agricultural subindustries, which were then aggregated, using a product-mix approach, to 2 main agricultural industries. For mining, 3 subindustries were maintained for petroleum and 21 subindustries for the 5 other mining industries, while for new construction, state inputs were estimated for 24 subindustries. For mining and construction, the state inputs for the subindustries were then aggregated, using the product-mix approach, to 6 mining industries and one new construction industry, respectively. In all, regional technology data were assembled for 217 subindustries, which were then aggregated to the 79 input-output industries used for this study.

Agricultural Technologies

The agricultural sector was disaggregated into 17 (or sometimes just 10) subindustries for the purposes of data assembly, and most inputs were assembled for each of these 17 or 10 subindustries. The 17 agricultural subindustries, listed in the appendix, table A-2, of the fourth volume [182, pp. 134-145] were used in a 1955 study by the Farm Income Branch of the Economic Research Service (ERS), U.S. Department of Agriculture (USDA) [257]. Some of the MRIO agricultural input data were assembled at this level of detail, then aggregated to the 10 agricultural subindustries identified in the detailed 1963 input-output study. Other data were assembled just for the 10 subindustries or for the 2 agricultural input-output industries. All data were finally aggregated to the 2 agricultural industries used in this study: IO-1, Livestock & livestock products, and IO-2, Other agricultural products. For the other 2 industries that belong to the agricultural sector (IO-3, Forestry & fishery products, and IO-4, Agricultural, forestry, & fishery services), inputs were estimated as part of the general estimation of service-industry inputs (described in a later section of this chapter).

Major Data Sources. For the state data, the major data source used was a set of unpublished worksheets providing 1963 state farm total production expenses for 47 different inputs. The worksheets were prepared by the Farm Income Branch of the ERS [257]. Although they provided detailed state data, only total farm production expenses were given and only purchased, domestically produced, inputs were covered. The state data that could be used directly with no further adjustments except to determine the industry producing the input and the agricultural subindustry consuming it were limited to the following four categories: Harness and saddlery, hired hauling of milk, cotton ginning, and sugar and sirup tolls. For the remaining 43 categories, the data had to be separated both by the industry producing the input and by the agricultural subindustry consuming it; the inputs had to be split; and, sometimes, other adjustments were also required. (A complete summary table with detailed comments on these adjustments is provided in *State Estimates of Technology, 1963* [182, pp. 54–81].) In addition, special estimates had to be made for nonpurchased inputs, for imports, and for transportation, trade, and insurance margins on all purchased inputs. To make the estimates, nine data sources were used. The data from these sources were used to make the state input estimates for the 2 agricultural input-output industries (IO-1 and IO-2), employing the procedures outlined in the next section.

Specific Estimation Procedure. Each of the 47 basic farm expenditures in the 1963 state estimates provided by the Farm Income Branch was separated into its component inputs, by both 79 producing industries and 17 or 10 agricultural consuming industries. (This procedure is represented in diagrammatic form in figure 2–2 in *State Estimates of Technology, 1963* [182, p. 51].) The step-by-step procedure used to obtain state inputs follows:

Step 1. A determination of the component inputs was made for each of the 47 state 1963 farm expenditures categories. The 1955 agricultural input-output study was used to determine the inputs. According to that study [257, p. 14], the category "Miscellaneous expenses of greenhouses and nurseries by state," for example, was composed of expenditures for coal (IO-7.00), cordage (IO-17.09), paperboard and paper (IO-25.00), burlap materials (IO-17.10), plastics materials (IO-32.04), clay pots (IO-36.09), commissions (IO-69.01), and advertising (IO-73.02).

Step 2. The consuming industry of each input was determined. In the example given above, all of the purchases except plastics materials were made by IO-2.07, Forest, greenhouse, & nursery products.

Step 3. The producing industry for the component inputs was determined. The numbers listed in parentheses after the expenditures categories in step 1 show the assigned producing industries for that example.

Step 4. The 1963 state figures for the 47 categories were separated into component input figures.

Step 5. Data so obtained for each of the 47 broad categories were summed to obtain a single number for each cell in the 79× 10 matrix of 1963 agricultural inputs.

Step 6. All data for the 17 consuming subindustries were aggregated to the 10 consuming subindustries.

Step 7. Data were converted from purchaser to producer values, using the detailed 1963 national unpublished transportation, trade, and insurance margins [277].

Step 8. All data for the 10 consuming subindustries were aggregated to the 2 respective input-output industries.

Step 9. Data on the 1963 national transferred (competitive) imports of agricultural commodities and the transportation, trade, and insurance margins on those imports (provided by the OBE for the 10 agricultural subindustries [265]) were allocated to states. The import data were then aggregated to the 2 respective input-output industries.

Step 10. The imputed values of nonpurchased inputs were estimated, for milk fed to calves, manure (nonpoultry) used for fertilizer, manure (poultry) used for fertilizer, animal work power, nonpurchased seed, and nonpurchased feed. These estimates were added to the purchased input data obtained in step 8.

Step 11. All state agricultural input data were reconciled with the respective OBE 79-industry estimates for the 2 agricultural industries by distributing the OBE national 1963 data to the states in proportion to the state estimates.

Step 12. The value added figure for each state for each of the 2 agricultural industries was checked to be certain it was 5 percent or more of total output.

Step 13. All the state inputs were again reconciled with the OBE 79-industry estimates.

The estimation of the margins (step 7), imports (step 9), and value added (step 12) is described in the last section of this chapter. A detailed table providing information on the producing industry, consuming industry, and special comments on all data sources and estimation procedures is available in *State Estimates of Technology, 1963* [182, pp. 54–81].

Mining Technologies

The mining sector consists of 6 input-output industries: IO-5, Iron & ferroalloy ores mining; IO-6, Nonferrous metal ores mining; IO-7, Coal mining; IO-8, Crude petroleum & natural gas; IO-9, Stone & clay mining & quarrying; and IO-10, Chemical & fertilizer mineral mining. For each mining industry except IO-8, a state input structure was estimated, using, in general, data from the *Census of Mineral Industries, 1963* (*CMI*) [236], combined with data from a report by Wang and Kokat [299] and national transportation and trade margins [277]. Data for IO-8 had to be estimated using a different procedure from that used for the other five mining industries; therefore, that estimation method will be explained first.

IO-8, Crude Petroleum and Natural Gas. A special estimation procedure for the state inputs on current account for IO-8, Crude petroleum & natural gas, was required for two reasons: (1) The nondisclosure rules of the Bureau of the Census (Census) resulted in the suppression in the *CMI* of any cost data for a single plant in a state. Because of the oligopolistic nature of the industry, considerable amounts of state data were therefore suppressed. (2) Purchases are made from only a few industries, with over four-fifths of the total purchases in 1963 representing payments for land rentals (IO-71, Real estate & rental) and imports and to factors of production (value added). Most major expenditures by the petroleum firms, such as those for well construction and drilling apparatus and other equipment, are made on capital account and therefore do not show up directly as part of the current account inputs from IO-1 through IO-79. Value added, of course, does include huge depreciation expenditures on plant and equipment.

For these two reasons, a product-mix calculation was made, using national input data and state output estimates for the three standard industrial classification (SIC) subindustries: SIC 1311, Crude petroleum (component); SIC 1311, Natural gas (component); and SIC 1321, Natural gas liquids. The national input coefficients, which were for 1958, were obtained from the Wang-Kokat report [299]. State 1963 establishment outputs, obtained from worksheets compiled by the JFA staff [42], were used to weight the 1958 national input coefficients. The corresponding elements of the resulting state input vectors for the three subindustries were then summed to obtain one input vector for each state. When data on fuels and purchased electricity were available directly from the *CMI* [236], those data were used to replace the original elements in the rows for IO-7, Coal mining; IO-31, Petroleum refining & related industries; and IO-68, Electric, gas, water, & sanitary services. The national 1963 transportation, trade, and insurance margins were used to obtain the state estimates for rows 65, 69, and 70, respectively, and the value added row was obtained as a residual. Both of these adjustments are described later in the chapter. These estimated 1963 state input vectors for IO-8 were used to allocate the respective 1963 OBE national input data for the industry.

Other Mining Industries. With the exception of the estimation of inputs for IO-8, the specific method used to determine the input structure for input-output mining industry j, composed of SIC industries x, y, and z, is illustrated in figure 3-1 in *State Estimates of Technology, 1963* [182, p. 93]. Data were estimated for seven different categories of inputs: (1) Materials inputs, (2) Fuels and purchased electric energy, (3) Intraindustry purchases, (4) Contract mining services, (5) Purchased services, (6) Transportation and trade, and (7) Value added. For the estimation of inputs for the first four categories, the unpublished JFA estimates of 3-digit and selected 4-digit SIC state mining outputs (for subcomponents of the 6 mining industries) were used as distribution factors. Estimates for the 9 census regions were nearly always given in the *CMI,* but sometimes the state data were suppressed. In such cases, the one or more state figures given in addition to the regional total were subtracted from the regional total and used without alteration; the remainder for the region was distributed to the states for which data had been suppressed in proportion to the relative value of their 1963 state establishment outputs.

The step-by-step procedure for estimating the seven different categories of inputs follows:

Step 1. Materials inputs were those purchased by a mining industry from the manufacturing sector, IO-13 through IO-64 (except IO-31, Petroleum refining & related industries) and IO-82, Office supplies. These inputs were tabulated from the *CMI* tables [236], using the information listed on the line "Supplies and purchases for resale," with appropriate use of the special JFA state establishment output estimates where necessary.

Step 2. Direct input coefficients from the Wang-Kokat report [299] were used to disaggregate the total state cost-of-supplies figures to the appropriate input-output industries. In their report, Wang and Kokat provide 1958 direct inputs that represent actual engineering estimates or process analyses for 48 detailed SIC subindustries of the 6 mining industries. (In 1968, when this data assembly was done, no detailed mining information existed for 1963.) To make these coefficients consistent with the *CMI* figures assembled in step 1, the Wang-Kokat data were converted from producer to purchaser values, using the 1958 national transportation and trade margins estimated from the Wang-Kokat data, and aggregated to 21 SIC industries. Then, it was assumed that each of the 21 SIC industries in each region had the same input structure for cost of supplies as the national structure for that industry. The appropriate input coefficients for the manufacturing sector (defined in step 1) inputs in purchaser prices were therefore added to obtain a total, and the coefficients were taken as a ratio to this sum. The state cost-of-supplies figures for the respective SIC subindustries were then distributed according to the resulting proportions. The result was a set of state estimates of materials inputs for each of 5 mining input-output industries in purchaser prices.

Step 3. The categories "Other fuels" and "Undistributed energy" were taken from the same *CMI* table [236] and were allocated to IO-31, Petroleum refining & related industries. They were distributed to states, using the JFA state establishment output distributions. Purchased electric energy was treated in the same way but was allocated to IO-68, Electric, gas, water, & sanitary services.

Step 4. The category "Purchased fuels" represents the combined purchases from IO-31 (petroleum and natural gas), IO-68 (only the gas subindustry), and IO-7 (coal). To obtain separate estimates for each of the three components, the regional totals for purchased fuels were therefore allocated to states, again using, where necessary, the JFA estimates of state establishment outputs [182, pp. 498-509]. Whenever individual fuels data were available by state, they were used to disaggregate the total figure. For a few SIC industries, the details were given in physical (tons, barrels, etc.), not dollar, units. In these cases, the purchased fuels category for each state was distributed, using the national distribution from the *CMI* of total fuel among the component types of fuel as weights for those SIC subindustries where this information was given [236, sec. 6, t. 3, pp. 8–13], and the regional physical quantity data were used to make further adjustments to the relevant state data. The coal estimates were allocated to IO-7, Coal mining; the fuel oil and gasoline estimates to IO-31, Petroleum refining & related industries; and the gas estimates to IO-68, Electric, gas, water, & sanitary services.

Step 5. Intraindustry purchases were estimated from the *CMI* categories "Minerals received for preparation," "Stone received for preparation," "Coal received for preparation," etc. These are the purchases by an industry of its own output for further cleaning, preparing, or processing. For regions where an intraindustry purchase was combined with the "Cost of supplies" figure, it had to be separated. This was done by (a) distributing the national figures for the "Cost of supplies" and ". . . received for preparation" categories to states, using state-to-national output ratios; (b) summing the state estimates of the figures for the two categories for the region where data were combined; (c) using the resulting two regional sums to separate the combined regional figure into two categories, and (d) allocating the regional figure for the two categories to the appropriate industry in the region, using the JFA state establishment output distributions [182, pp. 498–509]. The resulting state estimates were then allocated to the intraindustry cell of the appropriate SIC industry.

Step 6. Inputs from contract mining services were assigned to the intraindustry cell except for IO-5, where the inputs were assumed to come from IO-6; and IO-10, where they were assumed to come from IO-9. This industry-supply allocation was determined from information given in the Wang-Kokat report [299].

Step 7. The data estimated in steps 1 through 6 were converted from purchaser to producer values, using the national transportation, trade, and insurance margins obtained from the unpublished 1963 national OBE margin tables [277]. This procedure also obtained the inputs for rows 65, 69, and 70. This step is explained in more detail in the last section of this chapter.

Step 8. Inputs from all service industries except IO-68 were added to the other input estimates (steps 1 through 7) by allocating 1963 national OBE input data [269] to states, using the JFA state establishment output distributions [182, pp. 498–509]. It should be noted that no consistent sets of regional data could be found for the service inputs.

Step 9. The data for the relevant SIC industries were summed to obtain the total inputs of goods and services for each of the 5 input-output mining industries.

Step 10. Value added was estimated as a residual by subtracting the sum of the input estimates from the total state output for the corresponding industry, using the procedure described later in the chapter.

Step 11. Reconciliation with the national input-output estimates was the final step. For each input-output industry, the state input vectors were summed, and a state distribution of each input was used to allocate the national input to the states. This step was required to assure consistency between the regional and national input-output data.

Construction Technologies

The construction sector is comprised of 2 input-output industries: IO-11, New construction, and IO-12, Maintenance & repair construction. Adequate regional data were available for IO-11, but data for IO-12 were so fragmentary that no attempt was made to obtain actual state inputs. Instead, for that industry, detailed 1963 national OBE input coefficients [270] were weighted by JFA estimates of state establishment outputs [182, pp. 498–509] to obtain state input estimates, using the general estimation procedure for service-industry inputs, described later in this chapter. The remainder of this section will pertain only to the new construction industry.

General Description of Data Sources and Estimation Procedures. The new construction industry in 1963 represented 6 percent of total output, ranking fourth out of 79 industries and accounting for 57 percent of total gross private fixed capital formation (the remainder being for equipment purchases), or 11 percent of total final demand [269]. The need for regional input estimates is evident for reasons other than just its large proportion of total output. A brief review of the industry indicates that significant variations in inputs purchased by new construction firms will occur from state to state because of differences in demand by private users, industries, and government, as well as differences in the raw materials available (wood, brick, stone, concrete, etc.), with the resulting differences in inputs used to build such a wide variety of structures. These variations are undoubtedly intensified by the immobile, expensive, and long-lasting nature of the structures, the vast number of contractors and subcontractors operating in the industry, and the high weight content of inputs (which often necessitates use of locally available materials). All of these factors tend to hamper any attempts to standardize the production process for all regions of the country.

For one subindustry, state input data were available; for 6 subindustries, regional data were available; while national inputs had to be used for the remaining 17 subindustries. For all 24 subindustries, state input totals could be estimated, using state data specific to the subindustry as state allocation factors for the national subindustry totals. The resulting state, regional, or national input coefficient vectors were then weighted by the corresponding subindustry state establishment outputs to obtain state purchase vectors for each of the 24 subindustries. These estimates were made for each of the 87 input-output industries. The outputs and the distribution of the outputs among the 24 subindustries are given in table 4-2 in the fourth volume of this series [182,

p. 112]. The specific sources and procedures used to make the state estimates follow.

Specific Description of Data Sources and Estimation Procedures. Specific state input information was available for only one of the 24 new-construction subindustries. Regional data for 4 large multistate regions (Northeast, North Central, South, and West) were used for 6 of the subindustries, while the national input structure for the particular subindustry had to be used for the remaining 17. The specific input and output data used for each subcomponent are given in the fourth volume of this series [182, pp. 118-127]. The step-by-step procedure used to make the estimates with these data follows. (Also refer to figure 4-1 in the fourth volume of this series [182, p. 113].)

Step 1. For each of 51 regions, regional input coefficient data were assembled for the 24 subindustries, the qualifications for which are given in detail in the volume by Polenske et al. [182, pp. 118-127]. It should be noted that 1963 BLS technology data were used in the estimation procedure for 20 of the 24 subindustries. For the 4 others, the BLS survey pertained to a year other than 1963, and no other 1963 data seemed suitable.

Step 2. State output data were assembled for the 24 subindustries. As noted in the detailed discussion of these data in the volume by Polenske et al. [182, pp. 118-127], data other than those for 1963 were used for 11 of the 24 subindustries. For 8 of the 11, 1963 data were unavailable, while for the remaining 3, data from a prior or future year were assumed to be better proxies than 1963 data. This assumption was made, for example, for subindustry 6, Commercial construction, and subindustry 7, Private industrial building construction (component) because of a presumed one-year lag between the time contracts are awarded and the time construction is put in place. Contract-award data had to be used as a proxy for actual construction, because no data on actual construction were available.

Step 3. For each subindustry, the 1963 national OBE output total was allocated in proportion to the initial state output estimates to make the sum of those estimates consistent with the national data.

Step 4. Each column of input coefficients was multiplied by the appropriate state output. The result for each state was a set of 24 columns of construction inputs for the subindustries in that state.

Step 5. State input data for each subindustry were arranged into 24 matrices, each 87× 51, and adjusted to add to the national input flows for that subindustry. This was accomplished by taking percentage distributions of the original estimates in each of the 24 input matrices and allocating the national input flows to the data in the corresponding row of that matrix, on the assumption that discrepancies between the row sum of the state subindustry construction matrix and the national data occurred in the same direction in each state.

Step 6. The subindustry data were again rearranged into 51 matrices, each 87×24, and each row was summed to obtain total construction in the state. The estimation of the transportation, trade, and insurance margins, imports, and value added figures is explained in the last section of this chapter.

Manufacturing and Service Technologies

For the purpose of these calculations, the manufacturing sector is defined to include the 52 input-output manufacturing industries IO-13 through IO-64; and the service sector is defined to include the 14 typical service industries, IO-65 through IO-70 (excluding IO-74, Research & development, which is eliminated in the 1963 table), as well as 3 other industries, for which no state data could be found: IO-3, Forestry & fishery products; IO-4, Agricultural, forestry, & fishery services; and IO-12, Maintenance & repair construction. State input data were not assembled for industries in the manufacturing and service sector. For 6 of the 52 manufacturing industries and for 5 of the 17 service industries, the national input coefficients at the 80-order level were used directly, because no industry subcomponents were available even at the more detailed 370-industry level. The remaining 46 manufacturing industries and 12 service industries were separated into 100 and 41 subindustries, respectively, and a detailed product-mix procedure was used to estimate the state technology structures.

General Description of Data Sources and Estimation Procedures. The principal sources of data for these estimates were 152 of the input columns from the 370-order primary national OBE input-output flow table and 3-digit and 4-digit SIC JFA state establishment outputs. Both sets of data were published as tables C-10 and C-11, respectively, in the volume by Polenske et al. [182, pp. 272–305, 307–323]. The industrial mapping between the detailed 152 industries in the manufacturing and service sectors and the 69 industries used for the MRIO accounts is provided in table A-2, pages 134–145, of that volume.

If considerably more time and money had been available, state inputs could have been tabulated directly from census tapes for most of these industries. As it was, an assumption—not unreasonable—had to be made that input requirements per unit of output remain constant from state to state for each of the 152 detailed industries. The national direct primary input coefficient for the 152 manufacturing and service industries were then weighted by the corresponding state establishment outputs, and the industries within each state were aggregated to the 69 manufacturing and service industries used for this study.

Specific Description of Methodology. The step-by-step procedure used to obtain the variations in the state input coefficients is shown in figure 1-8 of the fourth volume of this series [182, p. 31]. Each of the vectors of direct input coefficients, a_{ij}^n, from the 370-order 1963 national primary input-output table was weighted by the amount of that output produced in a given state, x_j^h, to obtain vectors of state flows, x_{ij}^h, for each state h ($h = 1,2,\ldots,51$). The state flow vectors were then summed to the appropriate 69 manufacturing and service industries given in the OBE 80-order 1963 input-output table. When the 80-order flows for each state were divided by the respective 80-order state outputs, the input coefficients for each state, a_{ij}^h, were obtained. These differed from one another and from the national input coefficients because the mix of industries varies from state to state, and the variation in industry mix is taken into account by using the disaggregated state output weights with the detailed national input coefficients.

Final Adjustments to the Technology Inputs

So far, the data sources and estimation procedures for determining the technology inputs for the 79 industries have been explained mainly for rows 1 through 80 of each state input-output table. These estimates were placed in the appropriate state table, portrayed in figure 2-3, and the data for the remaining columns and rows (81 through 87) were calculated. Because the description of the content of each column and row is given in chapter 2, the calculations of the state estimates will only be summarized in this section, with emphasis on the methods of estimating the values for transferred imports, secondary products, and margins.

Transferred Imports

Data for directly allocated imports (row 80) had been estimated at the state level (51 regions) in the original set of MRIO accounts completed in 1970, but data for transferred imports (row 81) had been estimated only for 44 regions. The national transferred imports value for each industry was allocated to regions in proportion to the total regional consumption of the corresponding industry (in 1970, total regional consumption was available only for 44 regions). The 44-region transferred import estimates were allocated to the 51 regions, using the 1968 proportion of a customs region's share of the total import value of the region as an allocation factor. (Census import data for 1963 were not available.) For the regional allocations, the 1963 input-output transferred imports data were separated by production area and rest-of-state area, based upon data from JFA unpublished worksheets [48]. The 1968 customs region import data that were used as allocation factors were obtained from three tables in *Highlights of U.S. Exports and Imports:* Table I-1, "Customs District and Port of Unlading by Dry Cargo and Tanker Service" [246, pp. 13-16]; Table I-5, "General Imports and Imports for Consumption–U.S. Customs Regions and Districts: 1968 and 1967" [246, pp. 54-55]; and Table I-6, "General Imports–Selected Schedule A, Commodity Groupings and Commodities, by U.S. Customs Regions: 1968, Cumulative to Date" [246, pp. 56-57]. After the transferred imports for the 51 regions had been estimated, the values were placed into row 81 of each corresponding regional input-output table.

Secondary Products

It is not always clear whether an establishment or a product classification would be more appropriate as the unit of analysis for multiregional input-output tables. Ideally, the economic analyst should be able to manipulate the data from one classification to another as the need arises. Because the OBE (and until 1979 the BEA) used the establishment classification in compiling national input-output tables, that methodology will be summarized here. Full details are provided in the fourth volume of this series [182, pp. 13-30].[1]

An establishment is classified into an SIC category by the Census according to the product comprising the largest part of its output–this product being called its primary product. Sometimes an establishment produces one or more commodities in addition to its primary one–these being called secondary products of the establishment. The SIC categories are used to classify divisions, industries, and products in the economy. To determine the SIC code of an establishment, the values of shipments of all 7-digit products of an establishment are summed to the 4-digit level, and the establishment is assigned the industry code represented by the product with the largest 4-digit value of shipments.

Most of the data used to construct the 1963 national input-output table were obtained from various Census publications. To compile data for the manufacturing industries, for example, three of the eight basic tables given in the *Census of Manufactures, 1963* [234] were used. They are: (1) Table 5, "Industry-Product Analysis"; (2) Table 6, "Products and Product Classes–Value Shipped by All Manufacturing Establishments"; and (3) Table 7a, "Materials by Kind," and 7b, "Fuels and Electric Energy Consumed and Horsepower Rating of Power Equipment." In these tables, inputs are given by establishments and are not separated into the inputs required to produce primary commodities and those required to produce secondary commodities. On the other hand, information is given in the Census on the division of an establishment's output between its primary commodity and its secondary commodities.

There are a number of techniques for treating secondary products in input-output tables; five of the major ones are summarized in an unpublished paper by Alan Strout [209]. Because most of them are also briefly explained in the description of the 1958 input-output table [267], they will not be discussed here. Analysts in the United States use either the pure-product method or the secondary-product-table method. The pure-product method has been discussed by Edmonston [31], Koenig and Ritz [106], Chenery and Clark [20], Rijcheghem [188], Gigantes [56], Almon [2], and Kok [107]. For the MRIO accounts, the pure-product method was deemed too cumbersome. Also, it involves the use of considerable intuitive judgment to keep mechanical methods of calculating the tables from creating negative inputs. The secondary-product-table method, used for the national input-output tables, however, results in a combination (explained below) of the secondary output of an establishment with the inputs required by the establishment to produce its total primary and secondary output. A special means of handling the secondary products was therefore developed for the MRIO accounts. The method used for the national input-output tables must be described first, however.

In the United States, the secondary-product-table technique that had been developed for the 1947 BLS input-output table was used later by the OBE and until 1979 by the BEA for the assembly of national input-output tables. The technique actually involves the use of three tables. The first is called a primary table; the second a secondary table; the third a total transactions (or flows) table. In the official publications, only the total transactions table is published. It is obtained by adding the primary and the secondary tables.

A primary-product table is a product-by-establishment table. In this table, the elements in each row show the total amount of a given product purchased by each establishment regardless of which establishment produced the product. The elements in each column, on the other hand, show the total amount of a particular good consumed by establishments (grouped within a specific input-output industry) to produce the total output of the establishments—their primary and secondary products. The corresponding sums of the rows and columns of the table will therefore generally not be equal, because, while the row sum is the total amount of a given commodity produced, whether by the primary establishment or by other establishments, the column sum is the total amount of inputs purchased by specific establishments. Primary-product data for the manufacturing and service industries are given in table C-10 in the fourth volume of this series [182, pp. 272-305].

The secondary-product table is an establishment-by-product table that provides information on the value of goods produced by each of the establishments in the economy that are actually the products of another industry. The elements in each row of this table show the values of the output of the industry represented by that row of products classified under other industries, represented by the column in which the element occurs. The sum of the row of the table gives the total value of secondary goods produced by a given industry. In the OBE tables, these are referred to as transfers-out because they are products that are classified under other industries, and they are therefore transferred out from the industry where they are produced. On the other hand, the sum of each column specifies the total amount of a particular commodity that is produced by other than the primary-producing establishment in the economy. In the OBE tables, these are referred to as transfers-in because the values of these products are transferred into the primary industry and make up part of the input pattern of that industry. Although the distribution of the secondary output data can be compiled from information given in the Census of Manufactures, no information is given in the Census concerning the amount of inputs required to produce the secondary commodities exclusively. Rather, the input information given indicates the amount required to produce both the primary and secondary commodities of the establishment.

To obtain a balanced national input-output table (that is, a table in which the value of output of an input-output industry exactly equals the value of inputs purchased), the elements of the primary table are added to the corresponding ones in the secondary table, resulting in a total-transactions table. The secondary products are thus double-counted. This double-counting is not insignificant. In 1963, for 20 industries, 10 percent or more of their output was comprised of secondary commodities; and for another 20 industries (not always the same ones), 10 percent or more of the total output of the primary product was produced by establishments classified in other industries. The percentages can be compared for each of the 79 industries and for each of three years (1947, 1958, and 1963) by referring to table 1-1 in the fourth volume of this series [182, pp. 22-24].

As mentioned earlier, the corresponding elements in the primary and the secondary tables are added to obtain the total-transactions table for the national input-output tables. This obscures the input structure for each industry and is therefore not considered to be a satisfactory way to treat secondary products in the MRIO accounts. Instead, secondary-product tables were estimated for each state, the data were summed to obtain a total transfers-out column and a total transfers-in row, and that column and row were then placed into column and row 83, respectively, of the corresponding state input-output table. To estimate the state secondary-product data, the basic assumption was made that the amount an industry produces of another industry's output (transfers-out) as a proportion of its total output remains constant from one state to another. The national transfers-out were distributed to states, using the JFA state establishment outputs as allocation factors [182, pp. 498-509]. Due to time and budget limitations, the secondary-product data could not be compiled directly from the Census publications. The state secondary-product tables are available on computer tape [274]; the sums of those tables are provided in the state input-output tables. In this way, the secondary-product figures do not interfere with the technology inputs. The step-by-step procedure used to establish the state secondary product estimates is given in *State Estimates of Technology, 1963* [182, pp. 26-30].

Margins

Input-output tables can be constructed either in producer prices or purchaser prices. The difference between the two is the transportation, wholesale and retail trade, and insurance costs of transferring goods from the producer to the purchaser. As mentioned in chapter 2, all data in the MRIO accounts are in terms of producer prices. Some of the data for the technology inputs, however, were available only in terms of purchaser prices, and therefore had to be converted to producer prices. To make the conversion, three sets of margin tables were used: transportation, wholesale and retail trade, and insurance. The same national margins were applied to all regions, because regional margin data were not available.

For purposes of illustration, only the national transportation margin table will be discussed, because the other margins can be handled in a similar way. Each element in the transportation margin table represents the amount paid to transport goods from the producing industry to the purchasing industry. If "products" do not have to be transported to the purchasing industry, an entire row in the margin table will be blank. This occurs, for example, for industries in the service sector. For the MRIO accounts, the ratio of each margin element to the corresponding national producer value was calculated to obtain a table of fractions, representing the transportation markup. The values in the state producer-price table were then multiplied by the corresponding national margin to obtain a regional transportation-margin table. The values in each column of each regional margin table were summed to determine the total cost of shipping products to each industry in the region. These sums were then added to any "directly allocated" transportation costs of an industry (already in row 65 of the table) to obtain the total value paid to transport goods to the purchasing industry. For transportation, directly allocated costs include those that cannot be assigned to a particular mode of transportation as well as the amount consumers spend for passenger transportation. The cost of transporting goods to final consumers, however, is treated as a margin.

The same procedure was used for the wholesale and retail trade margins and for the insurance margins, with the regional estimates being placed in rows 69 and 70, respectively, of the appropriate state input-output table. Thus, the margin tables serve a dual role. First, they are used to convert data from purchaser to producer prices (or vice versa). Second, they are used to obtain margin cost estimates for the transportation, wholesale and retail trade, and insurance rows in the input-output tables.

State Input-Output Tables

The final adjustment to the input-output tables involved the following steps:

Step 1. The estimated technology inputs were placed into rows 1 through 80 and columns 1 through 79 of the appropriate state input-output table.

Step 2. The transportation, trade, and insurance margins were calculated and used to convert any inputs in purchaser prices to producer prices and to obtain estimates for rows 65, 69, and 70 of the state input-output tables.

Step 3. The value added figures for row 82 in the tables were obtained by subtracting the sum of the technology inputs for a particular industry from the state establishment output figure for the same industry. If the value added estimate represented less than 5 percent of the establishment output figure, the value added figure was augmented to the 5-percent control value, and all other technology inputs for the industry were reduced in proportion to their initial values so that the reduction in their sum exactly offset the addition to value added.

Step 4. The transferred import data were estimated for row 81 of each state input-output table.

Step 5. The values for inventory depletions, scrap production, and scrap purchases were determined and placed into rows 84, 85, and 86, respectively, and the values for the net trade balance were calculated and placed into column 81 of each state input-output table. The procedures for making these estimates were described in chapter 2.

Step 6. The estimates for the six components of final demand (refer to chapter 4) were summed to obtain a total for each industry in a given state, the corresponding values for inventory depletions were subtracted, and the resulting figures were placed into column 82 of the appropriate state input-output table.

Step 7. The elements in each row and column of a given state input-output table were summed to obtain gross regional consumption (column 87) and gross regional output (row 87).

As a final check on all the calculations, the 51 input-output tables were added, element by element, to obtain a national table, and the national table was checked against the control estimates (described in the National Control Table section of chapter 2).

Conclusion

A substantial amount of effort was spent in assembling the estimates for the state input-output tables and in documenting the data sources and estimation procedures used. Since the final revisions to the estimates were completed, in 1973, no major inconsistencies have been found. The data have been used in a wide variety of studies ranging from determination of employment and income multipliers for the state of Massachusetts to determination of the price and output effects of the 1974 Clean Air Standards. In general, the results of these studies seem reasonable. When a new set of MRIO accounts is assembled for a later year, a number of improvements in the estimation procedures may be possible. The manufacturing and service inputs could be determined, if money is available, on a state-by-state basis through direct tabulations from the Census tapes. On the other hand, new data sources will have to be found for the determination of inputs for agriculture (the 1955 data being outdated) and for mining and construction (the regional data for these two sectors also being outdated).

Interesting analyses can be made with the present set of data in terms of comparative regional technology studies. Before comparisons can be made over time, one or more additional sets of state input-output tables will be needed with inputs of all sets constructed using similar estimation procedures. Such comparable sets of tables will open the way for a rich variety of technological studies.

Note

1. It should be noted that beginning in 1979, the BEA switched to a product classification. Because the details of the new methodology are provided in the February 1979 issue of the *Survey of Current Business* [190, pp. 37-43], no discussion of it will be included here. Although a new methodology is now being used, the description presented here is relevant for the use of the 1947, 1958, 1963, and 1967 national input-output tables as well as for the MRIO accounts.

6 Interregional Trade-Flow Estimates

For the implementation of the multiregional input-output (MRIO) model, 1963 state-to-state trade-flow estimates were required in addition to technology and final demand data. The state-to-state commodity-trade flows were estimated at Jack Faucett Associates, Inc. (JFA) in terms of dollars and tons for six modes of transportation: rail, truck, air, water, other, and unknown. Although partial statistics on commodity-trade flows are regularly compiled and published by several government agencies, the JFA estimates represent the first attempt to integrate U.S. commodity-trade flows within the MRIO framework—or, for that matter, any other consistent regional framework. The state-to-state service-industry trade flows were estimated at the Federal Preparedness Agency in terms of dollars only.

A brief history of the estimation of the trade flows is presented in the next section of the chapter; the data sources and estimation methods used to obtain the interregional trade flows are given in the second section; and a summary of the adjustment procedure used to make the interregional trade flows consistent with the data in the state input-output tables is provided in the third section.

History of the Trade-Flow Data Estimation

The estimation of the trade flows was separated into five phases: the initial estimation of total interregional commodity-shipments data for 44 regions and 61 commodities; the disaggregation of these data to 51 regions and six modes of transportation; the estimation of interregional trade flows for the service industries; the estimation of the interregional transfers of electricity; and the development of a technique to improve the consistency between the trade-flow and input-output data. These five phases are summarized in table 6-1.

Initial Data Assembly

The 1963 MRIO commodity-trade flows were initially assembled during 1969-1970 by JFA staff members for 44 regions and for total interregional commodity shipments, but not for modal shipments. An extensive description of the methodology used was submitted by JFA to the Office of Business Economics (OBE) in a report entitled "1963 Interregional Commodity Trade Flows" [43]. The description was later rewritten by John M. Rodgers of the JFA staff and published in *State Estimates of Interregional Commodity Trade,*

Table 6–1
Trade-Flows Data Assembly

Phase	*Data Assembly and Reconciliation*	*Completion of Work*	*Sources of Funding*	*Place of Data Assembly or Reconciliation*[a]	*Place Data Available*	*Comments*
1	44-region 1963 commodity trade flows for 61 industries	1970	BLS, OBE, OCD, DOT, EDA	JFA and HERP	NTIS[b]	At the same time, data were assembled for 76 production and rest-of-state areas and 9 census regions.[c]
2	51-region 1963 commodity trade flows for 61 industries and for 6 modes of transportation	1972	DOT	JFA and HERP (and MIT)	NTIS	The data for the 6 transportation modes were not reconciled with the regional input-output control totals.
3	51-region 1963 service-industry trade flows	1972	FPA (and DOT)	FPA (and MIT)	FPA (and MIT)	A number of adjustments were made in 1975 at MIT to the trade flows provided by the FPA before they were reconciled with the regional input-output control totals.
4	51-region 1963 and 1970 electric industry (IO-68.01) trade flows	1974	DOT	MIT	MIT	The trade flows for the combined gas (IO-68.02) and water utilities (IO-68.03) were obtained as a residual by subtracting the elements for IO-68.01 from the corresponding FPA estimates for IO-68.
5	New reconciliation of 1963 commodity trade-flow tables for 79 commodities and services with regional input-output control totals	1975	DOT	MIT	MIT	Additional reconciliation procedures may be developed.

NOTE: A list of abbreviations is provided at the front of the book.

[a]Data assembled at JFA or FPA were reconciled with the input-output data by the MRIO staff members at HERP and MIT.

[b]In September 1978, a request was made to the NTIS to remove the 44-region data from circulation.

[c]All 1963 interregional trade data assembled in 1970, except the 76 production and rest-of-state area figures, are obsolete. The 1963 data assembled in 1972 should be used instead.

1963 [192], which also contains the 1963 state-to-state trade data for 61 commodities and 51 regions that had been assembled as of 1972. In addition to the JFA report, computer tapes containing the 44-region commodity-trade flows were submitted to the OBE and were later made available through the National Technical Information Service (NTIS) [41]. Three origin-destination flow measures were prepared for 1963 and are now available on the NTIS tapes: (1) census region to census region; (2) state to state (44 region—explained in the following paragraph); and (3) production area (or rest-of-state area) to production area (or rest-of-state area). Because the 44-region commodity-trade estimates, representing the second set of data, are now obsolete, the 51-region trade estimates given in the Rodgers volume, cited above, should be used instead. The data in the first and third sets of statistics were not revised and are still usable. The second set of these data—the 1963 dollar values of state-to-state commodity trade—was used at the Harvard Economic Research Project (HERP) for the implementation of the MRIO model in 1970.

For 1963, Census of Transportation statistics were available for 76 production and rest-of-state areas. However, in those statistics, the data for 12 of the 51 regions (50 states plus the District of Columbia) were combined, because some of the 76 production and rest-of-state areas overlap state boundaries. Because individual state-to-state commodity shipments could not be accurately estimated from the census information, no attempt was made to disaggregate the data for the 12 states from the 5 regions into which they were combined. Instead, the total number of regions was reduced from 51 to 44. Thus, "state-to-state," at this point, actually means region-to-region. The state combinations were:

1. Massachusetts, Rhode Island, New Hampshire, and Connecticut
2. Pennsylvania and New Jersey
3. Michigan and Ohio
4. Indiana and Illinois
5. Delaware and Maryland.

Although assembly of the 44-region 1963 commodity-trade data was done by the JFA staff, reconciliation of these data with the 44 regional input-output tables was done by the HERP staff during 1970.

Disaggregation to 51 Regions and Six Modes

Some research analysts attempted to use the commodity-shipments data but encountered difficulties when the state they wanted to study was, say, Massachusetts, Connecticut, Michigan, or any one of the other 12 states included in the five combinations. As the initial data assembly was reviewed during 1970-1971, the need for estimates of state-to-state shipments became evident, but the need to maintain consistency in the estimates became equally evident. It was realized that the state-to-state estimates for the 12 states listed above would be less accurate than the combined state estimates. During 1972, the JFA staff disaggregated the 44-region commodity-shipments estimates to 51 regions. Estimates were also made for the six modes of transportation given earlier.

The 51-region (44-region) commodity trade-flow estimates, which represented the sum of all modal shipments, were adjusted by MRIO staff members to conform with the 51-region (44-region) input-output tables.[1] The modal shipments were not adjusted to conform with the input-output information, because the use of the modal data was not at that time high on the list of MRIO research priorities. Since the early 1970s, however, the MRIO and other research groups have been using the modal shipments data for studies outside the MRIO framework, which emphasizes the fact that the MRIO trade-flow data are useful for a wide variety of transportation studies.

The disaggregated data (total and modal shipments) are available on computer tape from the NTIS [176]. In addition, the total transportation shipments for each of the 61 commodities, which were reconciled with the input-output tables, are given in appendix D of *State Estimates of Interregional Commodity Trade, 1963* [192, pp. 67–443].

Although input-output (IO) data were assembled for 79 industries, the shipments data were initially assembled only for the 61 industries that transport commodities by the regular modes of transport (rail, truck, air, water, and so on). The 61 industries are IO-1 through IO-64, excluding IO-4, Agricultural, forestry, & fishery services; IO-11, New construction; and IO-12, Maintenance & repair construction. A complete list of the 87 input-output industry numbers and titles is given in the appendix, table A–1. These numbers, rather than the sequential numbers of the 61 industries, will be used in referring to the industries in this chapter. As mentioned previously, the original commodity-shipments data were assembled for 76 production and rest-of-state areas, 44 regions, and 9 regions; revisions that were completed in 1973, however, were made only at the 51-region level. The regional classifications are given in the appendix, table A–2.

Estimation of Service-Industry Trade Flows

The Federal Preparedness Agency (FPA) was the first government agency to set up the MRIO model and data for policy analyses.[2] It was implemented there in 1973. As members of the FPA staff implemented the model, they also assembled service-industry trade flows. The 1963 interregional transfers for almost all of the service industries were estimated. In 1975, the MRIO staff was provided with a computer tape containing the FPA data, but not with documentation concerning the procedure by which trade flows were assembled.

Two important discrepancies, which are thoroughly documented in a report by Ng [166], were found when an attempt was made to integrate the FPA service-industry trade flows into the MRIO accounting framework: (1) The values for the state transfers-out (STRO) had been distributed throughout the trade-flow matrices, rather than left as a separate row and column in the table. (2) For each matrix, the column sum (commodity consumption) was exactly the same as the row sum (commodity production), because the value of the net trade balance (NTB)–the dummy industry created to account for the difference between regional consumption and regional production for non-traded commodities–had not been subtracted from the value of total consumption to obtain the consumption controls used by the staff at the FPA for the trade-flow tables. The MRIO staff made adjustments for these two discrepancies.

From information obtained through discussions with members of the FPA staff, it appears that the trade flows were not assembled from a single data source, but were, instead, pieced together from miscellaneous sets of data, combined with intuitive judgments, on the interregional transfer of those services.

For reasons that have not been determined, no estimates were made at the FPA for IO-4, Agricultural, forestry, & fishery services; IO-11, New construction; and IO-12, Maintenance & repair construction. Since, for these industries, production does not equal consumption in all states, an NTB entry still exists for them in the input-output tables. An NTB entry also still exists for IO-3, Forestry & fishery products; but members of the MRIO staff decided that the initial IO-3 data assembled at JFA were not usable and that no logical assembly of trade flows could be made at this time.

Interregional Transfers of Electricity

As work on the MRIO model proceeded from the model-implementation to the policy-analysis stage, the need for additional trade-flow statistics at a subindustry level became evident. Especially high on the list of priorities in the early 1970s were interregional transfers of electricity–the energy crisis was here. Details on the data sources and procedures used to obtain state-to-state flows are given later.

Development of a Technique to Improve Consistency Between Data in the Interregional Trade and Input-Output Tables

The need to maintain consistency between the data in the interregional trade tables and those in the input-output tables was discussed in the section on

Commodity Trade-Flow Tables in chapter 2. When the initial policy analyses were made in 1970–1973, it was assumed that the lack of absolute consistency between relevant sums from these tables was causing some of the errors in the final results obtained in implementing the model. Inconsistencies greater than 1 percent still existed in the trade-flow tables for 11 of the 61 traded commodities [180, p. 180]. This meant that one or more of the row (column) sums in the trade tables was not the same as the corresponding column (row) control total from the input-output tables, and that the difference was greater than 1 percent.

The source of the consistency problem was not known. Inconsistencies could arise from four sources, two related to data errors and two to problems in data-assembly procedures. First, errors could exist in the trade-table estimates because of lack of data or inaccurate data. The data were considered to be the best available, and no major improvements to them were possible, partly because there is almost no way to reconstruct accurate data for years as distant as 1963. (This points up the need for a massive improvement in origin-destination statistics in general by restructuring the present sets of surveys and censuses to permit more accurate and more comprehensive data assembly for future years.)

Second, errors could exist in the input-output data. Here again, after a general review of the data, and considering the extensive revisions made to those data in 1972, it was decided that no other major improvements could be made, for reasons similar to those given for the trade-flow data.

Third, errors could result from the method used to implement the model. The method could perhaps have been altered so that inconsistencies did not create as much of a problem. But no satisfactory way to do this was apparent. In any case, altering the method of implementing the model seemed the wrong way to handle the inconsistencies, because it would adjust the end result without affecting the errors in the data input, and the data were being used for analyses other than the MRIO model implementation.

Fourth, errors could result from the lack of complete consistency between all the trade flows and the input-output data. This, of course, is due to data errors, but no method of improving the data estimates was available, given the time and budget constraints. The method of obtaining consistency between the two sets of data could, however, have been improved with additional investigation of the consistency requirements of the model.

The fourth possible source of the inconsistencies seemed to be the only reasonable one to try to alter. The research required to make this alteration in methodology is thoroughly described in Möhr's Ph.D. thesis [145] and two reports by him [144; 146]. This research entailed two studies. The first, an extensive statistical analysis of the MRIO trade data, was designed to gain some insight into the structure of the trade flows and, therefore, into the way in which those data could be altered to be consistent with the input-output control totals. The second study was a careful examination of the RAS procedure,[3] referred to in this book as the *d*istribute-the-*und*istributed (DUD) procedure. It was conducted to determine why the DUD procedure would not provide a convergent solution for some commodity matrices and what adjustments might be made to the data so that it would provide convergent solutions, or what alternative procedure might be adopted that would do so. Essentially, the nonconvergence was caused by a violation of the existence conditions of constrained biproportional matrices. A simplex algorithm was developed to prove necessary (but not sufficient) conditions, and the 11 trade matrices with infeasible solutions were modified in light of the results of the simplex algorithm until a feasible solution was obtained. A discussion of the combination of procedures adopted is provided in a later section of this chapter.

Interregional Trade-Data Sources

To assemble the 61 state-to-state 1963 commodity trade-flow tables, origin-destination data had to be obtained for each commodity. Supplemental information on regional output (converted to tons), imports by port of entry, and the regional demand for commodities was used to adjust the origin-destination figures to account for all commodities produced and consumed—thus shipped—in the United States. Principal data sources used for the trade-flow estimates for the agricultural, mining, and manufacturing sectors were *Census of Transportation, 1963* [239]; a commodity tabulation specially prepared for this research project by the U.S. Bureau of the Census (Census) [245]; *Carload Waybill Statistics, 1963* [86], *1964* [87], and *1966* [88]; *Minerals Yearbook, 1963* [283]; and *Waterborne Commerce of the United States, 1963* [258]. The sources of data used by the FPA for assembling service-industry trade flows are unknown.

A detailed discussion of all the data sources and the strengths and limitations of the data assembled from them follows. The data sources used are listed in table 2-3 of the fifth volume of this series [192, p. 17], with supplementary information being provided when special tabulations or special estimation procedures were used for estimating commodity flows.

Agricultural Sector

For the agricultural sector, commodity shipments were estimated only for IO-1, Livestock & livestock products, and IO-2, Other agricultural products. Interregional trade data initially obtained for IO-3, Forestry & fishery products, were eventually discarded; and no data were obtained for IO-4, Agricultural, forestry, & fishery services, for reasons already explained.

IO-1, Livestock and Livestock Products.

IO-2, Other Agricultural Products. Nearly all agricultural livestock and crop products are shipped either by rail or truck. According to estimates made at JFA, trucks are used exclusively for over 90 percent of livestock and livestock products and for at least 50 percent of all other agricultural commodities [192, p. 26]. Most of the remainder is shipped by rail.

Truck-Shipments Estimates. The principal source of statistics on trucking of agricultural commodities is a publication entitled *For-Hire Motor Carriers Hauling Exempt Agricultural Commodities* which is a tabulation by the Marketing Research Division of the U.S. Department of Agriculture (USDA) of a survey of truck operators exempt from Interstate Commerce Commission (ICC) regulations. The data used for this study were from the 1963 USDA survey of 1514 operators. Although most trucking of agricultural products is exempt from ICC regulations, and thus is covered by these statistics, the data do not contain actual origin-to-destination information and therefore had to be adjusted to obtain state-to-state shipments.

Data on major movements from state of origin to state of destination were obtained from the USDA trucking survey for each of 6 regions and each of 9 major agricultural commodities and arranged into a 51x51 trade matrix. For each region and commodity, statistics on total truck shipments from each shipping state were then allocated to the elements in each row of the matrix, using the row distribution percentages from the origin-destination trade tables just tabulated. For each commodity, the corresponding state-to-state shipments in the six regional state-to-state trade tables were added to obtain a total state-to-state shipments table for each. The corresponding data in the nine commodity tables were then aggregated into two major commodity groups and added to form state-to-state truck shipments for the two input-output agricultural industries. These data were then used to prorate independent estimates of total truck shipments, again using the row distributions, this time from the two tables of combined commodities.

The independent estimates of total national truck shipments of each commodity were obtained by determining major shipments of agricultural commodities by each mode of transport, including truck. Then the national truck shipments estimates were used to adjust the original estimates of total truck shipments from each shipping state, obtained from the survey.

Rail-Shipments Estimates. State-to-state rail shipments for the two input-output industries were estimated from data provided in *Carload Waybill Statistics, 1963* [86] and were expanded by a factor of 100, because the waybill data represent a 1 percent sample. For each of the two industries, total shipments were obtained by adding the corresponding data in the truck and rail state-to-state tables.

IO-3, Forestry and Fishery Products.

IO-4, Agricultural, Forestry, and Fishery Services. Initially, estimates were made for IO-3, Forestry & fishery products, but difficulties were encountered when the data were adjusted to be consistent with the commodity control totals from the input-output tables. The original set of trade data received from JFA contained estimates for IO-3, but the interregional flows represented only the shipments of fishing products (basically hatched fish) from one state to another. The value of the forestry portion of the industry is the value of stumpage, which is not shipped from state to state. As a result, difficulties were encountered in trying to reconcile the interregional trade flows with the state input-output data. This industry represents an obvious case where additional research is required. One possibility would be to construct separate input-output table rows and columns for the fishing and forestry industries—thus adding one more industry to the accounts—and to use the interregional flows already assembled for the fishing products, but to force production to equal consumption in each region through use of the DUD program only for the forestry products. Another possibility would be to perform the initial assembly of two separate sets of information, as just described, and then to add them together in order to maintain the same industry-numbering scheme used in the previous research.

For IO-4, Agricultural, forestry, & fishery services, no data were initially assembled, because, this being a service industry, it was assumed that all services were consumed in the state where they were produced. In addition, as was noted earlier, the estimates of interregional transfers of services received from the FPA in 1975 did not include IO-4 flows. Since there was insufficient time for the MIT staff to prepare reliable estimates, all services from IO-4 produced in a region are still assumed to be consumed in the same region, and any difference between production and consumption in a region is allocated to the net trade balance column in the respective state input-output table.

Mining Sector

Separate types of data sources were used for oil, coal, and the four other mining industries.

IO-7, Coal Mining. Two sources were used to obtain data for tonnage shipments of coal. For anthracite coal, statistics were taken from *Minerals Yearbook, 1963* [283]. For bituminous coal and lignite, they were tabulated from the publication *Bituminous Coal and Lignite: Changing Patterns in Distribution and Markets, 1962–1964* [282]. The corresponding trade flows for anthracite and bituminous and lignite coal were then combined to form the total trade flows for IO-7, Coal mining.

IO-8, Crude Petroleum and Natural Gas. Separate interregional tonnage estimates for IO-8, Crude petroleum & natural gas, were tabulated from a different source for each of the three components, crude petroleum, natural gas, and natural gas liquids. For crude petroleum, a Bureau of Mines publication on refinery receipts was used, and for natural gas, gas receipts data in *Minerals Yearbook, 1963* [283] were used. For natural gas liquids, estimates were made of the supply and demand in each state. The state supply (production) data were then distributed to the consuming states, using the demand proportions. Thus, the row distributions in the resulting trade table were identical at this stage. The corresponding trade flows for the three components were then combined to form the total trade flows for the industry.

Other Mining Industries. Except for the oil and coal estimates just mentioned, the basic interregional shipments data sources used for tonnage shipments from the mining industries were *Carload Waybill Statistics, 1963* [86], *1964* [87], and *1966* [88]. It was assumed that all shipments were by rail. Because it was determined that the 1966 waybill data were more reliable than those for 1963, the 1966 data were used extensively for estimating shipments of IO-6, Nonferrous metal ores mining; IO-9, Stone & clay mining & quarrying; and IO-10, Chemical & fertilizer mineral mining. The tonnage shipments for IO-5, Iron & ferroalloy ores mining, however, were estimated exclusively from the 1963 statistics, because the 1963 data were relatively reliable.

To estimate the total tonnage shipped by rail, the 1 percent waybill sample data were expanded by a factor of 100. Tonnage measures of state industry supply were obtained for each of these four mining industries, and the differences between the total consumption figures in the trade tables and the independently estimated total supply figures were allocated column by column, using the initial state-to-state shipments estimates as the base.

Manufacturing Sector

The interregional tonnage estimates for all manufacturing industries, except those for IO-13, Ordnance & accessories, and IO-26, Printing & publishing, were tabulated from three sources: a census tabulation prepared specially for this research project by the Census from the 1963 Census of Transportation [245], *Carload Waybill Statistics, 1963* [86], and *Census of Transportation, 1963* [239]. In terms of dollars, these sources accounted for 76, 13, and 11 percent, respectively, of the total shipments tabulated before adjustments. The procedures used to assemble the data will be described first for the two exceptions and then for the major group of other manufacturing industries.

IO-13, Ordnance and Accessories. This industry has been excluded from the 1963 Census of Transportation for national security reasons. Production data were assembled from estimates made earlier at JFA and contained in their report "1963 Output Measures for Input-Output Sectors by County" [45]. The production data were distributed to the consuming states, using the demand proportions. Thus, the row distributions for each region in the resulting trade table were identical at this stage.

IO-26, Printing and Publishing. The printing and publishing industry, IO-26, had been excluded from the 1963 Census of Transportation because many newspapers and advertising circulars are only shipped locally (shipments for all industries within a 25-mile radius were excluded from the census), while the U.S. mail is used for interregional shipments of most periodicals.

Because tonnage data were not available, the dollar figures were obtained first, and then the tonnage flows were calculated by dividing the dollar value by the average-price-per-ton data for each of the 3-digit standard industrial classification (SIC) industries. Value-of-shipments and price-per-ton data for the 3-digit SIC industries by state of origin were obtained from "1963 Manufacturing Industry Shipments Estimates for Counties, SMSAs, and States" [44]. For the five subindustries included in the local-shipments segment of the industry, all movements were considered to be made within the state; therefore, the entire tonnage or dollar figure was allocated to the diagonal (intraregional) element in the trade table. For lack of better data, the value-of-shipments data for the four subindustries included in the nonlocal-shipments segment of the industry were distributed to the consuming states, using the demand proportions. Thus, the row distributions in the trade table for this segment of the industry were identical at this stage, but not when added to the data for the local segment of the industry. The corresponding trade flows for the two components were then combined to form the total trade flows for the industry.

Other Manufacturing Industries. Most of the data needed to assemble interregional tonnage estimates for the remaining 50 manufacturing industries were tabulated from the 1963 Census of Transportation. The 1963 census, however, represents a very incomplete coverage for the following reasons:

1. It is a survey, not a complete census.
2. It covers only manufacturing industries, and even then excludes data for IO-13, Ordnance & accessories, and IO-26, Printing & publishing.
3. No local shipments (those within a 25-mile radius of the major producing area) are included.
4. It covers only shipments of domestic goods, excluding imported goods.

5. Data are provided only in tonnage, not dollar (value-of-shipments) terms.
6. Data that disclose information for individual plants are suppressed.

The procedure used to establish estimates for the manufacturing tonnage shipments was as follows:

Step 1. The interregional data, in general, were obtained from a 1963 Census of Transportation tabulation specially prepared for this research project by the Census [245]. These data accounted for 76 percent of the total other manufacturing shipments initially estimated.

Step 2. When an estimate could not be determined from this source, an estimate based upon adjustments made to data from *Carload Waybill Statistics, 1963* [86] was used. These waybill data, which represent only 1 percent of all rail shipments, were expanded by a factor of 100 to represent all rail shipments. They were then reclassified from the Transportation Commodity Codes (TCC) to SIC codes and further adjusted, using a detailed procedure explained by Rodgers [192, pp. 36–38], to represent transportation on all modes.

Although Rodgers estimated that errors for cells with relatively small volumes of shipments were enormous—50 to 100 percent of the true tonnage of shipments—it should be noted that the data had to be used for only about 11 percent of the flows [192, p. 38]. The five industries for which they represented over 30 percent of the total value of the initial trade flows are [192, pp. 42–43]:

IO-19, Miscellaneous fabricated textile products

IO-20, Lumber & wood products, except containers

IO-39, Metal containers

IO-57, Electronic components & accessories

IO-63, Optical, ophthalmic, & photographic equipment & supplies

Step 3. A set of interregional trade flows for the 9 census regions, rather than states, was tabulated from *Census of Transportation, 1963* [239]. These 9-region data were then distributed to the 51 regions, using a type of gravity formula, as explained in detail in Rodgers [192, pp. 38–40]. These data were used for approximately 13 percent of the estimates. The 8 industries for which they represented over 30 percent of the total value of the initial trade flows are [192, pp. 42–43]:

IO-15, Tobacco manufactures

IO-21, Wooden containers

IO-33, Leather tanning & industrial leather products

IO-51, Office, computing, & accounting machines

IO-54, Household appliances

IO-57, Electronic components & accessories

IO-60, Aircraft & parts

IO-61, Other transportation equipment

The data assembled from steps 2 and 3 are probably considerably less accurate than those assembled directly from the special census tabulation. They had to be used when no data were provided in the original tabulation. The way in which the data from these two steps were incorporated into the initial trade tables constructed from the special tabulation by the Census is illustrated in figure 5-1 in the fifth volume of this series [192, p. 41].

When the MRIO model is implemented, or if data from the specific industries listed in steps 2 and 3 are used for other purposes, the results relating to these industries should be examined with considerable care because of the possibility of large errors in the original data assembly. Even more important in some ways, these become industries for which special types of surveys or studies may be needed to determine interregional shipments unless the data-collection procedures now used by the Census itself can be improved.

Service Sector

As noted earlier, the 1963 trade flows for the service sector were assembled at the FPA, but no documentation exists on the numerous data sources and estimation procedures used to make the estimates. They were assembled only in terms of dollars, not in terms of physical quantities.

Because of the desire to separate the data for the electricity industry from the remainder of the data for IO-68, Electricity, gas, water, & sanitary services, trade flows for electricity were assembled by the MRIO staff in 1976. The trade-flow data were tabulated from the sales-for-resale statistics given in the Federal Power Commission (FPC) annual reports for 219 privately owned electric companies [49]. The data used were sales-for-resale or the amounts of electricity that each company sold to other power companies, both public and private, for resale. In this way, both intrastate and interstate sales were obtained. However, sales made directly to industry and private users were not obtainable; and these direct sales, calculated as being the difference between total state production and total state sales for resale, were assumed to remain within the state as a part of the intraregional trade. Because eighteen annual FPC 1963 reports were missing, the 1970 sales-for-resale data, which had been collected at the same time, were used in place of the missing 1963 data, instead of trying to assemble approximations to the data from reports for closer years, such as 1962 or 1964.

The procedure used to obtain state-to-state flows for electricity was straightforward. The 1963 sales-for-resale data, supplemented with the 1970 data for the above eighteen companies, were arranged into a 51 × 51 trade-flow matrix. Total income and other tax revenues paid by the electric utility companies in each state were estimated and were distributed according to the row distributions of data already in the trade-flow matrix. This procedure was used to adjust the data to a total production concept, comparable with the input-output control totals. Finally, the regional transfers-out were added to the table as a 52nd row and column.

The estimates were subtracted, cell by cell, from the FPA trade flows for IO-68, Electricity, gas, water, & sanitary services, to obtain trade flows for the remainder of the IO-68 industry. Trade flows for the electricity subindustry are not available on the computer tapes submitted to the National Technical Information Service. It should also be noted that although the electricity trade flows were assembled for 51 regions for both 1963 and 1970, only the 1963 trade flows were reconciled with the input-output data for the electricity industry and then only for the 9 census regions. The 9-region 1963 electricity data are given in the appendix, table B.3-19.

Adjustment of Interregional Trade Flows

The interregional trade estimates, prior to their adjustment using the DUD procedure, are referred to as PREDUD trade flows. The PREDUD flows are available both in tonnage and dollar units. Trade flows were estimated initially for the 61 nonservice industries mentioned earlier only for domestic shipments of commodities and in terms of tonnage flows. Four adjustments had to be made to transform the trade data to be consistent with the input-output data: (1) estimation of interregional shipments of foreign imports; (2) conversion of data from tons to dollars; (3) estimation of service-industry trade flows; and (4) adjustment of data in all 79 trade tables for consistency with the input-output data, using the DUD procedure. (The final estimates are sometimes referred to as the POSTDUD trade flows.) Each of these adjustments, except the third (which was discussed in the previous section), will be discussed here.

Foreign Imports

The tons of waterborne and overland imports were estimated for each input-output industry from *Waterborne Commerce of the United States, 1963* [258] and *Highlights of U.S. Exports and Imports* [246], by port or state of entry.

The figures for each industry by state of origin were then adjusted by prorating the value of competitive imports in the 1963 national input-output table [265], using the state import figures as distribution factors. Because no information on the destination of these imports was available, they were allocated to consuming states, based upon the state-to-state commodity value distributions for domestically produced goods.

Tonnage-to-Dollar Conversion

As summarized in the previous section, all commodity trade flows, except those for IO-26, Printing & publishing, were first obtained as tonnage flows. The tonnage data for total domestic shipments from each producing region were converted to dollar measures using a set of average price-per-ton data for each commodity. Because of resource and data limitations, prices were estimated only for the 9 census regions, and all state shipments of a particular commodity originating within a given census region were transformed from tons to dollars using an identical regional average price.

National average (producer) prices were estimated for each of 61 commodities (IO-1 through IO-3, IO-5 through IO-10, and IO-13 through IO-64). Regional prices, however, were calculated as an average of the prices of the component commodities only for the 31 industries that consisted of two or more 3-digit SIC codes. Because the only data available to differentiate prices at a regional level were the regional industry value of shipments, no weighting was possible when an input-output industry was comprised of just one subindustry. Tons of commodity shipments by census region were used as weights.

Data on unit weights and values were obtained from *Agricultural Statistics, 1963* [253], *Minerals Yearbook, 1963* [283], *Census of Mineral Industries, 1963* [236], *Census of Manufactures, 1963* [234], worksheet data of the Interstate Commerce Commission [85], and miscellaneous advertising catalogs, such as *Sears Roebuck.*

The national average price was calculated by dividing the national value of shipments of commodity k by an estimate of 1963 national total tons of commodity k shipped. If the industry consisted of more than one 3-digit or 4-digit industry, a weighted price was obtained, using the national industry value of shipments as weights. For the 31 industries for which this weighting could be done, regional prices were also calculated, using regional industry value of shipments as weights. The regional prices for the remaining 30 nonservice industries were assumed to be identical to the national prices. Additional commodity and geographical stratification would have been desirable, but could not be undertaken due to resource and time limitations.

Biproportional Matrix Adjustment Procedure

Numerous attempts have been made to devise methods of adjusting input-output tables to permit updating the direct input coefficients from a base year to a more current year for use in policy analyses. One of the most frequently used methods is the RAS procedure. Because this procedure, with important modifications, is also the one used to adjust the interregional trade tables, a brief historical sketch is presented here concerning the basic mathematical formulation of the procedure and its modifications. Since adjustment of the trade flows was explained in detail in the Commodity Trade-Flow Tables section in chapter 2, only the modified RAS procedure is summarized here.

In 1941, Leontief published a theoretical description of a biproportional matrix change procedure [122]. To allow for changes in the input-output coefficients, he used a vector of row multipliers and another vector of column multipliers, which jointly allowed for productivity changes of commodity k—variations in commodity output—and productivity changes of industry k—variations in input-output coefficients, that is, technology.

History of RAS. When the row and column multipliers are not known, but fixed row and column control totals exist, the biproportional-matrix-change procedure becomes constrained. In his 1941 book, Leontief proposed a least-squares procedure to obtain another unknown set of multipliers, which he called "efficiency coefficients" and "investment coefficients" [122, pp. 107-109]. Two major problems with the least-squares estimates are that unless special restrictions are imposed, negative elements can result, and not all zero elements are preserved [5, p. 6].

Stone is responsible for the so-called RAS method [207, pp. 69-70], in which he took a simple iterative solution procedure proposed by Deming and Stephan [28, p. 440] and applied it to constrained biproportional matrix estimation problems, namely, updating national input-output tables. Bacharach extended Stone's work by analyzing the existence, uniqueness, and convergence properties of the biproportional matrix model. He provided a general solution to the existence problem. He also compared the model and the RAS procedure with other mathematical formulations and reviewed economic interpretations and applications of the procedure [5]. McMenanin and Haring give an updated appraisal of RAS applications [130], and Schneider does a comparison of several procedures for adjusting the matrices [199].

Theory of RAS. The biproportional-matrix-change model is set forth as follows by Stone [207, p. 70] and Bacharach [5]:

$$A^x = \hat{r} A \hat{s}$$

where

A = a known nonnegative $m \times n$ matrix that can be transformed by row and column multiplication into a nonnegative $m \times n$ matrix A^x

$\hat{r}$ = an unknown diagonal $m \times m$ matrix of row multipliers

$\hat{s}$ = an unknown diagonal $n \times n$ matrix of column multipliers

$\hat{}$ = a diagonal matrix.

The solution A^x is obtained by using known row totals, u, and known column totals, v, and the RAS procedure.

The existence question concerns whether or not a set of r and s multipliers can be found that can be used to transform A to A^x, where the sums of the rows and columns of A^x equal the row control totals u and the column control totals v. If a solution does exist, then A^x retains the type of A strictly, that is, the position of the positive elements in the two matrices are identical, because the multipliers r and s are strictly positive.

If matrix A is a square matrix of ones, a solution to the problem (A, u, v) always exists, and the solution is identical to the biproportional matrix solution resulting after a single cycle of the RAS procedure. This is not so if A contains any zeros. An existence problem exists only if A contains zeros. Bacharach's existence theorem, however, raises three questions: First, and most important, how are the relevant all-zero partitions of A to be determined? If all partitions are considered, there is a total of 2^{m+n}, which for any but small matrices makes testing of all partitions infeasible. Second, are boundary solutions necessary because some matrices can be included due to weak inequalities that have no biproportional solution? Third, does matrix A have to be transformed so it is not disconnected?

As noted earlier, for some trade-flow tables, the DUD procedure would not provide a convergent solution due to a violation of the existence conditions of constrained biproportional matrices. Möhr showed the necessary, but not sufficient, conditions for finding a solution to the existence problem (A, u, v), with one of the most important conditions being that the partial sum of the row total $\overset{*}{u}_c$ must be less than the partial sum of the column total $\bar{v}_c$. (The complete condition is stated in Möhr's thesis [145, p. 72].) These partial sums are determined by rearranging rows or columns of A so that all rows and columns in which zeros occur in the same places are grouped. Although the above is a necessary existence condition, it is not sufficient, and no means has yet been found to determine a sufficient condition.[4] Möhr did develop a set of evaluation and selection criteria to identify critical zeros through use of a simplex algorithm and to assign an order to the zeros according to the number of times they occur in critical partitions of the matrix. He was then able to assign values to the critical zero elements in the trade tables and obtain convergent solutions when the DUD procedure was again used. After Möhr completed his Ph.D. thesis in 1975, the procedure he developed was used by the MRIO staff to adjust the trade flows both for the 61 commodity tables and the 18 noncommodity trade tables.

Conclusion

Statistics on interregional trade flows are essential for the conduct of regional analyses, and of course the more comprehensive the data, the more valuable the data. Although these data are being collected by the Census for the manufacturing industries in each industrial census year, the present collection effort needs to be extended to include all industries that produce commodities. In addition, modifications need to be made in the definition of the data requested from establishments both in the Census of Transportation and the Census of Manufactures (and related census publications) so that the measures of production, inputs, and goods (and services) transported (transferred) can be directly related to one another. Special data sources and estimation methods may have to be found to determine interregional transfers for the service industries.

The consistency between the interregional trade flows and the input-output data in the MRIO accounts has proven to be extremely valuable for the regional analyses conducted thus far. The interregional trade flows specified by mode of transport have been used for many studies. As noted in chapter 3, the interregional trade estimates provided in the MRIO model enable a regional analyst to determine gross shipments to and from each region in the economy—information that is highly important for transportation forecasting and planning.

Notes

1. The Harvard Economic Research Project was closed June 30, 1972, and the multiregional staff members were transferred to the Department of Urban Studies and Planning (DUSP), Massachusetts Institute of Technology, where the MRIO work is being continued. Revisions to the 51-region data were begun at the HERP and continued at the DUSP.

2. The Office of Business Economics implemented the model earlier under a contract with the Economic Development Administration, but only for purposes of evaluating the model, not for policy purposes.

3. The name RAS is not an abbreviation but is derived from the fact that two adjustment parameters, R and S, are applied to the matrix A when this biproportional matrix procedure is used.

4. Two problems actually arise in connection with the existence condition: infeasible matrix problems and slow rate of convergence. Some matrices have feasible solutions, but the rate of convergence is so slow that they can be classified along with infeasible matrices. Möhr explains these two problems in more detail [145].

7 Projections of 1970 and 1980 Gross Regional Product

Since 1962, the projection of the gross national product has been part of the routine work of the Interagency Growth Project at the Bureau of Labor Statistics (BLS), U.S. Department of Labor. A brief discussion of that work was included in the Coordinated National Economic Accounts section in chapter 1. State projections, however, are still not made on an official basis. Prior to the present study, in fact, gross regional product projections were available only for a few states, such as for the state of Washington [213] and the state of West Virginia [138].

When the multiregional input-output (MRIO) model was implemented, the 1970 and 1980 final demand projections made for the present study were used as one of the three exogenous sets of variables for calculating 1970 and 1980 regional outputs and interregional trade.[1] As explained in chapter 3, the other two sets of exogenous variables were base-year (1963) technology and trade coefficients. The 1970 and 1980 projections of the gross regional product were made during 1968–1970 as estimates independent of the general MRIO model. Because any errors in the final demand projections will cause inaccuracies in the projected output and trade estimates, it is important to complete the description of the MRIO data assembly by summarizing the data sources and estimation procedures used to make the independent projections. A detailed description was provided in the third volume of this series, *State Projections of the Gross National Product, 1970, 1980* [198]. A brief history of the three phases of the calculations is provided first; then, the specifics on the data sources and projection procedures used for each of the components of the gross regional product are summarized.

History of the Data Estimation

The estimation of the 1970 and 1980 gross regional product was separated into three phases. During the first phase, all of the projections, described in detail in the next section, were made by members of the staff at Jack Faucett Associates, Inc. (JFA), and were adjusted to the BLS national totals. During the second and third phases, modifications of these estimates were made, principally by members of the staff at the Harvard Economic Research Project in consultation with the JFA staff members.

The second phase involved a detailed check of the state estimates for consistency with the respective 1970 and 1980 BLS national projections. First, the BLS national 1970 and 1980 projections were adjusted for consistency with the industry-composition definitions used in the MRIO model. In 1969, the BLS prepared three alternative national 1970 and 1980 projections [285].[2] The one used in the initial MRIO research was based upon an assumed 4.3 percent rate of growth in the real gross national product and a 4.0 percent unemployment rate. Next, the state estimates were checked for consistency with the adjusted national data. These consistent state final demand projections were then used in December 1970 for the initial implementation of the MRIO model.

In the spring of 1972, the BLS published revised 1970 national final demand "projections" to account for adjustments in the economy, mainly those resulting from a scaling-down of military expenditures in Vietnam. During the third phase of data estimation, these revised BLS 1970 national control totals (still with an assumed 4.3 percent rate of growth in the real gross national product and an unemployment rate of 4.0 percent [291]) were used as control totals for the 1970 state estimates. (The 1980 BLS control totals were unchanged.) This set of adjustments was made during 1971–1972, when extensive revisions were being made to all MRIO data. These 1970 and 1980 final state estimates are published in appendix C of the third volume of this series [198, pp. 116–259].

Because different data sources and estimation procedures were used to project the state final demands for the six basic components, each component will be discussed separately. The components are the same as those estimated for 1947, 1958, and 1963: personal consumption expenditures, gross private fixed capital formation, net inventory change, net foreign exports, state and local government purchases, and federal government purchases.

Data Sources and Projection Procedures

The basic approach was to use data sources and projection procedures compatible with the base year. Thus, personal consumption expenditures were projected using 32 types of consumer units, and state and local government purchases were separated into 25 functional categories. As a result, consistent gross regional product estimates are now available for five years (1947, 1958, 1963, 1970, and 1980) not only for the six basic components, but for certain subcomponents as well. The specific data sources and projection procedures used for each component will be briefly reviewed here. Full details are given in the third volume of this series [198].

Personal Consumption Expenditures

Personal consumption expenditures (PCE) is the largest final demand component, comprising 66 percent of the 1970 and 65 percent of the 1980 projected gross national product. Projections for each state were made by weighting regional data from the 1960-1961 Consumer Expenditures Survey (CES) [294] with state projections of 1970 and 1980 population made specifically for this research effort. Average personal consumption expenditures data for each of 126 commodities are available from the CES for four regions, three places of residence, two types of family, and ten income groups. These disaggregated average consumption data for each of the four regions were therefore initially available for 60 (3×2×10) types of consumer units but were aggregated to 32 types (two places of residence, two types of family, and eight income groups) for comparability with the population data and with the base-year estimates.

Three separate procedures were required to obtain the 1970 and 1980 state population projections. First, the number of households and unrelated individuals were available for 1970, but had to be projected for 1980. To do this, the 1970 and 1975 projections by the U.S. Bureau of the Census (Census) of the number of households by state were extrapolated to 1980. Because of instability in the past trends, a ratio method (developed by the Census) was used whereby the distribution of seven age classes by five household types, from the *Census of Population, 1960* [238], was applied to the 1980 Census population projection by age class [249]. The state sums of the total number of households were then adjusted to add to the 1980 national projections.

Second, the 1970 and 1980 total number of families and unrelated individuals were divided into rural and urban components. This was done by aging the distributions from the 1960 decennial census, using estimates of growth in the population of standard metropolitan statistical areas (SMSAs), developed by the National Planning Association [163], as determinants of the urban/rural split.

Third, the 1970 and 1980 urban families, rural families, urban unrelated individuals, and rural unrelated individuals were each separated into eight income classes. To accomplish this separation, the projected change in mean income between 1960 and 1970 and between 1960 and 1980 was used to shift the 1960 distribution [238]. The estimates of 1970 and 1980 mean family or household incomes were obtained by combining projections of 1970 and 1980 per capital income, provided by the National Planning Association [163], with projections of family size, based upon past trends.

Using the 1960-1961 CES data and the state population projections, the 1970 and 1980 PCE projections for each state were calculated by multiplying the 32 population projections for 1970 and 1980, respectively, by the 126 average 1960–1961 consumption expenditures for the corresponding consumer unit.

This provided the state estimates to which a few special adjustments were made for imputations, out-of-home-state expenditures, and expenditures by foreigners. State distribution factors were calculated for the allocation of both 1970 and 1980 national estimates of imputed consumption expenditures for the following four categories: food, clothing, and housing; financial intermediaries; food and fuel produced and consumed on farms; and rental value of owner-occupied housing. For out-of-home-state expenditures, the national totals for food, lodging, recreation, and all-expense tours were projected to 1970 and 1980 and were then distributed to states, while all transportation expenditures were assumed to be made in the state of residence. National 1963–1969 time-series data on expenditures made by Canadians, Mexicans, and other foreign visitors (obtained from the June 1964 through 1968 issues of the *Survey of Current Business*) were projected to 1970 and 1980, adjusted to the BLS controls for all foreign expenditures, and then distributed to states.[3] Details on the specific data sources and estimation procedures used for these estimates are provided in the third volume of this series [198, pp. 14–23].

Gross Private Domestic Investment

Gross private domestic investment, comprising 14 percent of the 1970 and 16 percent of the estimated 1980 gross national product, is not only a large component; it also has one of the greatest year-to-year fluctuations of any of the components. For the 1970 and 1980 projections, it was separated into four basic subcomponents: producers' durable equipment, plant construction, residential construction, and net inventory change. These represent all private investment, with all public investment being accounted for in the government sectors of final demand.

Producers' Durable Equipment. Equipment investment is made for either replacement or expansion purposes. Investment for either purpose can incorporate new technologies. For this study, these technological changes in capital were assumed to be constant for all states. Projected output by industry for each state therefore became the major variable determining the distribution of the BLS national investment estimates to the states.

Replacement Equipment Investment. For each industry in each state, the replacement of worn or outdated equipment was assumed to be a function of three factors: 1970 and 1980 state output projections for each industry;[4] 1966 national replacement-to-stock ratios; and 1966 national stock-to-output ratios. The national replacement and stock ratios were determined from 1966 values [36], the latest year for which data were available in 1969. (Attempts to project these values using time series resulted in some negative 1980 values and were therefore abandoned.) The projected 1970 and 1980 outputs were then multiplied by the products of the two ratios for the corresponding year to determine 1970 and 1980 replacement equipment investment.

Net Equipment Investment. For each consuming industry in each state, the 1970 and 1980 expansion (net) equipment investment was obtained by multiplying the corresponding 1969–1970 or 1979–1980 changes in output [47] by the 1966 stock-to-output ratios [36]. The 1969 and 1979 outputs were obtained by geometric interpolation between 1963 and 1970 and 1970 and 1980 estimates, respectively. If output decreased, net investment was constrained to be zero.

Total Equipment Investment. Total producers' equipment investment by consuming industry was obtained by summing the replacement and net investment estimates for each industry in each state. The estimates for each state then became column controls for a capital-flow table for the respective state. As explained in the Gross Private Fixed Capital Formation section in chapter 2, in a capital-flow table, each row shows the industry producing the capital and each column the industry consuming the capital. To transfer the equipment investment data from consuming industry to producing industry, each column of the 1963 national capital-flow matrix [38] was divided by the column sum, and the state-by-state consuming-industry equipment-investment totals were multiplied by the fractions in the respective industry column to obtain 51 state capital equipment tables for 1970 as well as 1980. (Row 11, New construction, is zero in these capital equipment tables.) The elements in each row of the tables were then summed to obtain total capital produced in each industry in each state, and the corresponding BLS national 1970 and 1980 capital equipment data were distributed in proportion to the state capital equipment totals for the respective year.

Plant Construction. For private plant construction, the same general assumptions were made and procedures used as for private equipment investment, with a separation into replacement and net components, but with plant stock and replacement ratios being used instead of those for equipment, and with no transformation from consuming to producing industry (through a capital-flow table) being necessary, because all plant investment is specified as being purchased directly from IO-11, New construction. The corresponding BLS national 1970 and 1980 private plant investment data were distributed in proportion to the estimated state data for the respective year, and the adjusted state data were placed as row 11 in the respective state capital vectors.

Residential Construction. For residential construction, two factors complicated the estimation process. First, almost no data exist on construction put in place. Second, it is known that total and per capita expenditures vary considerably over time (since housing starts are sensitive to mortgage and interest rates) and from state to state (with eight states accounting for over 50 percent of total residential construction expenditures). Because of these complications, residential construction expenditures for each state (1958 contract awards) were estimated by fitting a regression equation, using 1958 cross-sectional data with 1957-to-1958 changes in population and 1958 personal income as the exogenous variables. The regression coefficients obtained from this estimation were used with 1969-to-1970 and 1979-to-1980 projections of changes in state population [249] and the National Planning Association's projections of 1970 and 1980 personal income [163]. The 1970 and 1980 BLS national estimates of residential construction were then allocated to states using the state estimates as distribution factors.

Net Investment in Inventories. The 1970 projections of net inventory change by state and industry were assumed to be a function of the ratio of the 1963-to-1970 change in projected state output by industry to the change in the same period in projected national output. The 1980 projections were assumed to be a function of the ratio of the 1970–1980 change to the change in that period in projected national output. Although these two assumptions were necessary because of limited resources, the direct link of inventory accumulation only to changes in output seemed reasonable. The link was also in line with the long-run BLS projections, for which it was assumed that the economy would be operating at full employment in 1970 and 1980 and that the 1970 and 1980 output levels would be achieved with no major fluctuations in the annual growth rates.

Net Foreign Exports

Net foreign exports comprised 0.3 percent of the 1970 and 0.8 percent of the 1980 projected gross national product. State projections were made only for the gross foreign export component of net foreign exports. At the state level, the exports of goods and services can be estimated either by state of production or by state (port) of exit. The projections in this study were estimated by state of exit, because in the MRIO model, the total output in all regions, as well as interregional shipments between regions, is assumed to be a function of the demand in a region. The interregional shipments must include exports that are shipped. The demand data, therefore, must include estimates of exports by state of exit in order for the export production and shipments to be properly generated.

While the level and composition of gross foreign exports were assumed to be highly unstable because they are a function of the aggregate world demand and supply conditions–including the competitive position of domestic producers relative to foreign producers–the distribution of those exports by state of exit was assumed to be relatively stable over time. A base-period distribution was therefore assumed to be representative of the distribution for both projection years.

For commodity trade, the base distribution was a combination of 1969 regional control totals (in dollar terms) for 8 U.S. customs regions [246], used to allocate the projected 1970 and 1980 national totals, and the 1963 state exports (in tonnage terms) [252; 258], used to allocate the eight regional control totals for each year. The assumption was made that the value of exports and their tonnage are closely correlated. For IO-13, Ordnance & accessories; IO-42, Other fabricated metal products; and IO-50, Machine shop products, the distributions were based solely on state tonnage data. (Customs regions data could not be used due to an industry classification problem.)

For the service industries, the state distribution proxies and sources are given, industry by industry, in the third volume of this series [198, pp. 43–44]. The national totals for 1970 and 1980 were allocated to states using these distribution series.

No state distribution was made for the gross import portion of net foreign exports.

State and Local Government Purchases

The net purchases by state and local governments comprised 10 percent of the 1970 and 11 percent of the 1980 projected gross national product. Although these transactions account for all purchases by state and local agencies, some important items at the state and local level, such as purchases by state and local government enterprises, transfer payments, net interest payments, and grants-in-aid, are not included in the input-output final demand component. For the state projections, 7 major functional categories, separated into 25 subfunctions, were used, rather than the 11 used for the national projections or the 22 used for the MRIO base-year estimates. The major functional categories used were: (1) education; (2) highways; (3) hospitals, health, & sanitation; (4) natural resources; (5) local parks & recreation; (6) public enterprises; and (7) all other. All state projections were made in terms of fiscal-year expenditures and then converted to 1970 and 1980 calendar-year purchases by extrapolating the fiscal-year data to time periods 1970.5 and 1980.5, respectively, and distributing the corresponding national purchase data over these adjusted estimates of state purchases. For most functional categories, the parameters for the regression equations were calculated using historical 1957–1968 data. State-by-state data are available in the *Census of Governments, 1967* [231] for 1957–1967, but before that period, only for 1942; therefore, the time series could not be extended prior to 1957. The regressions used for the projections of all subfunctions of state and local government were of one of the following general forms:

$$\log E_t^h = a_0 + a_1 t \tag{7.1}$$

$$E_t^h = b_0 + b_1 t \tag{7.2}$$

where

E^h = expenditures (total or per capita) for state h

t = time

a_0, a_1, b_0, and b_1 = least-squares estimates (generally using 1957–1968 data).

The endogenous and exogenous variables and the data used for each subfunction are given in table 7-1.

The past and anticipated growth rates of all of the major functional and subfunctional categories vary drastically, as documented in the third volume of this series [198, pp. 56–79]. The 1970 and 1980 projections for each of the seven functions are given there as well.

Federal Government Purchases

Federal government purchases comprised 9.5 percent of the projected GNP for 1970 but were expected to decline and comprise only 7.3 percent of the projected GNP for 1980. Detailed state projections were made for 1970, then adjusted to obtain estimates for 1980. Because of the lack of historical time-series data, state projections were made for only two components: defense and nondefense. Each of the two components will be discussed here.

Defense Purchases in 1970. For 27 of the 52 manufacturing industries and 11 of the 27 nonmanufacturing industries, 1970 national defense expenditures were allocated in proportion to the 1967 total employment data from *County Business Patterns, 1967* (*CBP*) [244]. For 12 of the 52 manufacturing industries producing major defense goods, such as ordnance, petroleum, and aircraft, the 1970 national total was allocated to states according to state data from *Military Prime Contract Awards by Region and State, 1968* (*Prime Contracts*) [281], supplemented by *CBP* data. Of the total value of prime contracts in each state, 65 percent was assumed to remain in the state of origin of the prime contract,

Table 7–1
Regression Parameters for Twenty-Four Subfunctions of State and Local Government

Function and Subfunction	*Endogenous Variables*	*Exogenous Variables*	*Years Covered by Time-Series Data*
1. Education			
1.1 Higher	$\log E_t^h$	t	1957–1968
1.2 Elementary, secondary, and other	E_t^h	$(P_{5\text{-}17})_{t-1}^h$	1957–1968
2. Highways			
2.1 Capital outlays	E_t^h	t	1957–1968
2.2 Current operation	E_t^h	t	1957–1968
3. Hospitals, health, & sanitation			
3.1 Hospitals, health, & other	$\log E_t^h$	t	1957, 1960–1968
3.2 Sanitation	E_t^h	t	1957–1968
4. Natural resources[a]	–	–	–
5. Local parks & recreation			
5.1 National per capita	$\log PEN_t$	t	1957–1968
5.2 State total	E_t^h	$E_{1968}^h, \frac{PEN_t}{PEN_{1968}}, \frac{P_t^h}{P_{1968}^h}$	1957–1968
6. Enterprises			
6.1 Water-supply systems[b]	CO_t^h	P_t^h	1961–1968 (July 1st for population)
6.2 Gas-supply systems			

Table 7–1 continued

Function and Subfunction	*Endogenous Variables*	*Exogenous Variables*	*Years Covered by Time-Series Data*
6.2a National total	CON_t	t	1957–1968
6.2b State total	CO_t^h	$CO^h_{1967}, \frac{CON_t}{CON_{1967}}$	1957–1968
6.3 Electricity			
6.3a National total	CON_t	P_t	1957–1968
6.3b State total	CO_t^h	$CO^h_{1967}, (P_t - P_{1967})^h$	1957–1968
6.4 Transit facilities[c]	–	–	
6.5 Sewerage			
6.5a National per capita	PE_t^h	t	1957–1968
6.5b State total	CO_t^h	PE_t^h, P_t^h	1957–1968
6.6 Housing and urban renewal			
6.6a National total	CON_t	P_t	1957–1968
6.6b State total	CO_t^h	$CO^h_{1967}, (P_t - P_{1967})^h$	1957–1968
6.7 Water transportation & terminals			
6.7a National total	CON_t	t	1957–1968

6.7b State total–1967	CO^h_{1967}	$0.60DE_{1967}$	1967
6.7c State total	CO^h_t	$CO^h_{1967}, \frac{CON_t}{CON_{1967}}$	1957–1968
6.8 Air transportation			
6.8a National total	CON_t	t	1957–1968
6.8b State total–1967	CO^h_{1967}	$0.67DE_{1967}$	1967
6.8c State total	CO^h_t	$CO^h_{1967}, \frac{CON_t}{CON_{1967}}$	1957–1968
6.9 Highway toll facilities	CO^h_t	t	1960–1968
7. All other			
7.1 Police			
7.1a National per capita	PEN_t	t	1957–1968
7.1b State per capita	PE^h_t	$PE^h_{1967}, \frac{PEN_t}{PEN_{1967}}$	1957–1968
7.1c State total	${}^pE^h_t$	PE^h_t, p^h_t	1957–1968
7.2 Fire	E^h_t	Y^h_t	1957–1968
7.3 Correction	${}^cE^h_t$	$\frac{{}^cE^h_t}{{}^pE^h_t}, {}^pE^h_t$	1957–1968
7.4 Public welfare	$\log E^h_t$	t	1957, 1962, 1967

Table 7–1 continued

Function and Subfunction	*Endogenous Variables*	*Exogenous Variables*	*Years Covered by Time-Series Data*
7.5 General government	$\log E_t^h$	t	1957, 1962, 1967
7.6 Other	$\log E_t^h$	t	1957, 1962, 1967
7.7 Libraries[d]	–	–	–

[a]The national 1970 and 1980 projections for this subfunction were distributed in proportion to actual 1967 state data for the subfunction [231].
[b]Civilian population only was used for the population parameter.
[c]Projections of capital outlays for 1970 and 1980 were obtained directly from local transit authorities in Boston, Chicago, Cleveland, New Jersey, New York, Philadelphia, San Francisco, Washington, D.C., and Atlanta.
[d]State library expenditures were projected to be 0.03 percent of the sum of the previous six categories both for 1970 and 1980.

NOTATIONS

t = time

CO_t^h = capital outlay of state h in year t

CON_t = national capital outlay in year t

DE_t = direct general expenditures in year t

E_t^h = expenditures in state h in year t

${}^cE_t^h$ = correction expenditures in state h in year t

${}^pE_t^h$ = police expenditures in state h in year t

P_t^h = population of state h in year t

$(P_{5\text{-}17})_t^h$ = population in age-class 5 to 17 for state h in year t

PE_t^h = per capita expenditures in state h in year t

PEN_t = per capita expenditures for the nation in year t

with the remaining 35 percent being distributed to other states in proportion to employment data from the *CBP* [244]. For 11 of the 52 manufacturing industries, the 1970 national total was allocated according to data from "Shipments of Defense-Oriented Industries, 1967" (Shipments) [250], supplemented by *CBP* data. The national defense purchases for 9 nonmanufacturing industries were allocated using civilian and military employment in the Department of Defense, by state, as of June 30, 1969, as the distribution factors.[5] Details on the industries for which the four major data sources were used are provided in tables 6-1 through 6-4 in *State Projections of the Gross National Product, 1970, 1980* [198, pp. 84-88].

Nondefense Purchases in 1970. Although the federal budget for the nondefense purchases category is specified in terms of functions, such as space research, education, and welfare, this category of direct federal purchases is so small that the BLS projections do not include detail by function. Over 70 percent of the purchases are concentrated in only six industries: IO-11, New construction; IO-13, Ordnance & accessories; IO-56, Radio, TV, & communication equipment; IO-60, Aircraft & parts; IO-77, Medical, educational services, & nonprofit organizations; and IO-84, Government industry. Of these, IO-11 accounts for 23 percent and IO-84 for 28 percent of the total. Most state allocations were made using the following sources:

1. State-by-state nondefense employment figures [251]—12 industries
2. *County Business Patterns, 1967* data [244]—18 industries
3. Combination of *Shipments* [250] and *CBP* [244] data—13 industries
4. Equal-weight distribution of production and consumption data—6 industries.

For the remaining 13 industries, unique data sources and methodologies were used, all of which are described in detail in the third volume of this series [198, pp. 93-95].[6]

Total Purchases in 1980. For 1980, the composition of the 1970 state purchases was adjusted where appropriate to reflect expected changes between 1970 and 1980, and the 1980 national total for each industry was distributed in proportion to the 1970 state estimates.

Conclusion

All 1970 and 1980 state projections except those for personal consumption expenditures were made in terms of producer prices. To convert the PCE state estimates from purchaser to producer prices, the same BLS 1970 and 1980 national margins [198, pp. 25-27] were applied to estimates for all states in the respective year. The procedure used for this conversion is the same as that described in the Margins section in chapter 5 for the 1947, 1958, and 1963 estimates.

In addition, all final demand projections were made in terms of constant 1958 dollars and then converted to constant 1963 dollars using the 1958/1963 price deflators given in the third volume of this series [198, pp. 108–110].

Although the MRIO projections were completed ten years ago, these are the only gross regional product projections that have been made in such detail for all states. As soon as actual data for 1980 become available, the 1980 projections should be compared with the actual data to determine ways in which the present projection techniques can be improved. Some possibilities for improvements were given in the third volume. The need for more up-to-date projections is great, and it is evident that private consulting groups will soon be expanding their present very limited state projection series.

Notes

1. The terms *final demand* and *gross regional product* will be used interchangeably throughout the chapter.

2. For a full description of the BLS final demand estimation procedures, refer to *The Structure of the U.S. Economy in 1980 and 1985* [292].

3. As noted in the Personal Consumption Expenditures section in chapter 2, the expenditures made by foreigners are distinguished from those made by U.S. residents in constructing the BLS tables, while they are not distinguished in assembling data for the OBE tables.

4. The 1970 and 1980 state output projections were made independent of the MRIO model and were based upon the relationship of state-to-national output in 1947, 1958, and 1963, with modifications being made for erratic historical patterns [47].

5. No 1970 defense purchases were made by 2 of the manufacturing industries and 11 of the nonmanufacturing industries.

6. No 1970 nondefense purchases were made by 19 of the input-output industries.

Appendix A: Industrial and Regional Classifications

Table A-1
Input-Output Industry Numbers, Titles, and Related SIC Codes

Industry Number	*Industry Title*	*Related SIC Codes (1957 edition)*[a]
1	Livestock & livestock products	013, pt. 014, 0193, pt. 02, pt. 0729
2	Other agricultural products	011, 012, pt. 014, 0192, 0199, pt. 02
3	Forestry & fishery products	074, 081, 082, 084, 086, 091
4	Agricultural, forestry, & fishery services	071, 0723, pt. 0729, 085, 098
5	Iron & ferroalloy ores mining	1011, 106
6	Nonferrous metal ores mining	102, 103, 104, 105, 108, 109
7	Coal mining	11, 12
8	Crude petroleum & natural gas	1311, 1321
9	Stone & clay mining & quarrying	141, 142, 144, 145, 148, 149
10	Chemical & fertilizer mineral mining	147
11	New construction	138, pt. 15, pt. 16, pt. 17, pt. 6561
12	Maintenance & repair construction	pt. 15, pt. 16, pt. 17
13	Ordnance & accessories	19
14	Food & kindred products	20
15	Tobacco manufactures	21
16	Broad & narrow fabrics, yarn & thread mills	221, 222, 223, 224, 226, 228
17	Miscellaneous textile goods & floor coverings	227, 229
18	Apparel	225, 23 (excluding 239), 3992
19	Miscellaneous fabricated textile products	239
20	Lumber & wood products, except containers	24 (excluding 244)
21	Wooden containers	244
22	Household furniture	251
23	Other furniture & fixtures	25 (excluding 251)
24	Paper & allied products, except containers & boxes	26 (excluding 265)

25	Paperboard containers & boxes	265
26	Printing & publishing	27
27	Chemicals & selected chemical products	281 (excluding alumina pt. of 2819), 286, 287, 289
28	Plastics & synthetic materials	282
29	Drugs, cleaning, & toilet preparations	283, 284
30	Paints & allied products	285
31	Petroleum refining & related industries	29
32	Rubber & miscellaneous plastics products	30
33	Leather tanning & industrial leather products	311, 312
34	Footwear & other leather products	31 (excluding 311, 312)
35	Glass & glass products	321, 322, 323
36	Stone & clay products	324, 325, 326, 327, 328, 329
37	Primary iron & steel manufacturing	331, 332, 3391, 3399
38	Primary nonferrous metals manufacturing	2819 (alumina only), 333, 334, 335, 336, 3392
39	Metal containers	3411, 3491
40	Heating, plumbing, & fabricated structural metal products	343, 344
41	Screw machine products, bolts, nuts, etc., & metal stampings	345, 346
42	Other fabricated metal products	342, 347, 348, 349 (excluding 3491)
43	Engines & turbines	351
44	Farm machinery & equipment	352
45	Construction, mining, oil field machinery & equipment	3531, 3532, 3533
46	Materials handling machinery & equipment	3534, 3535, 3536, 3537
47	Metalworking machinery & equipment	354
48	Special industry machinery & equipment	355
49	General industrial machinery & equipment	356
50	Machine shop products	359
51	Office, computing, & accounting machines	357
52	Service industry machines	358

(continued)

Table A–1 *continued*

Industry Number	*Industry Title*	*Related SIC Codes (1957 edition)*[a]
53	Electric transmission & distribution equipment & electrical industrial apparatus	361, 362
54	Household appliances	363
55	Electric lighting & wiring equipment	364
56	Radio, TV, & communication equipment	365, 366
57	Electronic components & accessories	367
58	Miscellaneous electrical machinery, equipment, & supplies	369
59	Motor vehicles & equipment	371
60	Aircraft & parts	372
61	Other transportation equipment	373, 374, 375, 379
62	Professional, scientific, & controlling instruments & supplies	381, 382, 384, 387
63	Optical, ophthalmic, & photographic equipment & supplies	383, 385, 386
64	Miscellaneous manufacturing	39 (excluding 3992)
65	Transportation & warehousing	40, 41, 42, 44, 45, 46, 47
66	Communications, except radio & TV broadcasting	481, 482, 489
67	Radio & TV broadcasting	483
68	Electric, gas, water, & sanitary services	49
69	Wholesale & retail trade	50 (excluding manufacturers sales offices), 52, 53, 54, 55, 56, 57, 58, 59, pt. 7399
70	Finance & insurance	60, 61, 62, 63, 64, 66, 67
71	Real estate & rental	65 (excluding 6541 and pt. 6561)
72	Hotels & lodging places; personal & repair services, except automobile repair	70, 72, 76 (excluding 7694 and 7699)
73	Business services	6541, 73 (excluding 7361, 7391, and pt. 7399), 7694, 7699, 81, 89 (excluding 8921)

74	Research & development	(eliminated in 1963 study)
75	Automobile repair & services	75
76	Amusements	78, 79
77	Medical, educational services, & nonprofit organizations	0722, 7361, 80, 82, 84, 86, 8921
78	Federal government enterprises	....
79	State & local government enterprises	....
80a	Directly allocated imports of goods & services	....
80b	Transferred imports of goods & services	....
81	Business travel, entertainment, & gifts	....
82	Office supplies	....
83	Scrap, used, & secondhand goods	....
84	Government industry	....
85	Rest of the world industry	....
86	Household industry	....
87	Inventory valuation adjustment	....

[a]These are the SIC codes assigned to industries in the 1958 input-output study. They differ slightly from those assigned in the 1963 study.

Table A-2
Regional Classification

Region[a] *Number*	*State*[b] *Number*	*State*[b] *Name*
1	6	Connecticut
	18	Maine
	20	Massachusetts
	28	New Hampshire
	38	Rhode Island
	44	Vermont
2	29	New Jersey
	31	New York
	37	Pennsylvania
3	12	Illinois
	13	Indiana
	21	Michigan
	34	Ohio
	48	Wisconsin
4	14	Iowa
	15	Kansas
	22	Minnesota
	24	Missouri
	26	Nebraska
	33	North Dakota
	40	South Dakota
5	7	Delaware
	8	District of Columbia
	9	Florida
	10	Georgia
	19	Maryland
	32	North Carolina
	39	South Carolina
	45	Virginia
	47	West Virginia
6	1	Alabama
	16	Kentucky
	23	Mississippi
	41	Tennessee
7	3	Arkansas
	17	Louisiana
	35	Oklahoma
	42	Texas
8	2	Arizona
	5	Colorado
	11	Idaho
	25	Montana
	27	Nevada
	30	New Mexico
	43	Utah
	49	Wyoming
9	4	California
	36	Oregon
	46	Washington
	50	Alaska
	51	Hawaii

[a]The names of the 9 census regions are:

1 New England
2 Middle Atlantic
3 East North Central
4 West North Central
5 South Atlantic
6 East South Central
7 West South Central
8 Mountain
9 Pacific

[b]The sequential order of the 51 states is the same for all published MRIO tables.

Table A–3
Multiregional Input-Output Classification for Nineteen Industries

Industry No.		
MRIO	*BEA*	*Industry Title*
1	1	Livestock & livestock products
2	2	Other agricultural products
3	7	Coal mining
4	8	Crude petroleum & natural gas
5		Other mining
	5	Iron & ferroalloy ores mining
	6	Nonferrous metal ores mining
	9	Stone & clay mining and quarrying
	10	Chemical & fertilizer mineral mining
6		Construction
	11	New construction
	12	Maintenance & repair construction
7		Food, tobacco, fabrics, & apparel
	14	Food & kindred products
	15	Tobacco manufactures
	16	Fabrics
	17	Textile products
	18	Apparel
	19	Misc. textile products
	33	Leather tanning & products
	34	Footwear, leather products
8		Transportation equipment & ordnance
	13	Ordnance & accessories
	59	Motor vehicles, equipment
	60	Aircraft & parts
	61	Other transportation equipment
9		Lumber & paper
	20	Lumber & wood products
	21	Wooden containers
	22	Household furniture
	23	Other furniture
	24	Paper & allied products
	25	Paperborad containers
	26	Printing & publishing
10	31	Petroleum, related industries
11		Plastics & chemicals
	27	Chemicals, selected products
	28	Plastics & synthetics
	29	Drugs & cosmetics
	30	Paint & allied products
	32	Rubber, misc. plastics
12		Glass, stone, & clay products
	35	Glass & glass products
	36	Stone & clay products
13	37	Primary iron, steel, manufacturing
14	38	Primary nonferrous manufacturing
15		Machinery & equipment
	39	Metal containers
	40	Fabricated metal products

Table A-3 continued

Industry No.		
MRIO	*BEA*	*Industry Title*
	41	Screw machine products, etc.
	42	Other fabricated metal products
	43	Engines & turbines
	44	Farm machinery & equipment
	45	Construction machinery & equipment
	46	Materials handling, machinery & equipment
	47	Metalworking machinery & equipment
	48	Special machinery & equipment
	49	General machinery & equipment
	50	Machine shop products
	51	Office, computing machines
	52	Service industry machines
	53	Electricity transmission equipment
	54	Household appliances
	55	Electric lighting equipment
	56	Radio, TV, etc., equipment
	57	Electronic components
	58	Misc. electrical machinery
	62	Professional, scientific instruments
	63	Medical, photographic equipment
	64	Misc. manufacturing
16		Services
	3	Forestry & fishery products
	4	Agriculture, forestry, & fishery services
	66	Communications, excl. broadcasting
	67	Radio & TV broadcasting
	69	Wholesale & retail trade
	70	Finance & insurance
	71	Real estate & rental
	72	Hotels; repair services, excl. auto
	73	Business services
	74	Research & development
	75	Automobile repair & services
	76	Amusements
	77	Medical & educational services, nonprofit organizations
	78	Federal government enterprises
	79	State & local government enterprises
17	65	Transportation & warehousing
18		Gas, water, & sanitary services
	68.02	Gas utilities
	68.03	Water & sanitary services
19	68.01	Electric utilities

Appendix B
Base 1963 and Projected 1970 and 1980 Multiregional Data

TABLE B.1-1

1963 INPUT-OUTPUT TRANSACTIONS
NEW ENGLAND
(THOUSANDS OF 1963 DOLLARS)

INDUSTRY TITLE	1	2	3	4	5	6	7	8	9
1 LIVESTOCK, PRDTS.	24122	34604	0	0	0	108	575634	118	141
2 OTHER AGRICULTURE PRDTS.	91932	20787	0	0	3	17669	335883	353	421
3 COAL MINING	243	41	0	0	0	0	4035	516	9702
4 CRUDE PETRO.,NATURAL GAS	0	0	0	0	0	0	0	0	0
5 OTHER MINING	40	3871	0	0	685	36260	430	29	10297
6 CONSTRUCTION	5957	3819	0	0	370	1131	13557	4586	9548
7 FOOD,TOBAC.,FAB.,APPAREL	176074	2453	0	0	98	16379	2178279	22829	64767
8 TRANSPORT EQPT.,ORDNANCE	136	145	0	0	407	2792	950	499004	438
9 LUMBER & PAPER	869	6621	0	0	188	227540	186098	18704	1018643
10 PETROLEUM, RELATED INDS.	3633	5077	0	0	1394	71613	17007	8393	19187
11 PLASTICS & CHEMICALS	4886	29158	0	0	2759	92172	450240	42534	165845
12 GLASS, STONE,CLAY PRDTS.	225	1338	0	0	119	277803	31511	12397	7692
13 PRIMARY IRON & STEEL MFR	0	0	0	0	682	88058	3895	111815	18714
14 PRIMARY NONFERROUS MFR.	3	1	0	0	74	72353	321	91452	4285
15 MACHINERY & EQUIPMENT	2558	1057	0	0	3878	555890	134121	431704	74452
16 SERVICES	63373	28580	0	13739	6307	552676	571892	184388	401829
17 TRANSPORT. & WAREHOUSING	12503	5623	0	66245	4831	129176	146812	36822	117431
18 GAS & WATER SERVICES	409	637	0	0	450	4652	14436	4266	19119
19 ELECTRIC UTILITIES	2582	420	0	0	1277	8934	35294	12153	28801
20 WAGES & SALARIES	55425	40575	0	0	21221	1023688	1475681	894082	1003327
21 DIRECT ALLOCATED IMPORTS	11	7	0	0	11	755	64660	823	1013
22 TRANSFERRRD IMPORTS	15545	3445	359	284649	37599	0	105492	12629	158586
23 OTHER VALUE ADDED	186340	190634	0	0	16192	1335071	821122	327186	525761
24 SECONDARY TRANSFERS-OUT	0	0	22	827	6021	0	53821	116901	52150
25 INVENTORY DEPLETION	0	1316	0	0	2	0	17304	6091	713
26 SCRAP (NET PURCHASES)	0	0	0	0	159	2081	-9153	-4954	17870
27 REGIONAL OUTPUT (OUTLAY)	646866	380209	380	365459	104730	4516801	7229321	2834820	3730731

TABLE B.1-1

1963 INPUT-OUTPUT TRANSACTIONS
NEW ENGLAND
(THOUSANDS OF 1963 DOLLARS)

INDUSTRY TITLE	10	11	12	13	14	15	16	17	18
1 LIVESTOCK, PRDTS.	3	290	18	9	22	464	6719	84	11
2 OTHER AGRICULTURE PRDTS.	9	1347	726	26	66	2964	9747	276	32
3 COAL MINING	62	5115	1171	8540	485	2135	9339	349	442
4 CRUDE PETRO.,NATURAL GAS	37647	1180	0	0	0	0	2034	181	54997
5 OTHER MINING	3591	14862	38144	22650	2942	1227	221	36	0
6 CONSTRUCTION	1630	8750	1921	3321	3724	15445	601730	48940	17675
7 FOOD,TOBAC.,FAB.,APPAREL	339	102041	6960	1158	5934	85881	147913	7065	769
8 TRANSPORT EQPT.,ORDNANCE	7	372	122	29	66	6700	57108	18935	52
9 LUMBER & PAPER	6940	78468	16400	1748	8821	166073	281249	5433	611
10 PETROLEUM, RELATED INDS.	17747	14433	3972	3520	2527	33967	130910	67123	3722
11 PLASTICS & CHEMICALS	2629	624371	25403	9099	31671	288183	174992	12617	2256
12 GLASS, STONE,CLAY PRDTS.	1840	13569	71869	879	3677	110776	19795	415	3
13 PRIMARY IRON & STEEL MFR	58	9566	7320	108850	4780	640332	802	10032	1
14 PRIMARY NONFERROUS MFR.	185	8639	2103	11020	528471	399108	838	733	0
15 MACHINERY & EQUIPMENT	1195	55371	12375	23505	28926	1567513	241578	17120	201
16 SERVICES	19672	281923	42013	34253	76206	813921	3874291	204424	22368
17 TRANSPORT. & WAREHOUSING	26840	63761	27534	24111	24755	133470	229118	129080	5628
18 GAS & WATER SERVICES	1701	15916	6695	6162	5805	16727	111188	4311	129794
19 ELECTRIC UTILITIES	716	23624	4972	7209	11613	45874	265605	5314	1458
20 WAGES & SALARIES	13395	540289	157392	144061	218455	2990318	6749617	612000	121615
21 DIRECT ALLOCATED IMPORTS	20	32596	1387	62	556	48082	43277	20548	74
22 TRANSFERRRD IMPORTS	180113	38404	10240	24631	33765	64044	36236	94713	800
23 OTHER VALUE ADDED	20902	661709	100589	88983	150835	1431508	8977636	425794	57464
24 SECONDARY TRANSFERS-OUT	5778	100227	19107	32516	20095	221453	893668	51490	112762
25 INVENTORY DEPLETION	0	536	162	149	2772	8193	0	0	0
26 SCRAP (NET PURCHASES)	46	302	376	11489	43432	-24073	2280	-2912	0
27 REGIONAL OUTPUT (OUTLAY)	343065	2697660	558970	567979	1210402	9070286	22867888	1734100	532733

TABLE B.1-1

1963 INPUT-OUTPUT TRANSACTIONS
NEW ENGLAND
(THOUSANDS OF 1963 DOLLARS)

INDUSTRY TITLE	19	20	21	22	23	24	25	26	27
1 LIVESTOCK, PRDTS.	17	103773	0	0	-8327	47211	0	0	785021
2 OTHER AGRICULTURE PRDTS.	52	177544	0	0	6905	35716	0	0	702457
3 COAL MINING	45065	12639	0	0	803	0	0	0	100681
4 CRUDE PETRO.,NATURAL GAS	3568	0	0	0	0	0	0	0	99606
5 OTHER MINING	0	989	0	0	1970	2741	0	0	140986
6 CONSTRUCTION	38126	0	0	-102725	3846625	0	0	0	4524131
7 FOOD,TOBAC.,FAB.,APPAREL	1417	5032882	0	0	165824	87235	0	0	8106298
8 TRANSPORT EQPT.,ORDNANCE	59	919313	0	0	2072235	127035	0	0	3705903
9 LUMBER & PAPER	1373	505743	0	0	230297	516917	0	0	3278735
10 PETROLEUM, RELATED INDS.	10894	537120	0	0	31252	10445	0	0	993934
11 PLASTICS & CHEMICALS	3230	454917	0	0	122929	109499	0	0	2649390
12 GLASS, STONE,CLAY PRDTS.	4	29294	0	0	12380	29322	0	0	624907
13 PRIMARY IRON & STEEL MFR	2	692	0	0	15018	30295	0	0	1050913
14 PRIMARY NONFERROUS MFR.	570	851	0	0	26756	68693	0	0	1216454
15 MACHINERY & EQUIPMENT	2069	696063	0	0	2453661	445430	0	0	6748666
16 SERVICES	52557	14220172	0	31409	1111107	278959	0	431	22886480
17 TRANSPORT. & WAREHOUSING	31985	656569	0	0	223960	11492	0	466	2108213
18 GAS & WATER SERVICES	35608	270808	0	0	5031	3287	0	0	656999
19 ELECTRIC UTILITIES	62022	354171	0	0	54014	3482	0	0	929537
20 WAGES & SALARIES	136617	209196	0	5349953	2747272	0	0	0	24504176
21 DIRECT ALLOCATED IMPORTS	120	402872	0	-740936	124062	0	0	0	0
22 TRANSFERRRD IMPORTS	3500	0	0	-1133717	0	0	0	28968	0
23 OTHER VALUE ADDED	518174	-67300	0	-5349953	-31074	0	0	0	10387573
24 SECONDARY TRANSFERS-OUT	120922	0	0	0	0	0	0	0	1807759
25 INVENTORY DEPLETION	0	0	0	0	0	0	0	0	37237
26 SCRAP (NET PURCHASES)	0	-14128	0	0	-362040	0	0	-29865	-369089
27 REGIONAL OUTPUT (OUTLAY)	1067948	24504176	0	-1945968	12850661	1807759	0	0	97676976

TABLE B.1-2

1963 INPUT-OUTPUT TRANSACTIONS
MIDDLE ATLANTIC
(THOUSANDS OF 1963 DOLLARS)

INDUSTRY TITLE	1	2	3	4	5	6	7	8	9
1 LIVESTOCK, PRDTS.	119881	78673	17	2	13	387	1896766	211	635
2 OTHER AGRICULTURE PRDTS.	434060	58547	48	5	36	53075	1072927	629	1893
3 COAL MINING	415	153	180568	0	1392	0	9252	2275	12241
4 CRUDE PETRO.,NATURAL GAS	0	0	0	1117	0	0	0	0	0
5 OTHER MINING	88	447	0	0	14373	90655	1340	193	12263
6 CONSTRUCTION	20797	15307	3759	2058	2045	4025	40487	11754	20421
7 FOOD,TOBAC.,FAB.,APPAREL	361707	6752	1003	118	726	60008	8154525	76192	154807
8 TRANSPORT EQPT.,ORDNANCE	481	447	3313	21	2397	9813	3598	1736968	1296
9 LUMBER & PAPER	2420	19225	4112	31	1686	783708	634820	43518	3263570
10 PETROLEUM, RELATED INDS.	14134	16272	5251	356	5899	220893	54474	17765	43117
11 PLASTICS & CHEMICALS	13003	87612	16977	809	19330	323364	697801	142760	420035
12 GLASS, STONE,CLAY PRDTS.	837	5995	593	286	761	1025465	150178	50476	21064
13 PRIMARY IRON & STEEL MFR	0	0	8228	95	6229	363833	2365	539664	65528
14 PRIMARY NONFERROUS MFR.	21	9	17	0	376	252711	1932	168401	14440
15 MACHINERY & EQUIPMENT	8521	5203	38801	1228	27635	2071468	653116	1016509	192961
16 SERVICES	157587	120490	52306	32871	50079	1971943	2379068	446543	1377052
17 TRANSPORT. & WAREHOUSING	36811	20520	18600	90607	52579	460759	580025	117488	303217
18 GAS & WATER SERVICES	1140	1868	639	133	4250	16564	47362	9822	29872
19 ELECTRIC UTILITIES	7204	1233	16735	381	11706	31802	96793	27013	57691
20 WAGES & SALARIES	108000	88000	201787	25408	120786	3572798	4873362	1584213	2970901
21 DIRECT ALLOCATED IMPORTS	40	32	110	12	75	2696	304974	1467	4496
22 TRANSFERRRD IMPORTS	54222	132529	574	387771	235051	0	1264645	140752	509002
23 OTHER VALUE ADDED	526534	694244	128758	12282	110325	1010631	3719487	1064286	1600297
24 SECONDARY TRANSFERS-OUT	0	0	103	4653	24982	0	155929	319727	143912
25 INVENTORY DEPLETION	0	4201	0	0	5525	0	20538	13902	2252
26 SCRAP (NET PURCHASES)	0	0	186	0	856	5374	-7357	-18073	4102
27 REGIONAL OUTPUT (OUTLAY)	1867903	1357759	682486	560243	699112	12331973	26808400	7514457	11227065

TABLE B.1-2

1963 INPUT-OUTPUT TRANSACTIONS
MIDDLE ATLANTIC
(THOUSANDS OF 1963 DOLLARS)

INDUSTRY TITLE	10	11	12	13	14	15	16	17	18
1 LIVESTOCK, PRDTS.	25	1191	92	107	51	1227	19421	822	58
2 OTHER AGRICULTURE PRDTS.	74	9595	2322	319	151	9622	33124	2458	174
3 COAL MINING	1369	22243	14896	149580	2478	6907	31016	2386	2346
4 CRUDE PETRO.,NATURAL GAS	1343517	6700	0	0	0	0	7640	1336	306661
5 OTHER MINING	13331	90042	139801	397480	151075	3420	966	146	0
6 CONSTRUCTION	50151	38885	11511	53744	9950	42401	2514262	241149	94736
7 FOOD,TOBAC.,FAB.,APPAREL	5961	248682	25344	13928	12792	232149	515474	57775	4196
8 TRANSPORT EQPT.,ORDNANCE	110	1010	492	334	146	17058	186819	160213	276
9 LUMBER & PAPER	31855	267713	104162	20006	15917	538242	1057253	26275	3298
10 PETROLEUM, RELATED INDS.	244090	70036	16303	46158	15446	86424	521282	364243	19837
11 PLASTICS & CHEMICALS	85109	2070813	133111	131235	69121	894597	610848	55261	11804
12 GLASS, STONE,CLAY PRDTS.	6558	86240	270977	9132	8353	258064	68326	1960	15
13 PRIMARY IRON & STEEL MFR	208	31473	23802	1439765	5674	2005514	2970	46900	5
14 PRIMARY NONFERROUS MFR.	6608	43941	10196	137307	1150777	1052747	3168	6774	0
15 MACHINERY & EQUIPMENT	22277	255061	49853	286022	73039	4196898	991607	84454	1083
16 SERVICES	239756	1252879	209717	438805	212330	2284797	15602193	1030533	121691
17 TRANSPORT. & WAREHOUSING	160533	244283	113721	362972	89054	417162	958409	805553	31092
18 GAS & WATER SERVICES	39052	82077	53378	83100	21672	45890	404960	23683	723134
19 ELECTRIC UTILITIES	16430	88697	35460	97218	43358	121812	947991	29193	7732
20 WAGES & SALARIES	191015	1722185	759259	1681100	471503	7675129	24662624	3691000	504334
21 DIRECT ALLOCATED IMPORTS	173	48391	4482	743	1540	71330	166067	254161	407
22 TRANSFERRRD IMPORTS	259273	221261	59912	248823	592637	886997	190219	360272	5000
23 OTHER VALUE ADDED	552523	2705182	585691	1306152	444913	4258949	37515696	1705085	474960
24 SECONDARY TRANSFERS-OUT	31708	414605	53181	73700	78942	766535	3905558	192225	429527
25 INVENTORY DEPLETION	0	765	592	1880	6988	20618	0	0	0
26 SCRAP (NET PURCHASES)	1041	7749	4326	153455	108342	-69452	6293	-15727	0
27 REGIONAL OUTPUT (OUTLAY)	3302749	10031702	2682579	7133065	3586247	25825024	90924208	9128128	2742365

TABLE B.1-2

1963 INPUT-OUTPUT TRANSACTIONS
MIDDLE ATLANTIC
(THOUSANDS OF 1963 DOLLARS)

INDUSTRY TITLE	19	20	21	22	23	24	25	26	27
1 LIVESTOCK, PRDTS.	46	331316	0	0	-12567	135484	0	0	2573856
2 OTHER AGRICULTURE PRDTS.	138	584401	0	0	322599	114039	0	0	2700235
3 COAL MINING	121268	38993	0	0	69407	4221	0	0	673405
4 CRUDE PETRO.,NATURAL GAS	9601	0	0	0	2397	3357	0	0	1682326
5 OTHER MINING	0	3336	0	0	60563	20033	0	0	999553
6 CONSTRUCTION	101559	0	0	-1032554	10110181	0	0	0	12356630
7 FOOD,TOBAC.,FAB.,APPAREL	3780	16673514	0	0	1414797	312996	0	0	28337216
8 TRANSPORT EQPT.,ORDNANCE	157	2998553	0	0	4420782	283936	0	0	9828222
9 LUMBER & PAPER	3650	1659311	0	0	895676	2589502	0	0	11965951
10 PETROLEUM, RELATED INDS.	29082	1726419	0	0	266214	238499	0	0	4022193
11 PLASTICS & CHEMICALS	3177	1486519	0	0	1443020	346556	0	0	9062863
12 GLASS, STONE,CLAY PRDTS.	10	96043	0	0	169304	120439	0	0	2351075
13 PRIMARY IRON & STEEL MFR	6	2168	0	0	285656	404637	0	0	5234721
14 PRIMARY NONFERROUS MFR.	1522	2769	0	0	254180	171355	0	0	3279252
15 MACHINERY & EQUIPMENT	5516	2268223	0	0	9587760	1170483	0	0	23007712
16 SERVICES	140011	47051088	0	-10047	4280302	1029663	0	2168	80473840
17 TRANSPORT. & WAREHOUSING	85976	2222837	0	0	1194705	62065	0	2342	8431311
18 GAS & WATER SERVICES	95796	891390	0	0	15493	18502	0	0	2609778
19 ELECTRIC UTILITIES	165706	1133774	0	0	172634	9411	0	0	3119975
20 WAGES & SALARIES	449927	759076	0	16106893	8615841	0	0	0	80835152
21 DIRECT ALLOCATED IMPORTS	325	1337887	0	-2460304	260896	0	0	0	0
22 TRANSFERRRD IMPORTS	3500	0	0	-5698033	0	0	0	145592	0
23 OTHER VALUE ADDED	1325943	-386326	0	-16106893	-104809	0	0	0	43143920
24 SECONDARY TRANSFERS-OUT	439892	0	0	0	0	0	0	0	7035178
25 INVENTORY DEPLETION	0	0	0	0	0	0	0	0	77260
26 SCRAP (NET PURCHASES)	0	-46153	0	0	-814828	0	0	-150102	-829968
27 REGIONAL OUTPUT (OUTLAY)	2986588	80835152	0	-9200939	42910208	7035178	0	0	342971648

TABLE B.1-3

1963 INPUT-OUTPUT TRANSACTIONS
EAST NORTH CENTRAL
(THOUSANDS OF 1963 DOLLARS)

INDUSTRY TITLE	1	2	3	4	5	6	7	8	9
1 LIVESTOCK, PRDTS.	581860	235089	10	10	15	417	3333761	511	485
2 OTHER AGRICULTURE PRDTS.	2168320	156080	30	30	44	57814	1381368	1523	1446
3 COAL MINING	624	178	41545	1	1738	0	9173	11095	18137
4 CRUDE PETRO.,NATURAL GAS	0	0	0	5103	0	0	0	0	0
5 OTHER MINING	276	46610	0	0	21819	117327	3133	1379	16480
6 CONSTRUCTION	54671	94016	2374	12346	2650	4341	37747	51626	23868
7 FOOD,TOBAC.,FAB.,APPAREL	562881	9021	639	683	926	67049	4125384	414318	183350
8 TRANSPORT EQPT.,ORDNANCE	1245	3089	3092	103	3343	9474	3858	9218685	1217
9 LUMBER & PAPER	3989	11574	2506	190	2212	945900	651889	126884	3124986
10 PETROLEUM, RELATED INDS.	36433	185754	4035	2089	10262	252179	53114	56427	50696
11 PLASTICS & CHEMICALS	31543	262139	12292	3184	27404	360538	362481	788052	512604
12 GLASS, STONE,CLAY PRDTS.	1540	10958	582	1096	1398	1076817	175133	306223	37389
13 PRIMARY IRON & STEEL MFR	0	0	6583	483	10369	379721	1202	2530354	93567
14 PRIMARY NONFERROUS MFR.	86	80	16	0	701	255773	925	474708	19794
15 MACHINERY & EQUIPMENT	17398	68329	30095	6070	38264	2167695	495531	3771919	236138
16 SERVICES	424768	1051099	34856	93353	70034	2076839	1727823	1650511	1097371
17 TRANSPORT. & WAREHOUSING	118869	62178	6617	42525	52188	485937	581959	500097	335396
18 GAS & WATER SERVICES	2270	6893	466	997	5709	17811	49465	35400	39414
19 ELECTRIC UTILITIES	14348	4551	12207	2861	15419	34223	76877	93822	71382
20 WAGES & SALARIES	139208	160792	136511	43897	182714	3413142	2691432	4810862	3065212
21 DIRECT ALLOCATED IMPORTS	276	6503	71	69	93	2895	331223	3555	3482
22 TRANSFERRRD IMPORTS	14865	7916	873	173481	215973	0	53979	24660	533561
23 OTHER VALUE ADDED	844103	2562162	142036	181394	151627	2860021	2845683	4538485	1652639
24 SECONDARY TRANSFERS-OUT	0	0	148	6388	30583	0	276494	515777	199393
25 INVENTORY DEPLETION	0	17326	0	0	7628	0	11005	18537	2165
26 SCRAP (NET PURCHASES)	0	0	157	0	1353	6181	761	-85405	23012
27 REGIONAL OUTPUT (OUTLAY)	5019572	4962338	437741	576354	854464	14592096	19281392	29860000	11343186

TABLE B.1-3

1963 INPUT-OUTPUT TRANSACTIONS
EAST NORTH CENTRAL
(THOUSANDS OF 1963 DOLLARS)

INDUSTRY TITLE	10	11	12	13	14	15	16	17	18
1 LIVESTOCK, PRDTS.	31	1262	112	187	71	1641	26207	308	69
2 OTHER AGRICULTURE PRDTS.	91	8513	2353	559	213	8943	24298	1087	207
3 COAL MINING	1646	17828	18138	213810	2053	10763	28052	1645	1685
4 CRUDE PETRO.,NATURAL GAS	1606505	6197	0	0	0	0	7579	2413	455649
5 OTHER MINING	17078	79442	185858	570015	92965	3929	785	139	0
6 CONSTRUCTION	60048	35983	14366	80040	11631	58273	2072878	259514	83725
7 FOOD,TOBAC.,FAB.,APPAREL	7189	404352	27267	24511	15933	259754	364065	28769	4878
8 TRANSPORT EQPT.,ORDNANCE	133	2078	647	606	189	33235	191359	70149	218
9 LUMBER & PAPER	40227	272789	124193	35289	20967	697398	788081	25477	3308
10 PETROLEUM, RELATED INDS.	295724	82424	20941	75574	13961	125504	416661	281924	15823
11 PLASTICS & CHEMICALS	101855	2351762	151258	200289	83753	1170762	464797	55583	5979
12 GLASS, STONE,CLAY PRDTS.	8426	72094	339648	16888	11210	325348	66191	2306	15
13 PRIMARY IRON & STEEL MFR	268	38235	29038	2349183	9567	3838710	2777	53722	4
14 PRIMARY NONFERROUS MFR.	7902	36606	11078	217313	1394613	1531131	2672	2362	0
15 MACHINERY & EQUIPMENT	26839	256031	62523	505871	135010	6537065	753917	84143	1038
16 SERVICES	277581	1216099	246789	709356	246281	3127550	11275584	920005	135552
17 TRANSPORT. & WAREHOUSING	158351	257604	146964	531600	92206	587676	690775	609366	41905
18 GAS & WATER SERVICES	46911	62298	65281	133955	22255	76756	313894	20893	1065516
19 ELECTRIC UTILITIES	19736	84404	43789	156712	44524	188574	745107	25754	5548
20 WAGES & SALARIES	216889	2021082	876656	2660233	601989	10288050	19576528	3123000	502966
21 DIRECT ALLOCATED IMPORTS	213	126773	4569	1304	1643	33877	114981	62909	482
22 TRANSFERRRD IMPORTS	2668	26687	35179	102993	123436	145567	52056	166826	17000
23 OTHER VALUE ADDED	676951	2538322	775649	2358277	531522	6276480	29613168	1696970	664697
24 SECONDARY TRANSFERS-OUT	44356	504474	82090	200283	176170	1474433	3687455	201653	435890
25 INVENTORY DEPLETION	0	1527	751	3098	8606	16525	0	0	0
26 SCRAP (NET PURCHASES)	1251	4374	5121	251066	130307	-97369	6361	-13415	0
27 REGIONAL OUTPUT (OUTLAY)	3618868	10509241	3270257	11399015	3771074	36720576	71286224	7683498	3442155

TABLE B.1-3

1963 INPUT-OUTPUT TRANSACTIONS
EAST NORTH CENTRAL
(THOUSANDS OF 1963 DOLLARS)

INDUSTRY TITLE	19	20	21	22	23	24	25	26	27
1 LIVESTOCK, PRDTS.	56	329355	0	0	4543	375936	0	0	4891938
2 OTHER AGRICULTURE PRDTS.	168	580352	0	0	423919	470310	0	0	5287670
3 COAL MINING	172432	40108	0	0	68784	2704	0	0	662139
4 CRUDE PETRO.,NATURAL GAS	13651	0	0	0	1656	19835	0	0	2118588
5 OTHER MINING	0	3491	0	0	47779	29769	0	0	1238273
6 CONSTRUCTION	128498	0	0	116750	11382451	0	0	0	14587796
7 FOOD,TOBAC.,FAB.,APPAREL	4632	14993404	0	0	624080	277752	0	0	22400832
8 TRANSPORT EQPT.,ORDNANCE	192	3648283	0	0	5689825	877533	0	0	19758544
9 LUMBER & PAPER	4470	1620939	0	0	605117	1866920	0	0	10975305
10 PETROLEUM, RELATED INDS.	35772	1693088	0	0	177120	286513	0	0	4172017
11 PLASTICS & CHEMICALS	3444	1496964	0	0	700296	416960	0	0	9563937
12 GLASS, STONE,CLAY PRDTS.	12	92608	0	0	85459	150271	0	0	2781612
13 PRIMARY IRON & STEEL MFR	7	2221	0	0	118181	662022	0	0	10126214
14 PRIMARY NONFERROUS MFR.	1870	2272	0	0	89086	206094	0	0	4255081
15 MACHINERY & EQUIPMENT	6767	2428488	0	0	6552838	1526893	0	0	25708864
16 SERVICES	170344	43541152	0	-25470	3090181	1010696	0	663	74169024
17 TRANSPORT. & WAREHOUSING	121540	1742775	0	0	1308239	52941	0	716	8528424
18 GAS & WATER SERVICES	136137	1309097	0	0	19710	25401	0	0	3456528
19 ELECTRIC UTILITIES	203579	1199568	0	0	167100	10996	0	0	3221082
20 WAGES & SALARIES	427544	516495	0	12776506	7957010	0	0	0	76188720
21 DIRECT ALLOCATED IMPORTS	381	1212924	0	-2161840	253616	0	0	0	0
22 TRANSFERRRD IMPORTS	0	0	0	-1742237	0	0	0	44516	0
23 OTHER VALUE ADDED	1676261	-209075	0	-12776506	-93282	0	0	0	49507584
24 SECONDARY TRANSFERS-OUT	433962	0	0	0	0	0	0	0	8269548
25 INVENTORY DEPLETION	0	0	0	0	0	0	0	0	87168
26 SCRAP (NET PURCHASES)	0	-55798	0	0	107792	0	0	-45896	239853
27 REGIONAL OUTPUT (OUTLAY)	3541721	76188720	0	-3812798	39381488	8269548	0	0	362196736

TABLE B.1-4

1963 INPUT-OUTPUT TRANSACTIONS
WEST NORTH CENTRAL
(THOUSANDS OF 1963 DOLLARS)

INDUSTRY TITLE	1	2	3	4	5	6	7	8	9
1 LIVESTOCK, PRDTS.	1967140	382475	0	16	12	181	4174010	125	129
2 OTHER AGRICULTURE PRDTS.	2349031	215881	3	47	39	21040	821337	373	385
3 COAL MINING	934	63	704	1	3129	0	5419	1529	2469
4 CRUDE PETRO.,NATURAL GAS	0	0	0	11826	0	0	0	0	0
5 OTHER MINING	440	12430	0	0	57243	79888	3034	167	2433
6 CONSTRUCTION	49872	71600	190	19706	2229	1848	22252	8000	5604
7 FOOD,TOBAC.,FAB.,APPAREL	687266	12993	49	1116	909	26542	2391869	57072	32715
8 TRANSPORT EQPT.,ORDNANCE	2349	5335	112	175	3141	5354	2055	1308393	337
9 LUMBER & PAPER	4896	5389	74	314	3436	384113	386786	32268	780426
10 PETROLEUM, RELATED INDS.	58110	280227	148	3357	12956	171300	27907	10757	11199
11 PLASTICS & CHEMICALS	49219	227765	447	6066	32477	174226	191633	112315	102899
12 GLASS, STONE,CLAY PRDTS.	1328	4609	21	2074	2705	470590	63305	40263	6306
13 PRIMARY IRON & STEEL MFR	0	0	197	1135	17125	170708	1319	341129	15813
14 PRIMARY NONFERROUS MFR.	192	156	0	0	1109	103624	211	105382	3630
15 MACHINERY & EQUIPMENT	18765	100333	1314	10735	44666	882009	227253	641483	46228
16 SERVICES	558272	1583239	2390	137832	117483	930818	940622	285420	292458
17 TRANSPORT. & WAREHOUSING	179904	57626	215	11115	22156	218383	435952	75632	73215
18 GAS & WATER SERVICES	2365	8772	1	1529	4610	7650	30314	6125	6889
19 ELECTRIC UTILITIES	14951	5791	26	4390	13300	14718	45617	16783	14664
20 WAGES & SALARIES	156443	146557	13847	50262	165173	1446420	1478771	906108	752427
21 DIRECT ALLOCATED IMPORTS	179	213	5	112	93	1263	126927	871	915
22 TRANSFERRRD IMPORTS	2431	961	166	33041	13776	0	7385	4073	82495
23 OTHER VALUE ADDED	1828034	3013515	15233	310504	216773	1256362	1542057	802298	388502
24 SECONDARY TRANSFERS-OUT	0	0	78	2313	11085	0	314218	71839	67705
25 INVENTORY DEPLETION	0	21536	0	0	30381	0	7030	5533	671
26 SCRAP (NET PURCHASES)	0	0	16	0	912	2470	-344	-11794	1068
27 REGIONAL OUTPUT (OUTLAY)	7932120	6157466	35237	607665	776918	6369508	13246940	4822144	2691580

TABLE B.1-4

1963 INPUT-OUTPUT TRANSACTIONS
WEST NORTH CENTRAL
(THOUSANDS OF 1963 DOLLARS)

INDUSTRY TITLE	10	11	12	13	14	15	16	17	18
1 LIVESTOCK, PRDTS.	8	347	32	8	7	264	27574	140	26
2 OTHER AGRICULTURE PRDTS.	24	2025	653	24	21	1547	9037	550	78
3 COAL MINING	474	3511	9292	7401	356	1819	12565	662	747
4 CRUDE PETRO.,NATURAL GAS	473715	1558	0	0	0	0	3119	2961	161667
5 OTHER MINING	3490	24319	74449	20192	24695	587	308	53	0
6 CONSTRUCTION	17599	7485	4633	2941	1303	9477	776071	113765	34429
7 FOOD,TOBAC.,FAB.,APPAREL	2037	83712	7506	1075	1570	45189	145869	13292	1843
8 TRANSPORT EQPT.,ORDNANCE	37	428	245	28	18	10293	81689	31171	93
9 LUMBER & PAPER	8957	63428	24240	1463	1780	96540	321195	10786	1306
10 PETROLEUM, RELATED INDS.	81962	18830	7655	2680	2349	18055	170328	122142	6744
11 PLASTICS & CHEMICALS	29917	504239	29522	7195	8333	191206	174451	22438	3079
12 GLASS, STONE,CLAY PRDTS.	1689	16720	98429	575	1158	48555	27299	1278	6
13 PRIMARY IRON & STEEL MFR	54	6424	10088	83325	836	650562	1140	22514	2
14 PRIMARY NONFERROUS MFR.	2330	6518	2077	8351	138216	220105	1019	812	0
15 MACHINERY & EQUIPMENT	7640	57127	19834	22528	14645	1135851	286064	36302	415
16 SERVICES	78699	279606	67426	29241	23027	504512	4460914	385234	51842
17 TRANSPORT. & WAREHOUSING	45274	59246	54078	19854	10119	97772	285782	252926	15224
18 GAS & WATER SERVICES	13541	12964	19665	5317	3122	12085	123055	10254	378792
19 ELECTRIC UTILITIES	5697	15912	15461	6220	6246	27997	295942	12639	2460
20 WAGES & SALARIES	57937	357636	231580	119164	70459	1614926	7710240	1405000	193202
21 DIRECT ALLOCATED IMPORTS	55	23153	1268	57	199	6562	49515	25259	181
22 TRANSFERRRD IMPORTS	433	4185	5365	4546	18732	19397	7522	23865	1300
23 OTHER VALUE ADDED	199165	554069	230551	88875	49289	954432	11520127	674899	244890
24 SECONDARY TRANSFERS-OUT	29640	127378	17249	30416	16357	206813	1737928	95568	178409
25 INVENTORY DEPLETION	0	230	279	128	917	2636	0	0	0
26 SCRAP (NET PURCHASES)	361	1480	584	9875	13976	-12216	2737	-5757	0
27 REGIONAL OUTPUT (OUTLAY)	1060736	2232530	932160	471479	407731	5864965	28231488	3258753	1276736

TABLE B.1-4

1963 INPUT-OUTPUT TRANSACTIONS
WEST NORTH CENTRAL
(THOUSANDS OF 1963 DOLLARS)

INDUSTRY TITLE	19	20	21	22	23	24	25	26	27
1 LIVESTOCK, PRDTS.	17	148980	0	0	207739	595976	0	0	7505207
2 OTHER AGRICULTURE PRDTS.	52	239951	0	0	471085	584574	0	0	4717757
3 COAL MINING	45114	19396	0	0	15495	217	0	0	131298
4 CRUDE PETRO.,NATURAL GAS	3572	0	0	0	811	32114	0	0	691342
5 OTHER MINING	0	1290	0	0	22974	18179	0	0	346170
6 CONSTRUCTION	38517	0	0	583546	4598888	0	0	0	6369956
7 FOOD,TOBAC.,FAB.,APPAREL	1421	5771209	0	0	289579	185015	0	0	9759849
8 TRANSPORT EQPT.,ORDNANCE	58	1337709	0	0	2756342	166971	0	0	5712335
9 LUMBER & PAPER	1368	604278	0	0	226680	534060	0	0	3493782
10 PETROLEUM, RELATED INDS.	10826	697648	0	0	74163	82679	0	0	1872021
11 PLASTICS & CHEMICALS	647	585600	0	0	174835	82584	0	0	2711091
12 GLASS, STONE,CLAY PRDTS.	4	34872	0	0	22054	51068	0	0	894907
13 PRIMARY IRON & STEEL MFR	2	1013	0	0	15116	26039	0	0	1364539
14 PRIMARY NONFERROUS MFR.	570	850	0	0	9546	22105	0	0	626804
15 MACHINERY & EQUIPMENT	2066	906373	0	0	2380823	246270	0	0	7088725
16 SERVICES	53686	16455187	0	21003	1390699	423904	0	90	29073600
17 TRANSPORT. & WAREHOUSING	32088	638371	0	0	427390	22720	0	97	3035137
18 GAS & WATER SERVICES	35681	498502	0	0	9177	9196	0	0	1199606
19 ELECTRIC UTILITIES	61968	504794	0	0	74912	3388	0	0	1163875
20 WAGES & SALARIES	140547	229549	0	8099720	3682377	0	0	0	29028336
21 DIRECT ALLOCATED IMPORTS	122	462532	0	-902036	202604	0	0	0	0
22 TRANSFERRRD IMPORTS	0	0	0	-235696	0	0	0	6022	0
23 OTHER VALUE ADDED	522158	-89269	0	-8099720	-53822	0	0	0	16168922
24 SECONDARY TRANSFERS-OUT	180061	0	0	0	0	0	0	0	3087057
25 INVENTORY DEPLETION	0	0	0	0	0	0	0	0	69341
26 SCRAP (NET PURCHASES)	0	-20489	0	0	320143	0	0	-6209	296815
27 REGIONAL OUTPUT (OUTLAY)	1130545	29028336	0	-533232	17319600	3087057	0	0	136408480

TABLE B.1-5

1963 INPUT-OUTPUT TRANSACTIONS
SOUTH ATLANTIC
(THOUSANDS OF 1963 DOLLARS)

INDUSTRY TITLE	1	2	3	4	5	6	7	8	9
1 LIVESTOCK, PRDTS.	177290	258676	16	2	16	331	1527117	108	210
2 OTHER AGRICULTURE PRDTS.	645142	71613	46	6	42	63409	2311084	321	627
3 COAL MINING	1258	68	102298	0	782	0	15203	1187	17256
4 CRUDE PETRO.,NATURAL GAS	0	0	0	5728	0	0	0	0	0
5 OTHER MINING	232	27654	143	0	28315	104609	1442	120	8853
6 CONSTRUCTION	18033	49382	4967	2611	2835	3453	48519	6884	20302
7 FOOD,TOBAC.,FAB.,APPAREL	567181	11365	965	159	905	58809	7866618	51521	144563
8 TRANSPORT EQPT.,ORDNANCE	307	1707	6410	26	3082	7700	2153	938839	964
9 LUMBER & PAPER	1815	13023	8453	47	1975	741375	573033	37582	1704543
10 PETROLEUM, RELATED INDS.	11963	108939	8361	429	7265	225257	45066	9093	37449
11 PLASTICS & CHEMICALS	19002	371740	25464	1320	25124	268529	1551976	92809	306613
12 GLASS, STONE,CLAY PRDTS.	512	6971	1209	421	755	1007390	119860	33733	23053
13 PRIMARY IRON & STEEL MFR	0	0	16609	615	10723	313644	699	270328	55111
14 PRIMARY NONFERROUS MFR.	30	47	30	0	1116	221304	580	90672	13788
15 MACHINERY & EQUIPMENT	5061	20832	62364	1846	41151	1804348	427559	561986	179836
16 SERVICES	309996	611134	71648	19148	48303	1726965	1848184	237452	703006
17 TRANSPORT. & WAREHOUSING	61509	56492	14948	6213	47835	400903	500424	62631	215016
18 GAS & WATER SERVICES	1040	4819	808	200	8539	14006	44789	5339	30933
19 ELECTRIC UTILITIES	6577	3182	21178	574	14802	26878	124357	14707	52339
20 WAGES & SALARIES	142606	264394	299445	17093	116498	2336480	3567899	950161	1606771
21 DIRECT ALLOCATED IMPORTS	36	38618	107	14	93	2309	195856	749	1612
22 TRANSFERRRD IMPORTS	18582	15429	0	24965	137637	0	250502	20831	225475
23 OTHER VALUE ADDED	438703	1648588	257668	29609	146161	2174143	5048528	515722	1180564
24 SECONDARY TRANSFERS-OUT	0	0	135	2668	14881	0	133251	71050	75950
25 INVENTORY DEPLETION	0	12520	0	0	583	0	7976	9165	1595
26 SCRAP (NET PURCHASES)	0	0	314	0	1073	5349	-54518	-10345	23202
27 REGIONAL OUTPUT (OUTLAY)	2426874	3597193	903585	113694	660491	11507191	26158160	3972643	6629632

TABLE B.1-5

1963 INPUT-OUTPUT TRANSACTIONS
SOUTH ATLANTIC
(THOUSANDS OF 1963 DOLLARS)

INDUSTRY TITLE	10	11	12	13	14	15	16	17	18
1 LIVESTOCK, PRDTS.	8	421	51	24	14	261	38714	402	28
2 OTHER AGRICULTURE PRDTS.	23	3223	525	71	41	1609	15145	1542	83
3 COAL MINING	244	19732	8584	32997	926	1074	22485	1024	582
4 CRUDE PETRO.,NATURAL GAS	199237	4099	0	0	0	0	4975	928	192373
5 OTHER MINING	7691	100154	105550	87919	60898	571	570	74	0
6 CONSTRUCTION	7836	25461	7139	11870	3102	8566	1350106	133114	31254
7 FOOD,TOBAC.,FAB.,APPAREL	1189	102320	8145	3087	3982	42574	268203	32220	1962
8 TRANSPORT EQPT.,ORDNANCE	24	517	354	75	42	5750	134631	82905	78
9 LUMBER & PAPER	15465	179224	56766	4352	4892	93429	494002	14985	1282
10 PETROLEUM, RELATED INDS.	55568	38252	10996	10028	5327	18596	263923	215845	5700
11 PLASTICS & CHEMICALS	13055	1527741	57508	28416	22046	161163	300268	30399	1694
12 GLASS, STONE,CLAY PRDTS.	3913	20631	173149	1943	2452	50266	45066	1126	6
13 PRIMARY IRON & STEEL MFR	124	20307	13685	313106	1325	569186	1814	26772	2
14 PRIMARY NONFERROUS MFR.	980	28815	3730	29044	363625	231756	1891	2189	0
15 MACHINERY & EQUIPMENT	4317	117248	28243	63855	13273	888521	499591	49017	397
16 SERVICES	51387	558625	115845	101652	58989	466739	7193738	569234	53980
17 TRANSPORT. & WAREHOUSING	41732	173141	82922	85410	26378	88164	466591	395837	17384
18 GAS & WATER SERVICES	6869	63848	31350	18183	7242	10317	200306	12351	449214
19 ELECTRIC UTILITIES	2890	62772	20946	21272	14488	26656	478458	15224	1916
20 WAGES & SALARIES	32029	1008846	398228	390486	125493	1427563	11927900	1886000	197860
21 DIRECT ALLOCATED IMPORTS	53	24771	1054	165	524	8203	89541	97604	195
22 TRANSFERRRD IMPORTS	152304	98675	5152	121172	239001	103008	26772	130840	0
23 OTHER VALUE ADDED	102143	1584153	386659	267537	148149	1093784	19271408	1092389	274490
24 SECONDARY TRANSFERS-OUT	19516	172110	33187	24506	21664	296055	1409422	134200	276583
25 INVENTORY DEPLETION	0	485	356	415	2140	4034	0	0	0
26 SCRAP (NET PURCHASES)	184	6029	2495	33693	33280	-14914	5281	-8533	0
27 REGIONAL OUTPUT (OUTLAY)	718778	5941598	1552620	1651277	1159293	5582931	44510800	4917687	1507064

TABLE B.1-5

1963 INPUT-OUTPUT TRANSACTIONS
SOUTH ATLANTIC
(THOUSANDS OF 1963 DOLLARS)

INDUSTRY TITLE	19	20	21	22	23	24	25	26	27
1 LIVESTOCK, PRDTS.	36	262682	0	0	16562	180725	0	0	2463691
2 OTHER AGRICULTURE PRDTS.	106	379445	0	0	535140	339838	0	0	4369080
3 COAL MINING	99775	19160	0	0	185865	5592	0	0	536093
4 CRUDE PETRO.,NATURAL GAS	7899	0	0	0	114	4509	0	0	419861
5 OTHER MINING	0	2109	0	0	26107	58369	0	0	621379
6 CONSTRUCTION	79113	0	0	-185660	9875955	0	0	0	11504842
7 FOOD,TOBAC.,FAB.,APPAREL	2903	9290243	0	0	699783	209805	0	0	19368496
8 TRANSPORT EQPT.,ORDNANCE	120	2212252	0	0	2840237	151044	0	0	6389217
9 LUMBER & PAPER	2800	1030017	0	0	577414	657699	0	0	6214174
10 PETROLEUM, RELATED INDS.	22370	1050979	0	0	144982	42049	0	0	2338437
11 PLASTICS & CHEMICALS	1035	1104897	0	0	751901	166359	0	0	6829058
12 GLASS, STONE,CLAY PRDTS.	7	57919	0	0	49121	72009	0	0	1671511
13 PRIMARY IRON & STEEL MFR	5	1152	0	0	82716	88843	0	0	1786767
14 PRIMARY NONFERROUS MFR.	1171	1735	0	0	45731	52636	0	0	1090869
15 MACHINERY & EQUIPMENT	4238	1586073	0	0	4136643	217081	0	0	10713479
16 SERVICES	107295	26928944	0	70454	2587941	691720	0	613	45132992
17 TRANSPORT. & WAREHOUSING	70536	1015567	0	0	1154151	33672	0	662	5018117
18 GAS & WATER SERVICES	78797	681748	0	0	28948	10610	0	0	1710256
19 ELECTRIC UTILITIES	127456	923247	0	0	153282	6835	0	0	2120035
20 WAGES & SALARIES	223545	802749	0	11378572	8834712	0	0	0	47935328
21 DIRECT ALLOCATED IMPORTS	247	737425	0	-1920577	721404	0	0	0	0
22 TRANSFERRRD IMPORTS	0	0	0	-1611522	0	0	0	41176	0
23 OTHER VALUE ADDED	1127144	-119990	0	-11378572	-154893	0	0	0	25134096
24 SECONDARY TRANSFERS-OUT	304217	0	0	0	0	0	0	0	2989395
25 INVENTORY DEPLETION	0	0	0	0	0	0	0	0	39269
26 SCRAP (NET PURCHASES)	0	-33031	0	0	-48043	0	0	-42452	-100937
27 REGIONAL OUTPUT (OUTLAY)	2260814	47935328	0	-3647305	33245760	2989395	0	0	206295536

TABLE B.1-6

1963 INPUT-OUTPUT TRANSACTIONS
EAST SOUTH CENTRAL
(THOUSANDS OF 1963 DOLLARS)

INDUSTRY TITLE	1	2	3	4	5	6	7	8	9
1 LIVESTOCK, PRDTS.	165222	233568	5	9	7	109	823974	54	87
2 OTHER AGRICULTURE PRDTS.	416393	35448	16	26	18	16103	711528	161	258
3 COAL MINING	659	20	80380	0	554	0	3713	354	5484
4 CRUDE PETRO.,NATURAL GAS	0	0	0	5656	0	0	0	0	0
5 OTHER MINING	147	15269	0	0	10148	44344	862	24	4903
6 CONSTRUCTION	16686	34529	2641	10525	1236	1094	14685	2228	8945
7 FOOD,T0BAC.,FAB.,APPAREL	304121	6591	361	597	411	16809	2333171	12740	57179
8 TRANSPORT EQPT.,ORDNANCE	275	971	3072	93	1333	3466	1009	294003	411
9 LUMBER & PAPER	1151	1285	2793	167	1048	199299	207845	10719	773358
10 PETROLEUM, RELATED INDS.	8766	45613	4009	1806	3646	96486	15693	3868	14241
11 PLASTICS & CHEMICALS	12358	158525	12209	3142	10203	100813	280104	28328	122524
12 GLASS, STONE,CLAY PRDTS.	339	4018	579	1074	359	316714	57483	7567	10179
13 PRIMARY IRON & STEEL MFR	0	0	5821	539	3683	128747	357	82428	23058
14 PRIMARY NONFERROUS MFR.	30	34	15	0	199	64217	172	39742	4585
15 MACHINERY & EQUIPMENT	4165	12916	30506	5668	16137	563966	164584	207539	72174
16 SERVICES	159913	293649	36502	73409	21710	577176	666597	93218	264175
17 TRANSPORT. & WAREHOUSING	32401	24414	9191	2714	13196	136077	185341	20636	84735
18 GAS & WATER SERVICES	738	3940	411	826	2058	4477	15255	2063	12548
19 ELECTRIC UTILITIES	4663	2602	10784	2371	4559	8598	31950	5821	22487
20 WAGES & SALARIES	75332	112668	140318	28119	48128	767458	1181542	281049	666686
21 DIRECT ALLOCATED IMPORTS	24	53	40	60	34	753	101274	375	655
22 TRANSFERRRD IMPORTS	9399	3763	0	3721	51963	0	11614	274	7318
23 OTHER VALUE ADDED	546058	1196549	138576	165999	77131	884854	1722288	293552	454423
24 SECONDARY TRANSFERS-OUT	0	0	56	1665	7026	0	85740	39996	38802
25 INVENT0RY DEPLETION	0	7660	0	0	1067	0	5835	3451	836
26 SCRAP (NET PURCHASES)	0	0	157	0	500	1770	-7032	-2991	10940
27 REGIONAL OUTPUT (OUTLAY)	1758840	2194084	478443	308186	276355	3933328	8615583	1427199	2660990

TABLE B.1-6

1963 INPUT-OUTPUT TRANSACTIONS
EAST SOUTH CENTRAL
(THOUSANDS OF 1963 DOLLARS)

INDUSTRY TITLE	10	11	12	13	14	15	16	17	18
1 LIVESTOCK, PRDTS.	4	126	23	22	10	135	21797	77	17
2 OTHER AGRICULTURE PRDTS.	11	1389	287	67	29	709	4632	236	51
3 COAL MINING	160	9451	6638	25903	932	801	12186	375	275
4 CRUDE PETRO.,NATURAL GAS	146792	1737	0	0	0	0	2547	911	123654
5 OTHER MINING	2924	40482	45288	69686	71509	532	207	27	0
6 CONSTRUCTION	5582	11886	3398	9696	2431	4717	425355	54612	16950
7 FOOD,TOBAC.,FAB.,APPAREL	730	73809	4058	2944	2735	24944	87541	6427	1187
8 TRANSPORT EQPT.,ORDNANCE	14	521	154	74	28	2260	50621	16226	40
9 LUMBER & PAPER	6238	74752	22193	4053	2829	64763	174162	5192	737
10 PETROLEUM, RELATED INDS.	31642	17248	4854	8483	5525	10121	94813	57247	2913
11 PLASTICS & CHEMICALS	9410	709331	23531	23136	15248	119255	96757	11115	453
12 GLASS, STONE,CLAY PRDTS.	1471	7496	63966	1730	1764	33510	16631	537	4
13 PRIMARY IRON & STEEL MFR	47	11375	5545	264457	1112	341038	882	10949	1
14 PRIMARY NONFERROUS MFR.	722	12998	1556	24392	252316	147462	698	662	0
15 MACHINERY & EQUIPMENT	2694	48029	12370	61542	11513	530758	169728	17258	224
16 SERVICES	28341	237087	48046	85089	31363	277498	2376373	188824	32206
17 TRANSPORT. & WAREHOUSING	16320	76746	34878	64596	16720	52352	186733	132710	10938
18 GAS & WATER SERVICES	4543	28537	15630	15838	6764	6696	70889	4735	288254
19 ELECTRIC UTILITIES	1911	29494	11279	18528	13531	15447	172513	5837	905
20 WAGES & SALARIES	18023	532696	147215	307487	109052	742257	4090432	671000	103393
21 DIRECT ALLOCATED IMPORTS	26	25436	569	156	431	2542	40877	19526	119
22 TRANSFERRRD IMPORTS	5872	6116	129	20422	819	6552	4200	27318	700
23 OTHER VALUE ADDED	69353	727151	192245	289847	94660	557523	6463504	335306	184405
24 SECONDARY TRANSFERS-OUT	18657	84690	15376	13989	12400	166954	668190	70018	144926
25 INVENTORY DEPLETION	0	324	166	362	1604	1399	0	0	0
26 SCRAP (NET PURCHASES)	121	2246	867	29560	25097	-6439	1894	-2819	0
27 REGIONAL OUTPUT (OUTLAY)	371608	2771153	660260	1342059	680423	3103786	15234164	1634305	912349

TABLE B.1-6

1963 INPUT-OUTPUT TRANSACTIONS
EAST SOUTH CENTRAL
(THOUSANDS OF 1963 DOLLARS)

INDUSTRY TITLE	19	20	21	22	23	24	25	26	27
1 LIVESTOCK, PRDTS.	10	101292	0	0	45443	131347	0	0	1523335
2 OTHER AGRICULTURE PRDTS.	29	157713	0	0	493571	207916	0	0	2046590
3 COAL MINING	25383	8911	0	0	7135	2961	0	0	192276
4 CRUDE PETRO.,NATURAL GAS	2010	0	0	0	434	17211	0	0	300951
5 OTHER MINING	0	809	0	0	26031	21556	0	0	354748
6 CONSTRUCTION	21315	0	0	-1417	3278412	0	0	0	3925505
7 FOOD,TOBAC.,FAB.,APPAREL	795	3653798	0	0	176749	89403	0	0	6857099
8 TRANSPORT EQPT.,ORDNANCE	33	835019	0	0	880449	61823	0	0	2151896
9 LUMBER & PAPER	767	394589	0	0	157062	236930	0	0	2341932
10 PETROLEUM, RELATED INDS.	6114	421284	0	0	58548	27773	0	0	940692
11 PLASTICS & CHEMICALS	284	444092	0	0	380121	84292	0	0	2645229
12 GLASS, STONE,CLAY PRDTS.	2	22682	0	0	11330	32374	0	0	591811
13 PRIMARY IRON & STEEL MFR	1	502	0	0	12073	77944	0	0	970557
14 PRIMARY NONFERROUS MFR.	320	673	0	0	12357	39692	0	0	602843
15 MACHINERY & EQUIPMENT	1159	615820	0	0	1243229	118388	0	0	3910366
16 SERVICES	29443	10319437	0	31965	844203	361799	0	63	17078080
17 TRANSPORT. & WAREHOUSING	17996	383590	0	0	213271	11124	0	68	1726746
18 GAS & WATER SERVICES	20051	270426	0	0	7648	6622	0	0	788951
19 ELECTRIC UTILITIES	34852	377375	0	0	53633	1823	0	0	830963
20 WAGES & SALARIES	54237	306183	0	5418063	2757840	0	0	0	18559168
21 DIRECT ALLOCATED IMPORTS	69	290057	0	-669705	186629	0	0	0	0
22 TRANSFERRRD IMPORTS	0	0	0	-164381	0	0	0	4200	0
23 OTHER VALUE ADDED	321723	-32461	0	-5418063	-39615	0	0	0	9225010
24 SECONDARY TRANSFERS-OUT	162492	0	0	0	0	0	0	0	1530977
25 INVENTORY DEPLETION	0	0	0	0	0	0	0	0	22704
26 SCRAP (NET PURCHASES)	0	-12613	0	0	160655	0	0	-4330	197582
27 REGIONAL OUTPUT (OUTLAY)	699084	18559168	0	-803538	10967209	1530977	0	0	79316032

TABLE B.1-7

1963 INPUT-OUTPUT TRANSACTIONS
WEST SOUTH CENTRAL
(THOUSANDS OF 1963 DOLLARS)

INDUSTRY TITLE	1	2	3	4	5	6	7	8	9
1 LIVESTOCK, PRDTS.	507086	298452	0	207	6	252	1106816	100	94
2 OTHER AGRICULTURE PRDTS.	512508	78133	0	617	21	36060	700986	297	281
3 COAL MINING	697	45	422	17	413	0	4329	543	6679
4 CRUDE PETRO.,NATURAL GAS	0	0	0	217022	0	0	0	0	0
5 OTHER MINING	144	9418	0	208	10848	94954	1328	40	4360
6 CONSTRUCTION	12012	38389	50	254110	1922	2643	13151	4270	7273
7 FOOD,TOBAC.,FAB.,APPAREL	427479	12188	16	14481	468	37162	1606637	25702	44104
8 TRANSPORT EQPT.,ORDNANCE	781	2890	53	2249	1844	8907	1117	494599	448
9 LUMBER & PAPER	809	2099	40	4136	1720	518645	214843	26763	794773
10 PETROLEUM, RELATED INDS.	14388	154134	70	42943	3943	230993	16740	7165	15758
11 PLASTICS & CHEMICALS	15254	145808	214	83688	15736	244881	104400	45652	115219
12 GLASS, STONE,CLAY PRDTS.	351	2532	10	28044	639	704721	55516	15425	10853
13 PRIMARY IRON & STEEL MFR	0	0	106	22038	7892	462655	482	124590	17519
14 PRIMARY NONFERROUS MFR.	64	85	0	0	515	146525	161	77536	3840
15 MACHINERY & EQUIPMENT	4292	43931	506	137985	22960	1323637	157564	395267	58646
16 SERVICES	212277	670284	709	1755938	32430	1339332	610717	165071	291534
17 TRANSPORT. & WAREHOUSING	54566	36362	98	48590	13225	319828	253475	36952	86329
18 GAS & WATER SERVICES	857	17163	0	20021	7227	10725	18719	3796	12058
19 ELECTRIC UTILITIES	5416	11331	7	57464	9073	20587	28988	10662	21460
20 WAGES & SALARIES	154444	237556	3380	734866	67344	1863695	849983	562939	691999
21 DIRECT ALLOCATED IMPORTS	953	38601	2	1438	48	1757	154462	693	685
22 TRANSFERRRD IMPORTS	28509	31620	0	22779	102672	0	254922	12251	28619
23 OTHER VALUE ADDED	697065	1480027	3520	3902289	136238	1565170	1048837	496888	510309
24 SECONDARY TRANSFERS-OUT	0	0	59	2346	16424	0	125382	50193	52483
25 INVENTORY DEPLETION	0	11492	0	0	802	0	2448	5676	863
26 SCRAP (NET PURCHASES)	0	0	4	0	748	4093	-757	-5468	10236
27 REGIONAL OUTPUT (OUTLAY)	2649951	3322540	9266	7353476	455158	8937223	7331248	2557601	2786421

TABLE B.1-7

1963 INPUT-OUTPUT TRANSACTIONS
WEST SOUTH CENTRAL
(THOUSANDS OF 1963 DOLLARS)

INDUSTRY TITLE	10	11	12	13	14	15	16	17	18
1 LIVESTOCK, PRDTS.	53	230	31	7	11	168	46750	336	24
2 OTHER AGRICULTURE PRDTS.	157	2703	410	22	33	885	7972	989	71
3 COAL MINING	3810	21493	9911	5955	1998	717	12000	942	374
4 CRUDE PETRO.,NATURAL GAS	3953304	5608	0	0	0	0	2878	10649	172858
5 OTHER MINING	9013	108090	74790	18738	175094	324	307	44	0
6 CONSTRUCTION	145460	23116	4767	2726	3637	6804	723544	120346	23345
7 FOOD,TOBAC.,FAB.,APPAREL	15927	76883	5657	965	2893	25660	159215	23102	1651
8 TRANSPORT EQPT.,ORDNANCE	285	527	239	25	30	2805	90683	61567	54
9 LUMBER & PAPER	36938	97842	27935	1363	1318	71148	317588	10346	1020
10 PETROLEUM, RELATED INDS.	615808	30732	7583	2662	12271	12170	167398	137916	3988
11 PLASTICS & CHEMICALS	248138	1013297	27748	6874	16266	111895	164432	18593	562
12 GLASS, STONE,CLAY PRDTS.	3745	14621	101920	618	1868	28957	28777	2403	5
13 PRIMARY IRON & STEEL MFR	120	31699	9007	82607	4432	507186	1067	17820	1
14 PRIMARY NONFERROUS MFR.	19445	44599	1760	7840	287583	155564	1200	2632	0
15 MACHINERY & EQUIPMENT	60194	128715	18082	20064	14680	664980	313242	35610	310
16 SERVICES	617964	383879	70512	34807	33786	332859	4382722	391393	44745
17 TRANSPORT. & WAREHOUSING	366072	138531	58883	27025	27316	64262	283759	312498	15264
18 GAS & WATER SERVICES	109213	84829	20325	4898	13291	7831	117600	17416	402902
19 ELECTRIC UTILITIES	45947	73442	15323	5730	26591	19593	281193	21468	1228
20 WAGES & SALARIES	413981	535767	203539	115580	122192	945971	7347543	1336000	291736
21 DIRECT ALLOCATED IMPORTS	366	25813	811	51	699	2494	51097	103116	165
22 TRANSFERRRD IMPORTS	58685	58652	20597	112117	42593	61035	61691	77723	2300
23 OTHER VALUE ADDED	1647453	1699621	270461	74230	154196	767390	11196108	1007850	108822
24 SECONDARY TRANSFERS-OUT	285232	536585	33344	18756	9086	187514	1201380	81113	244984
25 INVENTORY DEPLETION	0	248	270	117	2228	1855	0	0	0
26 SCRAP (NET PURCHASES)	2909	7899	875	9195	35177	-10727	3462	-6650	0
27 REGIONAL OUTPUT (OUTLAY)	8660217	5145419	984779	553972	989269	3969340	26963600	3785221	1316407

TABLE B.1-7

1963 INPUT-OUTPUT TRANSACTIONS
WEST SOUTH CENTRAL
(THOUSANDS OF 1963 DOLLARS)

INDUSTRY TITLE	19	20	21	22	23	24	25	26	27
1 LIVESTOCK, PRDTS.	23	159149	0	0	62772	196594	0	0	2379161
2 OTHER AGRICULTURE PRDTS.	70	236652	0	0	1221448	311941	0	0	3112255
3 COAL MINING	71459	12149	0	0	2175	57	0	0	157183
4 CRUDE PETRO.,NATURAL GAS	5657	0	0	0	17476	417623	0	0	4803076
5 OTHER MINING	0	1366	0	0	65630	62039	0	0	636736
6 CONSTRUCTION	53517	0	0	75823	7412399	0	0	0	8930302
7 FOOD,TOBAC.,FAB.,APPAREL	1925	5949434	0	0	762791	96281	0	0	9290621
8 TRANSPORT EQPT.,ORDNANCE	80	1403458	0	0	1694638	113169	0	0	3880449
9 LUMBER & PAPER	1855	657656	0	0	290454	318177	0	0	3397468
10 PETROLEUM, RELATED INDS.	14829	656657	0	0	722903	666453	0	0	3537502
11 PLASTICS & CHEMICALS	685	709064	0	0	729990	133448	0	0	3951846
12 GLASS, STONE,CLAY PRDTS.	5	36672	0	0	37784	49682	0	0	1125146
13 PRIMARY IRON & STEEL MFR	3	729	0	0	73836	24247	0	0	1388035
14 PRIMARY NONFERROUS MFR.	777	1110	0	0	87037	55636	0	0	893908
15 MACHINERY & EQUIPMENT	2810	1018193	0	0	1956791	137713	0	0	6516171
16 SERVICES	71225	17181168	0	125865	1449934	394817	0	381	30594336
17 TRANSPORT. & WAREHOUSING	50404	650452	0	0	848201	26245	0	412	3718749
18 GAS & WATER SERVICES	56433	448092	0	0	19880	9330	0	0	1402605
19 ELECTRIC UTILITIES	84518	581719	0	0	97882	4467	0	0	1424085
20 WAGES & SALARIES	138487	428029	0	8540327	4897750	0	0	0	30483104
21 DIRECT ALLOCATED IMPORTS	159	473965	0	-1226520	369145	0	0	0	0
22 TRANSFERRRD IMPORTS	0	0	0	-1002378	0	0	0	25612	0
23 OTHER VALUE ADDED	737305	-101542	0	-8540327	-50217	0	0	0	18811680
24 SECONDARY TRANSFERS-OUT	173037	0	0	0	0	0	0	0	3017917
25 INVENTORY DEPLETION	0	0	0	0	0	0	0	0	25999
26 SCRAP (NET PURCHASES)	0	-21064	0	0	320315	0	0	-26405	323841
27 REGIONAL OUTPUT (OUTLAY)	1465262	30483104	0	-2026210	23091008	3017917	0	0	143802208

TABLE B.1-8

1963 INPUT-OUTPUT TRANSACTIONS
MOUNTAIN
(THOUSANDS OF 1963 DOLLARS)

INDUSTRY TITLE	1	2	3	4	5	6	7	8	9
1 LIVESTOCK, PRDTS.	650580	178989	1	34	27	131	688389	45	35
2 OTHER AGRICULTURE PRDTS.	677202	56703	5	99	86	10725	169911	133	105
3 COAL MINING	130	19	4199	2	1119	0	1562	160	552
4 CRUDE PETRO.,NATURAL GAS	0	0	0	25242	0	0	0	0	0
5 OTHER MINING	34	279	0	0	228190	56493	412	2	352
6 CONSTRUCTION	10691	20033	443	40439	6635	1371	4804	1277	3647
7 FOOD,TOBAC.,FAB.,APPAREL	125969	10771	105	2282	2501	21356	512846	5194	8226
8 TRANSPORT EQPT.,ORDNANCE	759	1802	724	347	4686	3662	506	148946	286
9 LUMBER & PAPER	866	11361	633	646	8867	273564	81797	11168	308042
10 PETROLEUM, RELATED INDS.	13574	77202	944	6855	8492	115836	7067	2776	5509
11 PLASTICS & CHEMICALS	12976	67937	2874	11766	65132	119999	26852	14866	22584
12 GLASS, STONE,CLAY PRDTS.	577	511	135	3980	2021	345696	18063	2280	4179
13 PRIMARY IRON & STEEL MFR	0	0	1516	2629	27994	174529	186	26333	5484
14 PRIMARY NONFERROUS MFR.	157	155	4	0	1249	78205	106	34416	871
15 MACHINERY & EQUIPMENT	3519	28670	6671	21450	84872	650742	57713	127365	19080
16 SERVICES	132828	380453	6866	280722	134654	697678	198004	63579	168076
17 TRANSPORT. & WAREHOUSING	54543	18546	1063	11178	24617	163468	84147	10863	28823
18 GAS & WATER SERVICES	839	28391	66	3267	13253	5577	6755	1308	2460
19 ELECTRIC UTILITIES	5303	18744	1718	9377	33821	10709	9910	3927	6739
20 WAGES & SALARIES	111458	112542	22464	94061	345683	1003895	309782	380993	283434
21 DIRECT ALLOCATED IMPORTS	824	25807	11	230	223	914	15560	311	250
22 TRANSFERRRD IMPORTS	7002	2579	68	18027	10956	0	7236	1699	36629
23 OTHER VALUE ADDED	226868	713687	31057	645975	417364	1075246	359173	50443	180439
24 SECONDARY TRANSFERS-OUT	0	0	263	1645	5290	0	79867	16976	19429
25 INVENTORY DEPLETION	0	6151	0	0	10799	0	930	2858	625
26 SCRAP (NET PURCHASES)	0	0	30	0	5054	2184	-62	-910	-448
27 REGIONAL OUTPUT (OUTLAY)	2036698	1761331	81861	1181253	1443584	4811979	2641516	907007	1105407

TABLE B.1-8

1963 INPUT-OUTPUT TRANSACTIONS
MOUNTAIN
(THOUSANDS OF 1963 DOLLARS)

INDUSTRY TITLE	10	11	12	13	14	15	16	17	18
1 LIVESTOCK, PRDTS.	6	21	12	5	11	53	10733	61	17
2 OTHER AGRICULTURE PRDTS.	17	260	103	16	32	343	4039	264	52
3 COAL MINING	377	618	3742	7639	2515	218	5841	277	353
4 CRUDE PETRO.,NATURAL GAS	386164	246	0	0	0	0	1441	1150	119824
5 OTHER MINING	1495	8049	36787	20322	221993	69	179	24	0
6 CONSTRUCTION	14252	1311	1844	2740	4334	2023	393840	49875	19156
7 FOOD,TOBAC.,FAB.,APPAREL	1589	17030	1761	703	3410	7524	72516	6088	1215
8 TRANSPORT EQPT.,ORDNANCE	29	111	112	17	31	811	44074	14091	48
9 LUMBER & PAPER	4764	7829	8722	1003	1336	15256	138356	4856	790
10 PETROLEUM, RELATED INDS.	62238	2595	3481	2312	15091	3306	75031	56443	3476
11 PLASTICS & CHEMICALS	24285	87578	6959	5649	19994	27209	87699	10144	992
12 GLASS, STONE,CLAY PRDTS.	682	937	47916	446	2191	9102	15078	542	4
13 PRIMARY IRON & STEEL MFR	22	1737	4187	72168	2079	108507	517	9996	1
14 PRIMARY NONFERROUS MFR.	1899	1193	278	5943	337873	39232	586	288	0
15 MACHINERY & EQUIPMENT	5989	6296	8286	14463	9101	186106	155656	16282	244
16 SERVICES	61413	32766	28109	21449	30202	86925	2101563	173426	33376
17 TRANSPORT. & WAREHOUSING	35703	12085	28315	17664	29994	16225	127074	110150	10805
18 GAS & WATER SERVICES	10784	2564	6663	4211	16199	1890	57140	4405	279754
19 ELECTRIC UTILITIES	4537	3125	5496	4926	32408	5096	135593	5430	1161
20 WAGES & SALARIES	40003	97045	91445	98810	160727	283095	3740663	630000	129791
21 DIRECT ALLOCATED IMPORTS	39	6890	209	38	872	1497	26285	9352	121
22 TRANSFERRRD IMPORTS	365	10672	7659	2607	10760	8094	14532	12402	8400
23 OTHER VALUE ADDED	163935	51614	93784	52254	154089	206806	5308757	298481	162854
24 SECONDARY TRANSFERS-OUT	45834	120178	10560	9555	3371	102524	494038	40916	93277
25 INVENTORY DEPLETION	0	62	126	97	2572	833	0	0	0
26 SCRAP (NET PURCHASES)	287	270	108	7755	40904	-2538	1473	-2566	0
27 REGIONAL OUTPUT (OUTLAY)	866708	473081	396662	354790	1102088	1110207	13012705	1452380	865710

TABLE B.1-8

1963 INPUT-OUTPUT TRANSACTIONS
MOUNTAIN
(THOUSANDS OF 1963 DOLLARS)

INDUSTRY TITLE	19	20	21	22	23	24	25	26	27
1 LIVESTOCK, PRDTS.	10	77935	0	0	63119	152450	0	0	1822665
2 OTHER AGRICULTURE PRDTS.	31	116455	0	0	55047	166960	0	0	1258588
3 COAL MINING	17012	3545	0	0	1689	505	0	0	52073
4 CRUDE PETRO.,NATURAL GAS	1347	0	0	0	1666	65965	0	0	604045
5 OTHER MINING	0	720	0	0	110372	69806	0	0	755577
6 CONSTRUCTION	20997	0	0	248504	3957024	0	0	0	4805338
7 FOOD,TOBAC.,FAB.,APPAREL	839	2928485	0	0	109761	36635	0	0	3876804
8 TRANSPORT EQPT.,ORDNANCE	34	700529	0	0	734382	43293	0	0	1699280
9 LUMBER & PAPER	810	304538	0	0	126055	144269	0	0	1455527
10 PETROLEUM, RELATED INDS.	6366	324502	0	0	50814	65819	0	0	909729
11 PLASTICS & CHEMICALS	307	322801	0	0	109906	14134	0	0	1063643
12 GLASS, STONE,CLAY PRDTS.	2	18586	0	0	5266	22334	0	0	500527
13 PRIMARY IRON & STEEL MFR	1	273	0	0	4188	20448	0	0	462797
14 PRIMARY NONFERROUS MFR.	335	474	0	0	14755	64695	0	0	583716
15 MACHINERY & EQUIPMENT	1219	501726	0	0	1039147	45799	0	0	2990394
16 SERVICES	31962	8582602	0	-55472	705059	196322	0	62	14092626
17 TRANSPORT. & WAREHOUSING	12385	344931	0	0	163465	10126	0	67	1316234
18 GAS & WATER SERVICES	13484	205036	0	0	10059	6542	0	0	680647
19 ELECTRIC UTILITIES	36488	228603	0	0	50161	1929	0	0	615201
20 WAGES & SALARIES	51838	106544	0	4273099	2555448	0	0	0	14922820
21 DIRECT ALLOCATED IMPORTS	80	236749	0	-508403	182143	0	0	0	0
22 TRANSFERRRD IMPORTS	0	0	0	-163874	0	0	0	4187	0
23 OTHER VALUE ADDED	372720	-72030	0	-4273099	-39049	0	0	0	6181368
24 SECONDARY TRANSFERS-OUT	84307	0	0	0	0	0	0	0	1128030
25 INVENTORY DEPLETION	0	0	0	0	0	0	0	0	25053
26 SCRAP (NET PURCHASES)	0	-10183	0	0	187467	0	0	-4317	224508
27 REGIONAL OUTPUT (OUTLAY)	652574	14922820	0	-479146	10197943	1128030	0	0	62027184

TABLE B.1-9

1963 INPUT-OUTPUT TRANSACTIONS
PACIFIC
(THOUSANDS OF 1963 DOLLARS)

INDUSTRY TITLE	1	2	3	4	5	6	7	8	9
1 LIVESTOCK, PRDTS.	556717	119101	0	30	8	451	1552379	398	241
2 OTHER AGRICULTURE PRDTS.	603025	75856	0	91	27	54518	970070	1186	720
3 COAL MINING	697	68	212	2	24	0	6400	2312	9385
4 CRUDE PETRO.,NATURAL GAS	0	0	0	23814	0	0	0	0	0
5 OTHER MINING	88	3806	0	0	8786	112473	1251	139	7883
6 CONSTRUCTION	11405	39445	41	37512	2133	4785	23561	15370	28110
7 FOOD,TOBAC.,FAB.,APPAREL	380070	20698	10	2119	699	82442	2507435	82280	93814
8 TRANSPORT EQPT.,ORDNANCE	437	2105	51	329	2372	8992	1995	1966348	1730
9 LUMBER & PAPER	4036	41914	49	594	1611	1040037	391863	87613	2407470
10 PETROLEUM, RELATED INDS.	8825	80720	65	6365	6133	274972	30356	27562	42621
11 PLASTICS & CHEMICALS	10543	188081	199	11560	18656	369907	153959	191169	261878
12 GLASS, STONE,CLAY PRDTS.	879	2019	9	3935	796	1171501	149623	45925	37142
13 PRIMARY IRON & STEEL MFR	0	0	127	2327	4938	360700	773	450613	57468
14 PRIMARY NONFERROUS MFR.	68	120	0	0	699	257602	564	314615	10988
15 MACHINERY & EQUIPMENT	5948	27765	462	20356	26864	2167122	469972	1384645	185241
16 SERVICES	195916	595709	593	263415	34075	2378654	1157122	662136	1155943
17 TRANSPORT. & WAREHOUSING	62268	39503	74	29259	6791	527903	391005	132386	246436
18 GAS & WATER SERVICES	3453	50569	2	2921	6096	19363	30998	14010	26396
19 ELECTRIC UTILITIES	21828	33388	62	8385	9073	37156	47370	40842	56545
20 WAGES & SALARIES	232590	437410	3346	119278	109113	3185953	1603725	3439563	2049753
21 DIRECT ALLOCATED IMPORTS	159	105047	1	212	64	3134	155035	2769	1743
22 TRANSFERRRD IMPORTS	23268	22475	159	97865	25372	0	151823	32311	209844
23 OTHER VALUE ADDED	223219	1729630	2278	565387	135153	6246830	1770275	908921	1426508
24 SECONDARY TRANSFERS-OUT	0	0	97	2595	16625	0	118558	117082	74950
25 INVENTORY DEPLETION	0	12598	0	0	2513	0	2534	27186	4080
26 SCRAP (NET PURCHASES)	0	0	3	0	883	8832	681	-15715	13436
27 REGIONAL OUTPUT (OUTLAY)	2345439	3628027	7841	1198351	419504	18313328	11689329	9931666	8410327

TABLE B.1-9

1963 INPUT-OUTPUT TRANSACTIONS
PACIFIC
(THOUSANDS OF 1963 DOLLARS)

INDUSTRY TITLE	10	11	12	13	14	15	16	17	18
1 LIVESTOCK, PRDTS.	21	352	47	15	19	474	35658	585	29
2 OTHER AGRICULTURE PRDTS.	63	1723	839	46	58	2705	17263	1944	87
3 COAL MINING	1263	5400	12806	16657	1581	2037	25318	1410	808
4 CRUDE PETRO.,NATURAL GAS	1263994	1789	0	0	0	0	6360	576	182201
5 OTHER MINING	8993	29557	106870	44549	122435	902	653	77	0
6 CONSTRUCTION	46935	9291	6702	6317	4313	16022	1554564	138003	37731
7 FOOD,TOBAC.,FAB.,APPAREL	5419	89401	10224	2012	4682	71770	326308	41964	2052
8 TRANSPORT EQPT.,ORDNANCE	99	429	343	50	52	9672	164110	113850	102
9 LUMBER & PAPER	23297	71399	42137	2912	4675	175670	574714	15749	1442
10 PETROLEUM, RELATED INDS.	217610	25681	10961	5896	9889	30120	312305	240811	7345
11 PLASTICS & CHEMICALS	79802	633964	46570	16266	25382	275781	342833	31160	3253
12 GLASS, STONE,CLAY PRDTS.	4343	15901	155525	1294	3191	90819	52352	1074	7
13 PRIMARY IRON & STEEL MFR	138	9975	14066	183107	3849	890722	2278	26719	2
14 PRIMARY NONFERROUS MFR.	6217	12202	3158	18964	429822	369172	2135	4040	0
15 MACHINERY & EQUIPMENT	20329	74682	28190	41238	32305	1660082	612823	51119	458
16 SERVICES	212096	308417	105911	62935	64096	836744	8742341	623433	57578
17 TRANSPORT. & WAREHOUSING	128878	75710	82687	47427	32798	155768	551328	493906	17077
18 GAS & WATER SERVICES	36071	20355	27968	10970	12028	17605	232840	13957	426736
19 ELECTRIC UTILITIES	15176	23717	21072	12833	24064	46307	552977	17204	2661
20 WAGES & SALARIES	150496	516394	346685	242258	186631	3050263	15545237	2063000	306818
21 DIRECT ALLOCATED IMPORTS	146	25217	1638	107	726	9359	110136	171567	202
22 TRANSFERRRD IMPORTS	75386	83348	22765	77588	41557	255904	49673	118984	62700
23 OTHER VALUE ADDED	534180	610863	353238	167210	185346	1478551	20695200	1218962	181524
24 SECONDARY TRANSFERS-OUT	51940	279603	32215	35424	24009	502285	1643315	168032	362201
25 INVENTORY DEPLETION	0	323	397	255	2873	8108	0	0	0
26 SCRAP (NET PURCHASES)	961	1871	1235	20202	44888	-28989	7234	-9649	0
27 REGIONAL OUTPUT (OUTLAY)	2883851	2927563	1434248	1016534	1261268	9927853	52159952	5548476	1653010

TABLE B.1-9

1963 INPUT-OUTPUT TRANSACTIONS
PACIFIC
(THOUSANDS OF 1963 DOLLARS)

INDUSTRY TITLE	19	20	21	22	23	24	25	26	27
1 LIVESTOCK, PRDTS.	25	247989	0	0	50757	174181	0	0	2739478
2 OTHER AGRICULTURE PRDTS.	74	395287	0	0	698834	341975	0	0	3166388
3 COAL MINING	30338	10015	0	0	3541	46	0	0	130320
4 CRUDE PETRO.,NATURAL GAS	2402	0	0	0	2696	61051	0	0	1544883
5 OTHER MINING	0	2597	0	0	105733	39284	0	0	596076
6 CONSTRUCTION	48359	0	0	297497	15980835	0	0	0	18308928
7 FOOD,TOBAC.,FAB.,APPAREL	2009	10421972	0	0	694067	162540	0	0	15003987
8 TRANSPORT EQPT.,ORDNANCE	82	2535699	0	0	5460361	432332	0	0	10701542
9 LUMBER & PAPER	1940	1085039	0	0	726595	761136	0	0	7461892
10 PETROLEUM, RELATED INDS.	15214	1124417	0	0	341605	220230	0	0	3039704
11 PLASTICS & CHEMICALS	933	1116292	0	0	376204	98096	0	0	4252485
12 GLASS, STONE,CLAY PRDTS.	5	66432	0	0	54060	74173	0	0	1931003
13 PRIMARY IRON & STEEL MFR	3	860	0	0	43692	53270	0	0	2105627
14 PRIMARY NONFERROUS MFR.	801	1658	0	0	115030	70996	0	0	1618851
15 MACHINERY & EQUIPMENT	2916	1774650	0	0	5517710	385580	0	0	14490458
16 SERVICES	76724	30554208	0	-189701	2984493	863892	0	528	51747248
17 TRANSPORT. & WAREHOUSING	22562	1290783	0	0	877036	38078	0	570	5250231
18 GAS & WATER SERVICES	24094	725630	0	0	30414	10320	0	0	1742797
19 ELECTRIC UTILITIES	87226	754180	0	0	184613	4725	0	0	2001402
20 WAGES & SALARIES	170543	466179	0	9864631	8993575	0	0	0	53083440
21 DIRECT ALLOCATED IMPORTS	199	849669	0	-1954717	517587	0	0	0	0
22 TRANSFERRRD IMPORTS	0	0	0	-1386449	0	0	0	35426	0
23 OTHER VALUE ADDED	880354	-303904	0	-9864631	-76341	0	0	0	29068752
24 SECONDARY TRANSFERS-OUT	362976	0	0	0	0	0	0	0	3791905
25 INVENTORY DEPLETION	0	0	0	0	0	0	0	0	60868
26 SCRAP (NET PURCHASES)	0	-36212	0	0	-61208	0	0	-36523	-88069
27 REGIONAL OUTPUT (OUTLAY)	1729777	53083440	0	-3233370	43621888	3791905	0	0	233750224

TABLE B.2-1

1963 DIRECT INPUT COEFFICIENTS
NEW ENGLAND
(INPUT REQUIRED PER DOLLAR OF OUTPUT)

INDUSTRY TITLE	1	2	3	4	5	6	7	8	9
1 LIVESTOCK, PRDTS.	0.037	0.091	0.0	0.0	0.0	0.000	0.080	0.000	0.000
2 OTHER AGRICULTURE PRDTS.	0.142	0.055	0.0	0.0	0.000	0.004	0.047	0.000	0.000
3 COAL MINING	0.000	0.000	0.0	0.0	0.0	0.0	0.001	0.000	0.003
4 CRUDE PETRO.,NATURAL GAS	0.0	0.0	0.0	0.0	0.0	0.0	0.0	0.0	0.0
5 OTHER MINING	0.000	0.010	0.0	0.0	0.007	0.008	0.000	0.000	0.003
6 CONSTRUCTION	0.009	0.010	0.0	0.0	0.004	0.000	0.002	0.002	0.003
7 FOOD,TOBAC.,FAB.,APPAREL	0.272	0.006	0.0	0.0	0.001	0.004	0.302	0.008	0.017
8 TRANSPORT EQPT.,ORDNANCE	0.000	0.000	0.0	0.0	0.004	0.001	0.000	0.176	0.000
9 LUMBER & PAPER	0.001	0.017	0.0	0.0	0.002	0.050	0.026	0.007	0.273
10 PETROLEUM, RELATED INDS.	0.006	0.013	0.0	0.0	0.013	0.016	0.002	0.003	0.005
11 PLASTICS & CHEMICALS	0.008	0.077	0.0	0.0	0.026	0.020	0.062	0.015	0.044
12 GLASS, STONE,CLAY PRDTS.	0.000	0.004	0.0	0.0	0.001	0.062	0.004	0.004	0.002
13 PRIMARY IRON & STEEL MFR	0.0	0.0	0.0	0.0	0.007	0.019	0.001	0.040	0.005
14 PRIMARY NONFERROUS MFR.	0.000	0.000	0.0	0.0	0.001	0.016	0.000	0.032	0.001
15 MACHINERY & EQUIPMENT	0.004	0.003	0.0	0.0	0.037	0.123	0.019	0.153	0.020
16 SERVICES	0.098	0.075	0.0	0.038	0.060	0.122	0.079	0.065	0.108
17 TRANSPORT. & WAREHOUSING	0.019	0.015	0.0	0.181	0.046	0.029	0.020	0.013	0.031
18 GAS & WATER SERVICES	0.001	0.002	0.0	0.0	0.004	0.001	0.002	0.002	0.005
19 ELECTRIC UTILITIES	0.004	0.001	0.0	0.0	0.012	0.002	0.005	0.004	0.008
20 TOTAL	0.602	0.381	0.0	0.219	0.225	0.477	0.652	0.524	0.528

TABLE B.2-1

1963 DIRECT INPUT COEFFICIENTS
NEW ENGLAND
(INPUT REQUIRED PER DOLLAR OF OUTPUT)

INDUSTRY TITLE	10	11	12	13	14	15	16	17	18	19
1 LIVESTOCK, PRDTS.	0.000	0.000	0.000	0.000	0.000	0.000	0.000	0.000	0.000	0.000
2 OTHER AGRICULTURE PRDTS.	0.000	0.000	0.001	0.000	0.000	0.000	0.000	0.000	0.000	0.000
3 COAL MINING	0.000	0.002	0.002	0.015	0.000	0.000	0.000	0.000	0.001	0.042
4 CRUDE PETRO.,NATURAL GAS	0.110	0.000	0.0	0.0	0.0	0.0	0.000	0.000	0.103	0.003
5 OTHER MINING	0.010	0.006	0.068	0.040	0.002	0.000	0.000	0.000	0.0	0.0
6 CONSTRUCTION	0.005	0.003	0.003	0.006	0.003	0.002	0.026	0.028	0.033	0.036
7 FOOD,TOBAC.,FAB.,APPAREL	0.001	0.038	0.012	0.002	0.005	0.009	0.006	0.004	0.001	0.001
8 TRANSPORT EQPT.,ORDNANCE	0.000	0.000	0.000	0.000	0.000	0.001	0.002	0.011	0.000	0.000
9 LUMBER & PAPER	0.020	0.029	0.029	0.003	0.007	0.018	0.012	0.003	0.001	0.001
10 PETROLEUM, RELATED INDS.	0.052	0.005	0.007	0.006	0.002	0.004	0.006	0.039	0.007	0.010
11 PLASTICS & CHEMICALS	0.008	0.231	0.045	0.016	0.026	0.032	0.008	0.007	0.004	0.003
12 GLASS, STONE,CLAY PRDTS.	0.005	0.005	0.129	0.002	0.003	0.012	0.001	0.000	0.000	0.000
13 PRIMARY IRON & STEEL MFR	0.000	0.004	0.013	0.192	0.004	0.071	0.000	0.006	0.000	0.000
14 PRIMARY NONFERROUS MFR.	0.001	0.003	0.004	0.019	0.438	0.044	0.000	0.000	0.0	0.001
15 MACHINERY & EQUIPMENT	0.003	0.021	0.022	0.041	0.024	0.173	0.011	0.010	0.000	0.002
16 SERVICES	0.057	0.105	0.075	0.060	0.063	0.090	0.169	0.118	0.042	0.049
17 TRANSPORT. & WAREHOUSING	0.078	0.024	0.049	0.042	0.020	0.015	0.010	0.074	0.011	0.030
18 GAS & WATER SERVICES	0.005	0.006	0.012	0.011	0.005	0.002	0.005	0.002	0.244	0.033
19 ELECTRIC UTILITIES	0.002	0.009	0.009	0.013	0.010	0.005	0.012	0.003	0.003	0.058
20 TOTAL	0.358	0.491	0.483	0.469	0.613	0.478	0.270	0.307	0.451	0.270

TABLE B.2-2

1963 DIRECT INPUT COEFFICIENTS
MIDDLE ATLANTIC
(INPUT REQUIRED PER DOLLAR OF OUTPUT)

INDUSTRY TITLE	1	2	3	4	5	6	7	8	9
1 LIVESTOCK, PRDTS.	0.064	0.058	0.000	0.000	0.000	0.000	0.071	0.000	0.000
2 OTHER AGRICULTURE PRDTS.	0.232	0.043	0.000	0.000	0.000	0.004	0.040	0.000	0.000
3 COAL MINING	0.000	0.000	0.265	0.0	0.002	0.0	0.000	0.000	0.001
4 CRUDE PETRO.,NATURAL GAS	0.0	0.0	0.0	0.002	0.0	0.0	0.0	0.0	0.0
5 OTHER MINING	0.000	0.000	0.0	0.0	0.021	0.007	0.000	0.000	0.001
6 CONSTRUCTION	0.011	0.011	0.006	0.004	0.003	0.000	0.002	0.002	0.002
7 FOOD,TOBAC.,FAB.,APPAREL	0.194	0.005	0.001	0.000	0.001	0.005	0.304	0.010	0.014
8 TRANSPORT EQPT.,ORDNANCE	0.000	0.000	0.005	0.000	0.003	0.001	0.000	0.232	0.000
9 LUMBER & PAPER	0.001	0.014	0.006	0.000	0.002	0.064	0.024	0.006	0.291
10 PETROLEUM, RELATED INDS.	0.008	0.012	0.008	0.001	0.009	0.018	0.002	0.002	0.004
11 PLASTICS & CHEMICALS	0.007	0.065	0.025	0.001	0.028	0.026	0.026	0.019	0.037
12 GLASS, STONE,CLAY PRDTS.	0.000	0.004	0.001	0.001	0.001	0.083	0.006	0.007	0.002
13 PRIMARY IRON & STEEL MFR	0.0	0.0	0.012	0.000	0.009	0.030	0.000	0.072	0.006
14 PRIMARY NONFERROUS MFR.	0.000	0.000	0.000	0.0	0.001	0.020	0.000	0.022	0.001
15 MACHINERY & EQUIPMENT	0.005	0.004	0.057	0.002	0.040	0.168	0.024	0.136	0.017
16 SERVICES	0.084	0.089	0.077	0.059	0.072	0.160	0.089	0.060	0.123
17 TRANSPORT. & WAREHOUSING	0.020	0.015	0.027	0.162	0.076	0.037	0.022	0.016	0.027
18 GAS & WATER SERVICES	0.001	0.001	0.001	0.000	0.006	0.001	0.002	0.001	0.003
19 ELECTRIC UTILITIES	0.004	0.001	0.025	0.001	0.017	0.003	0.004	0.004	0.005

TABLE B.2-2

1963 DIRECT INPUT COEFFICIENTS
MIDDLE ATLANTIC
(INPUT REQUIRED PER DOLLAR OF OUTPUT)

INDUSTRY TITLE	10	11	12	13	14	15	16	17	18	19
1 LIVESTOCK, PRDTS.	0.000	0.000	0.000	0.000	0.000	0.000	0.000	0.000	0.000	0.000
2 OTHER AGRICULTURE PRDTS.	0.000	0.001	0.001	0.000	0.000	0.000	0.000	0.000	0.000	0.000
3 COAL MINING	0.000	0.002	0.006	0.021	0.001	0.000	0.000	0.000	0.001	0.041
4 CRUDE PETRO.,NATURAL GAS	0.407	0.001	0.0	0.0	0.0	0.0	0.000	0.000	0.112	0.003
5 OTHER MINING	0.004	0.009	0.052	0.056	0.042	0.000	0.000	0.000	0.0	0.0
6 CONSTRUCTION	0.015	0.004	0.004	0.008	0.003	0.002	0.028	0.026	0.035	0.034
7 FOOD,TOBAC.,FAB.,APPAREL	0.002	0.025	0.009	0.002	0.004	0.009	0.006	0.006	0.002	0.001
8 TRANSPORT EQPT.,ORDNANCE	0.000	0.000	0.000	0.000	0.000	0.001	0.002	0.018	0.000	0.000
9 LUMBER & PAPER	0.010	0.027	0.039	0.003	0.004	0.021	0.012	0.003	0.001	0.001
10 PETROLEUM, RELATED INDS.	0.074	0.007	0.006	0.006	0.004	0.003	0.006	0.040	0.007	0.010
11 PLASTICS & CHEMICALS	0.026	0.206	0.050	0.018	0.019	0.035	0.007	0.006	0.004	0.001
12 GLASS, STONE,CLAY PRDTS.	0.002	0.009	0.101	0.001	0.002	0.010	0.001	0.000	0.000	0.000
13 PRIMARY IRON & STEEL MFR	0.000	0.003	0.009	0.202	0.002	0.078	0.000	0.005	0.000	0.000
14 PRIMARY NONFERROUS MFR.	0.002	0.004	0.004	0.019	0.322	0.041	0.000	0.001	0.0	0.001
15 MACHINERY & EQUIPMENT	0.007	0.025	0.019	0.040	0.020	0.163	0.011	0.009	0.000	0.002
16 SERVICES	0.073	0.125	0.078	0.062	0.059	0.089	0.172	0.113	0.044	0.047
17 TRANSPORT. & WAREHOUSING	0.049	0.024	0.042	0.051	0.025	0.016	0.011	0.088	0.011	0.029
18 GAS & WATER SERVICES	0.012	0.008	0.020	0.012	0.006	0.002	0.004	0.003	0.264	0.032
19 ELECTRIC UTILITIES	0.005	0.009	0.013	0.014	0.012	0.005	0.010	0.003	0.003	0.055

TABLE B.2-3

1963 DIRECT INPUT COEFFICIENTS
EAST NORTH CENTRAL
(INPUT REQUIRED PER DOLLAR OF OUTPUT)

INDUSTRY TITLE	1	2	3	4	5	6	7	8	9
1 LIVESTOCK, PRDTS.	0.116	0.048	0.000	0.000	0.000	0.000	0.173	0.000	0.000
2 OTHER AGRICULTURE PRDTS.	0.432	0.032	0.000	0.000	0.000	0.004	0.072	0.000	0.000
3 COAL MINING	0.000	0.000	0.095	0.000	0.002	0.0	0.000	0.000	0.002
4 CRUDE PETRO.,NATURAL GAS	0.0	0.0	0.0	0.009	0.0	0.0	0.0	0.0	0.0
5 OTHER MINING	0.000	0.009	0.0	0.0	0.026	0.008	0.000	0.000	0.001
6 CONSTRUCTION	0.011	0.019	0.005	0.021	0.003	0.000	0.002	0.002	0.002
7 FOOD,TOBAC.,FAB.,APPAREL	0.112	0.002	0.001	0.001	0.001	0.005	0.214	0.014	0.016
8 TRANSPORT EQPT.,ORDNANCE	0.000	0.001	0.007	0.000	0.004	0.001	0.000	0.309	0.000
9 LUMBER & PAPER	0.001	0.002	0.006	0.000	0.003	0.065	0.034	0.004	0.276
10 PETROLEUM, RELATED INDS.	0.007	0.038	0.009	0.004	0.012	0.017	0.003	0.002	0.004
11 PLASTICS & CHEMICALS	0.006	0.053	0.028	0.006	0.032	0.025	0.019	0.026	0.045
12 GLASS, STONE,CLAY PRDTS.	0.000	0.002	0.001	0.002	0.002	0.074	0.009	0.010	0.003
13 PRIMARY IRON & STEEL MFR	0.0	0.0	0.015	0.001	0.012	0.026	0.000	0.085	0.008
14 PRIMARY NONFERROUS MFR.	0.000	0.000	0.000	0.0	0.001	0.018	0.000	0.016	0.002
15 MACHINERY & EQUIPMENT	0.003	0.014	0.069	0.011	0.045	0.149	0.026	0.126	0.021
16 SERVICES	0.085	0.213	0.080	0.162	0.083	0.142	0.090	0.055	0.097
17 TRANSPORT. & WAREHOUSING	0.024	0.013	0.015	0.074	0.062	0.033	0.030	0.017	0.030
18 GAS & WATER SERVICES	0.000	0.001	0.001	0.002	0.007	0.001	0.003	0.001	0.003
19 ELECTRIC UTILITIES	0.003	0.001	0.028	0.005	0.018	0.002	0.004	0.003	0.006

TABLE B.2-3

1963 DIRECT INPUT COEFFICIENTS
EAST NORTH CENTRAL
(INPUT REQUIRED PER DOLLAR OF OUTPUT)

INDUSTRY TITLE	10	11	12	13	14	15	16	17	18	19
1 LIVESTOCK, PRDTS.	0.000	0.000	0.000	0.000	0.000	0.000	0.000	0.000	0.000	0.000
2 OTHER AGRICULTURE PRDTS.	0.000	0.001	0.001	0.000	0.000	0.000	0.000	0.000	0.000	0.000
3 COAL MINING	0.000	0.002	0.006	0.019	0.001	0.000	0.000	0.000	0.000	0.049
4 CRUDE PETRO.,NATURAL GAS	0.444	0.001	0.0	0.0	0.0	0.0	0.000	0.000	0.132	0.004
5 OTHER MINING	0.005	0.008	0.057	0.050	0.025	0.000	0.000	0.000	0.0	0.0
6 CONSTRUCTION	0.017	0.003	0.004	0.007	0.003	0.002	0.029	0.034	0.024	0.036
7 FOOD,TOBAC.,FAB.,APPAREL	0.002	0.038	0.008	0.002	0.004	0.007	0.005	0.004	0.001	0.001
8 TRANSPORT EQPT.,ORDNANCE	0.000	0.000	0.000	0.000	0.000	0.001	0.003	0.009	0.000	0.000
9 LUMBER & PAPER	0.011	0.026	0.038	0.003	0.006	0.019	0.011	0.003	0.001	0.001
10 PETROLEUM, RELATED INDS.	0.082	0.008	0.006	0.007	0.004	0.003	0.006	0.037	0.005	0.010
11 PLASTICS & CHEMICALS	0.028	0.224	0.046	0.018	0.022	0.032	0.007	0.007	0.002	0.001
12 GLASS, STONE,CLAY PRDTS.	0.002	0.007	0.104	0.001	0.003	0.009	0.001	0.000	0.000	0.000
13 PRIMARY IRON & STEEL MFR	0.000	0.004	0.009	0.206	0.003	0.105	0.000	0.007	0.000	0.000
14 PRIMARY NONFERROUS MFR.	0.002	0.003	0.003	0.019	0.371	0.042	0.000	0.000	0.0	0.001
15 MACHINERY & EQUIPMENT	0.007	0.024	0.019	0.044	0.036	0.178	0.011	0.011	0.000	0.002
16 SERVICES	0.077	0.116	0.075	0.062	0.065	0.085	0.158	0.120	0.039	0.048
17 TRANSPORT. & WAREHOUSING	0.044	0.025	0.045	0.047	0.025	0.016	0.010	0.079	0.012	0.034
18 GAS & WATER SERVICES	0.013	0.006	0.020	0.012	0.006	0.002	0.004	0.003	0.310	0.038
19 ELECTRIC UTILITIES	0.005	0.008	0.013	0.014	0.012	0.005	0.010	0.003	0.002	0.057

TABLE B.2-4

1963 DIRECT INPUT COEFFICIENTS
WEST NORTH CENTRAL
(INPUT REQUIRED PER DOLLAR OF OUTPUT)

INDUSTRY TITLE	1	2	3	4	5	6	7	8	9
1 LIVESTOCK, PRDTS.	0.248	0.062	0.0	0.000	0.000	0.000	0.315	0.000	0.000
2 OTHER AGRICULTURE PRDTS.	0.296	0.035	0.000	0.000	0.000	0.003	0.062	0.000	0.000
3 COAL MINING	0.000	0.000	0.020	0.000	0.004	0.0	0.000	0.000	0.001
4 CRUDE PETRO.,NATURAL GAS	0.0	0.0	0.0	0.019	0.0	0.0	0.0	0.0	0.0
5 OTHER MINING	0.000	0.002	0.0	0.0	0.077	0.013	0.000	0.000	0.001
6 CONSTRUCTION	0.006	0.012	0.005	0.032	0.003	0.000	0.002	0.002	0.002
7 FOOD,TOBAC.,FAB.,APPAREL	0.087	0.002	0.001	0.002	0.001	0.004	0.181	0.012	0.012
8 TRANSPORT EQPT.,ORDNANCE	0.000	0.001	0.003	0.000	0.004	0.001	0.000	0.272	0.000
9 LUMBER & PAPER	0.001	0.001	0.002	0.001	0.005	0.060	0.029	0.007	0.290
10 PETROLEUM, RELATED INDS.	0.007	0.046	0.004	0.006	0.017	0.027	0.002	0.002	0.004
11 PLASTICS & CHEMICALS	0.006	0.037	0.013	0.010	0.044	0.027	0.014	0.023	0.038
12 GLASS, STONE,CLAY PRDTS.	0.000	0.001	0.001	0.003	0.004	0.074	0.005	0.008	0.002
13 PRIMARY IRON & STEEL MFR	0.0	0.0	0.006	0.002	0.023	0.027	0.000	0.071	0.006
14 PRIMARY NONFERROUS MFR.	0.000	0.000	0.0	0.0	0.001	0.016	0.000	0.022	0.001
15 MACHINERY & EQUIPMENT	0.002	0.016	0.037	0.018	0.060	0.138	0.017	0.133	0.017
16 SERVICES	0.070	0.258	0.068	0.227	0.157	0.146	0.071	0.059	0.109
17 TRANSPORT. & WAREHOUSING	0.023	0.009	0.006	0.018	0.030	0.034	0.033	0.016	0.027
18 GAS & WATER SERVICES	0.000	0.001	0.000	0.003	0.006	0.001	0.002	0.001	0.003
19 ELECTRIC UTILITIES	0.002	0.001	0.001	0.007	0.018	0.002	0.003	0.003	0.005

TABLE B.2-4

1963 DIRECT INPUT COEFFICIENTS
WEST NORTH CENTRAL
(INPUT REQUIRED PER DOLLAR OF OUTPUT)

INDUSTRY TITLE	10	11	12	13	14	15	16	17	18	19
1 LIVESTOCK, PRDTS.	0.000	0.000	0.000	0.000	0.000	0.000	0.001	0.000	0.000	0.000
2 OTHER AGRICULTURE PRDTS.	0.000	0.001	0.001	0.000	0.000	0.000	0.000	0.000	0.000	0.000
3 COAL MINING	0.000	0.002	0.010	0.016	0.001	0.000	0.000	0.000	0.001	0.040
4 CRUDE PETRO.,NATURAL GAS	0.447	0.001	0.0	0.0	0.0	0.0	0.000	0.001	0.127	0.003
5 OTHER MINING	0.003	0.011	0.080	0.043	0.061	0.000	0.000	0.000	0.0	0.0
6 CONSTRUCTION	0.017	0.003	0.005	0.006	0.003	0.002	0.027	0.035	0.027	0.034
7 FOOD,TOBAC.,FAB.,APPAREL	0.002	0.038	0.008	0.002	0.004	0.008	0.005	0.004	0.001	0.001
8 TRANSPORT EQPT.,ORDNANCE	0.000	0.000	0.000	0.000	0.000	0.002	0.003	0.010	0.000	0.000
9 LUMBER & PAPER	0.008	0.028	0.026	0.003	0.004	0.016	0.011	0.003	0.001	0.001
10 PETROLEUM, RELATED INDS.	0.077	0.008	0.008	0.006	0.006	0.003	0.006	0.037	0.005	0.010
11 PLASTICS & CHEMICALS	0.028	0.226	0.032	0.015	0.020	0.033	0.006	0.007	0.002	0.001
12 GLASS, STONE,CLAY PRDTS.	0.002	0.007	0.106	0.001	0.003	0.008	0.001	0.000	0.000	0.000
13 PRIMARY IRON & STEEL MFR	0.000	0.003	0.011	0.177	0.002	0.111	0.000	0.007	0.000	0.000
14 PRIMARY NONFERROUS MFR.	0.002	0.003	0.002	0.018	0.340	0.038	0.000	0.000	0.0	0.001
15 MACHINERY & EQUIPMENT	0.007	0.026	0.021	0.048	0.036	0.194	0.010	0.011	0.000	0.002
16 SERVICES	0.074	0.125	0.072	0.062	0.057	0.086	0.158	0.118	0.041	0.047
17 TRANSPORT. & WAREHOUSING	0.043	0.027	0.058	0.042	0.025	0.017	0.010	0.078	0.012	0.028
18 GAS & WATER SERVICES	0.013	0.006	0.021	0.011	0.008	0.002	0.004	0.003	0.297	0.032
19 ELECTRIC UTILITIES	0.005	0.007	0.017	0.013	0.015	0.005	0.010	0.004	0.002	0.055

TABLE B.2-5

1963 DIRECT INPUT COEFFICIENTS
SOUTH ATLANTIC
(INPUT REQUIRED PER DOLLAR OF OUTPUT)

INDUSTRY TITLE	1	2	3	4	5	6	7	8	9
1 LIVESTOCK, PRDTS.	0.073	0.072	0.000	0.000	0.000	0.000	0.058	0.000	0.000
2 OTHER AGRICULTURE PRDTS.	0.266	0.020	0.000	0.000	0.000	0.006	0.088	0.000	0.000
3 COAL MINING	0.001	0.000	0.113	0.0	0.001	0.0	0.001	0.000	0.003
4 CRUDE PETRO.,NATURAL GAS	0.0	0.0	0.0	0.050	0.0	0.0	0.0	0.0	0.0
5 OTHER MINING	0.000	0.008	0.000	0.0	0.043	0.009	0.000	0.000	0.001
6 CONSTRUCTION	0.007	0.014	0.005	0.023	0.004	0.000	0.002	0.002	0.003
7 FOOD,TOBAC.,FAB.,APPAREL	0.234	0.003	0.001	0.001	0.001	0.005	0.301	0.013	0.022
8 TRANSPORT EQPT.,ORDNANCE	0.000	0.000	0.007	0.000	0.005	0.001	0.000	0.237	0.000
9 LUMBER & PAPER	0.001	0.004	0.009	0.000	0.003	0.064	0.022	0.009	0.257
10 PETROLEUM, RELATED INDS.	0.005	0.030	0.009	0.004	0.011	0.020	0.002	0.002	0.006
11 PLASTICS & CHEMICALS	0.008	0.104	0.028	0.012	0.038	0.023	0.059	0.023	0.046
12 GLASS, STONE,CLAY PRDTS.	0.000	0.002	0.001	0.004	0.001	0.088	0.005	0.009	0.003
13 PRIMARY IRON & STEEL MFR	0.0	0.0	0.018	0.005	0.016	0.027	0.000	0.068	0.008
14 PRIMARY NONFERROUS MFR.	0.000	0.000	0.000	0.0	0.002	0.019	0.000	0.023	0.002
15 MACHINERY & EQUIPMENT	0.002	0.006	0.069	0.016	0.062	0.157	0.016	0.142	0.027
16 SERVICES	0.128	0.170	0.079	0.168	0.073	0.150	0.071	0.060	0.106
17 TRANSPORT. & WAREHOUSING	0.025	0.016	0.017	0.055	0.072	0.035	0.019	0.016	0.032
18 GAS & WATER SERVICES	0.000	0.001	0.001	0.002	0.013	0.001	0.002	0.001	0.005
19 ELECTRIC UTILITIES	0.003	0.001	0.023	0.005	0.022	0.002	0.005	0.004	0.008

TABLE B.2-5

1963 DIRECT INPUT COEFFICIENTS
SOUTH ATLANTIC
(INPUT REQUIRED PER DOLLAR OF OUTPUT)

INDUSTRY TITLE	10	11	12	13	14	15	16	17	18	19
1 LIVESTOCK, PRDTS.	0.000	0.000	0.000	0.000	0.000	0.000	0.001	0.000	0.000	0.000
2 OTHER AGRICULTURE PRDTS.	0.000	0.001	0.000	0.000	0.000	0.000	0.000	0.000	0.000	0.000
3 COAL MINING	0.000	0.003	0.006	0.020	0.001	0.000	0.001	0.000	0.000	0.044
4 CRUDE PETRO.,NATURAL GAS	0.277	0.001	0.0	0.0	0.0	0.0	0.000	0.000	0.128	0.003
5 OTHER MINING	0.011	0.017	0.068	0.053	0.053	0.000	0.000	0.000	0.0	0.0
6 CONSTRUCTION	0.011	0.004	0.005	0.007	0.003	0.002	0.030	0.027	0.021	0.035
7 FOOD,TOBAC.,FAB.,APPAREL	0.002	0.017	0.005	0.002	0.003	0.008	0.006	0.007	0.001	0.001
8 TRANSPORT EQPT.,ORDNANCE	0.000	0.000	0.000	0.000	0.000	0.001	0.003	0.017	0.000	0.000
9 LUMBER & PAPER	0.022	0.030	0.037	0.003	0.004	0.017	0.011	0.003	0.001	0.001
10 PETROLEUM, RELATED INDS.	0.077	0.006	0.007	0.006	0.005	0.003	0.006	0.044	0.004	0.010
11 PLASTICS & CHEMICALS	0.018	0.257	0.037	0.017	0.019	0.029	0.007	0.006	0.001	0.000
12 GLASS, STONE,CLAY PRDTS.	0.005	0.003	0.112	0.001	0.002	0.009	0.001	0.000	0.000	0.000
13 PRIMARY IRON & STEEL MFR	0.000	0.003	0.009	0.190	0.001	0.102	0.000	0.005	0.000	0.000
14 PRIMARY NONFERROUS MFR.	0.001	0.005	0.002	0.018	0.314	0.042	0.000	0.000	0.0	0.001
15 MACHINERY & EQUIPMENT	0.006	0.020	0.018	0.039	0.011	0.159	0.011	0.010	0.000	0.002
16 SERVICES	0.071	0.094	0.075	0.062	0.051	0.084	0.162	0.116	0.036	0.047
17 TRANSPORT. & WAREHOUSING	0.058	0.029	0.053	0.052	0.023	0.016	0.010	0.080	0.012	0.031
18 GAS & WATER SERVICES	0.010	0.011	0.020	0.011	0.006	0.002	0.005	0.003	0.298	0.035
19 ELECTRIC UTILITIES	0.004	0.011	0.013	0.013	0.013	0.005	0.011	0.003	0.001	0.056

TABLE B.2-6

1963 DIRECT INPUT COEFFICIENTS
EAST SOUTH CENTRAL
(INPUT REQUIRED PER DOLLAR OF OUTPUT)

INDUSTRY TITLE	1	2	3	4	5	6	7	8	9
1 LIVESTOCK, PRDTS.	0.094	0.107	0.000	0.000	0.000	0.000	0.096	0.000	0.000
2 OTHER AGRICULTURE PRDTS.	0.237	0.016	0.000	0.000	0.000	0.004	0.083	0.000	0.000
3 COAL MINING	0.000	0.000	0.168	0.0	0.002	0.0	0.000	0.000	0.002
4 CRUDE PETRO.,NATURAL GAS	0.0	0.0	0.0	0.018	0.0	0.0	0.0	0.0	0.0
5 OTHER MINING	0.000	0.007	0.0	0.0	0.037	0.011	0.000	0.000	0.002
6 CONSTRUCTION	0.009	0.016	0.006	0.034	0.004	0.000	0.002	0.002	0.003
7 FOOD,TOBAC.,FAB.,APPAREL	0.173	0.003	0.001	0.002	0.001	0.004	0.271	0.009	0.021
8 TRANSPORT EQPT.,ORDNANCE	0.000	0.000	0.006	0.000	0.005	0.001	0.000	0.206	0.000
9 LUMBER & PAPER	0.001	0.001	0.006	0.001	0.004	0.051	0.024	0.008	0.291
10 PETROLEUM, RELATED INDS.	0.005	0.021	0.008	0.006	0.013	0.025	0.002	0.003	0.005
11 PLASTICS & CHEMICALS	0.007	0.073	0.026	0.010	0.037	0.026	0.033	0.020	0.046
12 GLASS, STONE,CLAY PRDTS.	0.000	0.002	0.001	0.003	0.001	0.081	0.007	0.005	0.004
13 PRIMARY IRON & STEEL MFR	0.0	0.0	0.012	0.002	0.013	0.033	0.000	0.058	0.009
14 PRIMARY NONFERROUS MFR.	0.000	0.000	0.000	0.0	0.001	0.016	0.000	0.028	0.002
15 MACHINERY & EQUIPMENT	0.002	0.006	0.064	0.018	0.059	0.143	0.019	0.146	0.027
16 SERVICES	0.091	0.134	0.076	0.238	0.079	0.147	0.077	0.065	0.099
17 TRANSPORT. & WAREHOUSING	0.018	0.011	0.019	0.009	0.048	0.035	0.022	0.014	0.032
18 GAS & WATER SERVICES	0.000	0.002	0.001	0.003	0.007	0.001	0.002	0.001	0.005
19 ELECTRIC UTILITIES	0.003	0.001	0.023	0.008	0.017	0.002	0.004	0.004	0.008

TABLE B.2-6

1963 DIRECT INPUT COEFFICIENTS
EAST SOUTH CENTRAL
(INPUT REQUIRED PER DOLLAR OF OUTPUT)

INDUSTRY TITLE	10	11	12	13	14	15	16	17	18	19
1 LIVESTOCK, PRDTS.	0.000	0.000	0.000	0.000	0.000	0.000	0.001	0.000	0.000	0.000
2 OTHER AGRICULTURE PRDTS.	0.000	0.001	0.000	0.000	0.000	0.000	0.000	0.000	0.000	0.000
3 COAL MINING	0.000	0.003	0.010	0.019	0.001	0.000	0.001	0.000	0.000	0.036
4 CRUDE PETRO.,NATURAL GAS	0.395	0.001	0.0	0.0	0.0	0.0	0.000	0.001	0.136	0.003
5 OTHER MINING	0.008	0.015	0.069	0.052	0.105	0.000	0.000	0.000	0.0	0.0
6 CONSTRUCTION	0.015	0.004	0.005	0.007	0.004	0.002	0.028	0.033	0.019	0.030
7 FOOD,TOBAC.,FAB.,APPAREL	0.002	0.027	0.006	0.002	0.004	0.008	0.006	0.004	0.001	0.001
8 TRANSPORT EQPT.,ORDNANCE	0.000	0.000	0.000	0.000	0.000	0.001	0.003	0.010	0.000	0.000
9 LUMBER & PAPER	0.017	0.027	0.034	0.003	0.004	0.021	0.011	0.003	0.001	0.001
10 PETROLEUM, RELATED INDS.	0.085	0.006	0.007	0.006	0.008	0.003	0.006	0.035	0.003	0.009
11 PLASTICS & CHEMICALS	0.025	0.256	0.036	0.017	0.022	0.038	0.006	0.007	0.000	0.000
12 GLASS, STONE,CLAY PRDTS.	0.004	0.003	0.097	0.001	0.003	0.011	0.001	0.000	0.000	0.000
13 PRIMARY IRON & STEEL MFR	0.000	0.004	0.008	0.197	0.002	0.110	0.000	0.007	0.000	0.000
14 PRIMARY NONFERROUS MFR.	0.002	0.005	0.002	0.018	0.372	0.048	0.000	0.000	0.0	0.000
15 MACHINERY & EQUIPMENT	0.007	0.017	0.019	0.046	0.017	0.171	0.011	0.011	0.000	0.002
16 SERVICES	0.076	0.086	0.073	0.063	0.046	0.089	0.156	0.116	0.035	0.042
17 TRANSPORT. & WAREHOUSING	0.044	0.028	0.053	0.048	0.025	0.017	0.012	0.081	0.012	0.026
18 GAS & WATER SERVICES	0.012	0.010	0.024	0.012	0.010	0.002	0.005	0.003	0.316	0.029
19 ELECTRIC UTILITIES	0.005	0.011	0.017	0.014	0.020	0.005	0.011	0.004	0.001	0.050

TABLE B.2-7

1963 DIRECT INPUT COEFFICIENTS
WEST SOUTH CENTRAL
(INPUT REQUIRED PER DOLLAR OF OUTPUT)

INDUSTRY TITLE	1	2	3	4	5	6	7	8	9
1 LIVESTOCK, PRDTS.	0.191	0.090	0.0	0.000	0.000	0.000	0.151	0.000	0.000
2 OTHER AGRICULTURE PRDTS.	0.193	0.024	0.0	0.000	0.000	0.004	0.096	0.000	0.000
3 COAL MINING	0.000	0.000	0.046	0.000	0.001	0.0	0.001	0.000	0.002
4 CRUDE PETRO.,NATURAL GAS	0.0	0.0	0.0	0.030	0.0	0.0	0.0	0.0	0.0
5 OTHER MINING	0.000	0.003	0.0	0.000	0.024	0.011	0.000	0.000	0.002
6 CONSTRUCTION	0.005	0.012	0.005	0.035	0.004	0.000	0.002	0.002	0.003
7 FOOD,TOBAC.,FAB.,APPAREL	0.161	0.004	0.002	0.002	0.001	0.004	0.219	0.010	0.016
8 TRANSPORT EQPT.,ORDNANCE	0.000	0.001	0.006	0.000	0.004	0.001	0.000	0.194	0.000
9 LUMBER & PAPER	0.000	0.001	0.004	0.001	0.004	0.058	0.029	0.010	0.285
10 PETROLEUM, RELATED INDS.	0.005	0.047	0.008	0.006	0.009	0.026	0.002	0.003	0.006
11 PLASTICS & CHEMICALS	0.006	0.044	0.023	0.011	0.035	0.027	0.014	0.018	0.041
12 GLASS, STONE,CLAY PRDTS.	0.000	0.001	0.001	0.004	0.001	0.079	0.008	0.006	0.004
13 PRIMARY IRON & STEEL MFR	0.0	0.0	0.011	0.003	0.017	0.052	0.000	0.049	0.006
14 PRIMARY NONFERROUS MFR.	0.000	0.000	0.0	0.0	0.001	0.016	0.000	0.030	0.001
15 MACHINERY & EQUIPMENT	0.002	0.013	0.055	0.019	0.051	0.148	0.021	0.155	0.021
16 SERVICES	0.080	0.202	0.077	0.239	0.071	0.150	0.083	0.065	0.105
17 TRANSPORT. & WAREHOUSING	0.021	0.011	0.011	0.007	0.029	0.036	0.035	0.014	0.031
18 GAS & WATER SERVICES	0.000	0.005	0.000	0.003	0.016	0.001	0.003	0.001	0.004
19 ELECTRIC UTILITIES	0.002	0.003	0.001	0.008	0.020	0.002	0.004	0.004	0.008

TABLE B.2-7

1963 DIRECT INPUT COEFFICIENTS
WEST SOUTH CENTRAL
(INPUT REQUIRED PER DOLLAR OF OUTPUT)

INDUSTRY TITLE	10	11	12	13	14	15	16	17	18	19
1 LIVESTOCK, PRDTS.	0.000	0.000	0.000	0.000	0.000	0.000	0.002	0.000	0.000	0.000
2 OTHER AGRICULTURE PRDTS.	0.000	0.001	0.000	0.000	0.000	0.000	0.000	0.000	0.000	0.000
3 COAL MINING	0.000	0.004	0.010	0.013	0.002	0.000	0.000	0.000	0.000	0.049
4 CRUDE PETRO.,NATURAL GAS	0.456	0.001	0.0	0.0	0.0	0.0	0.000	0.003	0.131	0.004
5 OTHER MINING	0.001	0.021	0.076	0.034	0.177	0.000	0.000	0.000	0.0	0.0
6 CONSTRUCTION	0.017	0.004	0.005	0.005	0.004	0.002	0.027	0.032	0.018	0.037
7 FOOD,TOBAC.,FAB.,APPAREL	0.002	0.015	0.006	0.002	0.003	0.006	0.006	0.006	0.001	0.001
8 TRANSPORT EQPT.,ORDNANCE	0.000	0.000	0.000	0.000	0.000	0.001	0.003	0.016	0.000	0.000
9 LUMBER & PAPER	0.004	0.019	0.028	0.002	0.001	0.018	0.012	0.003	0.001	0.001
10 PETROLEUM, RELATED INDS.	0.071	0.006	0.008	0.005	0.012	0.003	0.006	0.036	0.003	0.010
11 PLASTICS & CHEMICALS	0.029	0.197	0.028	0.012	0.016	0.028	0.006	0.005	0.000	0.000
12 GLASS, STONE,CLAY PRDTS.	0.000	0.003	0.104	0.001	0.002	0.007	0.001	0.001	0.000	0.000
13 PRIMARY IRON & STEEL MFR	0.000	0.006	0.009	0.149	0.004	0.128	0.000	0.005	0.000	0.000
14 PRIMARY NONFERROUS MFR.	0.002	0.009	0.002	0.014	0.291	0.039	0.000	0.001	0.0	0.001
15 MACHINERY & EQUIPMENT	0.007	0.025	0.018	0.036	0.015	0.168	0.012	0.009	0.000	0.002
16 SERVICES	0.071	0.075	0.072	0.063	0.034	0.084	0.163	0.103	0.034	0.049
17 TRANSPORT. & WAREHOUSING	0.042	0.027	0.060	0.049	0.028	0.016	0.011	0.083	0.012	0.034
18 GAS & WATER SERVICES	0.013	0.016	0.021	0.009	0.013	0.002	0.004	0.005	0.306	0.039
19 ELECTRIC UTILITIES	0.005	0.014	0.016	0.010	0.027	0.005	0.010	0.006	0.001	0.058

TABLE B.2-8

1963 DIRECT INPUT COEFFICIENTS
MOUNTAIN
(INPUT REQUIRED PER DOLLAR OF OUTPUT)

INDUSTRY TITLE	1	2	3	4	5	6	7	8	9
1 LIVESTOCK, PRDTS.	0.319	0.102	0.000	0.000	0.000	0.000	0.261	0.000	0.000
2 OTHER AGRICULTURE PRDTS.	0.332	0.032	0.000	0.000	0.000	0.002	0.064	0.000	0.000
3 COAL MINING	0.000	0.000	0.051	0.000	0.001	0.0	0.001	0.000	0.000
4 CRUDE PETRO.,NATURAL GAS	0.0	0.0	0.0	0.022	0.0	0.0	0.0	0.0	0.0
5 OTHER MINING	0.000	0.000	0.0	0.0	0.159	0.012	0.000	0.000	0.000
6 CONSTRUCTION	0.005	0.011	0.005	0.034	0.005	0.000	0.002	0.001	0.003
7 FOOD,TOBAC.,FAB.,APPAREL	0.062	0.006	0.001	0.002	0.002	0.004	0.194	0.006	0.007
8 TRANSPORT EQPT.,ORDNANCE	0.000	0.001	0.009	0.000	0.003	0.001	0.000	0.165	0.000
9 LUMBER & PAPER	0.000	0.006	0.008	0.001	0.006	0.057	0.031	0.012	0.279
10 PETROLEUM, RELATED INDS.	0.007	0.044	0.012	0.006	0.006	0.024	0.003	0.003	0.005
11 PLASTICS & CHEMICALS	0.006	0.039	0.035	0.010	0.045	0.025	0.010	0.016	0.020
12 GLASS, STONE,CLAY PRDTS.	0.000	0.000	0.002	0.003	0.001	0.072	0.007	0.003	0.004
13 PRIMARY IRON & STEEL MFR	0.0	0.0	0.019	0.002	0.020	0.036	0.000	0.029	0.005
14 PRIMARY NONFERROUS MFR.	0.000	0.000	0.000	0.0	0.001	0.016	0.000	0.038	0.001
15 MACHINERY & EQUIPMENT	0.002	0.016	0.081	0.018	0.059	0.135	0.022	0.141	0.017
16 SERVICES	0.065	0.217	0.084	0.238	0.094	0.145	0.075	0.070	0.152
17 TRANSPORT. & WAREHOUSING	0.027	0.011	0.013	0.009	0.017	0.034	0.032	0.012	0.026
18 GAS & WATER SERVICES	0.000	0.016	0.001	0.003	0.009	0.001	0.003	0.001	0.002
19 ELECTRIC UTILITIES	0.003	0.011	0.021	0.008	0.024	0.002	0.004	0.004	0.006

TABLE B.2-8

1963 DIRECT INPUT COEFFICIENTS
MOUNTAIN
(INPUT REQUIRED PER DOLLAR OF OUTPUT)

INDUSTRY TITLE	10	11	12	13	14	15	16	17	18	19
1 LIVESTOCK, PRDTS.	0.000	0.000	0.000	0.000	0.000	0.000	0.001	0.000	0.000	0.000
2 OTHER AGRICULTURE PRDTS.	0.000	0.001	0.000	0.000	0.000	0.000	0.000	0.000	0.000	0.000
3 COAL MINING	0.000	0.001	0.009	0.022	0.002	0.000	0.000	0.000	0.000	0.026
4 CRUDE PETRO.,NATURAL GAS	0.446	0.001	0.0	0.0	0.0	0.0	0.000	0.001	0.138	0.002
5 OTHER MINING	0.002	0.017	0.093	0.057	0.202	0.000	0.000	0.000	0.0	0.0
6 CONSTRUCTION	0.016	0.003	0.005	0.008	0.004	0.002	0.030	0.034	0.022	0.032
7 FOOD,TOBAC.,FAB.,APPAREL	0.002	0.036	0.004	0.002	0.003	0.007	0.006	0.004	0.001	0.001
8 TRANSPORT EQPT.,ORDNANCE	0.000	0.000	0.000	0.000	0.000	0.001	0.003	0.010	0.000	0.000
9 LUMBER & PAPER	0.005	0.017	0.022	0.003	0.001	0.014	0.011	0.003	0.001	0.001
10 PETROLEUM, RELATED INDS.	0.072	0.005	0.009	0.007	0.014	0.003	0.006	0.039	0.004	0.010
11 PLASTICS & CHEMICALS	0.028	0.185	0.018	0.019	0.018	0.025	0.007	0.007	0.001	0.000
12 GLASS, STONE,CLAY PRDTS.	0.001	0.002	0.121	0.001	0.002	0.008	0.001	0.000	0.000	0.000
13 PRIMARY IRON & STEEL MFR	0.000	0.004	0.011	0.203	0.002	0.098	0.000	0.007	0.000	0.000
14 PRIMARY NONFERROUS MFR.	0.002	0.003	0.001	0.020	0.307	0.035	0.000	0.000	0.0	0.001
15 MACHINERY & EQUIPMENT	0.007	0.013	0.021	0.041	0.008	0.168	0.012	0.011	0.000	0.002
16 SERVICES	0.071	0.069	0.071	0.060	0.027	0.078	0.162	0.119	0.039	0.049
17 TRANSPORT. & WAREHOUSING	0.041	0.026	0.071	0.050	0.027	0.015	0.010	0.076	0.012	0.019
18 GAS & WATER SERVICES	0.012	0.005	0.017	0.012	0.015	0.002	0.004	0.003	0.323	0.021
19 ELECTRIC UTILITIES	0.005	0.007	0.014	0.014	0.029	0.005	0.010	0.004	0.001	0.056

TABLE B.2-9

1963 DIRECT INPUT COEFFICIENTS
PACIFIC
(INPUT REQUIRED PER DOLLAR OF OUTPUT)

INDUSTRY TITLE	1	2	3	4	5	6	7	8	9
1 LIVESTOCK, PRDTS.	0.237	0.033	0.0	0.000	0.000	0.000	0.133	0.000	0.000
2 OTHER AGRICULTURE PRDTS.	0.257	0.021	0.0	0.000	0.000	0.003	0.083	0.000	0.000
3 COAL MINING	0.000	0.000	0.027	0.000	0.000	0.0	0.001	0.000	0.001
4 CRUDE PETRO.,NATURAL GAS	0.0	0.0	0.0	0.020	0.0	0.0	0.0	0.0	0.0
5 OTHER MINING	0.000	0.001	0.0	0.0	0.021	0.006	0.000	0.000	0.001
6 CONSTRUCTION	0.005	0.011	0.005	0.031	0.005	0.000	0.002	0.002	0.003
7 FOOD,TOBAC.,FAB.,APPAREL	0.162	0.006	0.001	0.002	0.002	0.005	0.215	0.008	0.011
8 TRANSPORT EQPT.,ORDNANCE	0.000	0.001	0.007	0.000	0.006	0.000	0.000	0.199	0.000
9 LUMBER & PAPER	0.002	0.012	0.006	0.000	0.004	0.057	0.034	0.009	0.286
10 PETROLEUM, RELATED INDS.	0.004	0.022	0.008	0.005	0.015	0.015	0.003	0.003	0.005
11 PLASTICS & CHEMICALS	0.004	0.052	0.025	0.010	0.045	0.020	0.013	0.019	0.031
12 GLASS, STONE,CLAY PRDTS.	0.000	0.001	0.001	0.003	0.002	0.064	0.013	0.005	0.004
13 PRIMARY IRON & STEEL MFR	0.0	0.0	0.016	0.002	0.012	0.020	0.000	0.045	0.007
14 PRIMARY NONFERROUS MFR.	0.000	0.000	0.0	0.0	0.002	0.014	0.000	0.032	0.001
15 MACHINERY & EQUIPMENT	0.003	0.008	0.059	0.017	0.064	0.118	0.040	0.140	0.022
16 SERVICES	0.084	0.165	0.076	0.220	0.082	0.130	0.099	0.067	0.138
17 TRANSPORT. & WAREHOUSING	0.027	0.011	0.009	0.024	0.016	0.029	0.033	0.013	0.029
18 GAS & WATER SERVICES	0.001	0.014	0.000	0.002	0.015	0.001	0.003	0.001	0.003
19 ELECTRIC UTILITIES	0.009	0.009	0.008	0.007	0.022	0.002	0.004	0.004	0.007

TABLE B.2-9

1963 DIRECT INPUT COEFFICIENTS
PACIFIC
(INPUT REQUIRED PER DOLLAR OF OUTPUT)

INDUSTRY TITLE	10	11	12	13	14	15	16	17	18	19
1 LIVESTOCK, PRDTS.	0.000	0.000	0.000	0.000	0.000	0.000	0.001	0.000	0.000	0.000
2 OTHER AGRICULTURE PRDTS.	0.000	0.001	0.001	0.000	0.000	0.000	0.000	0.000	0.000	0.000
3 COAL MINING	0.000	0.002	0.009	0.016	0.001	0.000	0.000	0.000	0.000	0.018
4 CRUDE PETRO.,NATURAL GAS	0.438	0.001	0.0	0.0	0.0	0.0	0.000	0.000	0.110	0.001
5 OTHER MINING	0.003	0.010	0.075	0.044	0.097	0.000	0.000	0.000	0.0	0.0
6 CONSTRUCTION	0.016	0.003	0.005	0.006	0.003	0.002	0.030	0.025	0.023	0.028
7 FOOD,TOBAC.,FAB.,APPAREL	0.002	0.031	0.007	0.002	0.004	0.007	0.006	0.008	0.001	0.001
8 TRANSPORT EQPT.,ORDNANCE	0.000	0.000	0.000	0.000	0.000	0.001	0.003	0.021	0.000	0.000
9 LUMBER & PAPER	0.008	0.024	0.029	0.003	0.004	0.018	0.011	0.003	0.001	0.001
10 PETROLEUM, RELATED INDS.	0.075	0.009	0.008	0.006	0.008	0.003	0.006	0.043	0.004	0.009
11 PLASTICS & CHEMICALS	0.028	0.217	0.032	0.016	0.020	0.028	0.007	0.006	0.002	0.001
12 GLASS, STONE,CLAY PRDTS.	0.002	0.005	0.108	0.001	0.003	0.009	0.001	0.000	0.000	0.000
13 PRIMARY IRON & STEEL MFR	0.000	0.003	0.010	0.180	0.003	0.090	0.000	0.005	0.000	0.000
14 PRIMARY NONFERROUS MFR.	0.002	0.004	0.002	0.019	0.342	0.037	0.000	0.001	0.0	0.000
15 MACHINERY & EQUIPMENT	0.007	0.026	0.020	0.041	0.026	0.167	0.012	0.009	0.000	0.002
16 SERVICES	0.074	0.105	0.074	0.062	0.051	0.084	0.168	0.112	0.035	0.044
17 TRANSPORT. & WAREHOUSING	0.045	0.026	0.058	0.047	0.026	0.016	0.011	0.089	0.010	0.013
18 GAS & WATER SERVICES	0.013	0.007	0.020	0.011	0.010	0.002	0.004	0.003	0.258	0.014
19 ELECTRIC UTILITIES	0.005	0.008	0.015	0.013	0.019	0.005	0.011	0.003	0.002	0.050

TABLE B.3-1

1963 INTERREGIONAL TRADE FLOWS
LIVESTOCK AND LIVESTOCK PRODUCTS
(THOUSANDS OF 1963 DOLLARS)

	1 NEW ENGLAND	2 MIDDLE ATLANTIC	3 EAST NORTH CENTRAL	4 WEST NORTH CENTRAL	5 SOUTH ATLANTIC	6 EAST SOUTH CENTRAL	7 WEST SOUTH CENTRAL	8 MOUNTAIN	9 PACIFIC	10 COMMODITY PRODUCTION
1 NEW ENGLAND	232579	328237	10070	112	65203	4569	463	450	2220	643904
2 MIDDLE ATLANTIC	346637	838415	28294	89	466084	111183	63168	416	6521	1860808
3 EAST NORTH CENTRAL	94639	429696	2380936	847173	493388	375211	219788	46723	128429	5015983
4 WEST NORTH CENTRAI	12334	82197	1168027	4658674	158685	393272	743268	531619	191082	7939159
5 SOUTH ATLANTIC	73764	625500	497253	39678	839025	123204	114147	21178	87760	2421510
6 EAST SOUTH CENTRAI	13375	152029	358845	187012	226973	340972	292112	69690	117111	1758119
7 WEST SOUTH CENTRAI	5386	80162	273618	947088	177640	141224	624157	216042	186524	2651841
8 MOUNTAIN	1676	8188	143675	680353	16757	26282	256961	522467	384000	2040358
9 PACIFIC	4628	29423	31202	145002	19928	7414	65090	414075	1635821	2352583
10 COMMODITY CONSUMPTION	785018	2573848	4891921	7505182	2463683	1523330	2379153	1822659	2739469	26684256

TABLE B.3-2

1963 INTERREGIONAL TRADE FLOWS
OTHER AGRICULTURAL PRODUCTS
(THOUSANDS OF 1963 DOLLARS)

	1 NEW ENGLAND	2 MIDDLE ATLANTIC	3 EAST NORTH CENTRAL	4 WEST NORTH CENTRAL	5 SOUTH ATLANTIC	6 EAST SOUTH CENTRAL	7 WEST SOUTH CENTRAL	8 MOUNTAIN	9 PACIFIC	10 COMMODITY PRODUCTION
1 NEW ENGLAND	115396	147654	39188	2190	63589	6168	3426	909	2611	381129
2 MIDDLE ATLANTIC	169152	656075	141301	19144	316110	30702	17632	3148	7642	1360905
3 EAST NORTH CENTRAL	68391	536245	2738840	219433	768807	412574	158900	30227	34342	4967758
4 WEST NORTH CENTRAL	8798	51108	1104321	3610382	144587	247532	631723	114215	236594	6149261
5 SOUTH ATLANTIC	202168	758200	451319	63176	1778309	173237	108246	20934	48677	3604266
6 EAST SOUTH CENTRAL	51016	111934	219277	94536	717870	752312	199144	19096	31597	2196781
7 WEST SOUTH CENTRAL	31935	123265	152117	172118	399594	308738	1764289	82026	287303	3321384
8 MOUNTAIN	7682	54813	103046	179275	31565	30545	65261	567260	717862	1757308
9 PACIFIC	47917	260935	338246	357492	148639	84778	163624	420770	1799752	3622153
10 COMMODITY CONSUMPTION	702455	2700228	5287655	4717744	4369068	2046585	3112246	1258584	3166380	27360944

TABLE B.3-3

1963 INTERREGIONAL TRADE FLOWS
COAL MINING
(THOUSANDS OF 1963 DOLLARS)

	1 NEW ENGLAND	2 MIDDLE ATLANTIC	3 EAST NORTH CENTRAL	4 WEST NORTH CENTRAL	5 SOUTH ATLANTIC	6 EAST SOUTH CENTRAL	7 WEST SOUTH CENTRAL	8 MOUNTAIN	9 PACIFIC	10 COMMODITY PRODUCTION
1 NEW ENGLAND	380	0	0	0	0	0	0	0	0	380
2 MIDDLE ATLANTIC	43010	471519	44037	382	92823	0	0	0	31049	682820
3 EAST NORTH CENTRAL	0	3565	319739	89625	10176	11464	2804	0	0	437373
4 WEST NORTH CENTRAI	0	0	0	11573	0	0	23634	0	0	35207
5 SOUTH ATLANTIC	46937	188260	186227	18984	315767	33418	53395	31298	29336	903623
6 EAST SOUTH CENTRAL	10406	10412	112482	10755	117606	147494	69016	0	0	478171
7 WEST SOUTH CENTRAI	0	0	0	36	0	0	8416	811	0	9262
8 MOUNTAIN	0	0	0	11	0	0	0	19848	62276	82135
9 PACIFIC	0	0	0	0	0	0	0	143	7726	7869
10 COMMODITY CONSUMPTION	100734	673756	662484	131366	536372	192376	157265	52100	130388	2636841

TABLE B.3-4

1963 INTERREGIONAL TRADE FLOWS
CRUDE PETROLEUM AND NATURAL GAS
(THOUSANDS OF 1963 DOLLARS)

	1 NEW ENGLAND	2 MIDDLE ATLANTIC	3 EAST NORTH CENTRAL	4 WEST NORTH CENTRAL	5 SOUTH ATLANTIC	6 EAST SOUTH CENTRAL	7 WEST SOUTH CENTRAL	8 MOUNTAIN	9 PACIFIC	10 COMMODITY PRODUCTION
1 NEW ENGLAND	28859	215499	120807	0	0	0	0	0	0	365165
2 MIDDLE ATLANTIC	22407	391376	35225	0	110731	6	0	0	0	559744
3 EAST NORTH CENTRAL	137	9331	519092	34705	1940	10787	0	24	0	576017
4 WEST NORTH CENTRAL	44	5511	174424	385992	226	0	21789	19364	17	607366
5 SOUTH ATLANTIC	15	48212	24251	0	40911	212	0	0	0	113601
6 EAST SOUTH CENTRAL	919	55756	19989	92	37221	110589	83370	1	0	307936
7 WEST SOUTH CENTRAL	47189	929665	1001324	209721	228652	179259	4581953	49633	121428	7348824
8 MOUNTAIN	36	26976	223478	60833	180	99	115965	535023	219888	1182478
9 PACIFIC	0	0	0	0	0	0	0	0	1203551	1203551
10 COMMODITY CONSUMPTION	99606	1682326	2118589	691342	419861	300951	4803077	604045	1544884	12264683

TABLE B.3-5

1963 INTERREGIONAL TRADE FLOWS
OTHER MINING
(THOUSANDS OF 1963 DOLLARS)

	1 NEW ENGLAND	2 MIDDLE ATLANTIC	3 EAST NORTH CENTRAL	4 WEST NORTH CENTRAL	5 SOUTH ATLANTIC	6 EAST SOUTH CENTRAL	7 WEST SOUTH CENTRAL	8 MOUNTAIN	9 PACIFIC	10 COMMODITY PRODUCTION
1 NEW ENGLAND	98685	5836	0	0	97	146	66	0	0	104829
2 MIDDLE ATLANTIC	22899	601314	14198	0	18265	28530	12985	0	0	698191
3 EAST NORTH CENTRAL	5795	113298	684460	11678	20305	12921	3034	2126	147	853764
4 WEST NORTH CENTRAL	10574	107824	353776	234229	12331	19727	10163	0	27977	776600
5 SOUTH ATLANTIC	272	54732	47389	4941	499914	26493	25401	0	0	659142
6 EAST SOUTH CENTRAL	2782	29041	7447	0	4335	229221	3095	0	0	275921
7 WEST SOUTH CENTRAL	0	43643	4307	2014	36671	14023	336104	2074	16395	455232
8 MOUNTAIN	0	41919	106832	93358	29550	23215	245715	746054	158919	1445562
9 PACIFIC	0	2090	20043	0	0	523	264	5431	392724	421075
10 COMMODITY CONSUMPTION	141006	999697	1238451	346220	621469	354799	636827	755685	596162	5690316

TABLE B.3-6

1963 INTERREGIONAL TRADE FLOWS
CONSTRUCTION
(THOUSANDS OF 1963 DOLLARS)

	1 NEW ENGLAND	2 MIDDLE ATLANTIC	3 EAST NORTH CENTRAL	4 WEST NORTH CENTRAL	5 SOUTH ATLANTIC	6 EAST SOUTH CENTRAL	7 WEST SOUTH CENTRAL	8 MOUNTAIN	9 PACIFIC	10 COMMODITY PRODUCTION
1 NEW ENGLAND	4524131	0	0	0	0	0	0	0	0	4524131
2 MIDDLE ATLANTIC	0	12356630	0	0	0	0	0	0	0	12356630
3 EAST NORTH CENTRAL	0	0	14587796	0	0	0	0	0	0	14587796
4 WEST NORTH CENTRAL	0	0	0	6369956	0	0	0	0	0	6369956
5 SOUTH ATLANTIC	0	0	0	0	11504842	0	0	0	0	11504842
6 EAST SOUTH CENTRAL	0	0	0	0	0	3925505	0	0	0	3925505
7 WEST SOUTH CENTRAL	0	0	0	0	0	0	8930302	0	0	8930302
8 MOUNTAIN	0	0	0	0	0	0	0	4805338	0	4805338
9 PACIFIC	0	0	0	0	0	0	0	0	18308928	18308928
10 COMMODITY CONSUMPTION	4524131	12356630	14587796	6369956	11504842	3925505	8930302	4805338	18308928	85313424

TABLE B.3-7

1963 INTERREGIONAL TRADE FLOWS
FOOD, TOBACCO, FABRICS, AND APPAREL
(THOUSANDS OF 1963 DOLLARS)

	1 NEW ENGLAND	2 MIDDLE ATLANTIC	3 EAST NORTH CENTRAL	4 WEST NORTH CENTRAL	5 SOUTH ATLANTIC	6 EAST SOUTH CENTRAL	7 WEST SOUTH CENTRAL	8 MOUNTAIN	9 PACIFIC	10 COMMODITY PRODUCTION
1 NEW ENGLAND	3979601	1810960	388864	171840	503095	101135	52322	55354	164020	7227191
2 MIDDLE ATLANTIC	1893326	16708158	2893509	586588	2115999	462289	640996	358045	1143678	26802576
3 EAST NORTH CENTRAL	404373	2027792	13026957	855963	910852	598365	469663	223777	752972	19270704
4 WEST NORTH CENTRAI	372313	1273686	2240128	6756813	557112	419095	1009324	201239	406444	13236155
5 SOUTH ATLANTIC	1101923	4811242	2140791	671404	12730686	1471288	836426	408151	1983669	26155568
6 EAST SOUTH CENTRAI	225391	1022611	789081	176783	2128327	3368758	528446	179756	192212	8611365
7 WEST SOUTH CENTRAI	49511	173085	323048	291276	209475	358482	5425174	187677	307726	7325454
8 MOUNTAIN	24470	116266	198761	60282	36818	4180	48266	1755462	402217	2646722
9 PACIFIC	55435	393580	399821	188954	176247	73543	280056	507366	9651132	11726135
10 COMMODITY CONSUMPTION	8106343	28337376	22400960	9759903	19368608	6857137	9290673	3876826	15004070	123001904

TABLE B.3-8

1963 INTERREGIONAL TRADE FLOWS
TRANSPORTATION EQUIPMENT AND ORDNANCE
(THOUSANDS OF 1963 DOLLARS)

	1 NEW ENGLAND	2 MIDDLE ATLANTIC	3 EAST NORTH CENTRAL	4 WEST NORTH CENTRAL	5 SOUTH ATLANTIC	6 EAST SOUTH CENTRAL	7 WEST SOUTH CENTRAL	8 MOUNTAIN	9 PACIFIC	10 COMMODITY PRODUCTION
1 NEW ENGLAND	797055	756185	394468	57462	395941	26228	138225	25884	243445	2834893
2 MIDDLE ATLANTIC	653270	3159751	2011835	349359	778282	115473	108578	22122	316105	7514775
3 EAST NORTH CENTRAL	1202592	3568425	14900020	3215694	2371878	633200	949572	344502	2674650	29860528
4 WEST NORTH CENTRAL	98722	468229	1031877	1191984	100933	311774	907856	402181	288235	4821792
5 SOUTH ATLANTIC	132529	1215186	235529	54106	1744167	349867	134897	13638	92822	3972741
6 EAST SOUTH CENTRAL	83287	141661	326702	65080	183653	415050	77559	27191	106988	1427170
7 WEST SOUTH CENTRAL	49147	47999	435260	331651	88138	109889	1204624	133201	157322	2557230
8 MOUNTAIN	200869	71137	78494	116628	91911	17699	40408	115978	173870	906994
9 PACIFIC	488440	379670	344415	330383	634329	172721	318739	614589	6648129	9931414
10 COMMODITY CONSUMPTION	3705912	9828244	19758592	5712348	6389232	2151901	3880458	1699284	10701567	63827536

TABLE B.3-9

1963 INTERREGIONAL TRADE FLOWS
LUMBER AND PAPER
(THOUSANDS OF 1963 DOLLARS)

	1 NEW ENGLAND	2 MIDDLE ATLANTIC	3 EAST NORTH CENTRAL	4 WEST NORTH CENTRAL	5 SOUTH ATLANTIC	6 EAST SOUTH CENTRAL	7 WEST SOUTH CENTRAL	8 MOUNTAIN	9 PACIFIC	10 COMMODITY PRODUCTION
1 NEW ENGLAND	2135871	881565	286600	68864	198685	39524	56920	20911	45128	3734068
2 MIDDLE ATLANTIC	522105	8309219	699799	345990	704989	130874	230422	78538	213167	11235103
3 EAST NORTH CENTRAL	191816	1030490	8142203	604794	444529	292594	322490	115410	206544	11350870
4 WEST NORTH CENTRAL	26353	131783	371255	1801834	82243	71912	139108	30418	38012	2692917
5 SOUTH ATLANTIC	200568	950253	562601	171695	4130248	277689	241658	37037	64600	6636349
6 EAST SOUTH CENTRAL	50323	187329	327544	130109	341973	1345129	232489	21368	27054	2663317
7 WEST SOUTH CENTRAL	35953	115073	202069	128860	152518	95202	1969125	47891	41313	2788004
8 MOUNTAIN	8300	36693	62081	42483	12406	8995	18536	789381	124397	1103271
9 PACIFIC	107484	323680	321278	199192	146655	80039	186760	314591	6701762	8381440
10 COMMODITY CONSUMPTION	3278773	11966086	10975430	3493822	6214245	2341958	3397506	1455543	7461976	50585328

TABLE B.3-10

1963 INTERREGIONAL TRADE FLOWS
PETROLEUM AND RELATED INDUSTRIES
(THOUSANDS OF 1963 DOLLARS)

	1 NEW ENGLAND	2 MIDDLE ATLANTIC	3 EAST NORTH CENTRAL	4 WEST NORTH CENTRAL	5 SOUTH ATLANTIC	6 EAST SOUTH CENTRAL	7 WEST SOUTH CENTRAL	8 MOUNTAIN	9 PACIFIC	10 COMMODITY PRODUCTION
1 NEW ENGLAND	203980	72515	61923	61	155	0	3416	305	418	342771
2 MIDDLE ATLANTIC	136589	2350395	301654	10317	451182	5331	30364	2190	12137	3300159
3 EAST NORTH CENTRAL	1023	72989	2814594	465859	41403	175600	17814	4733	22134	3616148
4 WEST NORTH CENTRAL	7	249	68146	863492	265	6229	50392	44537	26948	1060266
5 SOUTH ATLANTIC	6855	122080	47389	5379	505655	7666	7187	15989	0	718199
6 EAST SOUTH CENTRAL	2057	27410	36570	18355	28669	220128	37964	109	45	371307
7 WEST SOUTH CENTRAL	643284	1334066	766269	393288	1307817	525064	3369992	202195	112281	8654256
8 MOUNTAIN	47	2	75035	115151	40	688	18579	587237	70338	867118
9 PACIFIC	108	42552	504	151	3289	0	1851	52449	2795452	2896355
10 COMMODITY CONSUMPTION	993950	4022258	4172085	1872051	2338474	940707	3537559	909744	3039753	21826576

TABLE B.3-11

1963 INTERREGIONAL TRADE FLOWS
PLASTICS AND CHEMICALS
(THOUSANDS OF 1963 DOLLARS)

	1 NEW ENGLAND	2 MIDDLE ATLANTIC	3 EAST NORTH CENTRAL	4 WEST NORTH CENTRAL	5 SOUTH ATLANTIC	6 EAST SOUTH CENTRAL	7 WEST SOUTH CENTRAL	8 MOUNTAIN	9 PACIFIC	10 COMMODITY PRODUCTION
1 NEW ENGLAND	934449	612139	357475	93541	261723	78459	110839	19966	228826	2697416
2 MIDDLE ATLANTIC	907499	4719730	1495502	315340	1464655	234536	243188	88039	560433	10028925
3 EAST NORTH CENTRAL	179851	1478863	5113612	893434	1129231	589001	454640	206965	461079	10506676
4 WEST NORTH CENTRAL	36600	123774	668242	683993	87644	183332	250399	82797	115639	2232420
5 SOUTH ATLANTIC	240347	1133653	756769	185624	2830693	390352	210460	15648	175157	5938704
6 EAST SOUTH CENTRAL	68231	319979	468386	160841	625944	779671	221219	37792	88063	2770125
7 WEST SOUTH CENTRAL	251039	612543	596236	259049	398751	357795	2335145	166871	167112	5144543
8 MOUNTAIN	3332	10953	21711	29937	4736	6189	37894	115162	244388	474301
9 PACIFIC	28066	51314	86093	89359	25743	25920	88101	330413	2211829	2936838
10 COMMODITY CONSUMPTICN	2649415	9062949	9564028	2711117	6829123	2645254	3951884	1063653	4252526	42729936

TABLE B.3-12

1963 INTERREGIONAL TRADE FLOWS
GLASS, STONE, AND CLAY PRODUCTS
(THOUSANDS OF 1963 DOLLARS)

	1 NEW ENGLAND	2 MIDDLE ATLANTIC	3 EAST NORTH CENTRAL	4 WEST NORTH CENTRAL	5 SOUTH ATLANTIC	6 EAST SOUTH CENTRAL	7 WEST SOUTH CENTRAL	8 MOUNTAIN	9 PACIFIC	10 COMMODITY PRODUCTION
1 NEW ENGLAND	410495	64519	29722	889	979	385	4409	2045	44964	558407
2 MIDDLE ATLANTIC	190921	1967165	126922	9523	273753	24224	12399	15281	58727	2678915
3 EAST NORTH CENTRAL	10680	192872	2402645	148271	162008	73200	68463	109681	100473	3268294
4 WEST NORTH CENTRAL	362	4338	73924	694120	4141	95116	37271	12018	10310	931601
5 SOUTH ATLANTIC	10736	108620	99822	7065	1100131	51264	33059	447	140949	1552092
6 EAST SOUTH CENTRAL	1538	12783	42092	17382	127361	335287	81259	13857	28574	660133
7 WEST SOUTH CENTRAL	175	520	6010	14984	3120	12211	888009	45271	15211	985512
8 MOUNTAIN	0	39	157	1799	0	125	91	249900	145704	397816
9 PACIFIC	2	226	326	877	25	0	189	52027	1386095	1439766
10 COMMODITY CONSUMPTION	624909	2351082	2781620	894910	1671516	591813	1125150	500528	1931008	12472538

TABLE B.3-13

1963 INTERREGIONAL TRADE FLOWS
PRIMARY IRON AND STEEL MANUFACTURE
(THOUSANDS OF 1963 DOLLARS)

	1 NEW ENGLAND	2 MIDDLE ATLANTIC	3 EAST NORTH CENTRAL	4 WEST NORTH CENTRAL	5 SOUTH ATLANTIC	6 EAST SOUTH CENTRAL	7 WEST SOUTH CENTRAL	8 MOUNTAIN	9 PACIFIC	10 COMMODITY PRODUCTION
1 NEW ENGLAND	245554	116161	144480	1128	31177	11478	696	2408	14598	567680
2 MIDDLE ATLANTIC	583813	3273990	2162658	111262	438172	130863	104343	41433	283840	7130375
3 EAST NORTH CENTRAL	127146	1306592	7326521	881495	521676	240234	417832	149638	424489	11395625
4 WEST NORTH CENTRAI	90	7488	116400	230847	4898	7305	24324	17757	62598	471705
5 SOUTH ATLANTIC	80689	437165	181875	36947	458416	128782	149651	14686	163373	1651583
6 EAST SOUTH CENTRAL	12021	72125	167135	69276	291823	427928	213577	35845	52551	1342282
7 WEST SOUTH CENTRAL	828	15070	14084	11716	20714	17107	425292	18706	30902	554418
8 MOUNTAIN	668	420	6017	9471	3648	4028	23465	158446	149704	355868
9 PACIFIC	104	5709	7042	12398	16244	2833	28856	23876	923572	1020633
10 CCMMODITY CONSUMPTICN	1050913	5234721	10126212	1364539	1786767	970557	1388035	462797	2105627	24490160

TABLE B.3-14

1963 INTERREGIONAL TRADE FLOWS
PRIMARY NONFERROUS MANUFACTURE
(THOUSANDS OF 1963 DOLLARS)

	1 NEW ENGLAND	2 MIDDLE ATLANTIC	3 EAST NORTH CENTRAL	4 WEST NORTH CENTRAL	5 SOUTH ATLANTIC	6 EAST SOUTH CENTRAL	7 WEST SOUTH CENTRAL	8 MOUNTAIN	9 PACIFIC	10 COMMODITY PRODUCTION
1 NEW ENGLAND	460017	260097	161260	93696	81829	36472	29552	20529	66740	1210192
2 MIDDLE ATLANTIC	435779	1702302	677495	49438	344535	113279	66760	39001	156993	3585583
3 EAST NORTH CENTRAL	103569	453484	2282734	229788	171970	138124	150466	64350	176356	3770842
4 WEST NORTH CENTRAL	45419	107535	104272	63561	33276	5665	20416	2846	24700	407689
5 SOUTH ATLANTIC	128175	368020	287731	42284	249590	26271	12663	1454	42886	1159074
6 EAST SOUTH CENTRAL	19817	101409	170972	16396	81674	181008	48172	9347	51614	680409
7 WEST SOUTH CENTRAL	3124	142673	196831	67200	14996	85035	209992	18068	251605	989523
8 MOUNTAIN	11195	83881	180149	24236	81921	6905	286651	337162	90401	1102502
9 PACIFIC	9361	59856	193642	40205	31080	10083	69237	90959	757557	1261980
10 COMMODITY CONSUMPTION	1216455	3279255	4255086	626805	1090870	602844	893909	583717	1618853	14167797

TABLE B.3-15

1963 INTERREGIONAL TRADE FLOWS
MACHINERY AND EQUIPMENT
(THOUSANDS OF 1963 DOLLARS)

	1 NEW ENGLAND	2 MIDDLE ATLANTIC	3 EAST NORTH CENTRAL	4 WEST NORTH CENTRAL	5 SOUTH ATLANTIC	6 EAST SOUTH CENTRAL	7 WEST SOUTH CENTRAL	8 MOUNTAIN	9 PACIFIC	10 COMMODITY PRODUCTION
1 NEW ENGLAND	2441083	2703473	1364729	472302	966447	141363	283863	146813	550108	9070182
2 MIDDLE ATLANTIC	2110114	10475236	4978597	984047	2631626	701425	1055344	462630	2425813	25824832
3 EAST NORTH CENTRAL	1408023	6769913	15776218	2830259	3056808	1510278	1591578	618255	3158634	36719968
4 WEST NORTH CENTRAL	128752	758947	1208028	1773618	433535	230460	382958	255387	693242	5864927
5 SOUTH ATLANTIC	245998	928290	744812	161887	2464230	281810	192299	139102	424421	5582851
6 EAST SOUTH CENTRAL	97740	453930	560907	172718	503884	785021	221222	61524	246774	3103720
7 WEST SOUTH CENTRAL	21059	174465	295657	361809	261913	168384	2110332	201179	374471	3969268
8 MOUNTAIN	15505	52903	125729	60105	29990	6795	52910	435832	330531	1110301
9 PACIFIC	280402	690593	654222	271990	365059	84835	625672	669675	6286483	9928931
10 COMMODITY CONSUMPTION	6748676	23007744	25708896	7088735	10713494	3910372	6516180	2990398	14490478	101174976

TABLE B.3-16

1963 INTERREGIONAL TRADE FLOWS
SERVICES
(THOUSANDS OF 1963 DOLLARS)

	1 NEW ENGLAND	2 MIDDLE ATLANTIC	3 EAST NORTH CENTRAL	4 WEST NORTH CENTRAL	5 SOUTH ATLANTIC	6 EAST SOUTH CENTRAL	7 WEST SOUTH CENTRAL	8 MOUNTAIN	9 PACIFIC	10 COMMODITY PRODUCTION
1 NEW ENGLAND	18036864	2347923	882422	376023	353330	187756	255065	93473	330842	22863696
2 MIDDLE ATLANTIC	3833081	70376864	5624926	1751452	3736188	1496037	2072989	499930	1522208	90913680
3 EAST NORTH CENTRAL	498756	3437137	61489040	2772879	1286483	972465	368838	100212	353301	71279104
4 WEST NORTH CENTRAL	66898	495402	2989234	21111520	163029	563380	1749479	787367	305959	28232272
5 SOUTH ATLANTIC	138325	2223269	1021167	181172	36807248	2512734	1050180	32314	549556	44515952
6 EAST SOUTH CENTRAL	29246	150845	728721	443954	1716115	10561523	1455627	12650	137032	15235714
7 WEST SOUTH CENTRAL	43623	230096	440725	1002237	691850	597226	22340288	1098196	523334	26967568
8 MOUNTAIN	22291	85244	92308	1268556	49569	19418	820974	9401568	1254603	13014533
9 PACIFIC	213817	1114441	888869	161252	322121	164870	476109	2064709	46762304	52168496
10 COMMODITY CONSUMPTION	22882896	80461232	74157408	29069040	45125920	17075408	30589552	14090418	51739152	365190912

TABLE B.3-17

1963 INTERREGIONAL TRADE FLOWS
TRANSPORTATION AND WAREHOUSING
(THOUSANDS OF 1963 DOLLARS)

	1 NEW ENGLAND	2 MIDDLE ATLANTIC	3 EAST NORTH CENTRAL	4 WEST NORTH CENTRAL	5 SOUTH ATLANTIC	6 EAST SOUTH CENTRAL	7 WEST SOUTH CENTRAL	8 MOUNTAIN	9 PACIFIC	10 COMMODITY PRODUCTION
1 NEW ENGLAND	850516	572341	113112	67929	72005	10120	15144	17165	15905	1734235
2 MIDDLE ATLANTIC	926937	4137779	2100898	161151	1405525	145539	143994	25233	81606	9128662
3 EAST NORTH CENTRAL	76657	1058266	3329505	534100	1206961	590720	387348	147504	352631	7683693
4 WEST NORTH CENTRAL	45610	163404	780246	742062	329932	207847	274416	211573	503581	3258672
5 SOUTH ATLANTIC	73164	1486279	733272	771410	1365405	241053	145403	49860	52063	4917909
6 EAST SOUTH CENTRAL	16316	156950	324538	287080	154737	413450	165731	26903	88629	1634334
7 WEST SOUTH CENTRAL	20788	208382	518551	241468	252495	50016	2338469	102005	53142	3785316
8 MOUNTAIN	28192	78743	44157	123124	34735	33678	154396	379809	575346	1452180
9 PACIFIC	70538	571189	586192	107541	197525	34737	94741	356498	3528589	5547550
10 COMMODITY CONSUMPTION	2108719	8433333	8530470	3035865	5019321	1727160	3719641	1316549	5251490	39142544

TABLE B.3-18

1963 INTERREGIONAL TRADE FLOWS
GAS AND WATER SERVICES
(THOUSANDS OF 1963 DOLLARS)

	1 NEW ENGLAND	2 MIDDLE ATLANTIC	3 EAST NORTH CENTRAL	4 WEST NORTH CENTRAL	5 SOUTH ATLANTIC	6 EAST SOUTH CENTRAL	7 WEST SOUTH CENTRAL	8 MOUNTAIN	9 PACIFIC	10 COMMODITY PRODUCTION
1 NEW ENGLAND	533932	0	0	0	0	0	0	0	0	533932
2 MIDDLE ATLANTIC	123084	2208876	199907	0	214695	0	0	0	0	2746562
3 EAST NORTH CENTRAL	0	330022	2938223	67528	110266	0	0	0	0	3446039
4 WEST NORTH CENTRAL	0	0	197172	933269	0	41377	74347	30094	0	1276258
5 SOUTH ATLANTIC	0	70946	32502	0	1205689	195807	3779	0	0	1508724
6 EAST SOUTH CENTRAL	0	0	88812	0	172715	495937	155377	0	0	912840
7 WEST SOUTH CENTRAL	0	0	0	43974	6934	55850	1131509	77243	0	1315510
8 MOUNTAIN	0	0	0	154866	0	0	37627	498776	172127	863396
9 PACIFIC	0	0	0	0	0	0	0	74551	1570713	1645264
10 TOTAL	657016	2609844	3456616	1199636	1710299	788971	1402640	680664	1742841	14248529

TABLE B.3-19

1963 INTERREGIONAL TRADE FLOWS
ELECTRIC UTILITIES
(THOUSANDS OF 1963 DOLLARS)

	1 NEW ENGLAND	2 MIDDLE ATLANTIC	3 EAST NORTH CENTRAL	4 WEST NORTH CENTRAL	5 SOUTH ATLANTIC	6 EAST SOUTH CENTRAL	7 WEST SOUTH CENTRAL	8 MOUNTAIN	9 PACIFIC	10 COMMODITY PRODUCTION
1 NEW ENGLAND	936036	117270	7494	0	0	0	0	0	0	1060799
2 MIDDLE ATLANTIC	12	2933162	2	0	861	0	36141	0	0	2970180
3 EAST NORTH CENTRAL	1	29095	3228947	1478	15640	261269	0	0	0	3536430
4 WEST NORTH CENTRAL	0	0	6	1029467	0	117	2148	19042	86311	1137090
5 SOUTH ATLANTIC	0	62324	7075	0	2117106	64514	0	0	0	2251018
6 EAST SOUTH CENTRAL	0	0	134	140711	1290	510832	47192	0	0	700159
7 WEST SOUTH CENTRAL	0	0	0	381	0	62	1348589	124621	0	1473653
8 MOUNTAIN	0	0	0	1	0	0	0	475429	182807	658237
9 PACIFIC	0	0	0	0	0	0	0	420	1746326	1746747
10 TOTAL	936050	3141851	3243658	1172037	2134897	836794	1434069	619514	2015444	15534316

TABLE B.4-1

1963 INTERREGIONAL TRADE COEFFICIENTS
LIVESTOCK AND LIVESTOCK PRODUCTS
(THOUSANDS OF 1963 DOLLARS)

	1 NEW ENGLAND	2 MIDDLE ATLANTIC	3 EAST NORTH CENTRAL	4 WEST NORTH CENTRAL	5 SOUTH ATLANTIC	6 EAST SOUTH CENTRAL	7 WEST SOUTH CENTRAL	8 MOUNTAIN	9 PACIFIC
1 NEW ENGLAND	0.296	0.128	0.002	0.000	0.026	0.003	0.000	0.000	0.001
2 MIDDLE ATLANTIC	0.442	0.326	0.006	0.000	0.189	0.073	0.027	0.000	0.002
3 EAST NORTH CENTRAL	0.121	0.167	0.487	0.113	0.200	0.246	0.092	0.026	0.047
4 WEST NORTH CENTRAL	0.016	0.032	0.239	0.621	0.064	0.258	0.312	0.292	0.070
5 SOUTH ATLANTIC	0.094	0.243	0.102	0.005	0.341	0.081	0.048	0.012	0.032
6 EAST SOUTH CENTRAL	0.017	0.059	0.073	0.025	0.092	0.224	0.123	0.038	0.043
7 WEST SOUTH CENTRAL	0.007	0.031	0.056	0.126	0.072	0.093	0.262	0.119	0.068
8 MOUNTAIN	0.002	0.003	0.029	0.091	0.007	0.017	0.108	0.287	0.140
9 PACIFIC	0.006	0.011	0.006	0.019	0.008	0.005	0.027	0.227	0.597
10 COMMODITY CONSUMPTION	1.000	1.000	1.000	1.000	1.000	1.000	1.000	1.000	1.000

TABLE B.4-2

1963 INTERREGIONAL TRADE COEFFICIENTS
OTHER AGRICULTURAL PRODUCTS
(THOUSANDS OF 1963 DOLLARS)

	1 NEW ENGLAND	2 MIDDLE ATLANTIC	3 EAST NORTH CENTRAL	4 WEST NORTH CENTRAL	5 SOUTH ATLANTIC	6 EAST SOUTH CENTRAL	7 WEST SOUTH CENTRAL	8 MOUNTAIN	9 PACIFIC
1 NEW ENGLAND	0.164	0.055	0.007	0.000	0.015	0.003	0.001	0.001	0.001
2 MIDDLE ATLANTIC	0.241	0.243	0.027	0.004	0.072	0.015	0.006	0.003	0.002
3 EAST NORTH CENTRAL	0.097	0.199	0.518	0.047	0.176	0.202	0.051	0.024	0.011
4 WEST NORTH CENTRAL	0.013	0.019	0.209	0.765	0.033	0.121	0.203	0.091	0.075
5 SOUTH ATLANTIC	0.288	0.281	0.085	0.013	0.407	0.085	0.035	0.017	0.015
6 EAST SOUTH CENTRAL	0.073	0.041	0.041	0.020	0.164	0.368	0.064	0.015	0.010
7 WEST SOUTH CENTRAL	0.045	0.046	0.029	0.036	0.091	0.151	0.567	0.065	0.091
8 MOUNTAIN	0.011	0.020	0.019	0.038	0.007	0.015	0.021	0.451	0.227
9 PACIFIC	0.068	0.097	0.064	0.076	0.034	0.041	0.053	0.334	0.568
10 COMMODITY CONSUMPTION	1.000	1.000	1.000	1.000	1.000	1.000	1.000	1.000	1.000

TABLE B.4-3

1963 INTERREGIONAL TRADE COEFFICIENTS
COAL MINING
(THOUSANDS OF 1963 DOLLARS)

	1 NEW ENGLAND	2 MIDDLE ATLANTIC	3 EAST NORTH CENTRAL	4 WEST NORTH CENTRAL	5 SOUTH ATLANTIC	6 EAST SOUTH CENTRAL	7 WEST SOUTH CENTRAL	8 MOUNTAIN	9 PACIFIC
1 NEW ENGLAND	0.004	0.0	0.0	0.0	0.0	0.0	0.0	0.0	0.0
2 MIDDLE ATLANTIC	0.427	0.700	0.066	0.003	0.173	0.0	0.0	0.0	0.238
3 EAST NORTH CENTRAL	0.0	0.005	0.483	0.682	0.019	0.060	0.018	0.0	0.0
4 WEST NORTH CENTRAL	0.0	0.0	0.0	0.088	0.0	0.0	0.150	0.0	0.0
5 SOUTH ATLANTIC	0.466	0.279	0.281	0.145	0.589	0.174	0.340	0.601	0.225
6 EAST SOUTH CENTRAL	0.103	0.015	0.170	0.082	0.219	0.767	0.439	0.0	0.0
7 WEST SOUTH CENTRAL	0.0	0.0	0.0	0.000	0.0	0.0	0.054	0.016	0.0
8 MOUNTAIN	0.0	0.0	0.0	0.000	0.0	0.0	0.0	0.381	0.478
9 PACIFIC	0.0	0.0	0.0	0.000	0.0	0.0	0.0	0.003	0.059
10 COMMODITY CONSUMPTION	1.000	1.000	1.000	1.000	1.000	1.000	1.000	1.000	1.000

TABLE B.4-4

1963 INTERREGIONAL TRADE COEFFICIENTS
CRUDE PETROLEUM AND NATURAL GAS
(THOUSANDS OF 1963 DOLLARS)

	1 NEW ENGLAND	2 MIDDLE ATLANTIC	3 EAST NORTH CENTRAL	4 WEST NORTH CENTRAL	5 SOUTH ATLANTIC	6 EAST SOUTH CENTRAL	7 WEST SOUTH CENTRAL	8 MOUNTAIN	9 PACIFIC
1 NEW ENGLAND	0.290	0.128	0.057	0.0	0.0	0.0	0.0	0.0	0.0
2 MIDDLE ATLANTIC	0.225	0.233	0.017	0.0	0.264	0.000	0.0	0.0	0.0
3 EAST NORTH CENTRAL	0.001	0.006	0.245	0.050	0.005	0.036	0.0	0.000	0.0
4 WEST NORTH CENTRAL	0.000	0.003	0.082	0.558	0.001	0.0	0.005	0.032	0.000
5 SOUTH ATLANTIC	0.000	0.029	0.011	0.0	0.097	0.001	0.0	0.0	0.0
6 EAST SOUTH CENTRAL	0.009	0.033	0.009	0.000	0.089	0.367	0.017	0.000	0.0
7 WEST SOUTH CENTRAL	0.474	0.553	0.473	0.303	0.545	0.596	0.954	0.082	0.079
8 MOUNTAIN	0.000	0.016	0.105	0.088	0.000	0.000	0.024	0.886	0.142
9 PACIFIC	0.0	0.0	0.0	0.0	0.0	0.0	0.0	0.0	0.779
10 COMMODITY CONSUMPTION	1.000	1.000	1.000	1.000	1.000	1.000	1.000	1.000	1.000

TABLE B.4-5

1963 INTERREGIONAL TRADE COEFFICIENTS
OTHER MINING
(THOUSANDS OF 1963 DOLLARS)

	1 NEW ENGLAND	2 MIDDLE ATLANTIC	3 EAST NORTH CENTRAL	4 WEST NORTH CENTRAL	5 SOUTH ATLANTIC	6 EAST SOUTH CENTRAL	7 WEST SOUTH CENTRAL	8 MOUNTAIN	9 PACIFIC
1 NEW ENGLAND	0.700	0.006	0.0	0.0	0.000	0.000	0.000	0.0	0.0
2 MIDDLE ATLANTIC	0.162	0.601	0.011	0.0	0.029	0.080	0.020	0.0	0.0
3 EAST NORTH CENTRAL	0.041	0.113	0.553	0.034	0.033	0.036	0.005	0.003	0.000
4 WEST NORTH CENTRAL	0.075	0.108	0.286	0.677	0.020	0.056	0.016	0.0	0.047
5 SOUTH ATLANTIC	0.002	0.055	0.038	0.014	0.804	0.075	0.040	0.0	0.0
6 EAST SOUTH CENTRAL	0.020	0.029	0.006	0.0	0.007	0.646	0.005	0.0	0.0
7 WEST SOUTH CENTRAL	0.0	0.044	0.003	0.006	0.059	0.040	0.528	0.003	0.028
8 MOUNTAIN	0.0	0.042	0.086	0.270	0.048	0.065	0.386	0.987	0.267
9 PACIFIC	0.0	0.002	0.016	0.0	0.0	0.001	0.000	0.007	0.659
10 COMMODITY CONSUMPTION	1.000	1.000	1.000	1.000	1.000	1.000	1.000	1.000	1.000

TABLE B.4-6

1963 INTERREGIONAL TRADE COEFFICIENTS
CONSTRUCTION
(THOUSANDS OF 1963 DOLLARS)

	1 NEW ENGLAND	2 MIDDLE ATLANTIC	3 EAST NORTH CENTRAL	4 WEST NORTH CENTRAL	5 SOUTH ATLANTIC	6 EAST SOUTH CENTRAL	7 WEST SOUTH CENTRAL	8 MOUNTAIN	9 PACIFIC
1 NEW ENGLAND	1.000	0.0	0.0	0.0	0.0	0.0	0.0	0.0	0.0
2 MIDDLE ATLANTIC	0.0	1.000	0.0	0.0	0.0	0.0	0.0	0.0	0.0
3 EAST NORTH CENTRAL	0.0	0.0	1.000	0.0	0.0	0.0	0.0	0.0	0.0
4 WEST NORTH CENTRAL	0.0	0.0	0.0	1.000	0.0	0.0	0.0	0.0	0.0
5 SOUTH ATLANTIC	0.0	0.0	0.0	0.0	1.000	0.0	0.0	0.0	0.0
6 EAST SOUTH CENTRAL	0.0	0.0	0.0	0.0	0.0	1.000	0.0	0.0	0.0
7 WEST SOUTH CENTRAL	0.0	0.0	0.0	0.0	0.0	0.0	1.000	0.0	0.0
8 MOUNTAIN	0.0	0.0	0.0	0.0	0.0	0.0	0.0	1.000	0.0
9 PACIFIC	0.0	0.0	0.0	0.0	0.0	0.0	0.0	0.0	1.000
10 COMMODITY CONSUMPTION	1.000	1.000	1.000	1.000	1.000	1.000	1.000	1.000	1.000

TABLE B.4-7

1963 INTERREGIONAL TRADE COEFFICIENTS
FOOD, TOBACCO, FABRICS, AND APPAREL
(THOUSANDS OF 1963 DOLLARS)

	1 NEW ENGLAND	2 MIDDLE ATLANTIC	3 EAST NORTH CENTRAL	4 WEST NORTH CENTRAL	5 SOUTH ATLANTIC	6 EAST SOUTH CENTRAL	7 WEST SOUTH CENTRAL	8 MOUNTAIN	9 PACIFIC
1 NEW ENGLAND	0.491	0.064	0.017	0.018	0.026	0.015	0.006	0.014	0.011
2 MIDDLE ATLANTIC	0.234	0.590	0.129	0.060	0.109	0.067	0.069	0.092	0.076
3 EAST NORTH CENTRAL	0.050	0.072	0.582	0.088	0.047	0.087	0.051	0.058	0.050
4 WEST NORTH CENTRAL	0.046	0.045	0.100	0.692	0.029	0.061	0.109	0.052	0.027
5 SOUTH ATLANTIC	0.136	0.170	0.096	0.069	0.657	0.215	0.090	0.105	0.132
6 EAST SOUTH CENTRAL	0.028	0.036	0.035	0.018	0.110	0.491	0.057	0.046	0.013
7 WEST SOUTH CENTRAL	0.006	0.006	0.014	0.030	0.011	0.052	0.584	0.048	0.021
8 MOUNTAIN	0.003	0.004	0.009	0.006	0.002	0.001	0.005	0.453	0.027
9 PACIFIC	0.007	0.014	0.018	0.019	0.009	0.011	0.030	0.131	0.643
10 COMMODITY CONSUMPTION	1.000	1.000	1.000	1.000	1.000	1.000	1.000	1.000	1.000

TABLE B.4-8

1963 INTERREGIONAL TRADE COEFFICIENTS
TRANSPORTATION EQUIPMENT AND ORDNANCE
(THOUSANDS OF 1963 DOLLARS)

	1 NEW ENGLAND	2 MIDDLE ATLANTIC	3 EAST NORTH CENTRAL	4 WEST NORTH CENTRAL	5 SOUTH ATLANTIC	6 EAST SOUTH CENTRAL	7 WEST SOUTH CENTRAL	8 MOUNTAIN	9 PACIFIC
1 NEW ENGLAND	0.215	0.077	0.020	0.010	0.062	0.012	0.036	0.015	0.023
2 MIDDLE ATLANTIC	0.176	0.321	0.102	0.061	0.122	0.054	0.028	0.013	0.030
3 EAST NORTH CENTRAL	0.325	0.363	0.754	0.563	0.371	0.294	0.245	0.203	0.250
4 WEST NORTH CENTRAL	0.027	0.050	0.052	0.209	0.016	0.145	0.234	0.237	0.027
5 SOUTH ATLANTIC	0.036	0.124	0.012	0.009	0.273	0.163	0.035	0.008	0.009
6 EAST SOUTH CENTRAL	0.022	0.014	0.017	0.011	0.029	0.193	0.020	0.016	0.010
7 WEST SOUTH CENTRAL	0.013	0.005	0.022	0.058	0.014	0.051	0.310	0.078	0.015
8 MOUNTAIN	0.054	0.007	0.004	0.020	0.014	0.008	0.010	0.068	0.016
9 PACIFIC	0.132	0.039	0.017	0.058	0.099	0.080	0.082	0.362	0.621
10 COMMODITY CONSUMPTION	1.000	1.000	1.000	1.000	1.000	1.000	1.000	1.000	1.000

TABLE B.4-9

1963 INTERREGIONAL TRADE COEFFICIENTS
LUMBER AND PAPER
(THOUSANDS OF 1963 DOLLARS)

	1 NEW ENGLAND	2 MIDDLE ATLANTIC	3 EAST NORTH CENTRAL	4 WEST NORTH CENTRAL	5 SOUTH ATLANTIC	6 EAST SOUTH CENTRAL	7 WEST SOUTH CENTRAL	8 MOUNTAIN	9 PACIFIC
1 NEW ENGLAND	0.651	0.074	0.026	0.020	0.032	0.017	0.017	0.014	0.006
2 MIDDLE ATLANTIC	0.159	0.694	0.064	0.099	0.113	0.056	0.068	0.054	0.029
3 EAST NORTH CENTRAL	0.059	0.086	0.742	0.173	0.072	0.125	0.095	0.079	0.028
4 WEST NORTH CENTRAL	0.008	0.011	0.034	0.516	0.013	0.031	0.041	0.021	0.005
5 SOUTH ATLANTIC	0.061	0.079	0.051	0.049	0.665	0.119	0.071	0.025	0.009
6 EAST SOUTH CENTRAL	0.015	0.016	0.030	0.037	0.055	0.574	0.068	0.015	0.004
7 WEST SOUTH CENTRAL	0.011	0.010	0.018	0.037	0.025	0.041	0.580	0.033	0.006
8 MOUNTAIN	0.003	0.003	0.006	0.012	0.002	0.004	0.005	0.542	0.017
9 PACIFIC	0.033	0.027	0.029	0.057	0.024	0.034	0.055	0.216	0.898
10 COMMODITY CONSUMPTION	1.000	1.000	1.000	1.000	1.000	1.000	1.000	1.000	1.000

TABLE B.4-10

1963 INTERREGIONAL TRADE COEFFICIENTS
PETROLEUM AND RELATED INDUSTRIES
(THOUSANDS OF 1963 DOLLARS)

	1 NEW ENGLAND	2 MIDDLE ATLANTIC	3 EAST NORTH CENTRAL	4 WEST NORTH CENTRAL	5 SOUTH ATLANTIC	6 EAST SOUTH CENTRAL	7 WEST SOUTH CENTRAL	8 MOUNTAIN	9 PACIFIC
1 NEW ENGLAND	0.205	0.018	0.015	0.000	0.000	0.0	0.001	0.000	0.000
2 MIDDLE ATLANTIC	0.137	0.584	0.072	0.006	0.193	0.006	0.009	0.002	0.004
3 EAST NORTH CENTRAL	0.001	0.018	0.675	0.249	0.018	0.187	0.005	0.005	0.007
4 WEST NORTH CENTRAL	0.000	0.000	0.016	0.461	0.000	0.007	0.014	0.049	0.009
5 SOUTH ATLANTIC	0.007	0.030	0.011	0.003	0.216	0.008	0.002	0.018	0.0
6 EAST SOUTH CENTRAL	0.002	0.007	0.009	0.010	0.012	0.234	0.011	0.000	0.000
7 WEST SOUTH CENTRAL	0.647	0.332	0.184	0.210	0.559	0.558	0.953	0.222	0.037
8 MOUNTAIN	0.000	0.000	0.018	0.062	0.000	0.001	0.005	0.645	0.023
9 PACIFIC	0.000	0.011	0.000	0.000	0.001	0.0	0.001	0.058	0.920
10 COMMODITY CONSUMPTION	1.000	1.000	1.000	1.000	1.000	1.000	1.000	1.000	1.000

TABLE B.4-11

1963 INTERREGIONAL TRADE COEFFICIENTS
PLASTICS AND CHEMICALS
(THOUSANDS OF 1963 DOLLARS)

	1 NEW ENGLAND	2 MIDDLE ATLANTIC	3 EAST NORTH CENTRAL	4 WEST NORTH CENTRAL	5 SOUTH ATLANTIC	6 EAST SOUTH CENTRAL	7 WEST SOUTH CENTRAL	8 MOUNTAIN	9 PACIFIC
1 NEW ENGLAND	0.353	0.068	0.037	0.035	0.038	0.030	0.028	0.019	0.054
2 MIDDLE ATLANTIC	0.343	0.521	0.156	0.116	0.214	0.089	0.062	0.083	0.132
3 EAST NORTH CENTRAL	0.068	0.163	0.535	0.330	0.165	0.223	0.115	0.195	0.108
4 WEST NORTH CENTRAL	0.014	0.014	0.070	0.252	0.013	0.069	0.063	0.078	0.027
5 SOUTH ATLANTIC	0.091	0.125	0.079	0.068	0.415	0.148	0.053	0.015	0.041
6 EAST SOUTH CENTRAL	0.026	0.035	0.049	0.059	0.092	0.295	0.056	0.036	0.021
7 WEST SOUTH CENTRAL	0.095	0.068	0.062	0.096	0.058	0.135	0.591	0.157	0.039
8 MOUNTAIN	0.001	0.001	0.002	0.011	0.001	0.002	0.010	0.108	0.057
9 PACIFIC	0.011	0.006	0.009	0.033	0.004	0.010	0.022	0.311	0.520
10 COMMODITY CONSUMPTION	1.000	1.000	1.000	1.000	1.000	1.000	1.000	1.000	1.000

TABLE B.4-12

1963 INTERREGIONAL TRADE COEFFICIENTS
GLASS, STONE, AND CLAY PRODUCTS
(THOUSANDS OF 1963 DOLLARS)

	1 NEW ENGLAND	2 MIDDLE ATLANTIC	3 EAST NORTH CENTRAL	4 WEST NORTH CENTRAL	5 SOUTH ATLANTIC	6 EAST SOUTH CENTRAL	7 WEST SOUTH CENTRAL	8 MOUNTAIN	9 PACIFIC
1 NEW ENGLAND	0.657	0.027	0.011	0.001	0.001	0.001	0.004	0.004	0.023
2 MIDDLE ATLANTIC	0.306	0.837	0.046	0.011	0.164	0.041	0.011	0.031	0.030
3 EAST NORTH CENTRAL	0.017	0.082	0.864	0.166	0.097	0.124	0.061	0.219	0.052
4 WEST NORTH CENTRAL	0.001	0.002	0.027	0.776	0.002	0.161	0.033	0.024	0.005
5 SOUTH ATLANTIC	0.017	0.046	0.036	0.008	0.658	0.087	0.029	0.001	0.073
6 EAST SOUTH CENTRAL	0.002	0.005	0.015	0.019	0.076	0.567	0.072	0.028	0.015
7 WEST SOUTH CENTRAL	0.000	0.000	0.002	0.017	0.002	0.021	0.789	0.090	0.008
8 MOUNTAIN	0.0	0.000	0.000	0.002	0.0	0.000	0.000	0.499	0.075
9 PACIFIC	0.000	0.000	0.000	0.001	0.000	0.000	0.000	0.104	0.718
10 COMMODITY CONSUMPTION	1.000	1.000	1.000	1.000	1.000	1.000	1.000	1.000	1.000

TABLE B.4-13

1963 INTERREGIONAL TRADE COEFFICIENTS
PRIMARY IRON AND STEEL MANUFACTURE
(THOUSANDS OF 1963 DOLLARS)

	1 NEW ENGLAND	2 MIDDLE ATLANTIC	3 EAST NORTH CENTRAL	4 WEST NORTH CENTRAL	5 SOUTH ATLANTIC	6 EAST SOUTH CENTRAL	7 WEST SOUTH CENTRAL	8 MOUNTAIN	9 PACIFIC
1 NEW ENGLAND	0.234	0.022	0.014	0.001	0.017	0.012	0.001	0.005	0.007
2 MIDDLE ATLANTIC	0.556	0.625	0.214	0.082	0.245	0.135	0.075	0.090	0.135
3 EAST NORTH CENTRAL	0.121	0.250	0.724	0.646	0.292	0.248	0.301	0.323	0.202
4 WEST NORTH CENTRAL	0.000	0.001	0.011	0.169	0.003	0.008	0.018	0.038	0.030
5 SOUTH ATLANTIC	0.077	0.084	0.018	0.027	0.257	0.133	0.108	0.032	0.078
6 EAST SOUTH CENTRAL	0.011	0.014	0.017	0.051	0.163	0.441	0.154	0.077	0.025
7 WEST SOUTH CENTRAL	0.001	0.003	0.001	0.009	0.012	0.018	0.306	0.040	0.015
8 MOUNTAIN	0.001	0.000	0.001	0.007	0.002	0.004	0.017	0.342	0.071
9 PACIFIC	0.000	0.001	0.001	0.009	0.009	0.003	0.021	0.052	0.439
10 COMMODITY CONSUMPTION	1.000	1.000	1.000	1.000	1.000	1.000	1.000	1.000	1.000

TABLE B.4-14

1963 INTERREGIONAL TRADE COEFFICIENTS
PRIMARY NONFERROUS MANUFACTURE
(THOUSANDS OF 1963 DOLLARS)

	1 NEW ENGLAND	2 MIDDLE ATLANTIC	3 EAST NORTH CENTRAL	4 WEST NORTH CENTRAL	5 SOUTH ATLANTIC	6 EAST SOUTH CENTRAL	7 WEST SOUTH CENTRAL	8 MOUNTAIN	9 PACIFIC
1 NEW ENGLAND	0.378	0.079	0.038	0.149	0.075	0.060	0.033	0.035	0.041
2 MIDDLE ATLANTIC	0.358	0.519	0.159	0.079	0.316	0.188	0.075	0.067	0.097
3 EAST NORTH CENTRAL	0.085	0.138	0.536	0.367	0.158	0.229	0.168	0.110	0.109
4 WEST NORTH CENTRAL	0.037	0.033	0.025	0.101	0.031	0.009	0.023	0.005	0.015
5 SOUTH ATLANTIC	0.105	0.112	0.068	0.067	0.229	0.044	0.014	0.002	0.026
6 EAST SOUTH CENTRAL	0.016	0.031	0.040	0.026	0.075	0.300	0.054	0.016	0.032
7 WEST SOUTH CENTRAL	0.003	0.044	0.046	0.107	0.014	0.141	0.235	0.031	0.155
8 MOUNTAIN	0.009	0.026	0.042	0.039	0.075	0.011	0.321	0.578	0.056
9 PACIFIC	0.008	0.018	0.046	0.064	0.028	0.017	0.077	0.156	0.468
10 COMMODITY CONSUMPTION	1.000	1.000	1.000	1.000	1.000	1.000	1.000	1.000	1.000

TABLE B.4-15

1963 INTERREGIONAL TRADE COEFFICIENTS
MACHINERY AND EQUIPMENT
(THOUSANDS OF 1963 DOLLARS)

	1 NEW ENGLAND	2 MIDDLE ATLANTIC	3 EAST NORTH CENTRAL	4 WEST NORTH CENTRAL	5 SOUTH ATLANTIC	6 EAST SOUTH CENTRAL	7 WEST SOUTH CENTRAL	8 MOUNTAIN	9 PACIFIC
1 NEW ENGLAND	0.362	0.118	0.053	0.067	0.090	0.036	0.044	0.049	0.038
2 MIDDLE ATLANTIC	0.313	0.455	0.194	0.139	0.246	0.179	0.162	0.155	0.167
3 EAST NORTH CENTRAL	0.209	0.294	0.614	0.399	0.285	0.386	0.244	0.207	0.218
4 WEST NORTH CENTRAL	0.019	0.033	0.047	0.250	0.040	0.059	0.059	0.085	0.048
5 SOUTH ATLANTIC	0.036	0.040	0.029	0.023	0.230	0.072	0.030	0.047	0.029
6 EAST SOUTH CENTRAL	0.014	0.020	0.022	0.024	0.047	0.201	0.034	0.021	0.017
7 WEST SOUTH CENTRAL	0.003	0.008	0.012	0.051	0.024	0.043	0.324	0.067	0.026
8 MOUNTAIN	0.002	0.002	0.005	0.008	0.003	0.002	0.008	0.146	0.023
9 PACIFIC	0.042	0.030	0.025	0.038	0.034	0.022	0.096	0.224	0.434
10 COMMODITY CONSUMPTION	1.000	1.000	1.000	1.000	1.000	1.000	1.000	1.000	1.000

TABLE B.4-16

1963 INTERREGIONAL TRADE COEFFICIENTS
SERVICES
(THOUSANDS OF 1963 DOLLARS)

	1 NEW ENGLAND	2 MIDDLE ATLANTIC	3 EAST NORTH CENTRAL	4 WEST NORTH CENTRAL	5 SOUTH ATLANTIC	6 EAST SOUTH CENTRAL	7 WEST SOUTH CENTRAL	8 MOUNTAIN	9 PACIFIC
1 NEW ENGLAND	0.788	0.029	0.012	0.013	0.008	0.011	0.008	0.007	0.006
2 MIDDLE ATLANTIC	0.168	0.875	0.076	0.060	0.083	0.088	0.068	0.035	0.029
3 EAST NORTH CENTRAL	0.022	0.043	0.829	0.095	0.029	0.057	0.012	0.007	0.007
4 WEST NORTH CENTRAL	0.003	0.006	0.040	0.726	0.004	0.033	0.057	0.056	0.006
5 SOUTH ATLANTIC	0.006	0.028	0.014	0.006	0.816	0.147	0.034	0.002	0.011
6 EAST SOUTH CENTRAL	0.001	0.002	0.010	0.015	0.038	0.619	0.048	0.001	0.003
7 WEST SOUTH CENTRAL	0.002	0.003	0.006	0.034	0.015	0.035	0.730	0.078	0.010
8 MOUNTAIN	0.001	0.001	0.001	0.044	0.001	0.001	0.027	0.667	0.024
9 PACIFIC	0.009	0.014	0.012	0.006	0.007	0.010	0.016	0.147	0.904
10 COMMODITY CONSUMPTION	1.000	1.000	1.000	1.000	1.000	1.000	1.000	1.000	1.000

TABLE B.4-17

1963 INTERREGIONAL TRADE COEFFICIENTS
TRANSPORTATION AND WAREHOUSING
(THOUSANDS OF 1963 DOLLARS)

	1 NEW ENGLAND	2 MIDDLE ATLANTIC	3 EAST NORTH CENTRAL	4 WEST NORTH CENTRAL	5 SOUTH ATLANTIC	6 EAST SOUTH CENTRAL	7 WEST SOUTH CENTRAL	8 MOUNTAIN	9 PACIFIC
1 NEW ENGLAND	0.403	0.068	0.013	0.022	0.014	0.006	0.004	0.013	0.003
2 MIDDLE ATLANTIC	0.440	0.491	0.246	0.053	0.280	0.084	0.039	0.019	0.016
3 EAST NORTH CENTRAL	0.036	0.125	0.390	0.176	0.240	0.342	0.104	0.112	0.067
4 WEST NORTH CENTRAL	0.022	0.019	0.091	0.244	0.066	0.120	0.074	0.161	0.096
5 SOUTH ATLANTIC	0.035	0.176	0.086	0.254	0.272	0.140	0.039	0.038	0.010
6 EAST SOUTH CENTRAL	0.008	0.019	0.038	0.095	0.031	0.239	0.045	0.020	0.017
7 WEST SOUTH CENTRAL	0.010	0.025	0.061	0.080	0.050	0.029	0.629	0.077	0.010
8 MOUNTAIN	0.013	0.009	0.005	0.041	0.007	0.019	0.042	0.288	0.110
9 PACIFIC	0.033	0.068	0.069	0.035	0.039	0.020	0.025	0.271	0.672
10 COMMODITY CONSUMPTION	1.000	1.000	1.000	1.000	1.000	1.000	1.000	1.000	1.000

TABLE B.4-18

1963 INTERREGIONAL TRADE COEFFICIENTS
GAS AND WATER SERVICES
(THOUSANDS OF 1963 DOLLARS)

	1 NEW ENGLAND	2 MIDDLE ATLANTIC	3 EAST NORTH CENTRAL	4 WEST NORTH CENTRAL	5 SOUTH ATLANTIC	6 EAST SOUTH CENTRAL	7 WEST SOUTH CENTRAL	8 MOUNTAIN	9 PACIFIC
1 NEW ENGLAND	0.813	0.0	0.0	0.0	0.0	0.0	0.0	0.0	0.0
2 MIDDLE ATLANTIC	0.187	0.846	0.058	0.0	0.126	0.0	0.0	0.0	0.0
3 EAST NORTH CENTRAL	0.0	0.126	0.850	0.056	0.064	0.0	0.0	0.0	0.0
4 WEST NORTH CENTRAL	0.0	0.0	0.057	0.778	0.0	0.052	0.053	0.044	0.0
5 SOUTH ATLANTIC	0.0	0.027	0.009	0.0	0.705	0.248	0.003	0.0	0.0
6 EAST SOUTH CENTRAL	0.0	0.0	0.026	0.0	0.101	0.629	0.111	0.0	0.0
7 WEST SOUTH CENTRAL	0.0	0.0	0.0	0.037	0.004	0.071	0.807	0.113	0.0
8 MOUNTAIN	0.0	0.0	0.0	0.129	0.0	0.0	0.027	0.733	0.099
9 PACIFIC	0.0	0.0	0.0	0.0	0.0	0.0	0.0	0.110	0.901
10 COMMODITY CONSUMPTION	1.000	1.000	1.000	1.000	1.000	1.000	1.000	1.000	1.000

TABLE B.4-19

1963 INTERREGIONAL TRADE COEFFICIENTS
ELECTRIC UTILITIES
(THOUSANDS OF 1963 DOLLARS)

	1 NEW ENGLAND	2 MIDDLE ATLANTIC	3 EAST NORTH CENTRAL	4 WEST NORTH CENTRAL	5 SOUTH ATLANTIC	6 EAST SOUTH CENTRAL	7 WEST SOUTH CENTRAL	8 MOUNTAIN	9 PACIFIC
1 NEW ENGLAND	1.000	0.037	0.002	0.0	0.0	0.0	0.0	0.0	0.0
2 MIDDLE ATLANTIC	0.000	0.934	0.000	0.0	0.000	0.0	0.025	0.0	0.0
3 EAST NORTH CENTRAL	0.000	0.009	0.995	0.001	0.007	0.312	0.0	0.0	0.0
4 WEST NORTH CENTRAL	0.0	0.0	0.000	0.878	0.0	0.000	0.001	0.031	0.043
5 SOUTH ATLANTIC	0.0	0.020	0.002	0.0	0.992	0.077	0.0	0.0	0.0
6 EAST SOUTH CENTRAL	0.0	0.0	0.000	0.120	0.001	0.610	0.033	0.0	0.0
7 WEST SOUTH CENTRAL	0.0	0.0	0.0	0.000	0.0	0.000	0.940	0.201	0.0
8 MOUNTAIN	0.0	0.0	0.0	0.000	0.0	0.0	0.0	0.767	0.091
9 PACIFIC	0.000	0.0	0.0	0.000	0.0	0.0	0.0	0.001	0.866
10 COMMODITY CONSUMPTION	1.000	1.000	1.000	1.000	1.000	1.000	1.000	1.000	1.000

TABLE B.5-1

1963 REGIONAL FINAL DEMANDS
(THOUSANDS OF 1963 DOLLARS)

INDUSTRY TITLE	1 NEW ENGLAND	2 MIDDLE ATLANTIC	3 EAST NORTH CENTRAL	4 WEST NORTH CENTRAL	5 SOUTH ATLANTIC	6 EAST SOUTH CENTRAL	7 WEST SOUTH CENTRAL	8 MOUNTAIN	9 PACIFIC	10 U.S. FINAL DEMAND
1 LIVESTOCK, PRDTS.	142657	454233	709834	952695	459969	278082	418515	293504	472927	4182414
2 OTHER AGRICULTURE PRDTS.	220165	1021039	1474581	1295610	1254423	859200	1770041	338462	1436096	9669617
3 COAL MINING	13442	112621	111596	35108	210617	19007	14381	5739	13602	536114
4 CRUDE PETRO.,NATURAL GAS	0	5754	21491	32925	4623	17645	435099	67631	63747	648916
5 OTHER MINING	5700	83932	81039	42443	86585	48397	129035	180897	147614	805642
6 CONSTRUCTION	3743900	9077627	11499201	5182434	9690295	3276995	7489222	4205628	16278332	70443632
7 FOOD,TOBAC.,FAB.,APPAREL	5285941	18401296	15895235	6245802	10199831	3919949	6808506	3074880	11278579	81110032
8 TRANSPORT EQPT.,ORDNANCE	3118583	7703272	10215641	4261022	5203533	1777290	3211266	1478204	8428392	45397200
9 LUMBER & PAPER	1252956	5144489	4092976	1365017	2265129	788581	1266286	574861	2572769	19323056
10 PETROLEUM, RELATED INDS.	578817	2231132	2156720	854490	1238010	507605	2046012	441135	1686252	11740173
11 PLASTICS & CHEMICALS	687345	3276095	2614220	843019	2023156	908505	1572502	446841	1590592	13962276
12 GLASS, STONE,CLAY PRDTS.	70996	385786	328338	107993	179049	66386	124138	46186	194665	1503537
13 PRIMARY IRON & STEEL MFR	46005	692461	782424	42168	172711	90519	98812	24909	97822	2047830
14 PRIMARY NONFERROUS MFR.	96300	428304	297452	32501	100102	52722	143783	79924	187684	1418771
15 MACHINERY & EQUIPMENT	3595153	13026466	10508220	3533465	5939797	1977437	3112697	1586671	7677940	50957840
16 SERVICES	15641647	52351008	47616560	18290784	30279056	11557403	19151775	9428510	34212880	238529696
17 TRANSPORT. & WAREHOUSING	892021	3479607	3103955	1088480	2203390	607985	1524898	518522	2205896	15624757
18 GAS & WATER SERVICES	279126	925385	1354207	516875	721306	284696	477302	221638	766364	5546899
19 ELECTRIC UTILITIES	411667	1315819	1377664	583093	1083363	432831	684067	280693	943518	7112715
20 TOTAL	36082416	120116352	114241360	45305936	73314960	27471232	50478336	23294832	90255680	580561152

TABLE B.5-2

PROJECTED 1970 REGIONAL FINAL DEMANDS
(THOUSANDS OF 1963 DOLLARS)

INDUSTRY TITLE	1 NEW ENGLAND	2 MIDDLE ATLANTIC	3 EAST NORTH CENTRAL	4 WEST NORTH CENTRAL	5 SOUTH ATLANTIC	6 EAST SOUTH CENTRAL	7 WEST SOUTH CENTRAL	8 MOUNTAIN	9 PACIFIC	10 U.S. FINAL DEMAND
1 LIVESTOCK, PRDTS.	142802	453323	720183	794162	447332	249799	367868	240484	420241	3836194
2 OTHER AGRICULTURE PRDTS.	197527	670066	1185185	815294	844370	421278	3223139	326832	1843978	9527669
3 COAL MINING	13985	218161	174691	23433	292584	25111	36496	7695	18458	810614
4 CRUDE PETRO.,NATURAL GAS	134	12339	24445	38590	4805	20389	508278	88499	69355	766834
5 OTHER MINING	5687	92852	101733	86596	98426	31526	126379	159890	150387	853476
6 CONSTRUCTION	3494967	11040210	13613536	5971146	10430808	4236261	8466451	4544981	12096020	73894368
7 FOOD,TOBAC.,FAB.,APPAREL	6363330	21695312	19413168	7355489	14216343	5209156	8990154	3635711	14572157	101450832
8 TRANSPORT EQPT.,ORDNANCE	4588845	11667014	13780632	5215422	8317188	2876110	6971512	2530860	12669172	68616752
9 LUMBER & PAPER	1555137	6271636	5291913	1740378	3214339	1140389	1948427	774821	3922958	25859984
10 PETROLEUM, RELATED INDS.	994249	3460552	2909843	1244391	1868711	670062	2983072	691140	2533088	17355104
11 PLASTICS & CHEMICALS	1050741	4956310	3952088	1208381	3093442	1537354	2965098	608186	2779252	22150848
12 GLASS, STONE,CLAY PRDTS.	80940	433572	376347	135116	225620	82652	157832	67246	232878	1792203
13 PRIMARY IRON & STEEL MFR	51330	878827	955669	58606	205375	131153	169594	30179	172521	2653254
14 PRIMARY NONFERROUS MFR.	73568	551873	292777	45912	203141	60679	192255	101061	340756	1862022
15 MACHINERY & EQUIPMENT	5093327	20990832	18678112	5599850	9570668	3647811	7508008	3130117	12022245	86240976
16 SERVICES	21344512	70738384	65836080	24406800	45196368	16325743	28186192	12832991	49290624	334157568
17 TRANSPORT. & WAREHOUSING	1358783	5388563	5187693	1856088	3428161	1106595	2303811	869859	3564153	25063696
18 GAS & WATER SERVICES	390777	2355833	3723584	1275846	222327	177765	251852	430058	1642469	10470514
19 ELECTRIC UTILITIES	576336	890862	107732	210540	2406157	850014	1387840	270151	919020	7618653
20 TOTAL	47376976	162766528	156325424	58082032	104286160	38799840	76744256	31340752	119259744	794981632

TABLE B.5-3

PROJECTED 1980 REGIONAL FINAL DEMANDS
(THOUSANDS OF 1963 DOLLARS)

INDUSTRY TITLE	1 NEW ENGLAND	2 MIDDLE ATLANTIC	3 EAST NORTH CENTRAL	4 WEST NORTH CENTRAL	5 SOUTH ATLANTIC	6 EAST SOUTH CENTRAL	7 WEST SOUTH CENTRAL	8 MOUNTAIN	9 PACIFIC	10 U.S. FINAL DEMAND
1 LIVESTOCK, PRDTS.	166771	517602	792818	828065	537038	277332	409828	268979	517975	4316408
2 OTHER AGRICULTURE PRDTS.	257120	833582	1489395	1046831	1087526	534521	4324191	405967	2442536	12421669
3 COAL MINING	22781	251898	208199	35629	325423	34353	52429	19625	66797	1017134
4 CRUDE PETRO.,NATURAL GAS	103	10101	22490	35068	4544	18559	460928	79419	64808	696020
5 OTHER MINING	9724	175090	128387	92265	152762	45265	361826	259545	189487	1414351
6 CONSTRUCTION	6369377	21679584	24309552	10041962	20931744	8366188	14196733	9116079	24334832	139346080
7 FOOD,TOBAC.,FAB.,APPAREL	8668498	28453200	26598400	9822462	20789648	7500282	13268505	5133810	22017088	142251936
8 TRANSPORT EQPT.,ORDNANCE	5083634	14346129	18124112	7065687	12122770	4029973	9321210	3476166	15602418	89172096
9 LUMBER & PAPER	2090949	8355956	7197003	2417284	4999866	1710052	3010907	1164489	5770279	36716784
10 PETROLEUM, RELATED INDS.	1221078	4062004	3472610	1456757	2553020	881090	3241394	878934	3166709	20933584
11 PLASTICS & CHEMICALS	1522179	7090604	5617709	1819518	4864511	2339433	4421246	985852	4491480	33152528
12 GLASS, STONE,CLAY PRDTS.	96485	693367	454150	141214	273334	96576	183731	69943	260676	2269476
13 PRIMARY IRON & STEEL MFR	79505	890806	1169710	70881	263234	157590	209776	57103	243338	3141943
14 PRIMARY NONFERROUS MFR.	147932	623357	416211	69767	271884	87317	260625	142128	459707	2478928
15 MACHINERY & EQUIPMENT	7578023	31636208	27469344	9092465	17332128	6416536	12756209	5692216	21516864	139490032
16 SERVICES	32860128	108997840	104812480	38466448	79376288	27624928	47216864	21333008	85229952	545917952
17 TRANSPORT. & WAREHOUSING	2050697	7545313	7908640	2797768	5563582	1739364	3508330	1353875	5610896	38078464
18 GAS & WATER SERVICES	570542	3326438	5483367	1847303	369696	281147	400617	657043	2673231	15609387
19 ELECTRIC UTILITIES	841460	1257898	158647	304842	4001071	1344355	2207617	412736	1495768	12024397
20 TOTAL	69636992	240747008	235833264	87452224	175820096	63484864	119812960	51506928	196154864	1240449024

TABLE B.6-1

1963 REGIONAL OUTPUTS
(THOUSANDS OF 1963 DOLLARS)

INDUSTRY TITLE	1 NEW ENGLAND	2 MIDDLE ATLANTIC	3 EAST NORTH CENTRAL	4 WEST NORTH CENTRAL	5 SOUTH ATLANTIC	6 EAST SOUTH CENTRAL	7 WEST SOUTH CENTRAL	8 MOUNTAIN	9 PACIFIC	10 U.S. OUTPUT
1 LIVESTOCK, PRDTS.	646866	1867903	5019572	7932120	2426874	1758840	2649951	2036698	2345439	26684256
2 OTHER AGRICULTURE PRDTS.	378893	1353558	4945011	6135930	3584673	2186424	3311048	1755180	3615429	27266144
3 COAL MINING	380	682486	437741	35237	903585	478443	9266	81861	7841	2636841
4 CRUDE PETRO.,NATURAL GAS	365459	560243	576354	607665	113694	308186	7353476	1181253	1198351	12264683
5 OTHER MINING	104728	693587	846836	746538	659908	275288	454356	1432785	416990	5631016
6 CONSTRUCTION	4516801	12331973	14592096	6369508	11507191	3933328	8937223	4811979	18313328	85313424
7 FOOD,TOBAC.,FAB.,APPAREL	7212017	26787856	19270384	13239910	26150176	8609748	7328800	2640586	11686795	122926304
8 TRANSPORT EQPT.,ORDNANCE	2828730	7500555	29841456	4816611	3963478	1423747	2551925	904150	9904480	63735136
9 LUMBER & PAPER	3730018	11224813	11341020	2690909	6628036	2660154	2785558	1104782	8406247	50571536
10 PETROLEUM, RELATED INDS.	343065	3302749	3618868	1060736	718778	371608	8660217	866708	2883851	21826576
11 PLASTICS & CHEMICALS	2697124	10030937	10507715	2232300	5941113	2770829	5145171	473020	2927240	42725440
12 GLASS, STONE,CLAY PRDTS.	558808	2681987	3269506	931882	1552264	660094	984509	396536	1433851	12469438
13 PRIMARY IRON & STEEL MFR	567831	7131186	11395917	471350	1650862	1341697	553855	354693	1016279	24483664
14 PRIMARY NONFERROUS MFR.	1207629	3579259	3762468	406814	1157153	678819	987041	1099516	1258395	14137097
15 MACHINERY & EQUIPMENT	9062094	25804416	36704048	5862329	5578897	3102387	3967486	1109373	9919745	101110784
16 SERVICES	22743936	90472656	70863520	28054288	44250912	15137119	26794800	12934145	51868832	363120128
17 TRANSPORT. & WAREHOUSING	1734100	9128128	7683498	3258753	4917687	1634305	3785221	1452380	5548476	39142544
18 GAS & WATER SERVICES	532733	2742365	3442155	1276736	1507064	912349	1316407	865710	1653010	14248529
19 ELECTRIC UTILITIES	1069928	2967824	3540753	1124092	2246998	693280	1462648	637824	1683748	15427098
20 TOTAL	60301136	220844512	241658944	87253712	125459360	48936640	89038960	36139184	136088336	1045720832

TABLE B.6-2

PROJECTED 1970 REGIONAL OUTPUTS
(THOUSANDS OF 1963 DOLLARS)

INDUSTRY TITLE	1 NEW ENGLAND	2 MIDDLE ATLANTIC	3 EAST NORTH CENTRAL	4 WEST NORTH CENTRAL	5 SOUTH ATLANTIC	6 EAST SOUTH CENTRAL	7 WEST SOUTH CENTRAL	8 MOUNTAIN	9 PACIFIC	10 U.S. OUTPUT
1 LIVESTOCK, PRDTS.	763731	2215452	5968288	9295343	2895872	2092073	3131090	2385950	2781541	31529328
2 OTHER AGRICULTURE PRDTS.	407586	1439707	5399814	6804562	3914860	2371466	4466729	2067024	4290155	31161904
3 COAL MINING	494	967474	544802	50411	1267046	679535	14880	105901	10193	3640736
4 CRUDE PETRO.,NATURAL GAS	549922	813941	857694	898773	159233	414105	10409754	1723064	1729648	17556128
5 OTHER MINING	128687	946246	1167474	1059004	851984	355230	588184	1795633	479098	7371542
6 CONSTRUCTION	4557870	15549364	17860064	7556332	13024041	5132211	10527685	5361934	14918639	94488144
7 FOOD,TOBAC.,FAB.,APPAREL	8889644	32947616	24009168	16271753	33849744	11157014	9540222	3222452	15040120	154927760
8 TRANSPORT EQPT.,ORDNANCE	4311486	11157462	43601488	7545391	6197333	2203561	4475312	1381032	15196259	96069328
9 LUMBER & PAPER	4795339	14490861	14990503	3509555	8886850	3634853	3887666	1431882	11133315	66760816
10 PETROLEUM, RELATED INDS.	513235	4819689	4888362	1439195	1027069	506732	12352157	1214840	4053401	30814672
11 PLASTICS & CHEMICALS	3847817	14336998	15076411	3206075	8446600	4016039	7772478	682794	4277442	61662656
12 GLASS, STONE,CLAY PRDTS.	661887	3377095	4174406	1173396	1860806	834749	1219334	440428	1434453	15176556
13 PRIMARY IRON & STEEL MFR	818256	10312155	16616729	688297	2370629	1951939	822154	484571	1410701	35475424
14 PRIMARY NONFERROUS MFR.	1711563	5124933	5413690	584002	1661581	977562	1418491	1568071	1785950	20245840
15 MACHINERY & EQUIPMENT	13650916	39585632	57053664	9047551	8504795	4881396	6826912	1731968	14766394	156049232
16 SERVICES	31117168	123995376	98228352	37815856	64084064	21406464	38606064	17605968	72615264	505474560
17 TRANSPORT. & WAREHOUSING	2485854	13251719	11269162	4743136	7150676	2407341	5476713	2084882	7943789	56813264
18 GAS & WATER SERVICES	735656	4966018	7035383	2443875	1406735	990912	1454935	1496938	2946237	23476688
19 ELECTRIC UTILITIES	1409006	3167550	3070493	971451	4051074	1060180	2462213	755816	2023817	18971600
20 TOTAL	81356128	303465216	337225984	115103968	171611008	67073376	125452976	47541152	178836432	1427666176

TABLE B.6-3

PROJECTED 1980 OUTPUTS
(THOUSANDS OF 1963 DOLLARS)

INDUSTRY TITLE	1 NEW ENGLAND	2 MIDDLE ATLANTIC	3 EAST NORTH CENTRAL	4 WEST NORTH CENTRAL	5 SOUTH ATLANTIC	6 EAST SOUTH CENTRAL	7 WEST SOUTH CENTRAL	8 MOUNTAIN	9 PACIFIC	10 U.S. OUTPUT
1 LIVESTOCK, PRDTS.	1030192	3009841	8116619	12616389	3963398	2872481	4290390	3287345	3951763	43138416
2 OTHER AGRICULTURE PRDTS.	557797	1971759	7375729	9259903	5409952	3278444	6146056	2854479	5946063	42800176
3 COAL MINING	745	1383150	791097	77131	1836525	996328	23034	191459	18656	5318125
4 CRUDE PETRO., NATURAL GAS	759562	1136111	1189438	1229620	225254	575005	13912499	2376809	2441366	23845664
5 OTHER MINING	203183	1494705	1775106	1599877	1370615	565147	1002406	2894093	746256	11651390
6 CONSTRUCTION	7997406	28624192	30850352	12461119	25234432	9803623	17323744	10413395	28999696	171708000
7 FOOD, TOBAC., FAB., APPAREL	12264208	45257264	33428720	22524112	48308464	15929777	13922460	4610915	22463536	218709488
8 TRANSPORT EQPT., ORDNANCE	5472753	14392785	57371856	10050597	8424768	2961648	5994089	1783398	19443632	125895552
9 LUMBER & PAPER	7000928	21226768	22098496	5180098	13785498	5583583	5998527	2256719	17265984	100396640
10 PETROLEUM, RELATED INDS.	684917	6490004	6595276	1915554	1477460	712249	16378325	1697819	5637710	41589312
11 PLASTICS & CHEMICALS	5764117	21470496	22533184	4810892	12782670	6072193	11671796	1076500	6789488	92971344
12 GLASS, STONE, CLAY PRDTS.	1057484	5642499	6565523	1812738	3186735	1401015	1909761	768136	2449375	24793264
13 PRIMARY IRON & STEEL MFR	1236276	15393232	24790304	1047909	3641434	3039906	1286894	795479	2229461	53460896
14 PRIMARY NONFERROUS MFR.	2634128	7823408	8268572	893179	2552272	1510405	2165973	2410469	2728724	30987120
15 MACHINERY & EQUIPMENT	21420720	62504064	89486256	14486303	14104083	7987729	11231047	2936079	24783440	248939760
16 SERVICES	48124160	193328864	154489184	59154752	109064096	35487760	62616560	28862688	122868960	813997056
17 TRANSPORT. & WAREHOUSING	3728014	19985088	17233952	7284613	10921661	3697045	8317613	3255523	12426435	86849952
18 GAS & WATER SERVICES	1093359	7278878	10437143	3604414	2236899	1540079	2216168	2306366	4757768	35471072
19 ELECTRIC UTILITIES	2103733	4758706	4713239	1478433	6661490	1670634	3861113	1196476	3292161	29735984
20 TOTAL	123133696	463171840	508110080	171487648	275187712	105685056	190268464	75974160	289240320	2202259211

TABLE B.7-1

PROJECTED 1980 TRADE FLOWS
LIVESTOCK AND LIVESTOCK PRODUCTS
(THOUSANDS OF 1963 DOLLARS)

	1 NEW ENGLAND	2 MIDDLE ATLANTIC	3 EAST NORTH CENTRAL	4 WEST NORTH CENTRAL	5 SOUTH ATLANTIC	6 EAST SOUTH CENTRAL	7 WEST SOUTH CENTRAL	8 MOUNTAIN	9 PACIFIC	10 COMMODITY PRODUCTION
1 NEW ENGLAND	370901	136560	406	3	7183	23986	2653	1541	4867	548100
2 MIDDLE ATLANTIC	552794	348813	1141	2	51348	583705	361963	1422	14296	1915485
3 EAST NORTH CENTRAL	150925	178770	96052	22841	54356	1969837	1259414	159852	281547	4173594
4 WEST NORTH CENTRAL	19670	34197	47120	125607	17482	2064655	4259032	1818823	418899	8805486
5 SOUTH ATLANTIC	117634	260232	20060	1070	92434	646815	654080	72457	192392	2057175
6 EAST SOUTH CENTRAL	21329	63250	14477	5042	25005	1790084	1673841	238431	256736	4088196
7 WEST SOUTH CENTRAL	8589	33351	11038	25535	19570	741421	3576509	739143	408906	5564062
8 MOUNTAIN	2672	3407	5796	18344	1846	137980	1472420	1787510	841822	4271797
9 PACIFIC	7381	12241	1259	3910	2195	38922	372972	1416669	3586121	5441670
10 COMMODITY CONSUMPTION	1251894	1070821	197350	202354	271421	7997406	13632885	6235850	6005586	36865568

TABLE B.7-2

PROJECTED 1980 TRADE FLOWS
OTHER AGRICULTURAL PRODUCTS
(THOUSANDS OF 1963 DOLLARS)

	1 NEW ENGLAND	2 MIDDLE ATLANTIC	3 EAST NORTH CENTRAL	4 WEST NORTH CENTRAL	5 SOUTH ATLANTIC	6 EAST SOUTH CENTRAL	7 WEST SOUTH CENTRAL	8 MOUNTAIN	9 PACIFIC	10 COMMODITY PRODUCTION
1 NEW ENGLAND	338597	298826	8641	1074	37974	43070	52552	3246	1109	785089
2 MIDDLE ATLANTIC	496329	1327785	31157	9388	188773	214400	270435	11239	3247	2552753
3 EAST NORTH CENTRAL	200674	1085268	603924	107606	459112	2881102	2437135	107934	14592	7897350
4 WEST NORTH CENTRAL	25815	103435	243507	1770474	86343	1728572	9689056	407837	100530	14155570
5 SOUTH ATLANTIC	593206	1534468	99518	30981	1061961	1209759	1660229	74750	20683	6285554
6 EAST SOUTH CENTRAL	149693	226536	48351	46359	428694	5253573	3054365	68188	13426	9289185
7 WEST SOUTH CENTRAL	93704	249467	33542	84404	238627	2155991	27059792	292897	122076	30330496
8 MOUNTAIN	22542	110933	22722	87914	18850	213303	1000934	2025560	305022	3807779
9 PACIFIC	140600	528088	74584	175308	88764	592028	2509588	1502476	764720	6376158
10 COMMODITY CONSUMPTION	2061159	5464805	1165947	2313507	2609096	14291800	47734080	4494129	1345404	81479936

TABLE B.7-3

PROJECTED 1980 TRADE FLOWS
COAL MINING
(THOUSANDS OF 1963 DOLLARS)

	1 NEW ENGLAND	2 MIDDLE ATLANTIC	3 EAST NORTH CENTRAL	4 WEST NORTH CENTRAL	5 SOUTH ATLANTIC	6 EAST SOUTH CENTRAL	7 WEST SOUTH CENTRAL	8 MOUNTAIN	9 PACIFIC	10 COMMODITY PRODUCTION
1 NEW ENGLAND	7208	0	0	0	0	0	0	0	0	7208
2 MIDDLE ATLANTIC	814835	2856662	244984	3959	608328	0	0	0	4409829	8938598
3 EAST NORTH CENTRAL	0	21599	1778765	929345	66688	128421	510332	0	0	3435150
4 WEST NORTH CENTRAL	0	0	0	120001	0	0	4301714	0	0	4421715
5 SOUTH ATLANTIC	889222	1140559	1036013	196853	2069416	374354	9718550	27550592	4166567	47142144
6 EAST SOUTH CENTRAL	197143	63081	625756	111525	770743	1652239	12561866	0	0	15982353
7 WEST SOUTH CENTRAL	0	0	0	368	0	0	1531744	713841	0	2245953
8 MOUNTAIN	0	0	0	114	0	0	0	17471632	8844898	26316640
9 PACIFIC	0	0	0	0	0	0	0	126039	1097301	1223340
10 COMMODITY CONSUMPTION	1908408	4081900	3685519	1362165	3515176	2155014	28624192	45862112	18518592	109713104

TABLE B.7-4

PROJECTED 1980 TRADE FLOWS
CRUDE PETROLEUM AND NATURAL GAS
(THOUSANDS OF 1963 DOLLARS)

	1 NEW ENGLAND	2 MIDDLE ATLANTIC	3 EAST NORTH CENTRAL	4 WEST NORTH CENTRAL	5 SOUTH ATLANTIC	6 EAST SOUTH CENTRAL	7 WEST SOUTH CENTRAL	8 MOUNTAIN	9 PACIFIC	10 COMMODITY PRODUCTION
1 NEW ENGLAND	6403965	1007392	1097787	0	0	0	0	0	0	8509144
2 MIDDLE ATLANTIC	4972184	1829565	320092	0	2936386	137	0	0	0	10058365
3 EAST NORTH CENTRAL	30420	43618	4717039	253899	51459	253719	0	6792	0	5356946
4 WEST NORTH CENTRAL	9817	25762	1585005	2823875	5997	0	244821	5394523	191	10089992
5 SOUTH ATLANTIC	3319	225377	220370	0	1084898	4984	0	0	0	1538949
6 EAST SOUTH CENTRAL	203950	260644	181639	670	987032	2601182	936748	256	0	5172122
7 WEST SOUTH CENTRAL	10471499	4345905	9099124	1534294	6063449	4216372	51483152	13827411	1407318	102448528
8 MOUNTAIN	8020	126106	2030765	445045	4780	2330	1302993	149052704	2548432	155521168
9 PACIFIC	0	0	0	0	0	0	0	0	13948802	13948802
10 COMMODITY CONSUMPTION	22103168	7864370	19251824	5057783	11134002	7078724	53967712	168281680	17904736	312643840

TABLE B.7-5

PROJECTED 1980 TRADE FLOWS
OTHER MINING
(THOUSANDS OF 1963 DOLLARS)

	1 NEW ENGLAND	2 MIDDLE ATLANTIC	3 EAST NORTH CENTRAL	4 WEST NORTH CENTRAL	5 SOUTH ATLANTIC	6 EAST SOUTH CENTRAL	7 WEST SOUTH CENTRAL	8 MOUNTAIN	9 PACIFIC	10 COMMODITY PRODUCTION
1 NEW ENGLAND	5055115	29132	0	0	192	1811	264	0	0	5086514
2 MIDDLE ATLANTIC	1172991	3001501	90979	0	36249	353473	52258	0	0	4707451
3 EAST NORTH CENTRAL	296835	565534	4385838	264968	40298	160083	12210	86806	9512	5822085
4 WEST NORTH CENTRAL	541649	538210	2266901	5314438	24471	244407	40903	0	1807165	10778144
5 SOUTH ATLANTIC	13951	273196	303656	112111	992129	328230	102228	0	0	2125499
6 EAST SOUTH CENTRAL	142512	144962	47715	0	8604	2839893	12455	0	0	3196141
7 WEST SOUTH CENTRAL	0	217850	27600	45688	72778	173731	1352663	84672	1059068	3034048
8 MOUNTAIN	0	209244	684552	2118205	58645	287616	988890	30457152	10265498	45069808
9 PACIFIC	0	10432	128431	0	0	6475	1064	221718	25368320	25736432
10 COMMODITY CONSUMPTION	7223054	4990059	7935673	7855409	1233365	4395718	2562933	30850352	38509568	105556144

TABLE B.7-6

PROJECTED 1980 TRADE FLOWS
CONSTRUCTION
(THOUSANDS OF 1963 DOLLARS)

	1 NEW ENGLAND	2 MIDDLE ATLANTIC	3 EAST NORTH CENTRAL	4 WEST NORTH CENTRAL	5 SOUTH ATLANTIC	6 EAST SOUTH CENTRAL	7 WEST SOUTH CENTRAL	8 MOUNTAIN	9 PACIFIC	10 COMMODITY PRODUCTION
1 NEW ENGLAND	36557792	0	0	0	0	0	0	0	0	36557792
2 MIDDLE ATLANTIC	0	21205888	0	0	0	0	0	0	0	21205888
3 EAST NORTH CENTRAL	0	0	7563982	0	0	0	0	0	0	7563982
4 WEST NORTH CENTRAL	0	0	0	20212272	0	0	0	0	0	20212272
5 SOUTH ATLANTIC	0	0	0	0	5576485	0	0	0	0	5576485
6 EAST SOUTH CENTRAL	0	0	0	0	0	21813936	0	0	0	21813936
7 WEST SOUTH CENTRAL	0	0	0	0	0	0	9310841	0	0	9310841
8 MOUNTAIN	0	0	0	0	0	0	0	60793984	0	60793984
9 PACIFIC	0	0	0	0	0	0	0	0	160625248	160625248
10 COMMODITY CONSUMPTION	36557792	21205888	7563982	20212272	5576485	21813936	9310841	60793984	160625248	343660288

TABLE B.7-7

PROJECTED 1980 TRADE FLOWS
FOOD, TOBACCO, FABRICS, AND APPAREL
(THOUSANDS OF 1963 DOLLARS)

	1 NEW ENGLAND	2 MIDDLE ATLANTIC	3 EAST NORTH CENTRAL	4 WEST NORTH CENTRAL	5 SOUTH ATLANTIC	6 EAST SOUTH CENTRAL	7 WEST SOUTH CENTRAL	8 MOUNTAIN	9 PACIFIC	10 COMMODITY PRODUCTION
1 NEW ENGLAND	9393932	690020	68357	205922	170890	2946	7840	10077	136221	10686205
2 MIDDLE ATLANTIC	4469236	6366214	508640	702930	718756	13467	96043	65179	949843	13890309
3 EAST NORTH CENTRAL	954531	772638	2289965	1025732	309395	17432	70372	40736	625355	6106156
4 WEST NORTH CENTRAL	878853	485305	393785	8096943	189238	12209	151231	36634	337558	10581756
5 SOUTH ATLANTIC	2601112	1833200	376323	804568	4324315	42862	125325	'74300	1647469	11829476
6 EAST SOUTH CENTRAL	532040	389640	138710	211846	722943	98139	79179	32723	159635	2364854
7 WEST SOUTH CENTRAL	116871	65950	56788	349047	71154	10443	812875	34165	255571	1772863
8 MOUNTAIN	57763	44300	34940	72238	12506	122	7232	319565	334047	882713
9 PACIFIC	130857	149963	70283	226431	59867	2142	41962	92361	8015419	8789286
10 COMMODITY CONSUMPTION	19135184	10797231	3937790	11695658	6579063	199763	1392058	705739	12461119	66903616

TABLE B.7-8

PROJECTED 1980 TRADE FLOWS
TRANSPORTATION EQUIPMENT AND ORDNANCE
(THOUSANDS OF 1963 DOLLARS)

	1 NEW ENGLAND	2 MIDDLE ATLANTIC	3 EAST NORTH CENTRAL	4 WEST NORTH CENTRAL	5 SOUTH ATLANTIC	6 EAST SOUTH CENTRAL	7 WEST SOUTH CENTRAL	8 MOUNTAIN	9 PACIFIC	10 COMMODITY PRODUCTION
1 NEW ENGLAND	3419982	776923	131143	33758	344172	20711	109347	21257	379507	5236801
2 MIDDLE ATLANTIC	2803034	3246405	668847	205243	676523	91184	85894	18168	492777	8288074
3 EAST NORTH CENTRAL	5160054	3666287	4953602	1889170	2061759	500009	751185	282929	4169514	23434512
4 WEST NORTH CENTRAL	423596	501618	343054	700272	87736	246194	718185	330299	449330	3800283
5 SOUTH ATLANTIC	568652	1248511	78303	31786	1516120	276274	106714	11201	144701	3982263
6 EAST SOUTH CENTRAL	357366	145546	108614	38234	159641	327746	61355	22331	166783	1387615
7 WEST SOUTH CENTRAL	210879	49316	144705	194840	76614	86774	952952	109394	245249	2070721
8 MOUNTAIN	861886	73088	26096	68517	79894	13976	31966	95249	271046	1521717
9 PACIFIC	2095785	390082	114503	194095	551391	136390	252148	504743	10363774	14602911
10 COMMODITY CONSUMPTION	15901235	10097777	6568867	3355915	5553850	1699257	3069744	1395570	16682681	64324896

TABLE B.7-9

PROJECTED 1980 TRADE FLOWS
LUMBER AND PAPER
(THOUSANDS OF 1963 DOLLARS)

	1 NEW ENGLAND	2 MIDDLE ATLANTIC	3 EAST NORTH CENTRAL	4 WEST NORTH CENTRAL	5 SOUTH ATLANTIC	6 EAST SOUTH CENTRAL	7 WEST SOUTH CENTRAL	8 MOUNTAIN	9 PACIFIC	10 COMMODITY PRODUCTION
1 NEW ENGLAND	38774336	484814	91548	28623	132277	113293	18328	10880	7765	39661872
2 MIDDLE ATLANTIC	9478224	4569629	223535	143807	469355	375146	74194	40863	36679	15411431
3 EAST NORTH CENTRAL	3482199	566715	2600843	251376	295951	838712	103839	60047	35539	8235221
4 WEST NORTH CENTRAL	478409	72474	118589	748914	54754	206134	44791	15826	6541	1746430
5 SOUTH ATLANTIC	3641095	522589	179710	71363	2749763	795985	77812	19270	11115	8068702
6 EAST SOUTH CENTRAL	913550	103021	104627	54079	227673	3855771	74859	11117	4655	5349351
7 WEST SOUTH CENTRAL	652688	63284	64546	53559	101541	272894	634039	24917	7109	1874577
8 MOUNTAIN	150671	20179	19830	17658	8259	25783	5968	410707	21404	680462
9 PACIFIC	1951250	178007	102625	82792	97637	229430	60135	163679	1153141	4018696
10 COMMODITY CONSUMPTION	59522432	6580712	3505854	1452170	4137209	6713149	1093964	757305	1283947	85046736

TABLE B.7-10

PROJECTED 1980 TRADE FLOWS
PETROLEUM AND RELATED INDUSTRIES
(THOUSANDS OF 1963 DOLLARS)

	1 NEW ENGLAND	2 MIDDLE ATLANTIC	3 EAST NORTH CENTRAL	4 WEST NORTH CENTRAL	5 SOUTH ATLANTIC	6 EAST SOUTH CENTRAL	7 WEST SOUTH CENTRAL	8 MOUNTAIN	9 PACIFIC	10 COMMODITY PRODUCTION
1 NEW ENGLAND	5178644	683483	218105	436	327	0	3377	1330	346	6086049
2 MIDDLE ATLANTIC	3467728	22153472	1062488	73838	954033	82814	30019	9552	10057	27844000
3 EAST NORTH CENTRAL	25983	687953	9913587	3334025	87546	2727881	17611	20639	18340	16833552
4 WEST NORTH CENTRAL	183	2351	240024	6179775	561	96767	49820	194223	22329	6786034
5 SOUTH ATLANTIC	174025	1150659	166913	38494	1069216	119091	7105	69725	0	2795228
6 EAST SOUTH CENTRAL	52234	258350	128808	131363	60621	3419602	37533	473	38	4089021
7 WEST SOUTH CENTRAL	16331712	12574144	2698960	2814652	2765404	8156656	3331719	881750	93038	49648032
8 MOUNTAIN	1198	22	264290	824102	85	10691	18368	2560881	58283	3737921
9 PACIFIC	2729	401067	1775	1081	6954	0	1830	228725	2316347	2960510
10 COMMODITY CONSUMPTION	25234432	37911504	14694952	13397765	4944748	14613503	3497382	3967299	2518778	120780368

TABLE B.7-11

PROJECTED 1980 TRADE FLOWS
PLASTICS AND CHEMICALS
(THOUSANDS OF 1963 DOLLARS)

	1 NEW ENGLAND	2 MIDDLE ATLANTIC	3 EAST NORTH CENTRAL	4 WEST NORTH CENTRAL	5 SOUTH ATLANTIC	6 EAST SOUTH CENTRAL	7 WEST SOUTH CENTRAL	8 MOUNTAIN	9 PACIFIC	10 COMMODITY PRODUCTION
1 NEW ENGLAND	9870166	7606954	434670	79452	246625	73388	74115	7722	28831	18421920
2 MIDDLE ATLANTIC	9585506	58651328	1818445	267843	1380161	219376	162612	34051	70612	72189936
3 EAST NORTH CENTRAL	1899687	18377600	6217859	758864	1064087	550928	304005	80048	58094	29311168
4 WEST NORTH CENTRAL	386591	1538118	812544	580970	82588	171481	167435	32024	14570	3786321
5 SOUTH ATLANTIC	2538674	14087731	920188	157665	2667394	365120	140728	6052	22069	20905616
6 EAST SOUTH CENTRAL	720693	3976327	569530	136615	589834	729274	147923	14617	11096	6895909
7 WEST SOUTH CENTRAL	2651615	7611977	724988	220031	375748	334668	1561444	64541	21055	13566069
8 MOUNTAIN	35196	136113	26399	25427	4463	5789	25338	44542	30792	334058
9 PACIFIC	296447	637674	104685	75900	24258	24245	58910	127795	278680	1628592
10 COMMODITY CONSUMPTION	27984576	112623840	11629310	2302766	6435159	2474268	2642511	411392	535798	167039616

TABLE B.7-12

PROJECTED 1980 TRADE FLOWS
GLASS, STONE, AND CLAY PRODUCTS
(THOUSANDS OF 1963 DOLLARS)

	1 NEW ENGLAND	2 MIDDLE ATLANTIC	3 EAST NORTH CENTRAL	4 WEST NORTH CENTRAL	5 SOUTH ATLANTIC	6 EAST SOUTH CENTRAL	7 WEST SOUTH CENTRAL	8 MOUNTAIN	9 PACIFIC	10 COMMODITY PRODUCTION
1 NEW ENGLAND	473647	269033	138755	4796	2971	1189	23526	5430	52696	972044
2 MIDDLE ATLANTIC	220294	8202754	592531	51359	831096	74768	66151	40576	68825	10148354
3 EAST NORTH CENTRAL	12323	804245	11216682	799659	491846	225938	365268	291239	117750	14324950
4 WEST NORTH CENTRAL	418	18088	345113	3743550	12570	293583	198854	31913	12083	4656172
5 SOUTH ATLANTIC	12388	452928	466017	38102	3339927	158230	176381	1187	165184	4810344
6 EAST SOUTH CENTRAL	1775	53304	196504	93744	386659	1034889	433542	36794	33487	2270698
7 WEST SOUTH CENTRAL	202	2167	28058	80813	9472	37691	4737785	120210	17827	5034225
8 MOUNTAIN	0	162	734	9702	0	387	486	663565	170757	845793
9 PACIFIC	2	940	1522	4727	76	1	1007	138148	1624430	1770854
10 COMMODITY CONSUMPTION	721048	9803623	12985916	4826453	5074617	1826675	6003000	1329062	2263039	44833424

TABLE B.7-13

PROJECTED 1980 TRADE FLOWS
PRIMARY IRON AND STEEL MANUFACTURE
(THOUSANDS OF 1963 DOLLARS)

	1 NEW ENGLAND	2 MIDDLE ATLANTIC	3 EAST NORTH CENTRAL	4 WEST NORTH CENTRAL	5 SOUTH ATLANTIC	6 EAST SOUTH CENTRAL	7 WEST SOUTH CENTRAL	8 MOUNTAIN	9 PACIFIC	10 COMMODITY PRODUCTION
1 NEW ENGLAND	321032	242967	567075	3450	21773	26444	2004	35043	2746	1222534
2 MIDDLE ATLANTIC	763265	6848009	8488310	340140	306010	301480	300644	602875	53400	18004128
3 EAST NORTH CENTRAL	166228	2732921	28756160	2694834	364327	553445	1203904	2177308	79861	38728992
4 WEST NORTH CENTRAL	117	15662	456861	705727	3420	16828	70084	258370	11777	1538845
5 SOUTH ATLANTIC	105491	914391	713850	112951	320148	296684	431191	213691	30736	3139133
6 EAST SOUTH CENTRAL	15717	150860	655994	211786	203803	985851	615383	521565	9887	3370844
7 WEST SOUTH CENTRAL	1083	31520	55278	35817	14466	39410	1225398	272182	5814	1680968
8 MOUNTAIN	874	879	23617	28954	2548	9280	67610	2305460	28164	2467387
9 PACIFIC	136	11941	27638	37902	11344	6526	83143	347414	173756	699801
10 COMMODITY CONSUMPTION	1373941	10949151	39744784	4171561	1247840	2235947	3999362	6733909	396141	70852640

TABLE B.7-14

PROJECTED 1980 TRADE FLOWS
PRIMARY NONFERROUS MANUFACTURE
(THOUSANDS OF 1963 DOLLARS)

	1 NEW ENGLAND	2 MIDDLE ATLANTIC	3 EAST NORTH CENTRAL	4 WEST NORTH CENTRAL	5 SOUTH ATLANTIC	6 EAST SOUTH CENTRAL	7 WEST SOUTH CENTRAL	8 MOUNTAIN	9 PACIFIC	10 COMMODITY PRODUCTION
1 NEW ENGLAND	3288792	113957	656540	2693107	815745	455925	205807	336019	89551	8655445
2 MIDDLE ATLANTIC	3115511	745835	2758286	1421005	3434649	1416073	464937	638370	210652	14205320
3 EAST NORTH CENTRAL	740447	198686	9293708	6604819	1714360	1726654	1047886	1053269	236633	22616464
4 WEST NORTH CENTRAL	324711	47114	424522	1826941	331724	70823	142179	46575	33143	3247733
5 SOUTH ATLANTIC	916356	161242	1171441	1215384	2488148	328409	88188	23801	57545	6450514
6 EAST SOUTH CENTRAL	141677	44431	696079	471275	814202	2262730	335483	152988	69255	4988121
7 WEST SOUTH CENTRAL	22331	62510	801359	1931531	149498	1063004	1462442	295732	337601	6126009
8 MOUNTAIN	80040	36751	733440	696611	816668	86316	1996319	5518613	121300	10086057
9 PACIFIC	66924	26225	788375	1155613	309831	126049	482188	1488806	1016484	5460495
10 COMMODITY CONSUMPTION	8696789	1436751	17323744	18016288	10874825	7535983	6225430	9554175	2172164	81836160

TABLE B.7-15

PROJECTED 1980 TRADE FLOWS
MACHINERY AND EQUIPMENT
(THOUSANDS OF 1963 DOLLARS)

	1 NEW ENGLAND	2 MIDDLE ATLANTIC	3 EAST NORTH CENTRAL	4 WEST NORTH CENTRAL	5 SOUTH ATLANTIC	6 EAST SOUTH CENTRAL	7 WEST SOUTH CENTRAL	8 MOUNTAIN	9 PACIFIC	10 COMMODITY PRODUCTION
1 NEW ENGLAND	1181310	232464	1077241	4766935	729723	80197	168488	139283	73025	8448669
2 MIDDLE ATLANTIC	1021144	900737	3929827	9931975	1987028	397926	626404	438903	322021	19555952
3 EAST NORTH CENTRAL	681383	582127	12452868	28565776	2308065	856797	944688	586546	419301	47397552
4 WEST NORTH CENTRAL	62307	65260	953550	17901104	327344	130743	227306	242289	92026	20001936
5 SOUTH ATLANTIC	119045	79821	587913	1633928	1860635	159874	114140	131968	56341	4743666
6 EAST SOUTH CENTRAL	47299	39032	442749	1743240	380461	445351	131307	58368	32759	3320567
7 WEST SOUTH CENTRAL	10191	15002	233375	3651730	197759	95526	1252596	190861	49710	5696751
8 MOUNTAIN	7503	4549	99244	606643	22644	3855	31405	413479	43877	1233199
9 PACIFIC	135694	59382	516407	2745189	275640	48128	371370	635329	834515	5621655
10 COMMODITY CONSUMPTION	3265877	1978374	20293168	71546528	8089301	2218396	3867706	2837025	1923575	116019952

TABLE B.7-16

PROJECTED 1980 TRADE FLOWS
SERVICES
(THOUSANDS OF 1963 DOLLARS)

	1 NEW ENGLAND	2 MIDDLE ATLANTIC	3 EAST NORTH CENTRAL	4 WEST NORTH CENTRAL	5 SOUTH ATLANTIC	6 EAST SOUTH CENTRAL	7 WEST SOUTH CENTRAL	8 MOUNTAIN	9 PACIFIC	10 COMMODITY PRODUCTION
1 NEW ENGLAND	90206	35505	17493	134703	51574	43187	25032	12171	14534	424405
2 MIDDLE ATLANTIC	19170	1064225	111506	627422	545354	344117	203446	65097	66869	3047209
3 EAST NORTH CENTRAL	2494	51976	1218932	993328	187782	223686	36198	13049	15520	2742965
4 WEST NORTH CENTRAL	335	7491	59257	7562773	23797	129588	171697	102526	13440	8070904
5 SOUTH ATLANTIC	692	33620	20243	64901	5372586	577977	103066	4208	24141	6201435
6 EAST SOUTH CENTRAL	146	2281	14446	159037	250494	2429353	142858	1647	6020	3006282
7 WEST SOUTH CENTRAL	218	3479	8737	359031	100986	137373	2192511	143000	22990	2968325
8 MOUNTAIN	111	1289	1830	454435	7235	4467	80572	1224207	55114	1829259
9 PACIFIC	1069	16852	17621	57765	47019	37923	46726	268852	2054224	2548051
10 COMMODITY CONSUMPTION	114442	1216719	1470064	10413395	6586827	3927673	3002107	1834757	2272852	30838832

TABLE B.7-17

PROJECTED 1980 TRADE FLOWS
TRANSPORTATION AND WAREHOUSING
(THOUSANDS OF 1963 DOLLARS)

	1 NEW ENGLAND	2 MIDDLE ATLANTIC	3 EAST NORTH CENTRAL	4 WEST NORTH CENTRAL	5 SOUTH ATLANTIC	6 EAST SOUTH CENTRAL	7 WEST SOUTH CENTRAL	8 MOUNTAIN	9 PACIFIC	10 COMMODITY PRODUCTION
1 NEW ENGLAND	418516	71456	16627	195687	446642	17628	7190	14474	14311	1202530
2 MIDDLE ATLANTIC	456120	516600	308816	464238	8718415	253521	68365	21277	73431	10880782
3 EAST NORTH CENTRAL	37721	132124	489412	1538615	7486732	1029000	183904	124376	317306	11339190
4 WEST NORTH CENTRAL	22444	20401	114690	2137707	2046556	362058	130286	178398	453135	5465676
5 SOUTH ATLANTIC	36002	185561	107785	2222251	8469553	419901	69034	42042	46848	11598977
6 EAST SOUTH CENTRAL	8029	19595	47705	827011	959829	720207	78685	22684	79751	2763495
7 WEST SOUTH CENTRAL	10229	26016	76223	695614	1566214	87124	1110250	86010	47819	3705500
8 MOUNTAIN	13872	9831	6491	354691	215460	58666	73304	320255	517711	1570281
9 PACIFIC	34710	71313	86166	309799	1225240	60510	44981	300599	3175116	5308434
10 COMMODITY CONSUMPTION	1037643	1052897	1253913	8745613	31134640	3008615	1765999	1110114	4725427	53834864

TABLE B.7-18

PROJECTED 1980 TRADE FLOWS
ELECTRICITY, GAS, AND WATER SERVICES
(THOUSANDS OF 1963 DOLLARS)

	1 NEW ENGLAND	2 MIDDLE ATLANTIC	3 EAST NORTH CENTRAL	4 WEST NORTH CENTRAL	5 SOUTH ATLANTIC	6 EAST SOUTH CENTRAL	7 WEST SOUTH CENTRAL	8 MOUNTAIN	9 PACIFIC	10 COMMODITY PRODUCTION
1 NEW ENGLAND	14592756	121588	10582	0	0	0	0	0	0	14724926
2 MIDDLE ATLANTIC	1048519	3303155	181238	0	3654558	0	298299	0	0	8485769
3 EAST NORTH CENTRAL	12	69309	7223592	63167	2127766	38336272	0	0	0	47820128
4 WEST NORTH CENTRAL	0	0	178763	3858603	0	1553937	1086399	841087	162675	7681466
5 SOUTH ATLANTIC	0	73033	39457	0	55381024	16738648	54324	0	0	72286496
6 EAST SOUTH CENTRAL	0	0	80706	416345	2949823	93374608	2622905	0	0	99444400
7 WEST SOUTH CENTRAL	0	0	0	39413	117570	2083456	27395216	2778053	0	32413712
8 MOUNTAIN	0	0	0	134837	0	0	540858	15246645	928458	16850784
9 PACIFIC	0	0	0	1	0	0	0	1701387	8619774	10321162
10 COMMODITY CONSUMPTION	15641286	3567086	7714339	4512364	64230752	152086944	31998000	20567168	9710908	310028800

Bibliography

1. Adamson, W.M. *Income in Counties of Alabama, 1929 and 1935.* University, Ala.: University of Alabama, 1939.
2. Almon, Clopper, Jr. "Investment in Input-Output Models and the Treatment of Secondary Products." In *Applications of Input-Output Analysis,* edited by A.P. Carter and A. Bródy. Amsterdam: North-Holland Publishing Co., 1970, pp. 103-116.
3. Almon, Clopper, Jr. "Prices in Input-Output." Paper presented at the 2nd US/USSR Exchange Symposium on Econometric Modeling, Skyland, Va., May 16-19, 1978.
4. Almon, Clopper, Jr.; Margaret B. Buckler; Lawrence M. Horwitz; and Thomas C. Reimbold. *1985: Interindustry Forecasts of the American Economy.* Lexington, Mass.: Lexington Books, D.C. Heath and Company, 1974.
5. Bacharach, Michael. *Biproportional Matrices and Input-Output Change.* Cambridge, England: Cambridge University Press, 1970.
6. Ballard, Kenneth P., and Robert M. Wendling. "The National-Regional Impact Evaluation System: A Spatial Model of U.S. Economic and Demographic Activity." Paper presented at the 25th Meeting of the Regional Science Association, Chicago, Ill., November 1978.
7. Battelle, Columbus Laboratories. "Interactions of Science and Technology in the Innovative Process: Some Case Studies." Prepared for the National Science Foundation. Columbus, Ohio: Battelle Columbus Laboratories. March 19, 1973. Unpublished.
8. Bon, Ranko. "Some Conditions of Macroeconomic Stability in Multiregional Models." Ph.D. dissertation, Massachusetts Institute of Technology, May 1975.
9. Borts, George H. "Review of Regional Growth Theory." *Journal of Economic Literature* 12 (1974): 546-547.
10. Bourque, Philip J., and Millicent Cox. "An Inventory of Regional Input-Output Studies in the United States." Occasional Paper No. 22. Seattle, Wash.: University of Washington, Graduate School of Business Administration, 1970.
11. Bourque, Philip J., and Gerald Hansen. "An Inventory of Regional Input-Output Studies in the United States." Occasional Paper No. 17. Seattle, Wash.: Graduate School of Business Administration, University of Washington, 1967.
12. Bourque, Philip J.; Edward J. Chambers; John S.Y. Chiu; Frederick L. Denman; Barney Dowdle; Guy G. Gordon; Morgan Thomas; Charles M.

Note: Material published by the U.S. Government Printing Office, Washington, D.C. 20402, is cited as: GPO, [date].

Tiebout; Eldon E. Weeks. "The Washington Interindustry Study for 1963." *University of Washington Business Review* 25 (February 1966): 5-10.

13. Carson, Carol S. "The History of the United States National Income and Product Accounts: The Development of an Analytical Tool." *Review of Income and Wealth* 21 (June 1975): 153-181.
14. Carter, Anne P. "The Economics of Technological Change." *Scientific American* 214 (April 1966): 25-31.
15. Carter, Anne P. "Changes in the Structure of the American Economy, 1947 to 1958 and 1962." *The Review of Economics and Statistics* 49 (May 1967): 209-224.
16. Carter, Anne P. *Structural Change in the American Economy.* Cambridge, Mass.: Harvard University Press, 1970.
17. Carter, Anne P. "Portrait: Wassily Leontief." *Challenge* (January/February 1976): 57-58.
18. Carter, Harold O., and D. Ireri. "Linkages of California-Arizona Input-Output Models to Analyze Water Transfer Patterns." In *Applications of Input-Output Analysis,* edited by A.P. Carter and A. Bródy. Amsterdam: North-Holland Publishing Co., 1970, pp. 139-167.
19. Chenery, Hollis. "Regional Analysis." In *The Structure and Growth of the Italian Economy,* edited by H. Chenery and P. Clark. Rome: United States Mutual Security Agency, 1953, pp. 96-115.
20. Chenery, Hollis, and Paul G. Clark. *Interindustry Economics.* New York: John Wiley & Sons, Inc., 1959.
21. CONSAD Research Corporation. "Impact Studies: Northeast Corridor Transportation Project." Vols. II and III. Prepared for the U.S. Department of Transportation, 1968 and 1969. Unpublished.
22. Coulter, H. Theresa. "The Usefulness of Two Multiregional Economic Models in Evaluating Transportation Policies." Prepared for the Federal Highway Administration, U.S. Department of Transportation, 1977. Unpublished.
23. Cumberland, John H. "A Regional Interindustry Study of Maryland." *Studies in Business and Economics* 8 (September 1954).
24. Czamanski, Stanislaw. *Regional and Interregional Social Accounting.* Lexington, Mass.: Lexington Books, D.C. Heath and Company, 1973.
25. Czamanski, Stanislaw, and Emil E. Malizia. "Applicability and Limitations in the Use of National Input-Output Tables for Regional Studies." *Papers of the Regional Science Association* 23 (1969): 65-77.
26. Davis, H. Craig. "A Multisector Input-Output Model of the Western States Emphasizing Heavy Water-Using Sectors." Ph.D. dissertation, University of California at Berkeley, 1967.
27. Del Duca, Patrick. "Accounting for the Regional Costs and Benefits of Improving Environmental Quality: An Input-Output Approach." B.A. dissertation, Harvard University, June 1978.

28. Deming, W.E., and F.F. Stephan. "On a Least-Squares Adjustment of a Sampled Frequency Table when the Expected Marginal Totals are Known." *Annals of Mathematical Statistics* 11 (1940): 427–444.
29. DiPasquale, Denise, and Karen R. Polenske. "Output, Income, and Employment Input-Output Multipliers." In *Impact Analysis: Methodology and Applications,* edited by Saul Pleeter. Leiden, The Netherlands: Martinus Nijhoff, forthcoming.
30. Dresch, Stephen P., and Robert D. Goldberg. "IDIOM: An Inter-Industry, National-Regional Policy Evaluation Model." *Annals of Economic and Social Measurement* 2 (1973): 323-356.
31. Edmonston, J. Harvey. "A Treatment of Multiple-Process Industries." *Quarterly Journal of Economics* 66 (November 1952): 557-571.
32. Evans, W. Duane, and Marvin Hoffenberg. "The Interindustry Relations Study for 1947." *The Review of Economics and Statistics* 34 (May 1952): 97-142.
33. Evans, W. Duane, and Marvin Hoffenberg. "The Nature and Uses of Interindustry-Relations Data and Methods." *Input-Output Analysis: An Appraisal. Studies in Income and Wealth.* Vol. 18. Princeton: Princeton University Press, 1955, pp. 53-135.
34. Evans, M.K., and L.R. Klein. *The Wharton Econometric Forecasting Model.* 2nd ed. Philadelphia: University of Pennsylvania, Economic Research Unit, 1968.
35. [Jack] Faucett Associates, Inc. "Capital Flow and Capital Expenditure Matrices–1963." Unpublished worksheets.
36. [Jack] Faucett Associates, Inc. "Capital Stocks Series, by 3-Digit SIC for Manufacturing Sectors, in Constant and Current Dollars." Data prepared for the Executive Office of the President, Office of Emergency Planning, National Resource Analysis Center, Resource Evaluation Division, 1969. Unpublished.
37. [Jack] Faucett Associates, Inc. "Compilation of Value of Manufacturing Industry Shipments: 1947, 1958, and 1963 from U.S. Bureau of the Census." Unpublished tabulations.
38. [Jack] Faucett Associates, Inc. "Development of a Matrix of Interindustry Transactions in Capital Goods in 1963." Appendix D. Prepared for the Bureau of Labor Statistics, U.S. Department of Labor, 1966. Unpublished.
39. [Jack] Faucett Associates, Inc. "Employment Effects of the Final System Plan." Prepared for the U.S. Railway Association, 1975. Unpublished.
40. [Jack] Faucett Associates, Inc. *Input-Output Transactions by Transportation Mode, 1947 and 1958.* U.S. Department of Transportation. Springfield, Va.: Clearinghouse for Federal, Scientific and Technical Information, Report No. PB 178 677, April 1968.
41. [Jack] Faucett Associates, Inc. "Interregional Trade Flow Data for 9 Regions, 44 Regions, and 76 Regions." Com-72-10818; Com-72-10819;

Com-72-10820. Springfield, Va.: National Technical Information Service, 1970.

42. [Jack] Faucett Associates, Inc. "Measures of 1947, 1958, and 1963 Output, Organized by Input-Output Sector and Within Input-Output Sector by State, in Current Dollars for Input-Output Sectors 1-79, 84, and 86." Unpublished worksheets.
43. [Jack] Faucett Associates, Inc. "1963 Interregional Commodity Trade Flows." Prepared for the Office of Business Economics, U.S. Department of Commerce, November 1970, revised March 1971. Unpublished.
44. [Jack] Faucett Associates, Inc. "1963 Manufacturing Industry Shipments Estimates for Counties, SMSAs, and States." Prepared for the Office of Civil Defense, U.S. Department of Defense, August 1968. Unpublished.
45. [Jack] Faucett Associates, Inc. "1963 Output Measures for Input-Output Sectors by County." Prepared for the Office of Civil Defense, U.S. Department of Defense, December 1968. Unpublished.
46. [Jack] Faucett Associates, Inc. "1963 Output Measures for Input-Output Sectors by Standard Metropolitan Statistical Areas and Non-Metropolitan State Areas." Prepared for the Institute for Defense Analyses, January 1967. Unpublished.
47. [Jack] Faucett Associates, Inc. "Projections of State Output by Input-Output Industry." n.d. Unpublished worksheets.
48. [Jack] Faucett Associates, Inc. "Transferred Imports Data, 1963." n.d. Unpublished worksheets, pp. 5-28.
49. [Jack] Faucett Associates, Inc. "Unpublished Estimates for 1963 Mineral Production." Prepared for the Bureau of Mines, U.S. Department of the Interior, October 1967. Unpublished.
50. Federal Power Commission. "Electric Utilities and Licenses (Class A & B): Annual Report." (Report for 219 Privately Owned Electric Companies), 1963.
51. Fencl, Zdenek, and Nathaniel Ng. "Comparison Tests of the Column Coefficient and the Gravity Coefficient Models." PB 235 881. Springfield, Va.: National Technical Information Service, April 1974.
52. Fox, Karl A., and T.K. Kumar. "The Functional Economic Area: Delineation and Implications for Economic Analysis and Policy." *Papers and Proceedings of the Regional Science Association* 15 (1965): 57-85.
53. Friedlaender, Ann F.; George Treyz; and Richard Tresch. "An Overview of a Quarterly Econometric Model for Massachusetts and Its Fiscal Structure." *The New England Journal of Business & Economics* 3 (Fall 1976): 57-73.
54. Garnick, Daniel H. "The Regional Statistics System." Paper presented at the Conference on Modeling the Multiregional Economic System: Perspectives for the Eighties. Fort Washington, Pa.: University of Pennsylvania, June 14-15, 1979.

55. Giarratani, Frank; James D. Maddy; and Charles F. Socher. *Regional and Interregional Input-Output Analysis: An Annotated Bibliography.* Morgantown, W.Va.: West Virginia University Library, 1976.
56. Gigantes, T. "The Representation of Technology in Input-Output Systems." In *Contributions to Input-Output Analysis,* edited by A.P. Carter and A. Bródy. Amsterdam: North-Holland Publishing Co., 1970, pp. 270-290.
57. Gilbert, Milton, and R.B. Bangs. "Preliminary Estimates of Gross National Product, 1929-41." *Survey of Current Business* 22 (May 1942): 9-13.
58. Glickman, Norman J. "Son of 'The Specification of Regional Econometric Models'." *Papers of the Regional Science Association* 32 (1974): 155-177.
59. Glickman, Norman J. *Econometric Analysis of Regional Systems.* New York: Academic Press, Inc., 1977.
60. Goldman, Morris R.; Martin L. Marimont; and Beatrice N. Vaccara. "The Interindustry Structure of the United States: A Report on the 1958 Input-Output Study." *Survey of Current Business* 44 (November 1964): 10-29.
61. Goldman, Morris R. "Comments on Czamanski and Malizia." *Papers of the Regional Science Association* 23 (1969): 81-82.
62. Goldman, Morris R. Bureau of Economic Analysis, U.S. Department of Commerce (letter from). "Input-Output and Census Cost Estimates." December 6, 1976.
63. Golladay, Frederick, and Robert Haveman, with the assistance of Kevin Hollenbeck. *The Economic Impacts of Tax-Transfer Policy: Regional and Distributional Effects.* New York: Academic Press, 1977.
64. Green, H. Albert. "'Q' Model: Personal Consumption Expenditures Submodel." U.S. Department of Agriculture, ESG Working Paper No. 4, March 1966.
65. Greenberger, Martin: Matthew A. Crenson; and Brian L. Crissey. *Models in the Policy Process: Public Decision Making in the Computer Era.* New York: Russel Sage Foundation, 1976.
66. Greytak, David. "An Interregional Interindustry Impact Model." In *Developmental Benefits of Water Resource Investments,* edited by C.L. Leven. Washington, D.C.: Institute for Water Resources, Office of the Chief of Engineers, U.S. Army Corps of Engineers, n.d., ch. 6, pp. 154-216, plus appendices.
67. Greytak, David. "Regional Impact of Interregional Trade in Input-Output Analysis." *Papers of the Regional Science Association* 25 (1970): 203-217.
68. Grubb, Herbert W. "The Structure of the Texas Economy." Austin, Texas: Office of Information Service, Office of the Governor, March 1973.
69. Gupta, S.; A. Schwartz; and R. Padula. "The World Bank Model for Global Interdependence: A Quantitative Framework for the World Development Report." *Journal of Policy Modeling* 1 (May 1979): 179-200.
70. Harris, Curtis C., Jr. "A Multiregional Multi-industry Forecasting Model." *Papers of the Regional Science Association* 25 (1970): 169-180.

71. Harris, Curtis C., Jr. *The Urban Economies, 1985.* Lexington, Mass.: Lexington Books, D.C. Heath and Company, 1973.
72. Harris, Curtis C., Jr. "A Multiregional Econometric Forecasting and Impact Model." Paper presented at 2nd US/USSR Exchange Symposium on Econometric Modeling, Skyland, Va., May 18, 1978.
73. Harvard Economic Research Project, "Capital Stock Matrix, 1947." Unpublished data.
74. Harvard Economic Research Project, "Capital Stock Matrix, 1958." Unpublished data.
75. Heilbroner, Robert L., and Lester C. Thurow. *The Economic Problem.* 5th ed. Englewood Cliffs, N.J.: Prentice-Hall, Inc., 1978.
76. Henderson, James M., and Anne O. Krueger. *National Growth and Economic Change in the Upper Midwest.* Minneapolis: University of Minnesota Press, 1965.
77. Hewings, Geoffrey J.D. "Regional Input-Output Analysis in the United States: A Bibliography." Discussion Paper No. 3. Canterbury, England: Center for Research in the Social Sciences, University of Kent, 1970.
78. Hicks, J.R. *The Social Framework: An Introduction to Economics.* 4th ed. Oxford: Clarendon Press, 1971.
79. Hirsch, Werner Z. "Interindustry Relations of a Metropolitan Area." *The Review of Economics and Statistics* 41 (November 1959): 360-369.
80. Hirsch, Werner Z. "Design and Use of Regional Accounts." *American Economic Review* 52 (May 1962): 365-373.
81. Hirsch, Werner Z. *Elements of Regional Accounts.* Baltimore: Johns Hopkins Press, 1964.
82. Hirsch, Werner Z. *Regional Accounts for Policy Decisions.* Baltimore: Johns Hopkins Press, 1966.
83. Hochwald, Werner, ed. *Design of Regional Accounts.* Baltimore: Johns Hopkins Press, 1961.
84. Houthakker, H.S., and Lester D. Taylor. *Consumer Demand in the United States, 1929-1970: Analyses and Projections.* Cambridge, Mass.: Harvard University Press, 1966.
85. Interstate Commerce Commission. "Unprinted Data on Unit Weight and Values," n.d.
86. Interstate Commerce Commission, Bureau of Economics. *Carload Waybill Statistics, 1963.* Washington, D.C., 1965.
87. Interstate Commerce Commission, Bureau of Economics. *Carload Waybill Statistics, 1964.* Washington, D.C., 1965.
88. Interstate Commerce Commission, Bureau of Economics. *Carload Waybill Statistics, 1966.* Washington, D.C., 1968.
89. Isard, Walter. "Interregional and Regional Input-Output Analysis: A Model of a Space Economy." *The Review of Economics and Statistics* 33 (November 1951): 318-328.

90. Isard, Walter. "Some Empirical Results and Problems of Regional Input-Output Analysis." In *Studies in the Structure of the American Economy,* edited by Wassily Leontief et al. New York: Oxford University Press, 1953, pp. 123–144.

91. Isard, Walter. *Location and Space Economy: A General Theory Relating to Industrial Location, Market Areas, Land Use, Trade, and Urban Structure.* Cambridge, Mass.: M.I.T. Press, 1956.

92. Isard, Walter. *Methods of Regional Analysis: An Introduction to Regional Science.* Cambridge, Mass.: M.I.T. Press, 1960.

93. Isard, Walter, and John H. Cumberland, eds. *Regional Economic Planning: Techniques of Analysis for Less Developed Areas.* Paris: European Productivity Agency, 1961.

—— Jack Faucett Associates, Inc.: See entries 35–49.

94. Jaszi, George. "An Economic Accountant's Ledger." Anniversary Issue, *The Economic Accounts of the United States: Retrospect and Prospect. Survey of Current Business* 51, no. 7, pt. II (July 1971): 183–227.

95. Kahn, Richard F. "The Relation of Home Investment to Unemployment." *The Economic Journal* 41 (June 1931): 173–198.

96. Kain, John F., and John R. Meyer, eds. *Essays in Regional Economics.* Cambridge, Mass.: Harvard University Press, 1971.

97. Kendrick, David. "Mathematical Models for Regional Planning." Discussion Paper No. 17. Austin, Texas: Center for Economic Development, University of Texas at Austin, December 1970.

98. Kendrick, John W., and C. Milton Jaycox. "The Concept and Estimation of Gross State Product." *Southern Economic Journal* 32 (October 1965): 153–168.

99. Kerr, Alex, and Robert B. Williamson. "Regional Economics in the U.S.: A Review Essay." *Growth and Change* 1 (January 1970): 5–19.

100. Keynes, John Maynard. *The General Theory of Employment, Interest, and Money.* London: MacMillan & Co., Ltd., 1936.

101. Kim Ungsoo; Cheol Park; and Sang Kyung Kwak. "An Application of the Interregional I/O Model for the Study of the Impact of the McClellan-Kerr Arkansas River Multiple Purpose Project." Prepared for the Institute for Water Resources, U.S. Army Corps of Engineers, 1975. Unpublished.

102. King, Willford I. *Employment Hours and Earnings in Prosperity and Depression, United States, 1920–1922.* New York: National Bureau of Economic Research, 1923.

103. King, Willford I. *The National Income and Its Purchasing Power.* New York: National Bureau of Economic Research, 1930.

104. Klein, Lawrence R. "The Specification of Regional Econometric Models." *Papers of the Regional Science Association* 23 (1969): 105–115.

105. Knauth, Oswald W. *Distribution of Income by States in 1919.* 2nd ed. New York: National Bureau of Economic Research, 1922.

106. Koenig, Lou P., and Philip M. Ritz. *Secondary Product Adjustment with Redistribution (SPAR).* NRAC Technical Report No. 67. Prepared for U.S. Army Engineer Mathematical Computation Agency, Corps of Engineers. National Planning Association, April 1967.
107. Kok, Frans. "Paper Recycling." Harvard Economic Research Project. 1971. Unpublished.
108. Kuczynski, Marguerite and Ronald L. Meek, eds. *Quesnay's Tableau Economique.* London: Macmillan Press Ltd., 1972.
109. Kuenne, Robert E. *The Theory of Economic Equilibrium.* Princeton, N.J.: Princeton University Press, 1963, ch. 7, pp. 420–427.
110. Kutscher, Ronald E. Assistant Commissioner, Office of Economic Growth, Bureau of Labor Statistics (letter from). "Estimates of Cost of Census and Other Statistical Data-Gathering." November 3, 1978.
111. Kuznets, Simon. "National Income." *Encyclopedia of the Social Sciences.* Vol. 11. New York: Macmillan, 1933, pp. 205-224.
112. Kuznets, Simon. *National Income, 1929–32.* New York: National Bureau of Economic Research, 1934.
113. Kuznets, Simon. *National Income and Capital Formation, 1919-1935: A Preliminary Report.* New York: National Bureau of Economic Research, 1937.
114. Lee, Tong Hun; John R. Moore; and David P. Lewis. *Regional and Interregional Intersectoral Flow Analysis: The Method and an Application to the Tennessee Economy.* Knoxville: University of Tennessee Press, 1973.
115. L'Esperance, Wilford L. *The Structure and Çontrol of a State Economy.* London: Pion Limited, forthcoming.
116. Leven, Charles L. "A Theory of Regional Social Accounting." *Papers and Proceedings of the Regional Science Association* 4 (1958): 221-237.
117. Leven, Charles L. "Regional Income and Product Accounts: Construction and Applications." In *Design of Regional Accounts,* edited by Werner Hochwald, Baltimore: Johns Hopkins Press, 1961, pp. 148–198.
118. Leven, Charles L. "Regional and Interregional Accounts in Perspective." *Papers of the Regional Science Association* 13 (1964): 127-144.
119. Leven, Charles L.; John B. Legler; and Perry Shapiro. *An Analytical Framework for Regional Development Policy.* Cambridge, Mass.: M.I.T. Press, 1970.
120. Leven, Maurice. *Income in the Various States: Its Sources and Distribution, 1919, 1920, and 1921.* New York: National Bureau of Economic Research, 1925.
121. Leontief, Wassily W. "Quantitative Input and Output Relations in the Economic System of the United States." *The Review of Economic Statistics* 18 (August 1936): 105–125.
122. Leontief, Wassily W. *The Structure of American Economy, 1919–1939: An Empirical Application of Equilibrium Analysis.* 2nd ed. New York: Oxford University Press, 1951.

123. Leontief, Wassily W. "Interregional Theory." In *Studies in the Structure of the American Economy,* edited by Wassily W. Leontief et al. New York: Oxford University Press, 1953, pp. 93-115.
124. Leontief, Wassily W. "Some Basic Problems of Empirical Input-Output Analysis." *Input-Output Analysis: An Appraisal. Studies in Income and Wealth.* Vol. 18. Princeton, N.J.: Princeton University Press, 1955, pp. 9-51.
125. Leontief, Wassily W., and Alan Strout. "Multiregional Input-Output Analysis." In *Input-Output Economics,* edited by Wassily W. Leontief. New York: Oxford University Press, 1966, pp. 223-257.
126. Leontief, Wassily W., et al. "The Economic Impact–Industrial and Regional–of an Arms Cut." *The Review of Economics and Statistics* 47 (August 1965): 217-241.
127. Leontief, Wassily W., et al. *The Future of the World Economy.* New York: Oxford University Press, 1977.
128. Liebling, Herman I. "Interindustry Economics and National Income Theory." *Input-Output Analysis: An Appraisal. Studies in Income and Wealth.* Vol. 18. Princeton, N.J.: Princeton University Press, 1955, pp. 291-320.
129. Luft, Harold S. "Computational Procedure for the Multiregional Model." Com-71-01148. Springfield, Va.: National Technical Information Service, September 1969.
130. McMenanin, D.G., and J.E. Haring. "An Appraisal of Nonsurvey Techniques for Estimating Regional Input-Output Models." *Journal of Regional Science* 14 (1974): 191-205.
131. Marshall, Alfred and Mary Paley. *The Economics of Industry.* 4th ed. London: Macmillan, 1881.
132. Marshall, Alfred. *Principles of Economics.* 8th ed. London: Macmillan, 1920.
133. Meyer, John R. "Regional Economics: A Survey." *American Economic Review* 53 (March 1963): 19-54.
134. Miernyk, William H. "An Interindustry Forecasting Model with Water Quantity and Quality Constraints." *Proceedings.* Fourth Annual Symposium on Water Resources Research. Columbus, Ohio: The Ohio State University, 1970.
135. Miernyk, William H. "Regional and Interregional Input-Output Models: A Reappraisal." In *Spatial, Regional, and Population Economics: Essays in Honor of Edgar M. Hoover,* edited by Mark Perlman, Charles L. Leven, and Benjamin Chinitz. New York: Gordon and Breach, 1972, pp. 263-292.
136. Miernyk, William H. "The Realism and Relevance of Regional Science." *Review of Regional Studies* 6 (1976): 1-10.
137. Miernyk, William H.; Ernest R. Bonner; John H. Chapman, Jr.; and Kenneth Shellhammer. *Impact of the Space Program on a Local Economy: An Input-Output Analysis.* Morgantown: West Virginia University Library, 1967.

138. Miernyk, William H.; Kenneth L. Shellhammer; Douglas M. Brown; Ronald L. Coccari; Charles J. Gallagher; and Wesley H. Wineman. *Simulating Regional Economic Development: An Interindustry Analysis of the West Virginia Economy.* Lexington, Mass.: Lexington Books, D.C. Heath and Company, 1970.
139. Ministry of International Trade and Industry [MITI]. "Interregional Input-Output Table for Japan." Tokyo: 1970. Unpublished.
140. Ministry of International Trade and Industry [MITI]. "Interregional Input-Output Table for Japan." Tokyo: 1975. Unpublished.
141. Ministry of International Trade and Industry [MITI]. "Interregional Input-Output Table for Japan." Tokyo: Vol. 108. n.d.
142. Mitchell, Wesley C.; Willford I. King; Frederick R. Macaulay; and Oswald W. Knauth. *Income in the United States: Its Amount and Distribution, 1909-1919. I, Summary.* New York: National Bureau of Economic Research, 1921.
143. Mitchell, Wesley C. (ed.); Willford I. King; Frederick R. Macaulay; and Oswald W. Knauth. *Income in the United States: Its Amount and Distribution, 1909-1919. II, Detailed Report.* New York: National Bureau of Economic Research, 1922.
144. Möhr, Malte. "Evaluation of the 1963 Interregional Commodity Trade Estimates." PB 244 587. Springfield, Va.: National Technical Information Service, May 1974.
145. Möhr, Malte. "A Consistency Problem of Multiregional Input-Output (MRIO), and Existence Conditions of Constrained Bioproportional Matrices." Ph.D. dissertation, Massachusetts Institute of Technology, May 1975.
146. Möhr, Malte. "A User's Guide to Constrained Biproportional Matrix Estimation." PB 253 583. Springfield, Va.: National Technical Information Service, September 1975.
147. Moore, Frederick T., and James M. Peterson. "Regional Analysis: An Interindustry Model of Utah." *The Review of Economics and Statistics* 37 (November 1955): 368-383.
148. Moses, Leon N. "A General Equilibrium Model of Production, Interregional Trade, and Location of Industry." *The Review of Economics and Statistics* 42 (November 1960): 373-397.
149. Moses, Leon N. "Regional Input-Output: A Method of Analyzing Regional Interdependence." Ph.D. dissertation, Harvard University, June 1952.
150. Moses, Leon N. "The Stability of Interregional Trading Patterns and Input-Output Analysis." *American Economic Review* 45 (December 1955): 803-832.
151. Nathan, Robert R., and John L. Martin. *State Income Payments, 1928-1937.* U.S. Department of Commerce, May 1939.
152. National Bureau of Economic Research. *The National Economic Accounts of the United States: Review, Appraisal, and Recommendations.* (A Report

by the National Accounts Review Committee.) New York: Arno Press, 1958.

153. National Bureau of Economic Research, Conference on Research in Income and Wealth. Harold Barger. *Outlay and Income in the United States, 1921–1938.* Vol. 4. Princeton, N.J.: Princeton University Press, 1942.

154. National Bureau of Economic Research, Conference on Research in Income and Wealth. Frank A. Hanna, Joseph A. Pechman, and Sidney M. Lerner. *Analysis of Wisconsin Income.* Vol. 9. Princeton, N.J.: Princeton University Press, 1948.

155. National Bureau of Economic Research, Conference on Research in Income and Wealth. *Input-Output Analysis: Technical Supplement.* Princeton, N.J.: Princeton University Press, 1954.

156. National Bureau of Economic Research, Conference on Research in Income and Wealth. *Input-Output Analysis: An Appraisal.* Vol. 18. Princeton, N.J.: Princeton University Press, 1955.

157. National Bureau of Economic Research, Conference on Research in Income and Wealth. *Studies in Income and Wealth.* Vol. 1. Princeton, N.J.: Princeton University Press, 1939.

158. National Bureau of Economic Research, Conference on Research in Income and Wealth. *Studies in Income and Wealth.* Vol. 6. Princeton, N.J.: Princeton University Press, 1943.

159. National Bureau of Economic Research, Conference on Research in Income and Wealth. *Studies in Income and Wealth.* Vol. 15. Princeton, N.J.: Princeton University Press, 1952.

160. National Bureau of Economic Research, Conference on Research in Income and Wealth. *Studies in Income and Wealth.* Vol. 16. Princeton, N.J.: Princeton University Press, 1954.

161. National Bureau of Economic Research, Conference on Research in Income and Wealth. *Studies in Income and Wealth.* Vol. 21. Princeton, N.J.: Princeton University Press, 1957.

162. National Bureau of Economic Research, Conference on Research in Income and Wealth. *Studies in Income and Wealth.* Vol. 22. Princeton, N.J.: Princeton University Press, 1958.

163. National Planning Association. *Projections to 1975, 1980, and 1985 of Population, Income, and Industry Employment.* Regional Economic Projections Series, Report No. 68-R-1. Washington, D.C.: The Association, 1969.

164. National Planning Association, Center for Economic Projections. *NPA Methodology for Long-Term National Economic Projections.* National Economic Projections Series, Report No. 69-N-1. Washington, D.C.: The Association, 1969.

165. National Science Foundation. *Reviews of Data on Science Resources.* Vol. 1, NSF 6, GPO, 1965.

166. Ng, Nathaniel K. "Regional Estimates of Electricity Technology and Trade, 1963." DOT Report No. 12. Prepared for the University Research Program, U.S. Department of Transportation, June 1976.
167. Ono, Mitsuo. "A Graphic Technique for Projecting Family Income Size Distribution." *American Statistical Association Proceedings of the Social Statistics Section* (August 1969).
168. Pai, Gregory G.Y. "Environmental Pollution Control Policy: An Assessment of Regional Economic Impacts." Ph.D. dissertation, Massachusetts Institute of Technology, June 1979.
169. Park, Se-hark, and A. David Sandoval. "Unconstrained and Constrained Dynamic Input-Output Models for Regional Energy Impact Analysis." Working Paper 77-WPIA-12. Regional Impact Division, Federal Energy Administration, May 1977.
170. Polenske, Karen R. "A Case Study of Transportation Models Used in Multiregional Analyses." Ph.D. dissertation, Harvard University, May 1966.
171. Polenske, Karen R. "A Multiregional Input-Output Model: Concept and Results." Prepared for a Seminar on Input-Output Models and Transportation Planning, Office of Economics and Systems Analysis, U.S. Department of Transportation, January 31, 1969.
172. Polenske, Karen R. "Empirical Implementation of a Multiregional Input-Output Gravity Trade Model." In *Contributions to Input-Output Analysis,* edited by A.P. Carter and A. Bródy. Vol. I. Amsterdam: North-Holland Publishing Co., 1970, pp. 143–163.
173. Polenske, Karen R. "An Empirical Test of Interregional Input-Output Models: Estimate of 1963 Japanese Production." *American Economic Review* 60 (May 1970): 76–82.
174. Polenske, Karen R. "The Implementation of a Multiregional Input-Output Model for the United States." In *Input-Output Techniques,* edited by A.P. Carter and A. Bródy. Amsterdam: North-Holland Publishing Co., 1972, pp. 171–189.
175. Polenske, Karen R. "Multiregional Interactions Between Energy and Transportation. In *Advances in Input-Output Analysis,* edited by Karen R. Polenske and Jiri V. Skolka. Cambridge, Mass.: Ballinger Publishing Co., 1976, pp. 433–460.
176. Polenske, Karen R. "Multiregional Research Publication List." Cambridge, Mass.: Massachusetts Institute of Technology, June 1977.
177. Polenske, Karen R. "Energy Analyses and the Determination of Multiregional Prices." *Papers of the Regional Science Association,* 43 (1980): 83–97.
178. Polenske, Karen R. "Regional Methods of Analysis for Stagnating Regions." In *Lectures on Regional Stagnation,* edited by Walter Buhr and Peter Friedrich. Baden-Baden, Germany, forthcoming.

179. Polenske, Karen R., and Ruth E. Rowan. "Multiregional Multipliers for Massachusetts and New England." *Northeast Regional Science Review* 7 (Spring 1977): 38-57.
180. Polenske, Karen R.; Carolyn W. Anderson; and Mary M. Shirley. "A Guide for Users of the U.S. Multiregional Input-Output Model." DOT Report No. 2. Prepared for the Office of Systems Analysis and Information, U.S. Department of Transportation. Cambridge, Mass.: Department of Urban Studies and Planning, June 1972.
181. Polenske, Karen R.; Carolyn W. Anderson; Richard Berner; William R. Buechner; Bo Carlsson; Orani Dixon; Peter Dixon; W. Norton Grubb; Frans J. Kok; Mary M. Shirley; James F. Smith; and Isabelle B. Whiston. *State Estimates of the Gross National Product, 1947, 1958, 1963.* Lexington, Mass.: Lexington Books, D.C. Heath and Company, 1972.
182. Polenske, Karen R.; Carolyn W. Anderson; Orani Dixon; Roger M. Kubarych; Mary M. Shirley; and John V. Wells. *States Estimates of Technology, 1963.* Lexington, Mass.: Lexington Books, D.C. Heath and Company, 1974.
183. Pucher, John R. "Projections of 1980 Freight Demands for Selected Midwestern Railroads." DOT Report No. 14. Prepared for the University Research Program, U.S. Department of Transportation. Cambridge, Mass.: Department of Urban Studies and Planning, M.I.T., September 1976.
184. Richardson, Harry W. *Input-Output and Regional Economics.* New York: John Wiley & Sons, 1972.
185. Richardson, Harry W. "The State of Regional Economics: A Survey Article." *International Regional Science Review* 3 (Fall 1978): 1-48.
186. Riefler, Roger F. "Interregional Input-Output: A State of the Arts Survey." In *Studies in Economic Planning Over Space and Time,* edited by George G. Judge and Takashi Takayama. Amsterdam: North-Holland Publishing Co., 1973, pp. 133-162.
187. Riefler, Roger F., and Charles M. Tiebout. "Interregional Input-Output: An Empirical California-Washington Model." *Journal of Regional Science* 10 (August 1970): 135-152.
188. Rijcheghem, W. van. "Exact Method for Determining the Technology Matrix in a Situation with Secondary Products." March 29, 1967. Unpublished.
189. Riley, Vera, and Robert Loring Allen. *Interindustry Economic Studies.* Baltimore: Johns Hopkins Press, 1955.
190. Ritz, Philip M. "The Input-Output Structure of the U.S. Economy, 1972." *Survey of Current Business* 59 (February 1979): 34-72.
191. Rodgers, John M. *State Estimates of Outputs, Employment, and Payrolls, 1947, 1958, 1963.* Lexington, Mass.: Lexington Books, D.C. Heath and Company, 1972.
192. Rodgers, John M. *State Estimates of Interregional Commodity Trade,*

1963. Lexington, Mass.: Lexington Books, D.C. Heath and Company, 1973.

193. Rosen, Sam. *National Income: Its Measurement, Determination, and Relation to Public Policy.* New York: Holt, Rinehart, and Winston, Inc., 1963.
194. Rowan, Ruth E. "Industry Employment Projections: an MRIO Model Simulation." Prepared for the Massachusetts Division of Employment Security. Cambridge, Mass.: Department of Urban Studies and Planning, M.I.T., December 1976.
195. Ruggles, Nancy and Richard. *The Design of Economic Accounts.* (General Series 89). New York: National Bureau of Economic Research, 1970.
196. Schaffer, William A. *On the Use of Input-Output Models for Regional Planning.* Leiden, The Netherlands: Martinus Nijhoff, 1976.
197. Schaffer, William A., and Chu Kong. "Nonsurvey Techniques for Constructing Regional Interindustry Models." *Papers of the Regional Science Association* 23 (1969): 83–101.
198. Scheppach, Raymond C. *State Projections of the Gross National Product, 1970, 1980.* Lexington, Mass.: Lexington Books, D.C. Heath and Company, 1972.
199. Schneider, Howard M. "An Evaluation of Two Alternative Methods for Updating Input-Output Tables." B.A. thesis, Harvard University, 1965.
200. Schwarz, Harry E. "The NAR Study: A Case Study in Systems Analysis." *Water Resources Research* 8 (June 1972): 751–754.
201. Shalizi, Zmarak M. "Multiregional Input-Output Multipliers and the Partitioned Matrix Solution of the Augmented MRIO Model." Ph.D. dissertation, Massachusetts Institute of Technology, October 1979.
202. Sonenblum, Sidney; Marshall K. Wood; and Philip M. Ritz. "Economic Projections and State Policy." Vol. A. Washington, D.C.: National Planning Association, Economic Programming Center, Central Economic and Demographic Study for New York State, November 1970.
203. Stevens, Benjamin H. "A Review of the Literature on Linear Methods and Models for Spatial Analysis." *Journal of the American Institute of Planners* 26 (1960): 253–259.
204. Stone, Richard. *Input-Output and National Accounts.* Paris: Organisation for Economic Co-operation and Development, 1961.
205. Stone, Richard. *Mathematics in the Social Sciences and Other Essays.* London: Chapman and Hall Ltd., 1966, pp. 118–151.
206. Stone, Richard and Giovanna. *Mathematical Models of the Economy and Other Essays.* London: Chapman and Hall Ltd., 1970.
207. Stone, Richard, and Alan Brown. *A Computable Model of Economic Growth (A Programme for Growth).* Vol. 1. London: Chapman and Hall Ltd., 1962.

208. Stone, Richard and Giovanna. *National Income and Expenditure.* 10th ed. London: Bowes & Bowes, 1977.
209. Strout, Alan. "A Flexible Input-Output Convention for Secondary Product Transactions." Harvard Economic Research Project. January 14, 1963. Unpublished.
210. Studenski, Paul. *The Income of Nations, Part One: History,* New York: New York University Press, 1958.
211. Studenski, Paul. *The Income of Nations, Part Two: Theory and Methodology.* New York: New York University Press, 1958.
212. Taskier, Charlotte E. "Alignment of the 450-Order (Input-Output) Industries, 1947, with the 1958 Interindustry Sales-Purchases Study Sectors." Prepared for the Harvard Economic Research Project, n.d.
213. Tiebout, Charles M. "Regional and Interregional Input-Output Models: An Appraisal." *Southern Economic Journal* 24 (1957): 140–147.
214. Tiebout, Charles M. "An Empirical Regional Input-Output Projection Model: The State of Washington, 1980." *The Review of Economics and Statistics* 51 (August 1969): 334-340.
215. Torene, Robert. "A General Purpose Disaggregate Data Base with Special Application to Transportation and Energy Planning and Analysis." Washington, D.C.: U.S. Bureau of the Census, Economic Surveys Division, Transportation Branch, June 2, 1978.
216. Treyz, George. "The Massachusetts Economic Policy Analysis Model." The Econometric Model Project, University of Massachusetts at Amherst, 1977.
217. Udis, Bernard, ed. "An Interindustry Analysis of the Colorado River Basin in 1960 with Projections to 1980 and 2010." Boulder: University of Colorado, Bureau of Economic Research, June 1968.
218. Ullman, Morris B., and Robert C. Klove. "The Geographic Area in Regional Economic Research." *Regional Income. Studies in Income and Wealth.* Vol. 21. Princeton, N.J.: Princeton University Press, 1957, pp. 87–111.
219. United Nations. *Input-Output Bibliography, 1955–1960.* New York: United Nations, 1961.
220. United Nations. *Input-Output Bibliography, 1960–1963.* Statistical Papers, Series M. No. 39. New York: United Nations, 1964.
221. United Nations. *Input-Output Bibliography, 1963–1966.* Statistical Papers, Series M. No. 46. New York: United Nations, 1967.
222. United Nations. *Input-Output Bibliography, 1966–1970.* 3 vols. Statistical Papers, Series M. No. 55. New York: United Nations, 1972.
223. United Nations, Department of Economic and Social Affairs. *A System of National Accounts: Studies in Methods.* Series F. No. 2. Rev. 3. New York: United Nations, 1968.

224. U.N. Economic Commission for Europe. "A Note on Some Aspects of National Accounting Methodology in Eastern Europe and the Soviet Union." In *Readings in the Concept & Management of Income,* edited by R.H. Parker and G.C. Harcourt. Cambridge, England: Cambridge University Press, 1969, pp. 370–398.
225. U.S. Bureau of the Census. *Census of Governments, 1942. City Finances, 1942 (Population over 25,000).* Vol. III, *Statistical Compendium,* GPO, 1944.
226. U.S. Bureau of the Census. *Census of Governments, 1942. County Finances, 1942 Compendium.* GPO, 1944.
227. U.S. Bureau of the Census. *Census of Governments, 1942. Finances of Townships and New England Towns, 1942.* GPO, 1944.
228. U.S. Bureau of the Census. *Census of Governments, 1942. State Finances, 1942.* Vol. III, *Statistical Compendium.* GPO, 1943.
229. U.S. Bureau of the Census. *Census of Governments, 1957.* Vol. III, no. 5, *Compendium of Government Finances,* GPO, 1959.
230. U.S. Bureau of the Census. *Census of Governments, 1962.* Vol. IV, no. 4, *Compendium of Government Finances,* GPO, 1964.
231. U.S. Bureau of the Census. *Census of Governments, 1967.* Vol. IV, *Compendium of Government Finances;* Vol. VI, *Historical Statistics on Governmental Finances and Employment.* GPO, 1969.
232. U.S. Bureau of the Census. *Census of Manufactures, 1947.* GPO, 1950.
233. U.S. Bureau of the Census. *Census of Manufactures, 1958.* GPO, 1961.
234. U.S. Bureau of the Census. *Census of Manufactures, 1963.* GPO, 1966.
235. U.S. Bureau of the Census. *Census of Manufactures, 1967.* GPO, 1971.
236. U.S. Bureau of the Census. *Census of Mineral Industries, 1963.* GPO, 1967.
237. U.S. Bureau of the Census. *Census of Population, 1950.* GPO, 1952.
238. U.S. Bureau of the Census. *Census of Population, 1960.* GPO, 1962.
239. U.S. Bureau of the Census. *Census of Transportation, 1963.* Vol. III, *Commodity Transportation Survey.* GPO, 1966.
240. U.S. Bureau of the Census. *Compendium of State Government Finances in 1947* (State Finances, 1947, no. 2). GPO, 1948.
241. U.S. Bureau of the Census. *Compendium of State Government Finances in 1962* (State Finances, 1962, no. 2). GPO, 1963.
242. U.S. Bureau of the Census. *County Business Patterns, 1959.* GPO, 1961.
243. U.S. Bureau of the Census. *County Business Patterns, 1964.* GPO, 1965.
244. U.S. Bureau of the Census. *County Business Patterns, 1967.* GPO, 1968.
245. U.S. Bureau of the Census. "Special Tabulation of 1963 State-to-State Flows for Input-Output Industries." Prepared for the Bureau of Public Roads. Unpublished.
246. U.S. Bureau of the Census. *Highlights of U.S. Exports and Imports.* Report FT-990. GPO (Dec., 1967; Nov. 1968; Dec. 1968; Dec. 1969).

247. U.S. Bureau of the Census. *Location of Manufacturing Plants, 1958.* GPO, 1961.
248. U.S. Bureau of the Census. *Location of Manufacturing Plants, 1963.* GPO, 1966.
249. U.S. Bureau of the Census. "Revised Projections of the Population of States, 1970 to 1985." *Current Population Reports.* Series P-25, No. 375. GPO, 1967.
250. U.S. Bureau of the Census. "Shipments of Defense-Oriented Industries, 1967." In *Current Industrial Reports* MA-175(67)-2. GPO, 1969.
251. U.S. Bureau of the Census. *Statistical Abstract of the United States, 1969.* GPO, 1969.
252. U.S. Bureau of the Census. *U.S. Exports–World Area, Country Schedule by Commodity Grouping and Method of Transportation.* (Revised through December 1968 Statistics.) Report FT-455. 1968 Annual. GPO, July 1969.
253. U.S. Department of Agriculture. *Agricultural Statistics, 1963.* GPO, 1963.
254. U.S. Congress, Senate, Joint Economic Committee. *The National Economic Accounts of the United States. Hearings before the Subcommittee on Economic Statistics on Sec. 5(a) of Public Law 304,* 79th Cong., 1st sess., October 29 and 30, 1957. GPO, 1957.
255. U.S. Department of Agriculture, Agricultural Marketing Service. "Net Change in Inventories in the Agricultural Sector, 1947, 1958, 1963." Unpublished worksheets prepared for *Farm Income Situation.*
256. U.S. Department of Agriculture, Agricultural Marketing Service and Agricultural Research Service; U.S. Department of Commerce, Bureau of the Census. *Farmers' Expenditures in 1955 by Regions for Production and Farm Living . . . with Tables on Off-Farm Income.* Statistical Bulletin No. 224, April 1958.
257. U.S. Department of Agriculture, Economic Research Service, Farm Income Branch. "Agricultural Industrial Relations Study, 1955." January 1959. Unpublished.
258. U.S. Department of the Army, Corps of Engineers. *Waterborne Commerce of the United States, 1963.* Washington, D.C: 1965.
259. U.S. Department of Commerce, Bureau of Economic Analysis. "Implementation and Evaluation of the MRIO Model." Prepared for the Economic Development Administration, U.S. Department of Commerce. Springfield, Virginia: National Technical Information Service, CPG-73-0003-PD, 1973.
260. U.S. Department of Commerce, Bureau of Economic Analysis. "The Input-Output Structure of the U.S. Economy: 1967." *Survey of Current Business* 54 (February 1974): 24–56.
261. U.S. Department of Commerce, Bureau of Economic Analysis. *Input-Output Table of the U.S. Economy: 1971.* BEA Staff Paper No. 28, March 1977.

262. U.S. Department of Commerce, Bureau of Economic Analysis. *Summary Input-Output Tables of the U.S. Economy: 1968, 1969, 1970.* BEA Staff Paper No. 27, September 1975.
263. U.S. Department of Commerce, Bureau of Economic Analysis, Regional Economic Analysis Division. *Industry-Specific Gross Output Multipliers for BEA Economic Areas.* GPO, January 1977.
264. U.S. Department of Commerce, Bureau of Foreign and Domestic Commerce, Division of Economic Research. *National Income, 1929–32.* Report submitted as Senate Doc. No. 124, 73rd Congress, 2nd Session. GPO, 1934.
265. U.S. Department of Commerce, Office of Business Economics. "Competitive Imports in the 1963 Input-Output Table, with Associated Trade, Transportation, and Insurance Margins." Unpublished worksheets.
266. U.S. Department of Commerce, Office of Business Economics. "Readings in Concepts and Methods of National Income Statistics." PB 194 900. Springfield, Va.: National Technical Information Service, 1971.
267. U.S. Department of Commerce, Office of Business Economics. "Industry Description Appendix I to Input-Output Study, 1958. November 1964. Unpublished.
268. U.S. Department of Commerce, Office of Business Economics. "The Input-Output Structure of the United States Economy: 1947." March 1970. Unpublished.
269. U.S. Department of Commerce, Office of Business Economics. "Input-Output Structure of the U.S. Economy: 1963." *Survey of Current Business* 49 (November 1969): 16–47.
270. U.S. Department of Commerce, Office of Business Economics. *Input-Output Structure of the U.S. Economy: 1963.* Vol. I, *Transactions Data for Detailed Industries.* GPO, 1969.
271. U.S. Department of Commerce, Office of Business Economics. *National Income, 1954 Edition.* GPO, 1954.
272. U.S. Department of Commerce, Office of Business Economics. *The National Income and Product Accounts of the United States, 1929-1965: Statistical Tables.* GPO, 1966.
273. U.S. Department of Commerce, Office of Business Economics. "The National Income and Product Accounts of the United States: Revised Estimates, 1929-64." *Survey of Current Business* 45 (August 1965): 6-56.
274. U.S. Department of Commerce, Office of Business Economics. "1963 Input-Output Data." Computer tapes, 1970.
275. U.S. Department of Commerce, Office of Business Economics. "State and Local General Government Net Purchases by Function and Industrial Origin, 1958." Unpublished worksheets, March 23, 1965.
276. U.S. Department of Commerce, Office of Business Economics. Anniversary Issue, *The Economic Accounts of the United States: Retrospect and Prospect. Survey of Current Business* 51, no. 7, pt. II (July 1971).

277. U.S. Department of Commerce, Office of Business Economics. "Trade, Transportation, and Insurance Margins for the 370-Order Flows in the 1963 Input-Output Table." Unpublished worksheets.
278. U.S. Department of Commerce, Office of Business Economics. "The Transactions Table of the 1958 Input-Output Study and Revised Direct and Total Requirements Data." *Survey of Current Business* 45 (September 1965): 33–49.
279. U.S. Department of Commerce, Office of Business Economics. *U.S. Income and Output.* GPO, 1958.
280. U.S. Department of Commerce, Office of Federal Statistics Policy and Standards. *Revolution in United States Government Statistics: 1926–1976.* GPO, October 1978.
281. U.S. Department of Defense, Directorate for Statistical Services. *Military Prime Contract Awards by Region and State, Fiscal Years 1966, 1967, 1968.* Washington, D.C., 1968.
282. U.S. Department of the Interior, Bureau of Mines. *Bituminous Coal and Lignite: Changing Patterns in Distribution and Markets, 1962–1964.* Washington, D.C., May 1965.
283. U.S. Department of the Interior. Bureau of Mines. *Minerals Yearbook, 1963.* Vols. I, III. GPO, 1964.
284. U.S. Department of Labor, Bureau of Labor Statistics. *Capital Flow Matrix, 1958.* GPO, 1968.
285. U.S. Department of Labor, Bureau of Labor Statistics. "Final Demand: Major Components and Total by IO Sector, 3% Basic Model (in Millions of 1958 Dollars at Producers' Prices) 1970 and 1980." 1969. Unpublished worksheets.
286. U.S. Department of Labor, Bureau of Labor Statistics. "Listing of the 1947 Input-Output Table, 450-Order." Unpublished.
287. U.S. Department of Labor, Bureau of Labor Statistics. "The 1947 Interindustry Relations Study: Industry Classification Manual." June 6, 1952; revised March 20, 1953. Unpublished.
288. U.S. Department of Labor, Bureau of Labor Statistics. "The 1947 Interindustry Relations Study: Industry Reports." Unpublished.
289. U.S. Department of Labor, Bureau of Labor Statistics. *Patterns of U.S. Economic Growth.* BLS Bulletin No. 1672. GPO, 1970.
290. U.S. Department of Labor, Bureau of Labor Statistics. *Projections 1970: Interindustry Relationships, Potential Demand, Employment.* BLS Bulletin No. 1536. GPO, 1966.
291. U.S. Department of Labor, Bureau of Labor Statistics. *Projections of the Post-Vietnam Economy, 1975.* BLS Bulletin No. 1733. GPO, 1972.
292. U.S. Department of Labor, Bureau of Labor Statistics. *The Structure of the U.S. Economy in 1980 and 1985.* BLS Bulletin No. 1816. GPO, 1974.
293. U.S. Department of Labor, Bureau of Labor Statistics. *Study of Consumer*

Expenditures, Incomes and Savings. Philadelphia: University of Pennsylvania, 1956.

294. U.S. Department of Labor, Bureau of Labor Statistics. *Survey of Consumer Expenditures, 1960-61.* GPO, 1966.
295. U.S. Department of Labor, Bureau of Labor Statistics, Division of Interindustry Economics. "Interindustry Flow of Goods and Services by Industry of Origin and Destination: Continental United States, 1947." GPO, October 1952.
296. U.S. Office of Management and Budget. *The Budget of the United States Government.* GPO. Annual.
297. Vaccara, Beatrice N. "Changes over Time in Input-Output Coefficints for the United States." In *Applications of Input-Output Analysis,* edited by A.P. Carter and A. Bródy. Amsterdam: North-Holland Publishing Co., 1970, pp. 238-260.
298. Walderhaug, Albert J. "State Input-Output Tables Derived from National Data." *Proceedings of the American Statistical Association* (August 1971): 77-86.
299. Wang, Kung-Lee, and Robert G. Kokat. *The Interindustry Structure of the U.S. Mining Industries, 1958.* Bureau of Mines Information Circular No. 8338. GPO, 1967.
300. Weber, Richard E. "A Synthesis of Methods Proposed for Estimating Gross State Product." *Journal of Regional Science* 19 (May 1979): 217-230.
301. Wilson, A.G. *Urban and Regional Models in Geography and Planning.* New York: John Wiley & Sons, Inc., 1974, ch. 8, pp. 112-126.
302. Young, Jeffrey K. "The Multiregional Input-Output Price Model: Transportation Case Study." MCP thesis, Massachusetts Institute of Technology, September 1978.

About the Author

Karen R. Polenske is an associate professor in the Department of Urban Studies and Planning at the Massachusetts Institute of Technology and a research associate at the Joint Center for Urban Studies. She received the B.A. in 1959 from Oregon State College in home economics, the M.A. in 1961 from the Maxwell School, Syracuse University, in the joint program of public administration and economics, and the Ph.D. in 1966 from Harvard University in economics. She then taught for four years in the Department of Economics at Harvard University and was a research associate at the Harvard Economic Research Project until 1972. She spent 1970–1971 at the University of Cambridge as a senior visitor at the Faculty of Economics and a member of High Table at King's College. During 1980, she has a fellowship at the Netherlands Institute for Advanced Studies in Wassenaar. She belongs to the American Economics Association and the Regional Science Association.

QUEEN MARY
COLLEGE
LIBRARY

WITHDRAWN
FROM STOCK
QMUL LIBRARY